Photographer's Guide to the Sony DSC-RX100 V

Photographer's Guide to the Sony DSC-RX100 V

Getting the Most from Sony's Pocketable Digital Camera

Alexander S. White

WHITE KNIGHT PRESS
HENRICO, VIRGINIA

The publisher does not assume responsibility for any damage or injury to property or person that results from the use of any of the advice, information, or suggestions contained in this book. Although the information in this book has been checked carefully for errors, the information is not guaranteed. Corrections and updates will be posted as needed at whiteknightpress.com.

Product names, brand names, and company names mentioned in this book are protected by trademarks, which are acknowledged.

Published by
White Knight Press
9704 Old Club Trace
Henrico, Virginia 23238
www.whiteknightpress.com
contact@whiteknightpress.com

ISBN: 978-1-937986-58-2 (paperback)
        978-1-937986-59-9 (ebook)

Printed in the United States of America

To my wife, Clenise.

Contents

CHAPTER 4: SHOOTING MENU   44

CHAPTER 5: PHYSICAL CONTROLS — 103

CHAPTER 6: PLAYBACK AND PRINTING — 119

Chapter 7: Custom and Setup Menus   131

CHAPTER 8: MOTION PICTURES   180

CHAPTER 9: WI-FI, APPLICATIONS, AND OTHER TOPICS   206

INTRODUCTION

This book is a guide to the operation of the Sony Cyber-shot DSC-RX100 V digital camera. It contains much of the same information as my earlier guide for the RX100 IV model, but I have revised it for the RX100 V with new illustrations and new or revised text where needed to cover this model's new or enhanced features.

The RX100 V camera continues in the tradition of the RX100 IV and earlier models with great portability, excellent image quality, and advanced features for taking stills and videos. It adds several enhancements, most notably a new autofocus system with 315 phase detection autofocus points that greatly increases the speed of autofocus. As a result, the RX100 V can shoot bursts of still images at speeds up to 24 frames per second while adjusting focus and exposure. The new model also includes an LSI (large scale integration) chip, which boosts the performance of the sensor and image processor, allowing the camera to shoot a burst of 150 shots that can be viewed right after shooting.

The RX100 V retains advanced features from the previous model, including a pop-up electronic viewfinder with resolution of 2.3 million dots. The lens has a wide-angle setting of 24mm, a bright f/1.8 aperture at the wide-angle end, and an f/2.8 aperture at the telephoto end. The camera has a tilting LCD screen, a built-in neutral density filter, and the ability to download camera apps that can add features and functions. Besides the ability to take short bursts of super-slow-motion video, the RX100 V comes with several features oriented to professional video production, including picture profiles with adjustments for gamma curve, knee, black level, and other settings, making this model suitable for use as a second or backup camera for serious videographers.

Despite the addition of several advanced features for still and video photography, the RX100 V retains the small size of the earlier RX100 models, which leaves the new model as possibly the greatest value available in a camera that can fit into most pockets.

My aim is to provide a complete guide to the camera's features, explaining how they work and when you might want to use them. The book is aimed largely at beginning and intermediate photographers who are not satisfied with the official documentation and prefer a more user-friendly explanation of the camera's controls and menus. For those seeking more advanced information, I discuss some topics that go beyond the basics, and I include in the appendices information about additional resources. I will provide updates and other information at my website, whiteknightpress. com, as warranted.

CHAPTER 1: PRELIMINARY SETUP

When you purchase your Sony DSC-RX100 V, the box should contain the camera itself, battery, charger, wrist strap, two adapters for attaching a shoulder strap (though no shoulder strap is supplied), micro USB cable, and several brief instruction pamphlets. There is no CD with software or user's guide; the software programs supplied by Sony are accessible through the Internet.

To install Sony's software for viewing and working with images and videos on Windows-based computers, go to the following Internet address: http://www.sony.co.jp/imsoft/Win/. If you have a Macintosh computer, you can get the software at http://www.sony.co.jp/imsoft/Mac/. You can download PlayMemories Home, a program for basic image editing, uploading, and management; Image Data Converter, a program for editing and processing images captured using the advanced Raw format; and Capture One Express, a special Sony-oriented version of Capture One, a sophisticated Raw-processing program from a company known as Phase One.

At the same websites, you also can install Sony's Remote Camera Control software, which lets you control the RX100 V from your computer when the camera is connected to the computer with its USB cable.

You might want to attach the wrist strap as soon as possible to help you keep a tight grip on the camera. The strap can be attached to the small mounting lug on either the left or right side of the camera. I have never attached the strap, though, because the camera is so small that I can hold it firmly without much risk of dropping it, even without a strap. See Appendix A for a discussion of custom grips that can also be of use. If you purchase an optional neck strap, you can attach it to the camera using the strap adapters provided by Sony in the box with the RX100 V.

Charging and Inserting the Battery

The Sony battery for the DSC-RX100 V is the NP-BX1. The standard procedure is to charge the battery while it's inside the camera. To do this, you use the supplied micro USB cable, which plugs into the camera and into the Sony charger or a USB port on your computer.

There are pluses and minuses to charging the battery while it is inside the camera. On the positive side, you don't need an external charger, and the camera can charge automatically when it's connected to your computer. Also, many automobiles have USB slots where you can plug in your RX100 V to keep up its charge. And, you can find portable charging devices with USB ports, as discussed in Appendix A.

On the negative side, with this system you cannot charge a battery outside of the camera, so you cannot be charging a spare battery while using the battery that is inside the camera. One solution to this situation is to purchase at least one extra battery and a device that will charge your batteries externally.

With the RX100 V, unlike some previous models, you can use the supplied battery charger as an AC adapter that will power the camera. So, if your battery runs completely down, you don't have to wait until you have recharged it to start using the camera again. You can plug the charger into the camera and into an AC outlet or USB power supply, and operate the camera directly from that power source. I'll discuss batteries, chargers, and other accessories in Appendix A.

To charge the battery, insert it into the camera and connect the charger. You first need to open the battery compartment door on the bottom of the camera and put in the battery. You can only insert it fully into the camera one way; what I do is look for the four gold-colored metal contact squares on the end of the battery and insert the battery so those four squares are positioned close to the front of the camera as the battery goes into the compartment, as shown in Figures 1-1 and 1-2. You may have to nudge aside the small blue latch that holds the battery in place, which is seen in Figure 1-3.

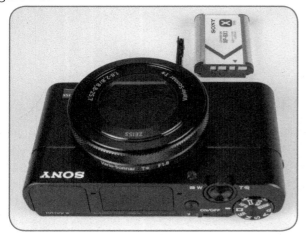

Figure 1-1. Battery Lined Up to Go Into Camera

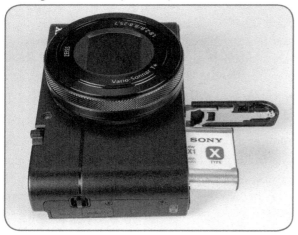

Figure 1-2. Battery Going Into Camera

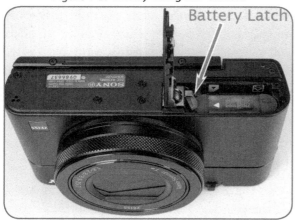

Figure 1-3. Battery Secured by Latch

With the battery inserted and secured by the latch, close the battery compartment door and slide the ridged latch on the door to the closed position. Then

plug the larger, rectangular end of the USB cable into the corresponding slot on the provided AC charger, which is model number AC-UUD12 in the United States. Plug the smaller end of the cable into the micro USB port on the upper part of the camera's right side as you hold it in shooting position, as shown in Figure 1-4.

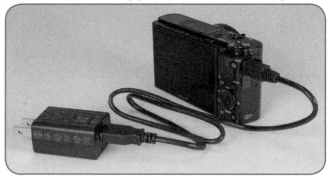

Figure 1-4. Charger Connected to Camera

Plug the charger's prongs into a standard electrical outlet. An orange lamp in the center of the power (On/Off) button on top of the camera will light up steadily while the battery is charging; when it goes out, the battery is fully charged. The full charging cycle should take about 150 minutes. If the charging lamp flashes, that indicates a problem with the charger or a problem with the temperature of the camera's environment.

To charge the battery using a USB power supply such as a USB port on a laptop computer, plug the large end of the camera's USB cable into that power source and the small end into the charging port on the camera, while the camera is turned off.

Choosing and Inserting a Memory Card

The RX100 V does not ship with a memory card. If you turn the camera on with no card inserted, you will see the message "NO CARD" in the upper left corner of the screen. If you ignore this message and press the shutter button to take a picture, don't be fooled into thinking that the camera is storing it in internal memory. The camera will temporarily store the image and play it back if you press the Playback button, but the image will not be permanently saved. (You cannot even operate the shutter with no card, if the Release w/o Card menu option is set to Disable, as discussed in Chapter 7.)

Some camera models have a small amount of built-in memory so you can take and store a few pictures even without a card, but the RX100 V does not have that safety net. (In an emergency, if you took one important picture with no card, you might be able to save it. First, don't turn off the camera. Second, play the image, and connect one end of a micro HDMI cable to the camera's HDMI port and the other end to a video capture device. Then capture the image to that device or to a computer connected to that device. I have done this using a Blackmagic Intensity Pro device, which saved the image to Photoshop. But that process is for emergencies only.)

To avoid the frustration of having a great camera that can't save images, you need to use a memory card. The RX100 V uses two types of memory storage. First, it can use all varieties of SD cards, which are about the size of a postage stamp. These cards come in several varieties; some examples are shown in Figure 1-5.

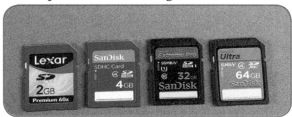

Figure 1-5. Memory Cards of Various Capacities

The standard card, called simply SD, comes in capacities from eight megabytes (MB) to two gigabytes (GB). A higher-capacity card, SDHC, comes in sizes from four GB to 32 GB. The newest, and highest-capacity card, SDXC (for extended capacity) comes in sizes of 48 GB, 64 GB, 128 GB, 256 GB, and 512 GB; this version of the card can have a capacity up to two terabytes (TB), theoretically, and SDXC cards generally have faster transfer speeds than the smaller-capacity cards. There also is a special variety of SD card called an Eye-Fi card, which I will discuss later in this chapter.

The RX100 V also can use micro SD cards, which are often used in smartphones and other small devices. These smaller cards operate the same as SD cards, but you need an adapter to use this tiny card in the RX100 V camera, as shown in Figure 1-6.

In addition to using SD cards, the RX100 V, being a Sony camera, also can use Sony's proprietary storage devices, known as Memory Stick cards. These cards are similar in size and capacity to SD cards, but with a slightly different shape, as shown in Figure 1-7.

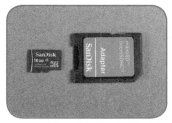

Figure 1-6. Micro SD Card with Adapter

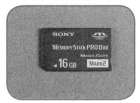

Figure 1-7. Sony Memory Stick Card

Memory Stick cards come in various types, according to their capacities. The ones that can be used in the RX100 V are the Memory Stick PRO Duo, Memory Stick PRO-HG Duo, and Memory Stick Micro (M2). The Memory Stick Micro, like the micro SD card, requires an adapter.

There is an important limitation on your choice of a memory card. To record video using the XAVC S format, which provides the highest quality, you have to use a memory card with a capacity of 4 GB or more and speed of Class 10, UHS Speed Class 1, or faster. If you want to record in that format using the highest quality of 100 megabits per second (Mbps), you have to use a card rated with the above specifications but in UHS Speed Class 3. These specifications are not just recommendations; if you try to record in a video format on a card that does not meet the requirements for that format, the camera will display an error message, as shown in Figure 1-8, and will not record the video.

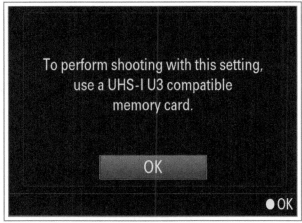

Figure 1-8. Error Message for Using Wrong Memory Card

The XAVC S format is worth using if you want high-quality video, and it is a good idea to get one of the high-powered cards that can support its use. Figure 1-9 shows three cards I have tested that can handle all video formats on the RX100 V—the San Disk Extreme PRO 32 GB SDHC card, the SanDisk Extreme 256 GB SDXC card, and the SanDisk Extreme PRO 512 GB card, all of which are rated in UHS Speed Class 3. This figure also shows two other cards that can handle all video formats except for the 100 Mbps versions of the XAVC S formats—the SanDisk Extreme Pro 64 GB SDXC card, rated in UHS Speed Class 1, and the Lexar Professional 128 GB SDXC card, rated in that same speed class.

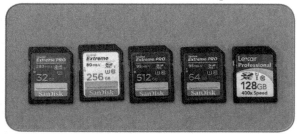

Figure 1-9. High-speed Memory Cards

If you do not care about using the XAVC S video format, the factors to consider in choosing a card are capacity and speed. If you're planning to record a good deal of HD video or a large number of Raw-format photos, you should get a large-capacity card, but don't get carried away—the largest cards have such huge capacities that you may be wasting money purchasing them.

There are several variables to consider in computing how many images or videos you can store on a particular size of card, such as which aspect ratio you're using (3:2, 4:3, 16:9, or 1:1), image size, and quality. Here are a few examples of what can be stored on a 64 GB SDXC card. If you're using the standard 3:2 aspect ratio, you can store about 2,850 Raw images (the highest quality), 4,150 high-quality JPEG images (Large size and Extra Fine quality), or about 9,600 of the lower-quality Standard images (Large size).

You can fit about 1 hour 15 minutes of the highest-quality XAVC S video on a 64 GB card. That same card will hold about 22 hours of video at the lowest-quality MP4 setting of 1280 x 720 pixels, which is still HD (high-definition) quality. Note, though, that the camera is limited to recording no more than about 29 minutes of video in any format in any one sequence. The highest-quality MP4 format (1920 x 1080 pixels at a bit rate of 28 megabits per second) can be recorded only for 20 minutes in one sequence, because of the four GB file size limit. A sequence using one of the highest-quality

XAVC S formats can be recorded for no more than about five minutes because of an issue with overheating of the sensor. All of these video formats and their limitations are discussed in Chapter 8.

The other major consideration is the speed of the card. High speed is important to get good results for recording continuous bursts of images and the highest-quality video with this camera. You should try to find a card that writes data at a rate of six MB/second or faster to record HD video. If you go by the class designation, a Class 4 card should be sufficient for shooting stills, and a Class 6 card should suffice for recording video, except for the requirements discussed above for recording XAVC S video.

You also may want to consider using an Eye-Fi card. This special type of device looks like an ordinary SDHC card, but it includes a tiny transmitter that lets it connect to a Wi-Fi network and send your images to your computer on that network as soon as the images are recorded by the camera. You also may be able to use Direct Mode, which lets the Eye-Fi card send your images directly to a computer, smartphone, tablet, or other device without needing a network, though Direct Mode can be tricky to set up.

I have tested a 16 GB Eye-Fi mobiPRO card with the RX100 V, and it worked as expected. Within a few seconds after I snapped a picture with this card in the camera, the image appeared in the Pictures/Eye-Fi folder on my computer. This card, shown in Figure 1-10, can handle Raw files and video files as well as the smaller JPEG files.

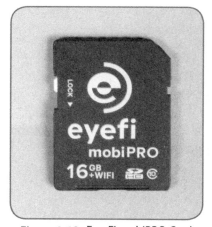

Figure 1-10. Eye-Fi mobiPRO Card

Of course, with the RX100 V Sony has included built-in Wi-Fi capability, as discussed in Chapter 9, so you do not need to use an Eye-Fi card or the equivalent to transfer images wirelessly. If you already have one or more wireless SD cards, you should be able to use them in your RX100 V, but there are other options for wireless transfer that may make more sense.

If you decide to use a Memory Stick card and want to use it with a card reader, be sure you have a reader that can accept those cards, which, as noted above, are not the same shape as SD cards.

Once you have chosen a card, open the same door on the bottom of the camera that covers the battery compartment, and slide the card in until it catches. An SD card is inserted with its label pointing toward the back of the camera, as shown in Figure 1-11; a Memory Stick card is inserted with its label pointing toward the front of the camera, as shown in Figure 1-12.

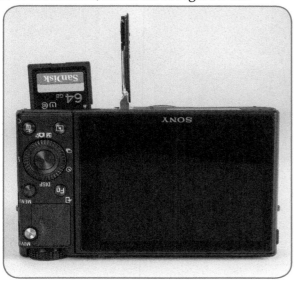

Figure 1-11. SD Card Going Into Camera

Once the card has been pushed down until it catches, close the compartment door and slide the latch to the outside position. To remove a card, push down on its edge until it releases and springs up, so you can grab it.

Although the card may work well when newly inserted in the camera, it's a good idea to format a card when first using it in the RX100 V, so it will have the correct file structure and will have any bad areas blocked off from use. To do this, turn on the camera by pressing the power button, then press the Menu button at the center right of the camera's back. Next, press the Right button (right edge of the Control wheel on the camera's back) multiple times until the small orange line near the top of the screen is positioned under the number 5,

while the menu's highlight lines are on the toolbox icon, as shown in Figure 1-13.

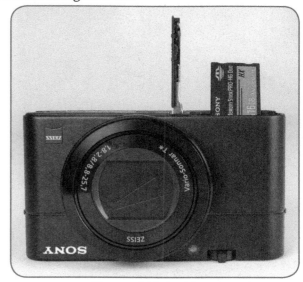

Figure 1-12. Memory Stick Card Going Into Camera

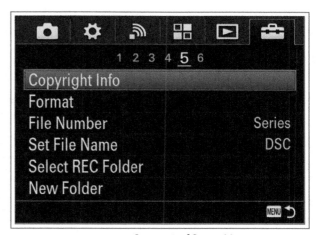

Figure 1-13. Screen 5 of Setup Menu

The toolbox icon stands for the Setup menu. The orange highlight bar should be on the top line of the menu, for the Copyright Info command. Press the Down button (bottom edge of Control wheel) until the Format command is highlighted, then press the button in the center of the Control wheel (called the "Center button" in this book). On the next screen, seen in Figure 1-14, highlight Enter and press the Center button again to carry out the command.

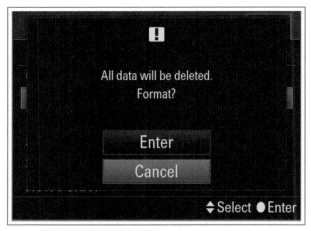

Figure 1-14. Format Confirmation Screen

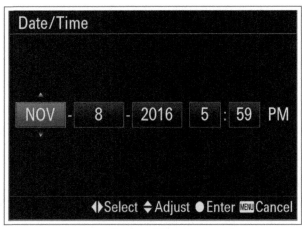

Figure 1-15. Date and Time Settings Screen

Setting the Language, Date, and Time

You need to have the date and time set correctly before you take pictures, because the camera records that information invisibly with each image and displays it later if you want. It is, of course, important to have the date (and the time of day) correctly recorded with your digital images. The camera may prompt you to set the date and time the first time you turn it on, but if not, carry out this procedure.

First, follow the same steps with the menu as noted above, but this time highlight the Date/Time Setup item on the fifth line of screen 4 of the Setup menu. Then press the Center button to move to the next screen. On that screen, select the Date/Time item and press the Center button. You will see a screen like the one in Figure 1-15.

On that screen, by pressing the Left and Right buttons or by turning the Control wheel, move through the month, day, year, and time settings, and change them by pressing the Up and Down buttons. When those settings have been made, press the Center button to confirm. You can adjust the Daylight Savings Time and Date Format settings on the previous screen if you need to. Then press the Menu button to exit from the menu system.

If you need to change the language the camera uses for menus and other messages, press the Menu button as discussed above to enter the menu system, and navigate to screen 4 of the Setup menu, as shown in Figure 1-16.

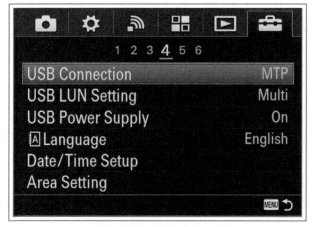

Figure 1-16. Screen 4 of Setup Menu

With the direction buttons, move if necessary to the Language item on the fourth line of the screen and press the Center button to select it. You then can select from the languages on the menu, as shown in Figure 1-17.

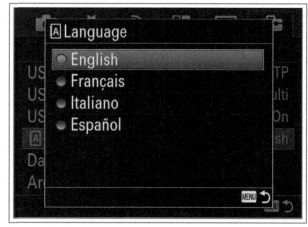

Figure 1-17. Language Selection Screen

CHAPTER 2: BASIC OPERATIONS

Now that the Sony RX100 V has the correct time and date set and a charged battery inserted along with a memory card, I'll discuss the steps for basic picture taking. For now, I won't discuss details about various options and why you might choose one over another. I'll just describe a reasonable set of steps that will get your camera into action and will save a usable image or video to your memory card.

Introduction to Main Controls

Before I discuss options for setting up the camera using the menu system and controls, I will introduce the main physical features of the camera. I won't discuss all of the controls here; I will cover them in more detail in Chapter 5. As I mention each item for the first time, I will describe its position and function; you may want to refer back to these images for a reminder about each control.

TOP OF CAMERA

On top of the camera are some of the most important controls and other features, as shown in Figure 2-1.

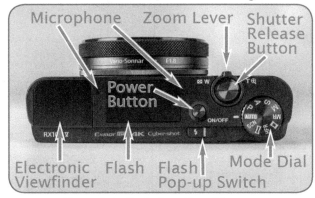

Figure 2-1. Controls on Top of Camera

The Mode dial selects a shooting mode for stills or video. For basic shooting without having to make other settings, turn the dial so the AUTO icon is next to the white marker; this sets the camera to its most automatic mode. The large, black shutter release button is used to take pictures. Press it halfway to evaluate

focus and exposure; press it all the way to take a picture. The zoom lever, surrounding the shutter button, is used to zoom the lens between its telephoto and wide-angle settings. The lever also is used to change the views of images in playback mode.

The power button turns the camera on and off. An orange light in the center of the button glows when the battery is being charged in the camera. A green light appears when the camera is powered on. The flash is stored inside the top of the camera; to use it, you have to pop it up using the flash pop-up switch behind the power button. The two small microphone openings are where the camera records sound for movies.

BACK OF CAMERA

Figure 2-2 shows the controls on the camera's back.

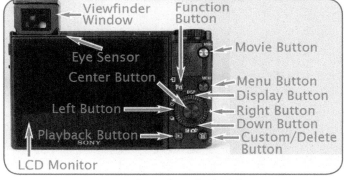

Figure 2-2. Controls on Back of Camera

The built-in electronic viewfinder (EVF) is stored inside the camera's top at the far left side until you pop it up using the Finder switch on the camera's left side. To the right of the viewfinder is a very small eye sensor, which detects the presence of your head for purposes of switching between the viewfinder and the LCD screen. The Movie button starts or stops a video recording. The Menu button calls up the menu screens with settings for shooting and other values, such as control button functions, audio features, and others. In shooting mode, the Function (Fn) button calls up a menu of camera settings for easy access. In playback mode, it activates the Send to Smartphone command, if the command is available. The Playback button puts the camera into playback mode so you can view recorded images, and it also can turn the camera on. The Custom/Delete button, marked with a C, can be programmed to call up any one of numerous functions. By default, in shooting mode it calls up help screens with information about menu options. In playback mode, it serves as the Delete button for erasing images.

The Control wheel sets values such as aperture and shutter speed and navigates through menus. In addition, its four edges act as buttons when you press them, to control items including flash mode, exposure compensation, continuous shooting, and the display screen. The Center button confirms selections and does other operations. The LCD screen—which displays the live view along with the camera's settings and plays back recorded images—tilts up or down to allow you to hold the camera in a high or low position to view a scene from unusual angles. It also can rotate 180 degrees forward to let you take a self-portrait.

FRONT OF CAMERA

Figure 2-3 shows the items on the camera's front.

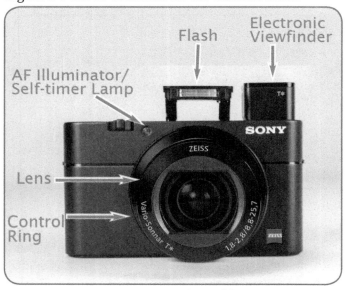

Figure 2-3. Items on Front of Camera

The AF Illuminator/Self-timer Lamp signals operation of the self-timer and provides illumination so the camera can use its autofocus system in dark areas. The Control ring, around the lens, can adjust items such as aperture, shutter speed, manual focus, and others, depending on the shooting mode and menu options

in effect. The lens has a 35mm equivalent focal length range of 24mm to 70mm and an aperture range of f/1.8 to f/11.0. (The actual focal length range of the lens is 8.8mm to 25.7mm; the "35mm equivalent" range is commonly used to state the focal length in a way that can easily be compared to lenses of other cameras.)

RIGHT SIDE OF CAMERA

On the right side of the camera are two small flaps, marked Multi and HDMI, as shown in Figure 2-4. Under those flaps are two ports, as shown in Figure 2-5.

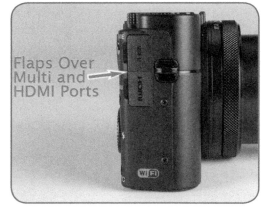

Figure 2-4. Right Side of Camera with Port Flaps Closed

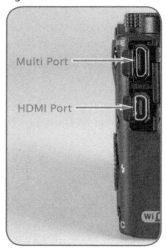

Figure 2-5. Right Side of Camera with Port Flaps Open

The Multi port or terminal is where you connect the micro USB cable that is supplied with the camera to charge the battery, to power the camera, to connect the camera to a computer to manage images, or to connect to a printer to print images directly from the camera. You also can connect a wired remote control to this port, as discussed in Appendix A. If you download the Remote Camera Control program from Sony's website, as mentioned in Chapter 1, you can connect the camera to your computer through this port and control the camera using that Sony software. The HDMI port is for connecting the camera to an HDTV to view images and videos. You can also use this port to output a "clean" video signal to a video recorder as discussed in Chapters 7 and 8, or to a monitor so you can view the shooting information from the camera in shooting mode.

LEFT SIDE OF CAMERA

The left side of the camera, shown in Figure 2-6, has two items of interest.

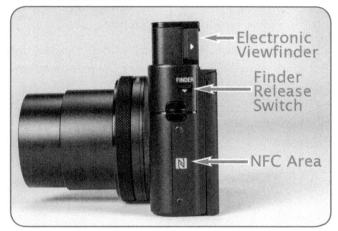

Figure 2-6. Left Side of Camera

The first is the Finder release switch, which you press down to release the electronic viewfinder so it will pop up. You then have to pull the viewfinder eyepiece out of its housing so you can see the live view through the camera's lens. When you are finished with the viewfinder, press the eyepiece back into the housing. You can then press the viewfinder down into the camera's body. When you do this, the camera will turn off or stay powered on, depending on the setting of the menu option called Function for VF Close, the first item on screen 3 of the Setup menu.

The other item of interest on the left side of the RX100 V is the NFC (near field communication) area, where you touch the camera against a smartphone or tablet with NFC capability to establish a Wi-Fi connection automatically. I will discuss this feature in Chapter 9.

BOTTOM OF CAMERA

Finally, as shown in Figure 2-7, on the bottom of the camera are the tripod socket, the battery/memory card compartment, and the speaker that produces sound for videos. There also is one other item that can't be seen unless the battery compartment is open—the access

lamp, located at the outside edge of the compartment, as shown in Figure 2-8.

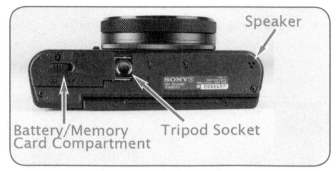

Figure 2-7. Bottom of Camera

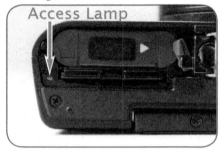

Figure 2-8. Access Lamp Inside Battery Compartment

That red lamp lights up when the camera is writing data to the memory card. When the camera has taken a long series of continuous shots, the lamp may stay illuminated for several seconds. During that time, do not remove the battery or the memory card.

Taking Pictures in Auto Mode

Now I'll discuss how to use these controls to take pictures and videos. Here's a list of steps to take if you want to set the camera to one of its most automatic modes and let it make (almost) all decisions for you. This is a good approach if you need to grab a quick shot without fiddling with too many settings.

1. Press the power button on top of the camera. The LCD screen will light up as the camera turns on.

2. Turn the Mode dial so the AUTO icon is next to the white indicator line, as shown in Figure 2-9.

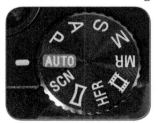

Figure 2-9. Mode Dial at AUTO

3. This sets the camera to the Auto shooting mode. If you see the help screen that describes the mode (called the Mode Dial Guide), as seen in Figure 2-10, press the Center button to dismiss it. (You can dispense with that help screen altogether using the Mode Dial Guide option on screen 2 of the Setup menu, as discussed in Chapter 7.)

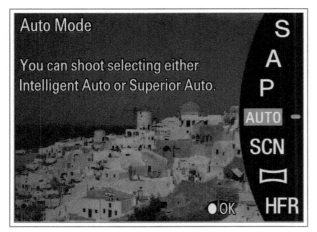

Figure 2-10. Mode Dial Guide

4. When you first select Auto mode, if the Mode Dial Guide is turned on, the camera will display the screen shown in Figure 2-11, letting you choose either Intelligent Auto mode (green camera icon) or Superior Auto mode (tan camera icon). For now, leave the green icon highlighted, and press the Center button to dismiss that screen.

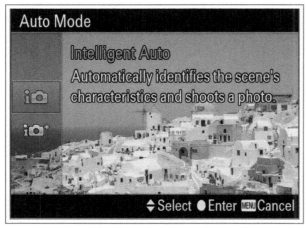

Figure 2-11. Screen to Select Intelligent Auto or Superior Auto

5. Press the Menu button to activate the menu system. As I discussed in Chapter 1, navigate through the menu screens by pressing the Right and Left buttons. You can tell which menu screen is active by looking at the small orange line (cursor) beneath the numbers. When a given screen is selected, navigate up and down through the options on that screen by pressing the Up and Down buttons or by turning the Control wheel right or left. When the orange selection bar is on the option you want, press the Center button to select that item. Then, pressing the Up and Down buttons or turning the Control wheel, highlight the value you want to set for that option, and press the Center button to confirm it. You can then continue making menu settings; when you are finished with the menu system, press the Menu button to go back to the live view, so you can take pictures.

6. Using the procedure described in Step 5, make the settings shown in Table 2-1 using the menu system.

Table 2-1. **Suggested Settings for Intelligent Auto Mode Still Images**

Image Size	L: 20M
Aspect Ratio	3:2
Quality	Extra Fine
Image Size (Dual Rec.)	L:17M
Quality (Dual Rec.)	Extra Fine
File Format	MP4
Record Setting	1920 x 1080 60p 28M
Dual Video REC	Off (not available)
HFR Settings	Default or As Needed
Drive Mode	Single shooting
Flash Mode	Autoflash
Red Eye Reduction	Off
Focus Mode	Single-shot AF
AF Illuminator	Auto
AF Drive Speed	Normal
AF Tracking Sensitivity	Normal
Center Lock-on AF	Off
Smile/Face Detection	Off
Auto Dual Rec	Off
Soft Skin Effect	Off
Auto Object Framing	Off
Auto Mode	Intelligent Auto
SteadyShot (Stills)	On
SteadyShot (Movies)	Standard
Color Space	sRGB
Auto Slow Shutter	On
Audio Recording	On
Micref Level	Normal
Wind Noise Reduction	Off
Memory	No setting needed

7. If you don't want to make all of these settings, don't worry; you are likely to get good images even if you don't adjust most of these settings at this point. Several of the settings apply only to video recording, but I have listed settings for them anyway, in case a video opportunity arises and you need to press the red button to make a recording. I have omitted some settings that are not available for adjustment in this shooting mode.

8. Press the Menu button again to make the menu disappear, if it hasn't done so already.

9. If you are shooting in dark conditions, press the flash pop-up switch to the right. That switch is located on top of the camera behind the power button. Then press the Right button on the Control wheel, marked with a lightning bolt. A vertical menu will appear at the left side of the screen, as shown in Figure 2-12.

10. Make sure Autoflash is highlighted with the orange selection block. If it is not, press the direction buttons or turn the Control wheel to highlight it, so the Flash Mode is set to Autoflash. Press the Center button to dismiss this menu.

11. Using a procedure like that in Steps 9 and 10, press the Left button, marked with a timer dial and an icon for a stack of images, and make sure the top option, showing a single rectangular frame, is selected, as shown in Figure 2-13. This sets the camera to take single shots, rather than continuous bursts.

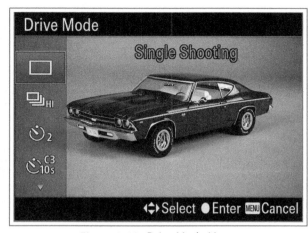

Figure 2-13. Drive Mode Menu

12. Aim the camera and compose the picture. Locate the zoom lever and push it to the left, toward the letter "W" on the camera, for a wider-angle shot, or to the right, toward the letter "T," to get a telephoto, zoomed-in shot.

13. Once the picture looks good, gently press the shutter button halfway and pause there. You should hear a beep and see one or more green focus brackets or small squares on the LCD, indicating sharp focus. Also look for a green disc in the extreme lower left corner of the screen. If that green disc lights up steadily, the image is in focus; if it flashes, the camera was unable to focus. In that case, you can re-aim and see if the autofocus system does better from a different distance or angle.

14. After you have made sure the focus is sharp, push the shutter button all the way to take the picture.

VARIATIONS FROM FULLY AUTOMATIC

Although the RX100 V takes care of the basic settings for you when it's set to Intelligent Auto mode, the camera lets you make a number of adjustments to fine-tune the shooting process when it's in this automatic mode or the Superior Auto shooting mode. (The Superior Auto mode is very similar to the Intelligent Auto mode. You can choose that mode when the mode dial is first turned to the AUTO setting, if the Mode Dial Guide menu option is on, or by using the Auto Mode option on screen 8 of the Shooting menu.)

Photo Creativity Feature

The Photo Creativity feature, available only in the Intelligent Auto and Superior Auto modes, is a simple way to make adjustments to the appearance of still

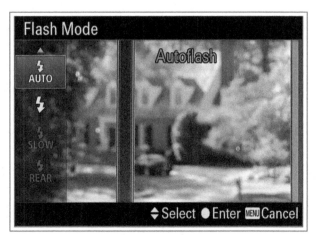

Figure 2-12. Flash Mode Menu

images and videos. I can understand why Sony presents these adjustments in this way, making them easy to use and giving them non-technical names such as "Background Defocus" and "Brightness," rather than "aperture control" and "exposure compensation." However, it is somewhat confusing (to me, at least) that these same adjustments are made using different controls in the other, less-automatic shooting modes.

In any event, for now I will discuss how to make these adjustments in the Intelligent Auto and Superior Auto modes. In Chapter 3, I will discuss all of the shooting modes, and in Chapters 4 and 5 I will discuss how to make similar settings in the more advanced shooting modes. For example, I will discuss aperture control in Chapter 3 in connection with Aperture Priority mode, and I will discuss exposure compensation in Chapter 5, in connection with the button that controls that function (the Down button, in the bottom position on the Control wheel).

With that introduction, here are details about how to make various settings in the two most automatic shooting modes using the Photo Creativity feature.

First, it's important to note that the Photo Creativity feature is not available if the Quality option on the Shooting menu is set to Raw or Raw & JPEG. So make sure that Quality is set to Extra Fine or Fine. (If you try to use Photo Creativity with Raw in effect, you will get an error message.) To use the Photo Creativity feature, press the Down button on the Control wheel—the button marked with the plus and minus icon and the camera icon with three plus signs at its right side, as shown in Figure 2-2, earlier. When you press that button, you will see some new icons and virtual controls appear on the display, as shown in Figure 2-14.

At the bottom of the screen are five blocks, each with an icon for a setting. When the blocks first appear, each of the four blocks at the left should show the word AUTO, and the block at the far right, with an icon of an artist's palette and brush, should say OFF. Use the Right and Left buttons to move through these five blocks; each one will be highlighted in orange when it is selected.

You can keep pressing the Right or Left button to wrap around to the other side of the group of icons if you want. For example, when the artist's palette is highlighted, you can press the Right button one more

time to move directly to the block at the far left of the screen.

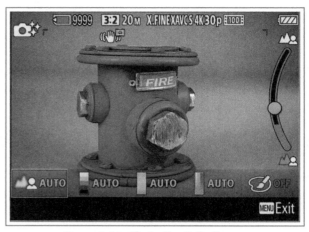

Figure 2-14. Photo Creativity Screen

When one of the blocks is highlighted in orange, you can change the value for that setting by turning the Control wheel or by pressing the Up or Down button to move an indicator disc or icon along a curved scale at the right side of the display. The display will change as appropriate to show the effect of your adjustment. For example, if you move the Color slider to the top of the curved scale, the image will appear more reddish, or "warm."

With the first four blocks, as you turn the wheel, a disc will move along the scale at the right of the screen. The disc will be green at first, but it will turn orange once the setting is changed. Also, the appearance of the icon for that block will change to show how the setting is changing, as seen in Figure 2-15.

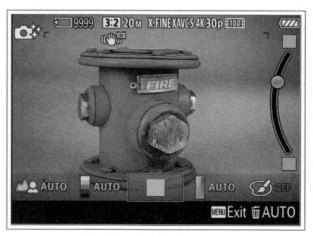

Figure 2-15. Icon Changed for Photo Creativity Setting

When a block is first selected, a label for its setting will appear briefly on the screen and then disappear. The settings that are controlled by the five blocks are as follows, from left to right:

Background Defocus. This first setting is designed to leave the foreground sharp while the background is blurry. This effect, some-times called "bokeh," can help separate the main subject from a background that might be distracting or unpleasant.

In technical terms, the camera's aperture (its opening to let in light) is opened up wider, which causes the depth of field to be shallower, allowing the background to go out of focus. When the disc is at the bottom of the scale, the aperture is opened as much as possible, resulting in a blurrier background; as the disc nears the top of the scale, the background should become sharper as the aperture narrows and depth of field increases. I will talk about this effect again in Chapter 3, in the discussion of the Aperture Priority shooting mode. Figure 2-16 is an example of an image with a defocused background.

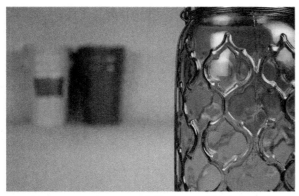

Figure 2-16. Image with Defocused Background

Brightness. The indicator disc starts in the middle of the scale. As you turn the Control wheel to move the disc higher, the image gets brighter; as it moves lower, the image darkens. In technical terms, this setting controls exposure compensation, which can be used in situations when the normal exposure calculated by the camera would not be ideal. For example, if a dark-colored subject, such as a group of apples, is photographed against a white background, the camera's automatic exposure control is likely to underexpose the dark object, because the camera takes into account the broad expanse of white tones in the image and decreases the exposure level. With the Brightness control, you can increase the brightness level so the subject will appear properly exposed, as shown in Figure 2-17.

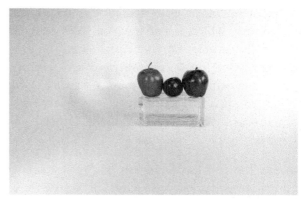

Figure 2-17. Image with Brightness Level Increased

Color. This third setting from the left lets you adjust the white balance of images, though Sony uses the term "Color" to simplify things. As I will discuss in Chapter 4, the white balance setting adjusts the camera's processing of colors according to the color temperature of the light source. For example, light from incandescent bulbs has a lower color temperature than light from a bright blue sky. The lower color temperatures are considered "warmer," with a reddish or yellowish cast, and the higher ones yield colors that are considered "cooler," with a more bluish appearance. (In this case, "warm" and "cool" have to do with the appearance, rather than the actual temperature, of the subjects.)

With this setting, again, the normal value is in the center of the curved scale. To make the colors of the scene appear cooler, or more bluish, turn the Control wheel to the left to move the indicator disc toward the bottom of the scale; reverse that process to make the colors warmer, or more reddish. Figure 2-18 shows the Color setting adjusted to the bluish side.

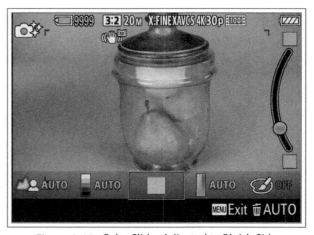

Figure 2-18. Color Slider Adjusted to Bluish Side

This adjustment does not change the actual white balance setting, which is fixed at Auto White Balance (AWB) for the automatic shooting modes; it merely tweaks the setting toward the warm or cool end of the scale. In some other shooting modes, as discussed in Chapter 4, you can make more precise adjustments to the camera's white balance through the White Balance menu option.

Vividness. The fourth setting from the left lets you adjust the intensity, or saturation, of colors in your images.

Again, the standard setting is in the middle of the scale; move the disc upward for more intense colors and downward for softer, less-saturated colors. In the more advanced shooting modes, you can adjust saturation in finer detail, along with contrast and sharpness, using the Creative Style menu option, as discussed in Chapter 4. Figure 2-19 shows Vividness set to its maximum.

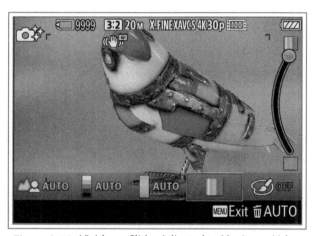

Figure 2-19. Vividness Slider Adjusted to Maximum Value

Picture Effect. The final option at the right, marked with an artist's palette, gives you access to the following settings: Toy Camera, Pop Color, Posterization Color, Posterization B/W, Retro Photo, Soft High-key, Partial Color: Red, Partial Color: Green, Partial Color: Blue, Partial Color: Yellow, and High Contrast Monochrome. These settings can produce dramatic effects, as indicated by their labels. The same settings are available through the Picture Effect item on the Shooting menu in advanced shooting modes, though there are some settings available through that menu item that cannot be made from the Photo Creativity system, such as different varieties of the Toy Camera setting as well as settings such as Watercolor and Illustration. I will discuss those settings and provide examples in Chapter 4.

You can combine more than one Photo Creativity setting to achieve various effects. For example, if you activate the Partial Color effect using the rightmost block at the bottom of the screen, you can then move the highlight to the Color or Vividness block and change the tint or intensity of the color that you selected for the Partial Color effect. Or, you can decrease the exposure of the image and also decrease the intensity of the colors by using the Brightness and Vividness controls together.

When you have moved a setting's control to the position you want, leave it there and take the picture with the control still on the screen. (Or, as noted above, you can go to another setting and adjust it as well before taking the picture.) Don't press the Menu button, because doing that will cancel the setting you just made.

To reset a setting to its original value, highlight its block and press the Custom/Delete (C) button. For the first four blocks, this action will reset the indicator to its default value (bottom of the scale for Background Defocus; middle of the scale for the other three). For the Picture Effect setting, this action will turn the selected effect off, leaving no effect active. To reset all five blocks at once, turn the Mode dial to another shooting mode (such as Scene or Program), then back to AUTO, and press the Down button to return to Photo Creativity. To exit from the Photo Creativity screen, press the Menu button.

Photo Creativity is a useful feature, and it is convenient to select one or more of its options while the camera is in Intelligent Auto or Superior Auto mode, so you don't have to invest too much effort into figuring out what settings to use. However, if you want to exercise more control over the settings, you can use one of the more advanced shooting modes with menu options and controls that let you make more precise adjustments.

FLASH

The RX100 V has a convenient built-in flash unit, which you may want to use on a regular basis. In Chapter 4 I'll provide details about the Flash Mode and Flash Compensation settings, as well as the prevention of "red eye" effects. In Appendix A, I'll discuss using external flash units, even though the camera has no flash shoe.

It's important to remember that the flash unit cannot pop up on its own, even if the flash mode is set to Fill-flash, which requires the flash to fire. You have to use the flash pop-up switch on top of the camera to release the flash before it can fire.

For this discussion, I'm assuming the camera is set to Intelligent Auto mode. In some other situations, such as with some of the Scene mode settings, the Flash menu will not appear; you will see an error message if you press the Right button when the shooting screen is active.

In Intelligent Auto mode, with the flash unit popped up, press the Right button once to call up the Flash Mode menu, then press the Up and Down buttons or turn the Control wheel to select a flash mode from that list. Press the Center button to confirm the selection. (You also can summon the Flash Mode menu from the Shooting menu: Flash Mode is the third item down on the third screen of the Shooting menu. See Chapter four for a discussion of all items on those menu screens.)

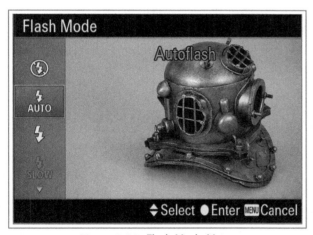

Figure 2-20. Flash Mode Menu

The vertical menu at the left of the screen, shown in Figure 2-20, has icons for the five flash modes—a lightning bolt with the "no" sign crossing it out, for Flash Off; a lightning bolt with the word "Auto," for Autoflash; a lightning bolt alone, for Fill-flash (meaning the flash will always fire); a lightning bolt with the word "Slow," for Slow Sync; and a lightning bolt with the word "Rear," for Rear Sync. When the camera is in Intelligent Auto mode, the last two choices will be dimmed; if you highlight one of them and press the Center button, the camera will display a message saying you cannot make that selection in this shooting mode.

I discussed earlier how to choose Autoflash. If you choose Fill-flash instead, you will see the lightning bolt icon on the screen at all times when the flash is popped up and the detailed display screen is selected. With this setting, the flash will fire regardless of whether the camera's exposure system believes flash is needed. You can use this setting when you are certain you want the flash to fire, such as in a dimly lighted room. This setting also can be of use in outdoor settings, such as when the sun is shining and you want to reduce the shadows on your subject's face. I will provide an illustration of the use of Fill-flash in Chapter 4.

When the camera is set for certain types of shooting, such as using the self-timer with multiple shots, the flash is forced off and cannot be used. If you turn on the flash with burst shooting, the use of flash will drastically limit the shooting speed. Instead of firing a rapid burst, the camera will take multiple images at a slow rate because the flash needs to recycle between shots. In some cases, such as with the Night Scene setting of Scene mode, you cannot even get the Flash Mode menu to appear; if you press the Flash button, the camera will display a message saying the flash is not available in that shooting mode, as shown in Figure 2-21.

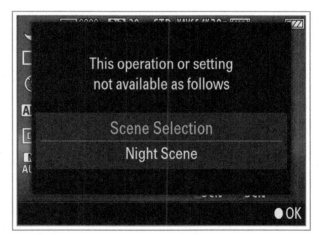

Figure 2-21. Error Message for Using Flash in Night Scene Mode

If you set the Mode dial to P, for Program mode, and then press the Flash button to select a flash mode, you will see the same five options for Flash Mode on the menu, but this time the Flash Off and Autoflash options will be dimmed because those selections are not available in that shooting mode.

In summary, when using Intelligent Auto (or Superior Auto) mode, if you don't want the flash to fire because you are in a museum or similar location, you can select the Flash Off mode. You also can just leave the flash stored inside the camera, so it cannot pop up and fire.

If you want to let the camera decide whether to fire the flash, you can select Autoflash mode. To make sure that the flash will fire no matter what, you can select Fill-flash mode. In Chapter 4, I'll explain the other flash options, Slow Sync and Rear Sync, and I'll discuss some other flash-related topics. For now, you have the basic information you need to select a flash mode when the camera is set to the Intelligent Auto or Superior Auto shooting mode.

DRIVE MODE: SELF-TIMER AND CONTINUOUS SHOOTING

The Drive Mode menu option includes more adjustments you can make when using Intelligent Auto mode. If you press the Control wheel's Left button, which is marked with a timer dial and an icon that looks like a stack of images, the camera will display a vertical menu for Drive Mode, as shown in Figure 2-22.

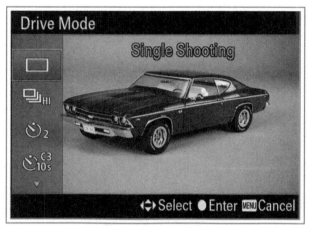

Figure 2-22. Drive Mode Menu

Navigate through these options by pressing the Up and Down buttons or by turning the Control wheel.

I will discuss the Drive Mode menu options more fully in Chapter 4. For now, you should be aware of a few of the choices. (I will skip over some others.) If you select the top option, represented by a single rectangular frame, the camera is set for single shooting mode; when you press the shutter button, a single image is captured. With the second option, whose icon looks like a stack of images, the camera is set for continuous shooting and takes a rapid burst of images while you hold down the

shutter button. You can use the Left and Right buttons to choose from Hi, Mid, or Lo for the speed of shooting.

If you choose the third option, whose icon is a timer dial with a number beside it, the camera uses the self-timer. Use the Left and Right buttons to choose two, five, or 10 seconds for the timer delay. After the timer has been set, press the shutter button. The shutter will be released after the specified number of seconds. The 10-second or five-second delay is useful when you need to place the camera on a tripod and join a group photo; the two-second delay is useful to make sure the camera is not jiggled by the action of pressing the shutter button. The two-second setting helps greatly when you are taking a picture for which focusing is critical, such as an extreme closeup. I will discuss the use of the self-timer and other Drive Mode options in more detail in Chapter 4.

The Drive Mode options also can be reached as the top item on screen 3 of the Shooting menu.

There are other settings that can be made when the camera is set to Intelligent Auto or Superior Auto mode, including Image Size, Aspect Ratio, Quality, Focus Mode, Face Detection, and others. I included suggested settings for those items in Table 2-1 earlier in this chapter, and I will discuss the details of those settings in Chapter 4.

Overview of Movie Recording

Now I'll discuss recording a short movie sequence with the RX100 V. With the camera powered on, turn the Mode dial to select Auto mode. There is a special Movie mode setting marked by the movie-film icon on the Mode dial, but you don't have to use that mode for shooting movies; I'll discuss the use of that option and provide more details about movie-recording options in Chapter 8.

Press the Menu button to get access to the menu system, and press the Right or Left button, if necessary, enough times to move the orange cursor under the number two while the camera icon for the Shooting menu is highlighted, as shown in Figure 2-23.

With the RX100 V, the main movie-related menu items are located on the Shooting menu; there is no separate Movie menu.

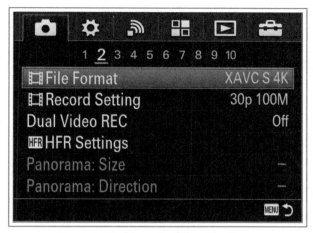

Figure 2-23. Screen 2 of Shooting Menu

On the top line of this Shooting menu screen, highlight File Format and press the Center button to go to the submenu with four choices for the format of movie recording. For now, be sure the fourth option, MP4, is highlighted; that format provides high quality for your videos without requiring a special memory card and is easy to edit or upload using a computer. (As discussed in Chapter 1, if you select XAVC S 4K or XAVC S HD for the movie format, you have to use a memory card with a speed of Class 10 or greater.) The AVCHD setting provides excellent quality but can be challenging to edit and work with using a computer.

For the rest of the settings, I will provide a table like the one included earlier in this chapter for shooting still images. The settings shown in Table 2-2 are standard ones for shooting high-quality movies.

Table 2-2.   **Suggested Shooting Menu Settings for Movies in Intelligent Auto Mode**

File Format	MP4
Record Setting	1920 x 1080 60p 28M
Dual Video REC	Off (not available)
Focus Mode	Automatic AF
AF Drive Speed	Normal
AF Tracking Sensitivity	Normal
Auto Dual Rec	Off
SteadyShot (Movies)	Standard
Auto Slow Shutter	On
Audio Recording	On
Micref Level	Normal
Wind Noise Reduction	Off

There are other Shooting menu settings that affect movie recording; I will discuss that topic in Chapter 8.

If you are going to be shooting a scene that includes people's faces, you may want to go to the Smile/Face Detection line on screen 7 of the Shooting menu and set the Face Detection item to On. You can leave the other items set as they were for shooting still images, as listed in Table 2-1 for still shooting.

Once you have made the above settings, aim the camera at your subject, and when you are ready to start recording, press and release the red Movie button at the upper right corner of the camera's back. (If you see an error message, go to screen 6 of the Custom menu, marked by a gear icon, and set the Movie Button option to Always.)

The screen will display a red REC icon in the lower left corner of the display, next to a counter showing the elapsed time in the recording, as shown in Figure 2-24.

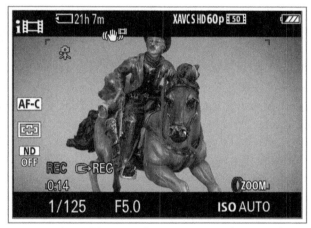

Figure 2-24. REC Icon on Screen During Video Recording

Hold the camera as steady as possible (or use a tripod), and pan (move the camera side to side) slowly if you need to. The camera will shoot until it reaches a recording limit, or until you press the Movie button again to stop the recording. (The maximum time for continuous recording of any one scene is about 29 minutes with most recording formats.) Don't be too concerned about the level of the sound that is being recorded, because you do not have much control over the audio volume while recording using the built-in microphone. I will discuss options for audio recording in Chapter 8.

The camera will automatically adjust exposure as lighting conditions change. You can zoom the lens in and out as needed, but you should do so sparingly if at all, to avoid distracting the audience and to avoid putting the sounds of zooming the lens on the sound track. When you are finished, press the Movie button again, and the recording will end.

Those are the basics for recording video with the RX100 V. I'll discuss movie options further in Chapter 8.

Viewing Pictures

Before I talk about more advanced settings for taking still pictures and movies, as well as other topics, I will discuss the basics of viewing your images in the camera.

REVIEWING WHILE IN SHOOTING MODE

When you take a still picture, it will appear on the camera's display for a short time, if you have the Custom menu's Auto Review option set to turn on this function. I'll discuss details of that setting in Chapter 7. By default, a new image stays on the screen for two seconds. If you prefer, you can set that display to last for five or 10 seconds, or to be off altogether.

REVIEWING IMAGES IN PLAYBACK MODE

To review images taken previously, enter playback mode by pressing the Playback button, to the lower left of the Control wheel. To view all still images and movies for a particular date, go to screen 1 of the Playback menu (marked with a triangle icon), set the View Mode option to Date View, and press the Center button on the selected date. If you prefer, you can set View Mode to show only stills, only MP4 movies, only AVCHD movies, or only XAVC S movies (either 4K or HD).

Once you choose a viewing option, you can scroll through images and movies by pressing the Left and Right buttons or by turning the Control wheel. Hold down the Left or Right button to move quickly through the items. You can enlarge the view of a still image by moving the zoom lever on top of the camera toward the T position, and you can scroll around in the enlarged image using the four direction buttons. When you first press the zoom lever to the right, the camera centers the enlarged image on the autofocus point, if there is one. If not, it zooms on the center of the image. (You can change that behavior using the Enlarge Initial Position option on screen 2 of the Playback menu.)

Press the zoom lever repeatedly in the other direction, toward the wide-angle setting, to return the image to normal size. You can immediately return an image to

normal size by pressing the Center button or the Menu button.

When viewing an image at normal size, press the zoom lever once to the left to see an index screen with either nine or 25 thumbnail images, depending on a Playback menu option. Another press of the lever to the left brings up either a calendar screen for selecting images or videos by date, or a screen for selecting a folder, depending on the View Mode option in effect. I'll discuss other playback options in Chapter 6.

To switch among views with varying amounts of information for your recorded images, press the Display button (Up button on the control wheel) until the view you prefer is shown.

PLAYING MOVIES

To play movies in the camera, move through your files by the methods described above until you find the movie you want to play. You should see a triangular playback icon inside a circle, as shown in Figure 2-25.

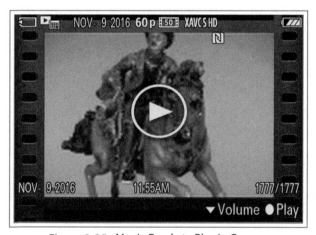

Figure 2-25. Movie Ready to Play in Camera

Press the Center button to start the movie playing. Then, as shown in Figure 2-26, you will see prompts at the bottom of the screen showing the controls you can use, including the Center button to pause. (You may have to press the Display button to show the icons.)

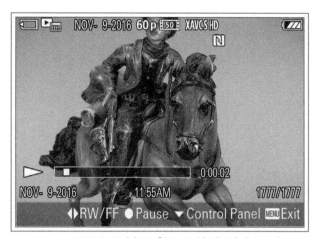

Figure 2-26. Initial Set of Movie Playback Controls

You also can press the Down button to bring up a more detailed set of controls on the screen, as shown in Figure 2-27.

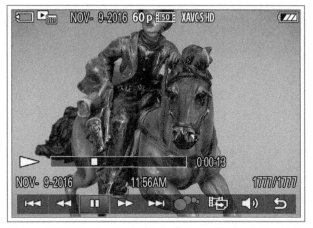

Figure 2-27. More Detailed Set of Movie Playback Controls

To change the volume, pause the movie and press the Down button to bring up the detailed controls; then navigate to the speaker icon, next to last at the right of those controls. Press the Center button to select volume, then use the Control wheel or the Right and Left buttons to adjust the volume. You also can adjust the volume before a movie starts playing, by pressing the Down button to bring up the volume control. To exit from playing the movie, press the Playback button. (I'll discuss other movie playback options in Chapter 8.)

If you want to play your movies on a computer or edit them with video-editing software, you can use the PlayMemories Home software that is provided through the Sony web site. You also can use any program that can deal with AVCHD and MP4 video files, such as Adobe Premiere Elements, Adobe Premiere Pro, Final Cut Express, Final Cut Pro, iMovie, or Windows Movie Maker, depending on what type of computer you are using.

Movies recorded by the RX100 V using the newest formats, XAVC S 4K and XAVC S HD, are saved as files with the .mp4 extension, and, in my experience, can be imported and edited with standard software that uses those files, such as iMovie for the Mac and Movie Maker for Windows-based computers. However, those files can be quite large, so you may need a computer with a large and fast storage drive and a powerful processor to edit those files efficiently.

CHAPTER 3: SHOOTING MODES

Until now, I have discussed the basics of taking quick shots and videos in Intelligent Auto or Superior Auto mode. The Sony RX100 V provides many other options and settings, though, for both still images and movies. To explain these features, I will discuss the shooting modes in this chapter and the Shooting menu options in Chapter 4.

To record still images, you need to select one of the available shooting modes on the Mode dial: Auto, Program Auto, Aperture Priority, Shutter Priority, Manual exposure, Scene Selection, Sweep Panorama, or Memory Recall. (The other two modes available are for movies.) So far, I have concentrated on procedures using Auto mode. This chapter will discuss all of the shooting modes, starting with a review of the first one.

Auto Mode

This is the mode to select for a quick shot when you don't have time to deal with settings such as ISO, white balance, aperture, shutter speed, or metering method. It's a good mode to choose when you hand the camera to someone to take a photo of you and your companions.

To set this mode, turn the Mode dial to the AUTO icon, as shown in Figure 3-1.

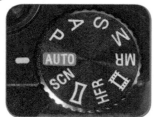

Figure 3-1. Mode Dial at AUTO

When you do this, the camera may display the Mode Dial Guide screen, showing Auto Mode selected on a graphic Mode dial display. If you press the Center button, the camera displays the screen shown in Figure 3-2, giving you the choice of selecting one of the two sub-modes: Intelligent Auto mode or Superior Auto mode.

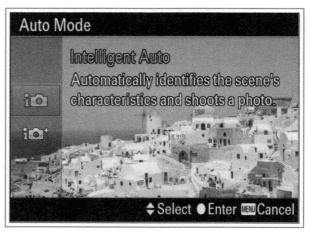

Figure 3-2. Screen to Select Intelligent Auto or Superior Auto

If the Mode Dial Guide option on screen 2 of the Setup menu is turned off, the camera will not automatically display the Mode Dial Guide. In that case, go to screen 8 of the Shooting menu and select the Auto Mode option, as shown in Figure 3-3.

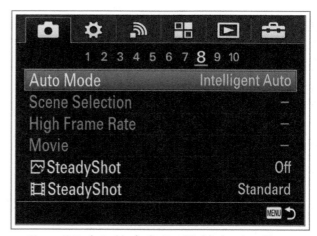

Figure 3-3. Auto Mode Option Highlighted on Menu

When you highlight that option and press the Center button, you will be able to choose either Intelligent Auto or Superior Auto for the shooting mode. I will discuss these two options next.

INTELLIGENT AUTO MODE

With this version of Auto mode, the camera makes several decisions for you and limits your options in some ways. For example, you can't set the ISO or white balance to any value other than Auto, and you can't choose a metering method or use exposure bracketing. You can, however, use quite a few features, as discussed in Chapter 2, including the Photo Creativity options, continuous shooting, Flash Mode, Focus Mode, and others. You also can use sophisticated options such as the Raw format for still images, which I will discuss in Chapter 4 along with other Shooting menu options.

In this mode (and Superior Auto mode, discussed next), the camera uses its programming to try to figure out what subject or scene you are shooting. Some subjects the camera will try to detect are Infant, Portrait, Night Portrait, Night Scene, Landscape, Backlight, Low Light, Spotlight, and Macro. It also will try to detect certain conditions, such as whether a tripod is in use, whether the subject is moving, and the brightness of the lighting, and it will display icons for those factors. So, if you see different icons when you aim at various subjects in this shooting mode, that means the camera is evaluating the scene for factors such as brightness, backlighting, the presence of human subjects, and the like, so it can use the best settings for the situation. Face detection must be turned on for the camera to recognize faces with the Infant setting or any of the Portrait settings.

For Figure 3-4, the camera evaluated a scene with a mannequin's head and appropriately used its Portrait setting. The Portrait scene-recognition icon is seen in the upper left corner of the screen.

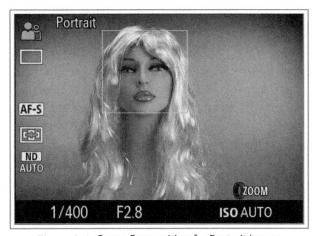

Figure 3-4. Scene Recognition for Portrait Image

Figure 3-5 shows the use of automatic scene recognition for a miniature knight figure closer to the lens. The camera interpreted the scene as a macro, or closeup shot, and switched automatically into Macro mode, indicated by the flower icon. In addition, the camera correctly detected that it was attached to a tripod, as indicated by the tripod icon to the lower right of the macro symbol.

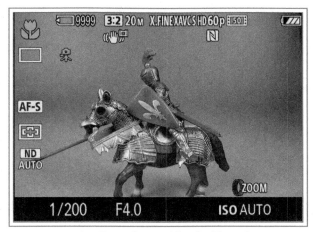

Figure 3-5. Scene Recognition for Macro Image

Of course, scene recognition depends on the camera's programming, which may not interpret every scene the same way you would. If that becomes a problem, you may want to make individual settings using one of the more advanced shooting modes, such as Program, Aperture Priority, Shutter Priority, or Manual. Or, you can use the SCN setting on the Mode dial and select a Scene mode setting that better fits the current situation.

SUPERIOR AUTO MODE

With many compact cameras, there is only one largely automatic shooting mode. The RX100 V, however, provides you with two choices, both of which provide high degrees of automation but which have one significant difference. The second version of Auto mode, called Superior Auto, is designated by the icon of a tan-colored camera with the letter "i" and a plus sign next to it, as shown in Figure 3-6.

Superior Auto mode includes all functions of Intelligent Auto mode, and adds one extra feature. In Superior Auto mode, as in Intelligent Auto mode, the camera uses its scene recognition capability to determine what subject matter or conditions are present, such as a portrait, a dimly lit scene, and the like. For many of these subjects, the camera operates the same way as in Intelligent Auto mode.

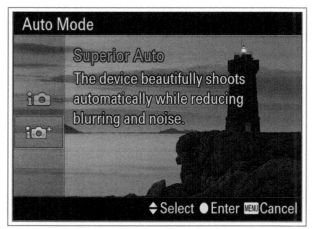

Figure 3-6. Superior Auto Mode Selection Screen

However, with situations involving dimly lit or backlit scenes, the camera takes a different approach: It will take a rapid burst of shots and combine them internally into a single image with higher quality than would be possible with a single shot. The higher quality can be achieved because the camera generally has to raise the ISO setting to a fairly high level, which introduces visual "noise" into the image. By taking multiple shots and then merging them, the camera can average out and cancel some of the noise, thereby increasing the quality of the resulting image.

One problem with this system is that you, the photographer, can't control when the camera uses this burst shooting technique. The camera will evaluate the lighting and use this technique if the lighting appears to be excessively dark or if backlighting is detected.

When the camera believes this option is appropriate, it fires a quick series of shots; you will hear the rapid firing of the shutter. Then, it will take longer than usual for the camera to process the multiple shots into a single image; you will likely see a message saying "Processing" on the screen for several seconds. When the camera is using this operation, which Sony calls "Overlay," you will see a small white icon in the upper left corner of the display that looks like a stack of frames with a plus sign at its upper right corner, as shown in Figure 3-7.

The multiple-shot feature of Superior Auto mode will not function when Quality is set to Raw or Raw & JPEG on the Shooting menu. If you change the Quality setting to one of those options when the camera is in

Superior Auto mode, the camera will take only a single shot, even if it detects backlighting or dim lighting.

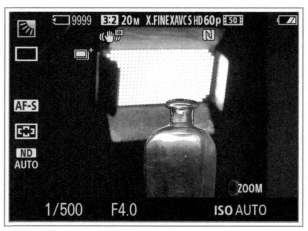

Figure 3-7. Overlay Icon on Shooting Screen

I have not found much advantage from using the Superior Auto setting. However, the overlay feature may improve the quality of an image, so it is not a bad idea to set the camera to the Superior Auto mode when you are shooting in low-light or backlit conditions. As a general rule, though, I prefer to use a mode such as Program, discussed below, and set my own values for items such as DRO, HDR, ISO, and metering mode.

Program Mode

Choose this mode by turning the Mode dial to the P setting, as shown in Figure 3-8.

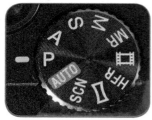

Figure 3-8. Mode Dial at P

Program mode (also called Program Auto mode) lets you control many settings on the camera, apart from shutter speed and aperture, which the camera chooses on its own. You can override the automatic exposure to a fair extent by using exposure compensation, as discussed in Chapter 5, as well as exposure bracketing, discussed in Chapter 4, and Program Shift, discussed later in this section. You don't have to make a lot of decisions if you don't want to, because the camera will make reasonable choices as defaults. The camera can choose a shutter speed as long as 30 seconds or as short as 1/32000 second, depending on the setting of the Shutter Type option on screen 4 of the Custom menu.

The Program Shift function, which is available only in Program mode, works as follows: When you aim the camera at your subject, the camera will display its chosen settings for shutter speed and aperture in the lower left corner of the display. At that point, turn the Control wheel on the back of the camera. The values for shutter speed and aperture will change, if possible under current conditions, to different values for both settings while keeping the same overall exposure of the scene.

You also can use the Control ring (the large ring around the lens) to make this setting, if the Control Ring option is set to the Standard setting through the Custom Key (Shooting) item on the Custom menu, as discussed in Chapter 7. If you use the Control ring for Program Shift, you will see two circular scales on the display, with shutter speed and aperture values that shift as you turn the ring, as shown in Figure 3-9. (A similar display is visible at the bottom of the screen if you use the Control wheel, but only if the Exposure Settings Guide menu option is turned on through screen 3 of the Custom menu.)

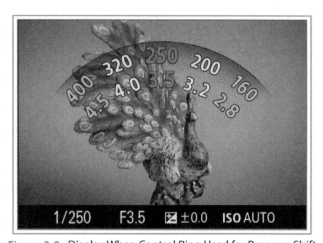

Figure 3-9. Display When Control Ring Used for Program Shift

With the Program Shift option, the camera "shifts" the original exposure to any of the matched pairs that appear as you turn the Control wheel. For example, if the original exposure was f/2.0 at 1/50 second, you may see equivalent pairs of f/2.5 at 1/30, f/2.8 at 1/25, and f/3.2 at 1/20, among others. When Program Shift is in effect, the P icon in the upper left corner of the screen will have an asterisk to its right, as shown in Figure 3-10.

To cancel Program Shift, turn the Control wheel or Control ring until the original settings are back in effect or release the flash by pressing the flash pop-up button. (Program Shift cannot function when the flash is in use.)

Program Shift is useful if, for example, you want to let the camera make the original exposure setting but you want a faster shutter speed to stop action or a wider aperture to blur the background. Of course, if you need to use a particular shutter speed or aperture, you probably should use Aperture Priority mode or Shutter Priority mode. However, Program Shift is a good option to have when you're taking pictures quickly using Program mode and you need a fast way to tweak the settings somewhat.

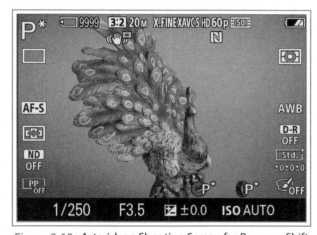

Figure 3-10. Asterisk on Shooting Screen for Program Shift

One important aspect of Program mode is that it expands the choices available through the Shooting menu, which controls many of the camera's settings. You will be able to make choices involving ISO sensitivity, metering method, DRO/HDR, white balance, Creative Style, and others that are not available in the Auto or Scene modes. I won't discuss those settings here; see Chapter 4 for information about all of the different selections that are available.

Aperture Priority Mode

You set the camera to the Aperture Priority shooting mode by turning the Mode dial to the A setting, as shown in Figure 3-11. In this mode, you select the aperture setting and the camera will select a shutter speed that will result in normal exposure, if possible.

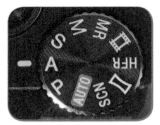

Figure 3-11. Mode Dial at A

The main reason to choose this mode is so you can select an aperture to achieve a broad depth of field, with objects in focus at different distances from the lens, or a shallow depth of field, with only one object in sharp focus and other parts of the image blurred to reduce distractions. With a narrow aperture (higher f-stop number) such as f/8.0, the depth of field will be relatively broad; with a wide aperture such as f/1.8, it will be shallower, resulting in the possibility of a blurred background.

In Figure 3-12 and Figure 3-13, I made the same shot with two very different aperture settings. I focused on the eye of the owl figurine in the foreground in each case. For Figure 3-12, the aperture of the RX100 V was set to f/1.8, the widest setting available.

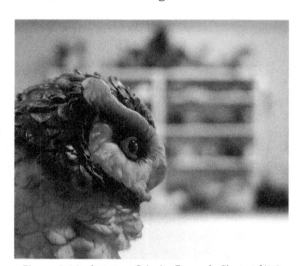

Figure 3-12. Aperture Priority Example Shot at f/1.8

With this setting, because the depth of field at this aperture was shallow, the objects in the background are blurry. I took Figure 3-13 with the camera's aperture set to f/11.0, the narrowest possible, resulting in a broader depth of field, and consequently bringing the background into sharper focus.

These two photos illustrate the effects of varying your aperture by setting it wide (low numbers) when you want to blur the background and narrow (high numbers) when you want to enjoy a broad depth of field and keep subjects at varying distances in sharp focus.

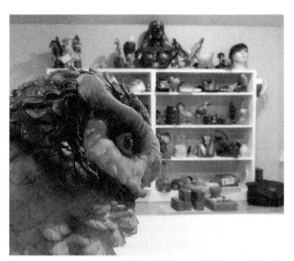

Figure 3-13. Aperture Priority Example Shot at f/11.0

The blurred background look, sometimes called "bokeh," can be useful to isolate your subject by de-emphasizing a distracting background, as illustrated in Figure 3-12.

Here are the steps to set the aperture. After moving the Mode dial to the A setting, use either the Control ring or the Control wheel to change the aperture. If the Control ring does not change the aperture, check the setting for the Control Ring in the Custom Key (Shooting) item on the Custom menu, as discussed in Chapter 7; that menu option has to be set to Standard or Aperture for the ring to carry out this function.

If you use the Control ring to set the aperture, the camera will display a circular scale showing the changing aperture values, as seen in Figure 3-14, and the selected value will also appear in the bottom center of the screen.

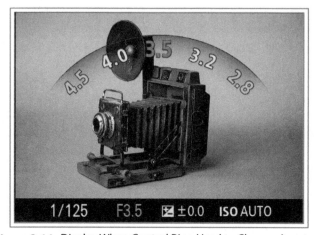

Figure 3-14. Display When Control Ring Used to Change Aperture

If you use the Control wheel instead, the camera will display a circular scale at the bottom of the screen, if the Exposure Settings Guide option on screen 3 of the Custom menu is turned on.

The available aperture settings range from f/1.8 to f/11.0, though the widest settings, such as f/1.8, are available only at the wide-angle focal lengths, as discussed later in this section. In Aperture Priority mode, the RX100 V can select shutter speeds from 1/32000 second to 30 seconds. The fastest speed available is 1/2000 second if the mechanical shutter is in use. If the flash is in use, the fastest setting available is 1/100 second with the electronic shutter and 1/2000 second with the mechanical shutter.

Although, in most cases, the camera will be able to select a corresponding shutter speed that results in a normal exposure, there may be times when this is not possible. For example, if you are taking pictures in a very bright location with the aperture set to f/1.8, the camera may not be able to set a shutter speed fast enough to yield a normal exposure, especially if you are using the mechanical shutter instead of the electronic shutter. In that case, the fastest possible shutter speed (1/2000) will flash on the display to show that a normal exposure cannot be made using the chosen aperture. The camera will let you take the picture, but it may be too bright to be usable. (The neutral density filter may activate to reduce brightness, depending on the ND Filter menu setting, as discussed in Chapter 4, but there still may be times when no shutter speed is available to make a good exposure.)

Similarly, if conditions are too dark for a good exposure at the aperture you have selected, the slowest possible shutter speed (30", meaning 30 seconds) will flash.

In situations where conditions are too bright or dark for a good exposure, the camera's display may become bright or dark, giving you notice of the problem. This will happen if the Live View Display item on screen 3 of the Custom menu is set to Setting Effect On. If that option is set to Setting Effect Off, the display will remain at normal brightness, even if the exposure settings would result in an excessively bright or dark image. I will discuss that menu option in Chapter 7.

As I noted earlier, not all apertures are available at all times. The widest aperture, f/1.8, is available only when the lens is zoomed out to its wide-angle setting (zoom lever moved toward the W). At the highest zoom levels, the widest aperture available is f/2.8.

To see an illustration of this point, here is a quick test. Zoom the lens out by moving the zoom lever all the way to the left, toward the W label. Then select Aperture Priority mode and set the aperture to f/1.8. Now zoom the lens in by moving the zoom lever to the right. After the zoom is finished, the aperture will have changed to f/2.8 because that is the limit for the aperture at the full-telephoto zoom level. (The aperture will change back to f/1.8 if you zoom back to the wide-angle setting.)

Shutter Priority Mode

In Shutter Priority mode, you choose the shutter speed and the camera will set the corresponding aperture to achieve a proper exposure of the image if it can.

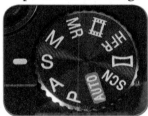

Figure 3-15. Mode Dial at S

In this mode, designated by the S position on the Mode dial, as shown in Figure 3-15, you can set the shutter to be open for a time ranging from 30 seconds to 1/32000 of a second, if the Shutter Type menu option is set to Auto or Electronic. If that option is set to Mechanical, the fastest setting available is 1/2000 second. If the flash is in use, the fastest setting available is 1/100 second with the electronic shutter and 1/2000 second with the mechanical shutter.

If you are photographing fast action, such as a baseball swing or a hurdles event at a track meet, and you want to stop the motion with a minimum of blur, you should select a fast shutter speed, such as 1/1000 of a second.

To illustrate the effects of different shutter speeds, I photographed a cup of uncooked rice being poured into a transparent pitcher, using very different shutter speeds for two different images. For Figure 3-16, I set the shutter speed to 1/2000 second. In that image, you can see many of the individual grains of rice appearing as if they are frozen in mid-air.

For Figure 3-17, I used a much slower shutter speed of 1/10 second, which resulted in an image that makes the grains of rice appear in a continuous stream, almost like a flow of milk.

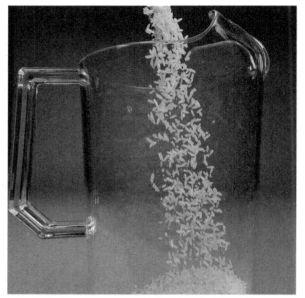

Figure 3-16. Shutter Speed Example at 1/2000 Second

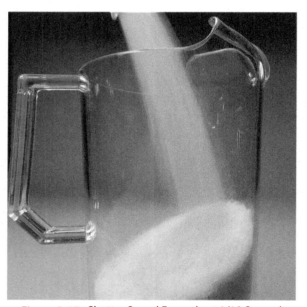

Figure 3-17. Shutter Speed Example at 1/10 Second

Choose this mode by turning the Mode dial to the S position, as seen in Figure 3-15. Select the shutter speed by turning the Control wheel or the Control ring. The Control Ring function must be set to Standard or Shutter Speed using the Custom Key (Shooting) option on the Custom menu for the ring to control shutter speed.

As with Aperture Priority mode, the camera will display a circular scale of shutter speeds as you turn the

Control wheel if you have the Exposure Settings Guide option turned on in the Custom menu. It will always display a circular scale when you use the Control ring to make the setting.

Although the Mode dial uses the letter "S" to stand for Shutter Priority, on the detailed display screen, as shown in Figure 3-18, the camera uses the notation Tv in the lower right corner, next to the icons showing that the Control ring or Control wheel can be used to make this setting. Tv stands for time value, a notation often used for this shooting mode.

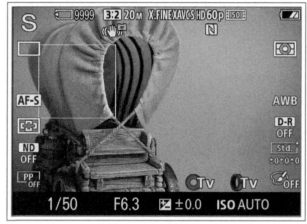

Figure 3-18. Tv Notation on Shooting Screen for Shutter Speed

As you cycle through various shutter speeds, the camera will select the appropriate aperture to achieve a proper exposure, if possible. As I discussed in connection with Aperture Priority mode, if you select a shutter speed for which the camera cannot select an aperture for a normal exposure, the display may (depending on the Live View Display menu option) change appearance to indicate how dark or light the resulting shot will be, and the aperture reading at the bottom of the display will flash. The flashing aperture means that proper exposure at that shutter speed is not possible at any available aperture, according to the camera's calculations.

For example, if you set the shutter speed to 1/320 second in a fairly dark indoor environment, the aperture number (which will be f/1.8, the widest setting, if the zoom is set to wide angle) may flash, indicating that proper exposure is not possible, and the display may be quite dark. As I discussed for Aperture Priority, you can still take the picture if you want to, though it may not be usable. A similar situation may take place if you select a slow shutter speed (such as four seconds) in a relatively bright location.

Manual Exposure Mode

One of the many features of the RX100 V that distinguish it from more ordinary compact cameras is its fully manual exposure mode, a great tool for photographers who want to have full control over exposure decisions.

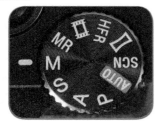

Figure 3-19. Mode Dial at M

To control exposure manually, set the Mode dial to the M indicator, as shown in Figure 3-19.

You now have to control both shutter speed and aperture by setting them yourself. To set the aperture, turn the Control ring around the lens (assuming the Control ring is set for this function through the Custom menu, as discussed in Chapter 7); to set the shutter speed, turn the Control wheel on the back of the camera.

If the Control ring is not set to control aperture, or if you prefer not to use the ring for that purpose, you can use the Control wheel to adjust both aperture and shutter speed. To do that, press the Down button to switch between the two selections.

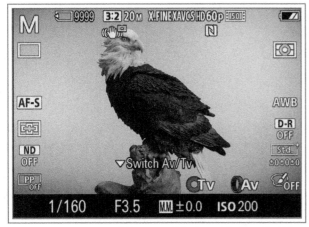

Figure 3-20. Manual Exposure Display with Specific ISO

When you press that button, either the shutter speed number or the aperture number on the display will turn orange for about 10 seconds to show that that value is currently being controlled by the Control wheel Also, the label beside the gray icon for the Control wheel in the lower right corner of the display will change between Av (for aperture value) and Tv (for time value) when you press the Down button to switch the wheel's function. Figure 3-20 shows the display when the Control wheel is controlling shutter speed.

As you adjust shutter speed and aperture, a third value, to the right of the aperture value, also may change. That value is a positive, negative, or zero number. The meaning of the number is different depending on the current ISO setting. (In Chapter 4, I'll provide more details about the ISO setting, which controls how sensitive the camera's sensor is to light. With a higher ISO value, the sensor is more sensitive and the image is exposed more quickly, so the shutter speed can be faster or the aperture more narrow, or both.)

To set the ISO value, press the Menu button to access the Shooting menu, go to the fifth screen, and highlight the ISO item. Press the Center button to bring up the ISO menu, as shown in Figure 3-21, and scroll through the selections using the Up and Down buttons or by turning the Control wheel.

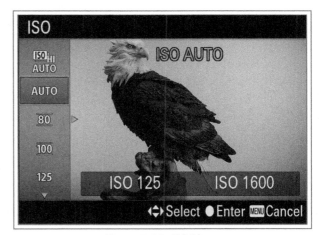

Figure 3-21. ISO Menu

Choose a low number like 125 to maximize image quality when there is plenty of light; use a higher number in dim light. Higher ISO settings are likely to cause visual "noise," or graininess, in your images. Generally speaking, you should try to set ISO no higher than 800 to ensure the highest image quality.

If the ISO value is set to a specific number, such as 125, 200, or 1000, then, in Manual exposure mode, the icon at the bottom center of the display is a box containing the letters "M.M.," which stand for "metered manual," as shown in Figure 3-20.

In this situation, the number next to the M.M. icon represents any deviation from what the camera's metering system considers normal exposure. So, even though you are setting the exposure manually, the camera will let you know whether the selected aperture and shutter speed will produce a standard exposure.

If the aperture, shutter speed, and ISO values you have selected will result in a darker exposure than normal, the M.M. value will be negative, and vice-versa. This value can vary only by +2.0 or -2.0 EV (exposure value) units; after that, the value will flash, meaning the camera considers the exposure excessively abnormal.

Of course, you can ignore the M.M. indicator; it is there only to give you an idea of how the camera would expose the image. You very well may want part or all of the scene to be darker or lighter than the metering would indicate to be "correct."

As with Aperture Priority and Shutter Priority modes, the camera's display will become unusually bright or dim to indicate that current settings would result in an abnormal exposure, but only when the Live View Display menu option on screen 3 of the Custom menu is set to Setting Effect On.

If, instead of a specific value, you have set ISO to Auto ISO, the icon at the bottom center of the screen changes. In this situation, the camera displays the exposure compensation icon, which contains a plus and minus sign, as shown in Figure 3-22.

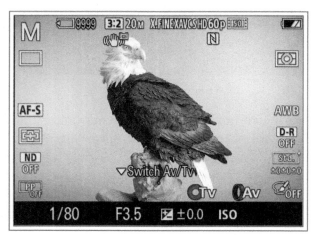

Figure 3-22. Manual Exposure Display with Auto ISO

The reason for this change is that, when you use Auto ISO in Manual exposure mode, the camera can likely produce a normal exposure by adjusting the ISO. There

is no need to display the M.M. value, which shows deviation from a normal exposure. Instead, the camera lets you adjust exposure compensation, so you can set the exposure to be darker or brighter than the camera's autoexposure system would produce.

To set exposure compensation in Manual mode, you cannot use the ordinary control for that purpose— the Down button—because that button toggles the function of the Control wheel for controlling aperture or shutter speed, as discussed above. To control exposure compensation in Manual mode, you can use the Exposure Compensation item on screen 4 of the Shooting menu, or you can assign exposure compensation to the Control ring or to the Custom, Center, Left, or Right button. You make that assignment using the Custom Key (Shooting) option on screen 5 of the Custom menu, as discussed in Chapter 7. You also can use the Function menu to adjust exposure compensation, if that adjustment has been included in that menu, as discussed in Chapter 7.

With Manual exposure mode, the settings for aperture and shutter speed are independent of each other. When you change one, the other one stays unchanged until you adjust it manually. But the effect of this system is different depending on whether you have selected a specific value for ISO as opposed to Auto ISO.

If you select a numerical value for ISO, which can range from 80 to 12800 or even higher when Multi Frame Noise Reduction is selected for the ISO setting, the camera leaves the creative decision about exposure entirely up to you, even if the resulting photograph would be washed out by excessive exposure or underexposed to the point of near-blackness.

However, if you select Auto ISO for the ISO setting, then, as discussed above, the camera will adjust the ISO to achieve a normal exposure if possible. In this case, Manual exposure mode becomes like a different shooting mode altogether. You might call this the "aperture and shutter speed priority mode," because you are able to set both aperture and shutter speed but still have the camera adjust exposure automatically by changing the ISO value.

The ability to use Auto ISO in Manual exposure mode is very useful. For example, suppose you are taking photographs of a craftsman using tools in a dimly lighted area. You may want to use a narrow aperture such as f/7.1 to achieve a broad depth of field and keep the tools and other items in focus, but you also may want to use a fast shutter speed, such as 1/100 second, to freeze action. If you use Aperture Priority mode, the camera will choose the shutter speed; with Shutter Priority mode, the camera will choose the aperture, and with Program mode, the camera will choose both values. Only by using Manual exposure mode with Auto ISO can you choose both aperture and shutter speed and still have the camera find a good exposure setting automatically.

Even with the ability to use Auto ISO, though, there may be situations in which the camera cannot produce a normal exposure. This could happen if you have limited the range of the Auto ISO setting by setting a narrow range between the minimum and maximum settings for Auto ISO. It also could happen if you have chosen extreme settings for aperture and shutter speed, such as 1/500 second at f/11.0 in dark conditions. In such situations, the ISO Auto label and the exposure compensation value at the bottom of the display will flash, indicating that a normal exposure cannot be achieved with these settings.

The range of apertures you can set in Manual mode is the same as for Aperture Priority mode: f/1.8 to f/11.0. (As in other modes, the widest aperture available is f/2.8 when the lens is zoomed in.)

The range of shutter speeds in Manual mode is largely the same as for Shutter Priority mode: 1/32000 second to 30 seconds if Shutter Type is set to Auto or Electronic and 1/2000 second to 30 seconds if Shutter Type is Mechanical. If the flash is in use, the fastest setting available is 1/100 second with the electronic shutter and 1/2000 second with the mechanical shutter. However, there is one important addition: In Manual mode, you can set the shutter speed to the BULB setting, just beyond the 30-second mark, as shown in Figure 3-23.

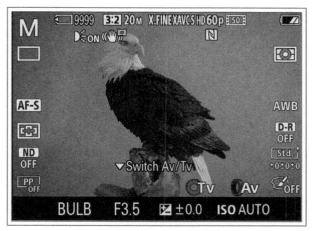

Figure 3-23. BULB Setting for Shutter Speed

With the BULB setting, you have to press and hold the shutter button to keep the shutter open. You can use this setting to take photos in dark conditions by holding the shutter open for a minute or more. One problem is that it is hard to avoid jiggling the camera, causing image blur, even if the camera is on a tripod. In Appendix A, I discuss using a remote control to trigger the camera. After the exposure ends, the camera will process the exposure for the same length of time as the exposure, to reduce the noise caused by long exposures. You will not be able to take another shot while this processing continues. (You can disable this setting with the Long Exposure Noise Reduction option on screen 6 of the Shooting menu.)

Another feature available in this mode is Manual Shift, which is similar to Program Shift, discussed earlier. To use Manual Shift, you first have to assign one of the control buttons (Custom, Center, Left, or Right) to the AEL (autoexposure lock) Hold or AEL Toggle function using the Custom Key (Shooting) option on screen 5 of the Custom menu, as discussed in Chapter 7. Then, after making your aperture and shutter speed settings, change the aperture or shutter speed setting while pressing the button assigned to the AEL function. (If you selected AEL Toggle, you don't have to hold down the button; just press it and release it.)

When you do this, the camera will make new settings with equivalent exposure, if possible. For example, if the original settings were f/3.5 at 1/160 second, when you select Manual Shift and change the aperture to f/3.2, the camera will reset the shutter speed to 1/200 second, maintaining the original exposure. In this way, you can tweak your settings to favor a particular shutter speed or aperture without affecting the overall exposure. An asterisk will appear in the lower right corner of the display while you activate the button that activates AEL.

With Manual Shift, if you select a new value for which there is no corresponding value available to maintain the exposure, the camera will not select new values. For example, if the original settings are f/1.8 and 1/250 second, and, using Manual Shift, you attempt to select a faster shutter speed, the camera will not choose any new values, because there is no available aperture setting that can maintain the original exposure setting.

I use Manual exposure mode often, for various purposes. One use is to take images at different exposures to combine into a composite HDR image. I will discuss that technique in Chapter 4. I also use Manual mode when using external flash with the RX100 V, as discussed in Appendix A, because the flash does not interact with the camera's autoexposure system.

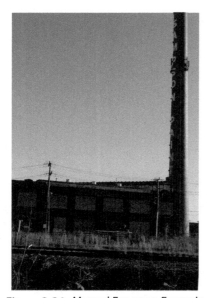

Figure 3-24. Manual Exposure Example

Manual mode also is useful for some special types of photography, such as making silhouettes. For example, in Figure 3-24, I adjusted exposure settings manually to photograph a factory with its smokestack, adjusting the shutter speed and aperture to reduce the exposure and give the scene a dark, silhouette-like appearance, emphasizing the subject's shape.

Scene Mode

Unlike other modes, Scene mode does not have a single defining feature, such as permitting control over one or more aspects of exposure. Instead, when you select Scene mode and then choose a scene type within that mode, you are telling the camera what sort of environment the picture is being taken in and what type of image you are looking for, and you are letting the camera make the decisions as to what settings to use to produce that result.

With most scene types, you cannot select several options that are available in the advanced shooting modes, such as Creative Style, Picture Effect, Metering Mode, White Balance, Focus Area, and ISO. There also are some settings that are available with certain scene types but not others, as discussed later in this chapter.

Although some photographers may feel that Scene mode limits creative decisions, I find it useful. You don't have to use the scene types only for their labeled purposes; some of them may offer settings that are useful for scenarios you regularly encounter.

You select Scene mode by turning the Mode dial to the SCN indicator, as shown in Figure 3-25.

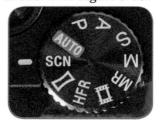

Figure 3-25. Mode Dial at SCN

Now, unless you want to use the setting that is already in place, you need to pick one from the list of 13 scene types. There are several ways to do this, depending on current menu settings.

If Mode Dial Guide is turned on through screen 2 of the Setup menu, then, whenever you turn the Mode dial to the SCN setting and press the Center button, the Scene Selection menu in Figure 3-26 appears.

If Mode Dial Guide is not turned on, or if the camera is already in Scene mode, you can use the Shooting menu to call up the Scene Selection screen. Navigate to screen 8 of the Shooting menu and choose the Scene Selection item, as shown in Figure 3-27.

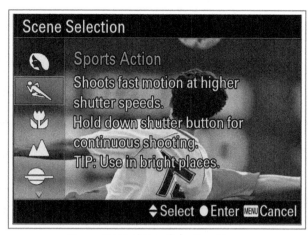

Figure 3-26. Scene Selection Menu

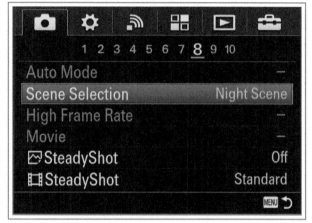

Figure 3-27. Scene Selection Item Highlighted on Menu

Once the Scene Selection menu is displayed, scroll through the 13 selections using the Up and Down buttons or the Control wheel. Press the Center button to select a setting and return to the shooting screen. You will see an icon representing that setting in the upper left corner of the display. (You may need to press the Display button to see the screen that shows the scene setting icon; the icon will disappear after a few seconds on some display screens.) For example, Figure 3-28 shows the display when the Gourmet setting is selected.

For each scene type the camera displays a screen with a description of the setting's uses as you move the selector over it, as shown in Figure 3-26, so you are not left to puzzle out what each icon represents. As you press the Up or Down button or turn the Control wheel to move the selector over the other scene types, when you reach the bottom or top edge of the screen, the selector wraps around to the first or last setting and continues going.

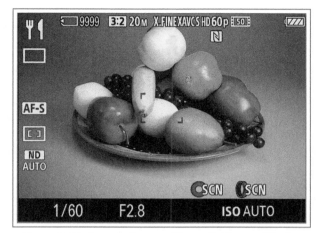

Figure 3-28. Icon for Gourmet Scene Setting on Display

There also are two more ways to select a scene type. If the Control ring is set to its Standard setting, then when the shooting screen is displayed in Scene mode, you can just turn the Control ring to cycle through the various scene types. You will see a circular display as the ring turns, as shown in Figure 3-29.

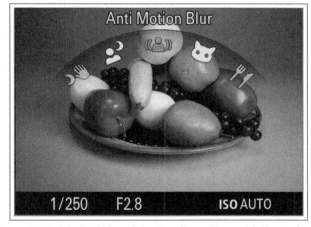

Figure 3-29. Display When Selecting Scene Type with Control Ring

After you stop turning the ring, the icon for the selected scene type will appear in the upper left corner. (If you are using manual focus or DMF (Direct Manual Focus) this will not work, because the Control ring will adjust focus and will not be available to display scene types.) Also, you can turn the Control wheel in Scene mode to change scene types, regardless of the function assigned to the Control ring. With that option, there is no circular display; the camera just cycles through the various scene icons in the upper left corner of the display.

That's all you have to do to select a scene type. But you need to know something about each option to decide whether it's one you would want to use. In general, each scene type carries with it a variety of values, including things like focus mode, flash status, range of shutter speeds, sensitivity to various colors, and others.

Note that some settings are designed for certain types of shooting, rather than particular subjects such as sunsets or fireworks. For example, the Anti Motion Blur and High Sensitivity settings are designed for difficult shooting environments, such as dimly lighted areas.

Portrait

The Portrait setting is designed to produce flesh tones with a softening effect, as shown in Figure 3-30. You should stand fairly close to the subject and set the zoom to fill the frame. If you have the Auto Object Framing option turned on through screen 7 of the Shooting menu, the camera may re-frame the portrait for you.

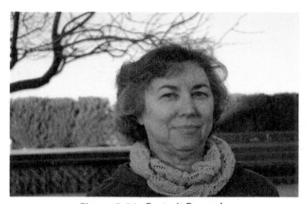

Figure 3-30. Portrait Example

The camera will try to use a wide aperture to blur the background. You can use Autoflash or Fill-flash if you want to even out the lighting or reduce shadows on your subject's face. If you want to improve the lighting, consider using off-camera flash with a softbox attachment.

If you are shooting a portrait in front of a busy background, such as a house, try to position the subject's head in front of a plain area, such as a light-colored wall, so the head will be seen clearly.

You can use the self-timer, but you cannot use bracketing or continuous shooting. You can use the self-portrait timer feature if it is turned on through screen 5 of the Custom menu. To use that feature, flip the LCD screen up so it is facing in the same direction as the lens, and turn the camera so the lens is facing you. Press the shutter button as you see your face, and

the shutter will fire after a three-second on-screen countdown.

Sports Action

The Sports Action setting is for use when lighting is bright and you need to freeze the action of athletes, children at play, pets, or other subjects. The camera may set a high ISO value so it can use a fast shutter speed to stop action. The flash is initially forced off, but you can turn on Fill-flash. The camera sets itself for continuous shooting so you can hold down the shutter button and capture a burst of images. In that way, you increase your chances of capturing the action at a perfect moment. You can switch to any of the three speeds of continuous shooting if you want, but you cannot set Drive Mode to single shooting or turn on the self-timer. (I'll discuss the Drive Mode options in Chapter 4.) The camera turns on continuous autofocus, so it adjusts focus automatically as the subject moves. You can switch to manual focus or direct manual focus (DMF), which are discussed in Chapter 4. You cannot turn on single autofocus.

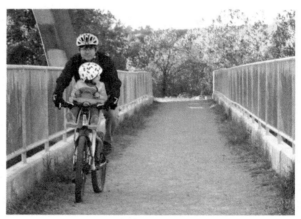

Figure 3-31. Sports Action Example

In Figure 3-31, I used this setting to photograph a bicycle rider who suddenly appeared on a trail coming toward me. The camera used a fast shutter speed of 1/1250 second at f/2.8 with an ISO setting of 640, with continuous shooting turned on. I held down the shutter button for a burst of 12 shots, and chose this one for the final version.

Macro

Although you can focus at close range in other shooting modes, it is convenient to use this setting to call up a group of options that are suited for extreme closeups of flowers, insects, or other small objects.

When you select the Macro option, the camera will let you set the flash to Forced Off, Autoflash, or Fill-flash. You cannot use continuous shooting or bracketing, but you can use the self-timer.

The camera initially uses single autofocus, but you don't have to use autofocus to take macro shots. You can use manual focus to focus on objects very close to the lens. You do, however, lose the benefit of automatic focus, and it can be tricky finding the correct focus manually. If you use the DMF setting, though, you can check focus by pressing the shutter button halfway and having the camera use its autofocus system. You also can take advantage of several aids to manual focusing with the RX100 V: Peaking, MF Assist, and Focus Magnifier, discussed in Chapters 4 and 7.

You don't have to use the Macro setting to shoot extreme closeups with the RX100 V. If you set the camera to one of its autofocus modes—either single-shot AF or continuous AF—it will focus on objects as close as two inches (five cm) when the lens is zoomed out and as close as 12 inches (30 cm) when the lens is zoomed in to its maximum telephoto range.

When shooting extreme closeups, you should use a tripod if possible because the depth of field is very shallow and you need to keep the camera steady to take a usable photograph. It's also a good idea to take advantage of the two-second or five-second self-timer. If you take the picture using the self-timer, you will not be touching the camera when the shutter is activated, so the chance of camera shake is minimized. You also can use a wired remote control, as discussed in Appendix A, or a remote control app that operates the camera through a wireless network, as discussed in Chapter 9.

If you need artificial illumination, consider using some sort of diffuser over the built-in flash, such as a handkerchief or piece of translucent plastic. Using the flash without some diffusion is likely to result in uneven illumination at such a close range. You might consider using a small lamp that can illuminate the subject without overwhelming it. Another approach is to use an off-camera flash triggered by an optical slave system, as discussed in Appendix A. In that case, you can attach a softbox to the flash to diffuse the light.

In Figure 3-32, I took a shot of the head of a small sculpture depicting the Roman goddess Diana in an art museum, holding the lens quite close, with no tripod.

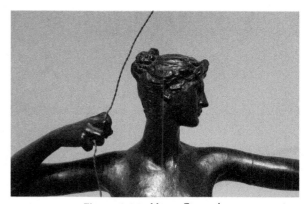
Figure 3-32. Macro Example

LANDSCAPE

Landscape is a Scene mode setting I use often. It is convenient to turn the Mode dial to the SCN position and pull up the Landscape setting when I'm at a scenic location. The camera lets you use Fill-flash in case you want to shoot an image of a person as part of your composition, and it boosts the brightness and intensity of the colors somewhat. Otherwise, it limits your choices; you cannot use continuous shooting, but you can use the self-timer. Figure 3-33 is an example taken using the Landscape setting for a shot of the skyline of Richmond, Virginia, with reflections in the James River.

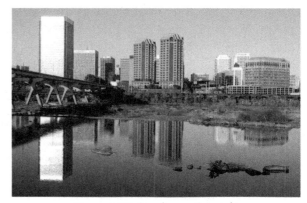
Figure 3-33. Landscape Example

SUNSET

This setting enhances reddish hues. You can use Fill-flash to take a portrait with the sunset or sunrise in the background. You cannot use continuous shooting, but you can use the self-timer. As I noted earlier, you don't have to limit this, or any Scene mode setting, to the subject its name implies. If you are photographing reddish leaves in autumn, you might use this option to create an enhanced view of the brightly colored foliage.

In Figure 3-34, I used the Sunset option to photograph a scene over the James River a few minutes before sunset.

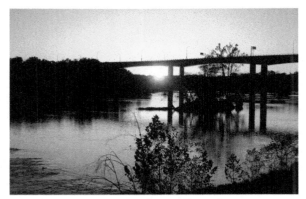

Figure 3-34. Sunset Example

NIGHT SCENE

The Night Scene option is designed to preserve the natural look of an evening setting. The camera disables the use of the flash completely; if the scene is quite dark, you should use a tripod to avoid camera motion during the long exposure that may be required. You cannot use continuous shooting, but you can use the self-timer. This setting is good for landscapes and other outdoor scenes after dark when flash would not help. The camera does not raise the ISO or use multiple shots, as it does with other modes used in dim lighting, such as Anti Motion Blur and Hand-held Twilight.

In Figure 3-35, I used the Night Scene setting to photograph a downtown view of Richmond, Virginia, about 20 minutes after sunset, with the moon at the upper left. The camera was on a tripod, and the shutter speed was 1/15 second at ISO 125, with aperture f/1.8.

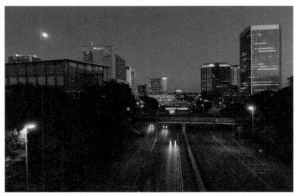

Figure 3-35. Night Scene Example

HAND-HELD TWILIGHT

This scene type is for taking pictures in low light without flash or tripod. With this special setting, the camera may boost the ISO to a higher level so it can use a fast shutter speed, and it takes a rapid burst of four shots. The camera combines these shots internally into one composite image to counteract the effects of high ISO, which often causes visible "noise," or grain, in an image.

Although the camera tries to select frames with minimal motion blur, the final result with this setting is more likely to show motion blur than a shot made with the Anti Motion Blur setting, discussed later in this section. If the Quality option on the Shooting menu is set to RAW or Raw & JPEG, the camera resets it to Fine while using this setting. However, you can set Quality to Extra Fine, and the camera will use that setting.

Hand-held Twilight is a good option if you are shooting a landscape or other static subject when you cannot use a tripod or flash and the light is dim. If you can use a tripod, you might be better off using the Night Scene setting, discussed above. Or, if you don't mind using flash, you could just use Intelligent Auto, Program, or one of the more ordinary shooting modes. Hand-held Twilight is a useful option when it's needed, but it will not yield the same overall quality as a shot at a lower ISO with the camera on a steady support.

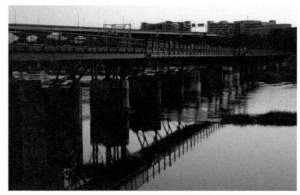

Figure 3-36. Hand-held Twilight Example

In Figure 3-36, I used this setting for a shot of a bridge across the river a few minutes after sunset, without using a tripod.

NIGHT PORTRAIT

This night-oriented setting is for situations when you are taking a portrait and are willing to use the camera's built-in flash. The main differences from the settings discussed above are that with Night Portrait, the camera takes only one shot and it activates the flash, in Slow Sync mode. You cannot set the Flash Mode to Flash Off. (However, you can leave the flash unit retracted, and the camera will let you take the shot without flash.)

I will discuss Slow Sync in more detail in Chapter 4. Basically, with this setting, the camera uses a slow shutter speed, so that as the flash illuminates the portrait subject, there is enough time for natural light to illuminate the background also. You can use the self-timer, but not continuous shooting. You also can use Raw quality if you wish, so this setting is a good choice for a high-quality portrait outdoors at night. Because of the slow shutter speed, you should use a tripod if possible to avoid motion blur.

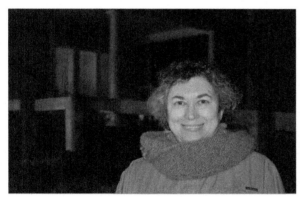

Figure 3-37. Night Portrait Example

In Figure 3-37, I used this setting for a portrait after dark, with some ambient light in the background. I used the flash, and the camera set the shutter speed to 1/4 second, an exposure long enough to allow some of the background scenery to appear.

ANTI MOTION BLUR

As noted earlier, this Scene mode setting is not meant for a particular subject, but for a certain type of situation. This option is useful when the lighting is dim or the lens is zoomed in to a telephoto setting. In either of those situations, the image is subject to blurring because of camera motion. In dim lighting, blurring can happen when the camera uses a slow shutter speed to expose the image properly, because it is hard to hold the camera steady enough for a sharply focused shot longer than about 1/30 second. In the telephoto

case, any camera motion is exaggerated because of the magnification of the image.

To counter the effects of this blurring, with Anti Motion Blur the camera raises the ISO to a higher-than-normal level so the camera can use a fast shutter speed and still let in enough light to expose the image properly. Because higher ISO settings result in increased visual noise, the camera takes a rapid burst of four shots and combines them internally into a single image with reduced noise. The camera also counteracts blur from motion of the subject to a fair extent, by analyzing the shots and rejecting those with motion blur as much as possible.

Anti Motion Blur is useful as the light is fading if you don't want to use flash. It is similar to the Hand-held Twilight setting, discussed above, but the camera is likely to use a higher ISO value with this option, which may result in more noise in the image. For Figure 3-38, I used this setting to capture an image of a man and his young helper, working on a project outdoors shortly after sunset. The camera used a very high ISO setting of 3200 and a shutter speed of 1/250 second along with its multiple-shot processing. As a result, the image does not show significant motion blur.

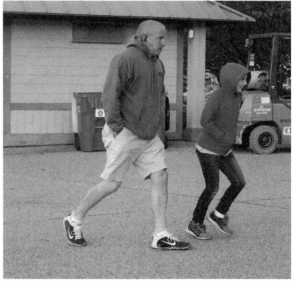

Figure 3-38. Anti Motion Blur Example

You should not expect good results if you use this setting with fast-moving subjects, because the camera will not be able to eliminate motion blur. With slower-moving subjects, though, the RX100 V can do a good job of reducing or avoiding blur. With this setting, you cannot set the Drive Mode options except for the self-timer, and you cannot use the flash. As with the Hand-held Twilight setting, if Quality is set to Raw or Raw & JPEG, the camera resets it to Fine while using this setting, though you can set Quality to Extra Fine if you want.

Pet

The Pet setting is for taking photos of cats, dogs, and other animals. It is similar to Sports Action in that the flash is off by default but can be set to Fill-flash. The Pet setting, though, lets you use the Soft Skin Effect setting on the Shooting menu, and does not let you use continuous shooting. I would recommend that you use this setting when you are shooting a relatively posed or calm shot of your dog, cat, or other pet; if the animal is running around, you might be better off with the Sports Action selection.

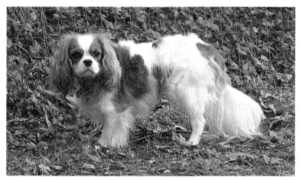

Figure 3-39. Pet Example

I used this setting for Figure 3-39, a shot of a normally very active spaniel, when she took a break to look around at her environment.

Gourmet

The Gourmet setting, according to Sony, is meant to let you shoot food so that it looks "delicious." In terms of settings, the RX100 V raises the brightness and vividness of colors to enhance the appearance of food. This setting is useful for people who write food blogs, or who like to record their meals for posterity. The camera lets you have the flash either forced off or set to Fill-flash. Continuous shooting is not available, but you can use the self-timer. In Figure 3-40, the color and brightness enhancements of this setting gave a boost to this image of a bowl of artificial fruit.

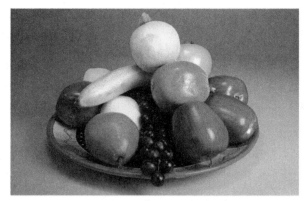

Figure 3-40. Gourmet Example

Fireworks

This scene type is designed to capture vivid images of fireworks bursts. It sets the camera to a two-second shutter speed and intensifies colors. If you can, you should set the camera on a tripod or other sturdy support and turn off the SteadyShot image stabilization option on the Shooting menu. The camera disables the flash and continuous shooting.

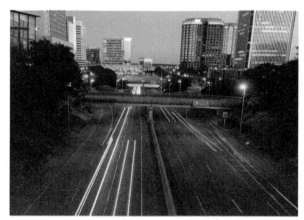

Figure 3-41. Fireworks Example

This setting is one you can also use as an alternative to the Night Scene setting when you are using a tripod after dark. You might want to try this approach to take advantage of the different color processing that the camera uses with this option. In Figure 3-41, I used this setting for a shot of a downtown expressway after sunset, to capture a few trails of automobile headlights and taillights during the two-second exposure.

High Sensitivity

This final Scene mode setting is another option for low-light shooting. The camera disables the flash and continuous shooting, but it allows use of the self-timer.

The camera is likely to use an ISO of 3200 or higher, all the way to the maximum of 25600 if the light is dim enough to require it. However, unlike the case with Hand-held Twilight and Anti Motion Blur, the camera takes only a single shot. As a result, there is no special processing of multiple images to reduce visual noise, so the image may be rather grainy. You cannot set Quality to Raw or Raw & JPEG.

If you need to shoot in dim light without a tripod and produce an image that is as smooth and noise-free as possible, you probably should use Hand-held Twilight or Anti Motion Blur instead of High Sensitivity. However, there might be occasions when you don't mind the grainy, noisy appearance that a high ISO can bring. It's good to have various choices available when you are confronted with a dimly lit location.

Note that you cannot set the ISO to 25600 with the ISO setting on the Shooting menu; as discussed in Chapter 4, the highest setting available on that menu is 12800. To get the camera to use the 25600 value for ISO, you have to use the Multi Frame Noise Reduction setting on the ISO menu or this High Sensitivity setting of Scene mode.

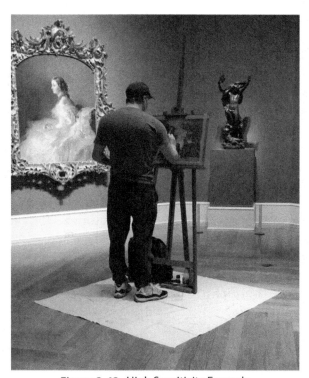

Figure 3-42. High Sensitivity Example

In Figure 3-42, I used the High Sensitivity setting to photograph an artist at work copying a painting in the art museum in a dimly lighted room. The camera set the

ISO to 3200 with a shutter speed of 1/80 second, so I was able to take the photograph without a tripod.

Sweep Panorama Mode

The next setting on the Mode dial is designed for the shooting of panoramic images. The RX100 V, like many other Sony cameras, has an excellent capability for automating the capture of panoramas. If you follow the fairly simple steps involved, the camera will stitch together a series of images internally to create a wide (or tall) view of a scenic vista or other subject that lends itself to panoramic depiction.

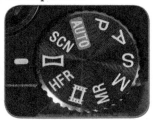

Figure 3-43. Mode Dial at Sweep Panorama

On the Mode dial, select the icon that looks like a squeezed rectangle, as seen in Figure 3-43. You will see a message telling you to press the shutter button and move the camera in the direction of the arrow that appears on the screen, as shown in Figure 3-44.

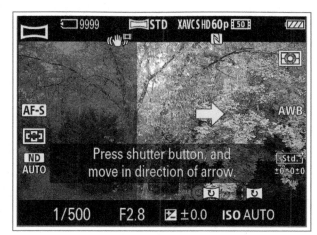

Figure 3-44. Message on Display for Sweep Panorama Mode

At that point, you can follow the directions and likely get excellent results. However, the camera also lets you make several choices for your panoramic images using the Shooting menu. Press the Menu button, and you will go to the menu screen that is currently displayed.

Navigate to the Shooting menu, which limits you to fewer choices than in most other shooting modes because several options are not appropriate for panoramas. For example, the Image Size, Aspect Ratio, and Quality settings are dimmed and unavailable. Also, options such as Drive Mode, Flash Mode, and Focus Area are of no use in this situation and cannot be selected. In addition, you will not be able to zoom the lens in; it will be fixed at its wide-angle position. (If the lens was zoomed in previously, it will zoom back out automatically when you switch the Mode dial to the Sweep Panorama selection.)

You will, however, see two options on the second screen of the Shooting menu that are not available for selection in any other shooting mode: Panorama Size and Panorama Direction, as shown in Figure 3-45.

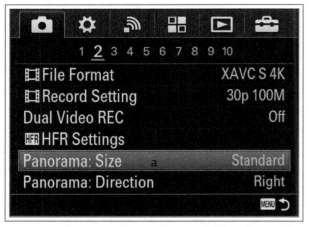

Figure 3-45. Panorama Size and Panorama Direction on Menu

Panorama Size has two options, Standard and Wide. With Standard, a horizontal panorama will have a size of 8192 by 1856 pixels, which is a resolution of about 15 megapixels (MP). If you choose Wide, a horizontal panorama will have a size of 12416 by 1856 pixels, resulting in a resolution of about 23 MP. (This figure is larger than the camera's maximum resolution of 20 MP because with the panorama settings, the camera is taking multiple images and stitching them together.)

A vertical panorama at the Standard setting is 3872 by 2160 pixels, or about 8.3 MP; a vertical panorama at the Wide setting is 5536 by 2160 pixels, or about 12 MP.

The Panorama Direction option selects Right, Left, Up, or Down for the direction in which you will sweep the camera. If the Control ring is set to the Standard option through the Custom Key (Shooting) item on the Custom menu and you are not using manual focus or DMF, you can turn the Control ring, and the camera will cycle

through the four arrows for the four directions, so you will not have to use the Shooting menu for that purpose. You also can turn the Control wheel to change the direction, regardless of the setting for the Control ring.

You can use the Direction settings with different orientations of the camera to get different results than usual. For example, if you set the direction to Up and hold the camera sideways while you sweep it to the right, you will create a horizontal panorama with 2160 pixels in its vertical dimension rather than the standard 1856.

Those are the main settings for most panoramas. There are a few other options you can select for panoramas on the Shooting menu, including Focus Mode, Metering Mode, White Balance, Creative Style, and SteadyShot. I will discuss all of these menu options in Chapter 4. My preferred settings for shooting panoramas are the ones shown in Table 3-1, at least as a starting point.

Table 3-1.   **Suggested Settings for Panoramas**

Focus Mode	Single-shot AF
Metering Mode	Multi
White Balance	Auto White Balance
Creative Style	Standard
SteadyShot (Still Images)	On (unless using a tripod)

One other setting you can make when shooting panoramas is exposure compensation, which is set using the Down button on the Control wheel. I will discuss that function in Chapter 5. In the context of shooting panoramas, this feature can be useful because the camera will not change the exposure if the camera is pointed at areas with varying brightness. For example, if you start sweeping from a dark area on the left, the camera will set the exposure for that area. If you then sweep the camera to the right over a bright area, that part of the panorama will be overexposed and possibly washed out in excessive brightness. To correct for this effect, you can reduce the exposure using negative exposure compensation. In this way, the initial dark area will be underexposed, but the brighter area should be properly exposed. Of course, you have to decide what part of the panorama is the most important one for having proper exposure.

Another way to deal with this issue is to point the camera at the bright area before starting the shot and press the shutter button half-way to lock the exposure, and then go back to the dark area at the left and start sweeping the camera. In that way, the exposure will be locked at the proper level for the bright area.

Once you have made the settings you want, follow the directions on the screen. Press and release the shutter button and start moving the camera at a steady rate in the direction you have chosen. I tend to shoot my panoramas moving the camera from left to right, but you may have a different preference. You will hear a steady clicking as the camera takes multiple shots during the sweep of the panorama. A white box and arrow will proceed across the screen; your task is to finish the camera's sweep at the same moment that the box and arrow finish their travel across the scene. If you move the camera either too quickly or too slowly, the panorama will not succeed; if that happens, just try again.

Panoramas usually work best when the scene does not contain moving objects such as cars or pedestrians because when items are in motion, the multiple shots are likely to capture images of the same object more than once in different positions.

It is advisable to use a tripod if possible so you can keep the camera steady in a single plane as it moves. If you don't have a tripod available, you might try using the electronic level that Sony provides with the RX100 V. You have to activate the level with the Display Button option on screen 2 of the Custom menu, as discussed in Chapter 7. Then press the Display button until the screen with the electronic level appears. Make sure the outer tips of the level stay green as much as possible, and the resulting panorama should benefit from the level shooting.

In addition to exposure, as discussed above, focus and white balance are fixed as soon as the first image is taken for the panorama.

When a panoramic shot is played back in the camera, it is initially displayed at a small size so the whole image can fit on the display screen. You can press the Center button to make the panorama scroll across the display at a larger size, using the full height of the screen.

Figure 3-46 is a sample panorama, shot from left to right using the Standard setting for Panorama Size.

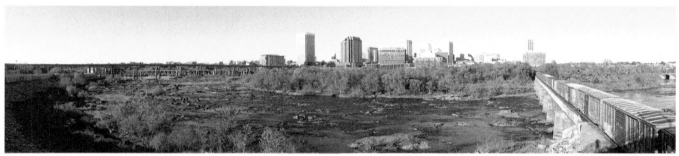

Figure 3-46. Panorama: James River, Richmond, Virginia, Using Standard Size Setting

Memory Recall Mode

There is one more shooting mode left to discuss, apart from Movie mode and HFR mode, which I will discuss in Chapter 8. This last mode, called Memory Recall, is a powerful tool that gives you expanded options for your photography.

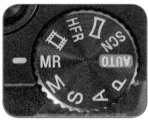

Figure 3-47. Mode Dial at MR

When you turn the Mode dial to the MR position (shown in Figure 3-47) and then select one of the seven groups of settings that can be stored there, you are, in effect, selecting a custom-made shooting mode that you create with your own favorite settings.

You can set up the camera just as you want it—with stored values for items such as shooting mode, shutter speed, aperture, zoom amount, white balance, ISO, and other settings—and later recall all of those values instantly just by turning the Mode dial to the MR position and selecting one of the seven stored memory registers on the Memory Recall screen, depending on which one you used to store the settings. With the RX100 V, unlike some other camera models, you can store settings for any shooting mode, including the Intelligent Auto and Scene modes.

Here is how this works. First, set up the camera with all of the settings you want to recall. For example, suppose you are going to do street photography. You may want to use a fast shutter speed, say 1/250 second, in black and white, at ISO 1250, using continuous shooting with autofocus, Large and Extra Fine JPEG images, and shooting in the 4:3 aspect ratio.

The first step is to make all of these settings. Set the Mode dial to Shutter Priority and use the Control wheel to set a shutter speed of 1/250 second. Then press the Menu button to call up the Shooting menu and, on screen 1, select L for Image Size, 4:3 for Aspect Ratio, and Extra Fine for Quality. Then move to screen 3 and choose continuous shooting (Mid speed) for Drive Mode. On screen 5, set ISO to 1250, and set the white balance to Daylight. Next, move to the Creative Style option on screen 6 and select the B/W setting, for black and white. You also may want to push the zoom lever all the way to the left for wide-angle shooting. You can set any other available Shooting menu options as you wish, but the ones listed above are the ones I will consider for now.

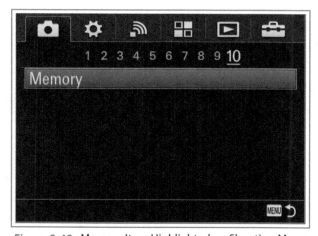

Figure 3-48. Memory Item Highlighted on Shooting Menu

Once these settings are made, navigate to the Memory item, shown in Figure 3-48, which is the final item on the last screen of the Shooting menu.

After you press the Center button, you will see a screen like the one in Figure 3-49, showing icons and values for all of the settings currently in effect.

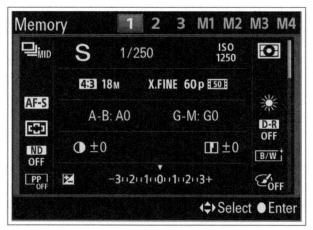

Figure 3-49. Memory Settings Screen

The word Memory appears at the upper left of the screen, and the indicators 1, 2, 3, M1, M2, M3, and M4 at the upper right. In the example shown here, the number 1 is highlighted. Now press the Center button, and you will have selected register 1 to store all of the settings you just made. Registers 1, 2, and 3 are stored in the camera's internal memory. Registers M1, M2, M3, and M4 are stored on the memory card that is currently inserted in the camera.

Note the short gray bar at the right side of the Memory screen shown in Figure 3-49. That bar indicates that you can scroll down through other screens to see additional settings that are in effect, such as ISO Auto Maximum and Minimum, AF Illuminator, AF Drive Speed, Center Lock-on AF, SteadyShot, and several others. Use the Up and Down buttons to scroll through those screens.

Next, to check how this worked, try making some very different settings, such as setting the camera for Manual exposure with a shutter speed of one second, Creative Style set to Vivid, continuous shooting turned off, the zoom lever moved all the way to the right for telephoto, and Quality set to Raw. Then turn the Mode dial back to the MR position and press the Center button while the number 1 is highlighted for Register 1. You will see that all of the custom settings you made have instantly returned, including the zoom position, shutter speed, and everything else. You can then continue shooting with those settings.

This is a wonderful feature, and it is more powerful than similar options on some other cameras, which can save menu settings but not values such as shutter speed and zoom position, or can save settings only for the less-automatic shooting modes, but not the Scene and

Auto modes. What is also quite amazing is that if you now switch back to Manual exposure mode, the camera will restore the settings that you had in that mode before you turned to the MR mode. (The position of the zoom lens will not revert to where it was, though.)

You can store settings from the Shooting menu, as well as the aperture, shutter speed, exposure compensation, and optical zoom settings. So, for example, you could set up one of the seven memory registers to recall Scene mode using the Macro setting, with the lens zoomed back to its wide-angle position. In that way, you could be ready for closeup shooting on a moment's notice. A Program Shift setting cannot be stored.

Note that you can recall the M1, M2, M3, or M4 settings only if the memory card that has those settings saved is inserted in the camera. On the positive side, this means that you can build up an inventory of different groups of settings, and store them in groups of four on different memory cards. If those cards are clearly labeled or indexed, you can select a card with the four settings you need for a particular shooting session.

This feature is powerful and useful. With a twist of the Mode dial and the press of a button, you can call up a complete group of settings tailored for a particular type of shooting. It is worth your while to experiment with this feature and develop various groups of settings that work well for your shooting needs.

CHAPTER 4: SHOOTING MENU

Much of the power of the Sony RX100 V comes from options on the Shooting menu, which gives you many ways to control the appearance of images and how you capture them. Depending on your preferences, you may not have to use this menu too much. You may prefer to use the camera's physical controls, with which you can make many settings, or you may use the Scene or Auto mode settings, which choose many options for you. However, it's nice to have this degree of control if you want it, and it is useful to understand the settings you can make. In addition, with the RX100 V, more than with many other cameras, you can control a fair number of settings on the Shooting menu even when the camera is in a Scene or Auto mode. Therefore, it is well worth exploring this powerful menu.

The Shooting menu is easy to use once you have played with it a bit. The available options can change depending on the setting of the Mode dial. For example, if the camera is set to Intelligent Auto mode, the Shooting menu options are limited because that mode is for a user who wants the camera to make many decisions without input. If the camera is in Sweep Panorama mode, the options are limited because of the specialized nature of that mode. For this discussion, I'm assuming you have the camera set to Program mode, because with that mode you have access to most of the options on the Shooting menu.

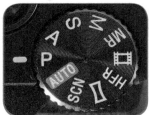

Figure 4-1. Mode Dial at P

Turn the Mode dial on top of the camera to P, which represents Program mode, as shown in Figure 4-1.

Enter the menu system by pressing the Menu button and move through the screens of the menu system by pressing the Right or Left button on the Control wheel. With each press of one of those buttons, the small orange line (cursor) at the top of the screen moves underneath a number that represents a menu screen.

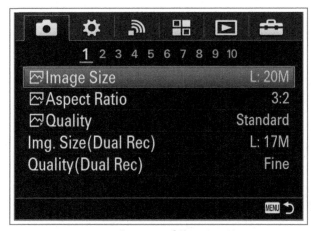

Figure 4-2. Screen 1 of Shooting Menu

When the menu system first appears, the cursor should sit beneath the number 1 while the camera icon, which represents the Shooting menu, is highlighted in the group of icons at the top of the screen, as shown in Figure 4-2. If a different screen is displayed, use the Right and Left buttons to navigate to that first screen. As you keep pressing the Right button, the cursor will move through all ten screens of the Shooting menu.

As you move through the menu screens on the RX100 V, after the Shooting menu comes the Custom menu, marked by a gear icon, then the Wi-Fi menu, headed by a wireless network icon. The last three menus are the Application menu, designated by a set of black and white blocks; the Playback menu, marked by a triangle icon; and, finally, the Setup menu, marked by a toolbox icon.

To navigate quickly through the six menu systems, you can press the Up button to move the orange highlight block into the line of menu icons at the top of the screen. When one of those icons is highlighted, you can use the Left and Right buttons to navigate directly from one menu system to another without going through the various screens of each menu.

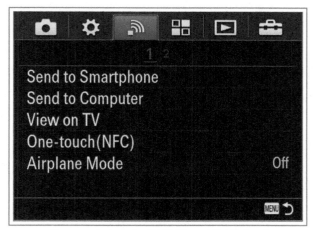

Figure 4-3. Icon for Wi-Fi Menu Highlighted

For example, in Figure 4-3, the Wi-Fi menu icon is highlighted. From there, you can press the Left button twice to move the highlight to the camera icon for the Shooting menu at the far left, as shown in Figure 4-4.

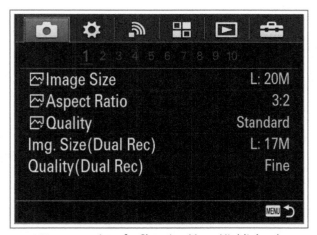

Figure 4-4. Icon for Shooting Menu Highlighted

Then you can press the Down button to move the highlight into the list of items on screen 1 of the Shooting menu, as shown earlier in Figure 4-2.

In this chapter, I am going to discuss only the Shooting menu; I will discuss the other five menus in Chapter six (Playback), Chapter 7 (Custom and Setup), and Chapter 9 (Wi-Fi and Application).

The Shooting menu contains many options divided into ten numbered screens. In most cases, each option (such as Image Size) occupies one line, with its name on

the left and its current setting (such as L: 20M) on the right. In other cases (such as Scene Selection, Movie, and Memory Recall), there may be only a small dash or nothing at all on the right side of the screen, meaning the selection is not currently applicable. For example, if the camera is in Program mode, the Scene Selection item on screen 8 of the Shooting menu will be followed by a dash because you cannot select a scene type in Program mode.

You also will see that some items on the menu screens are dimmed, as the Picture Effect and High ISO NR options are in Figure 4-5, for example. This means those options are not available for selection in the current context. In this case, Quality was set to Raw, and that setting conflicts with the two settings that are dimmed, so they cannot be selected.

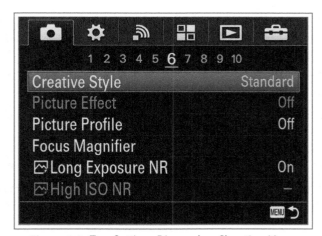

Figure 4-5. Two Settings Dimmed on Shooting Menu

In addition, some items are preceded by an icon that indicates whether they are used for still images, movies, or high frame rate (HFR) movies.

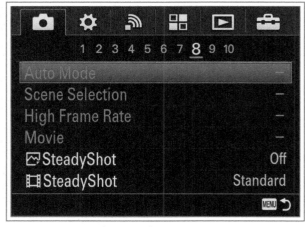

Figure 4-6. Icons for Items for Still images or Movies Only

For example, Figure 4-6 shows screen 8 of the Shooting menu, on which the first SteadyShot item is for still images and the second one is for movies, as indicated by the still-image and movie-film icons preceding those menu items.

To follow the discussion below of the options on the Shooting menu, leave the shooting mode set to Program, which gives you access to most of the options on that menu. (I'll also discuss the options that are available in other modes as I come to them.) I'll start at the top of screen 1 and discuss each option on the way down the list for each of the ten screens of this menu.

Image Size

This first option on the Shooting menu is related to the next two entries on the menu, Aspect Ratio and Quality, to control the overall appearance and "quality" of your images, in a broad sense. The Image Size setting controls the size in pixels of a still image recorded by the camera. The Sony RX100 V has an unusually large digital sensor for a camera of its size, and that sensor has a high maximum resolution, or pixel count. The sensor is capable of recording a still image with 5472 pixels, or individual points of light, in the horizontal direction and 3648 pixels vertically. When you multiply those two numbers together, the result is about 20 million pixels, often referred to as megapixels, MP, or M.

The resolution of still images is important mainly when it comes time to enlarge or print your images. If you need to produce large prints (say, eight by 10 inches or 20 by 25 cm), then you should select a high-resolution setting for Image Size. You also should choose the largest Image Size setting if you may need to crop out a small portion of the image and enlarge it for closer viewing. For example, if you are shooting photos of wildlife and the animal or bird you are interested in is in the distance, you may need to enlarge the image digitally to see that subject in detail. In that case, also, you should choose the highest setting for Image Size.

The available settings for Image Size with the RX100 V are L, M, S, and VGA, for Large, Medium, Small, and VGA, as shown in Figure 4-7. When you select one of the first three options, the camera displays a setting such as L:20M, meaning Large: 20 megapixels. The number of megapixels changes depending on the Aspect Ratio setting, discussed below. This is because

when the shape of the image changes, the number of horizontal pixels or the number of vertical pixels changes also to form the new shape.

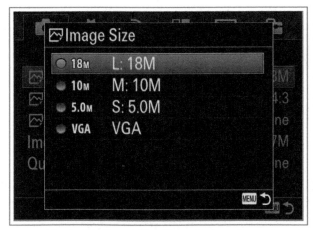

Figure 4-7. Image Size Menu Options Screen

For example, if the Aspect Ratio setting is 3:2, the maximum number of pixels is used because 3:2 is the aspect ratio of the camera's sensor. However, if you set Aspect Ratio to 16:9, the number of horizontal pixels (5472) stays the same, but the number of vertical pixels is reduced from 3648 to 3080 to form the 16:9 ratio of horizontal to vertical pixels. When you multiply those two numbers (5472 and 3080) together, the result is about 17 million pixels, which the camera states as 17M, as in Figure 4-8.

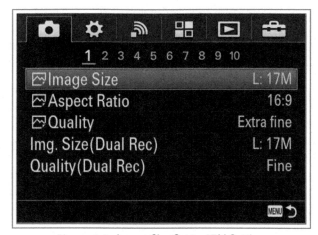

Figure 4-8. Image Size Set to 17M Setting

The VGA option, the smallest size possible, is available only if Aspect Ratio is set to 4:3. Otherwise, this choice does not even appear on the menu option for Image Size. VGA stands for video graphics array, the designation used for older-style computer screens, which have a 4:3 aspect ratio. The pixel count for this setting is very low—just 640 by 480 pixels, yielding a resolution of 0.3 M, much less than one megapixel. This very small size is suitable if you need to send images by e-mail or need to store a great many images on a memory card.

One of the few reasons to choose an Image Size smaller than L is if you are running out of space on your memory card and need to keep taking pictures in an important situation. Table 4-1 shows approximately how many images can be stored on a 64 GB memory card for various settings. (These numbers are somewhat different from those discussed in Chapter 1, which come from the Sony users guide. The numbers here come from readings taken with a freshly formatted card in my camera, for comparison.)

Table 4-1. **Number of Images That Fit on a 64 GB Card (Image Size vs. Quality at 3:2 Aspect Ratio)**

	Large	Medium	Small
Raw & JPEG	1968	2304	2506
Raw	2982	-----	-----
Extra Fine	4302	6752	9999+
Fine	5788	9999+	9999+
Standard	9922	9999+	9999+

As you can see, if you are using a 64 GB memory card, which is an increasingly common size, you can fit about 1900 images on the card even at the maximum settings of 3:2 for Aspect Ratio, Large for Image Size, and Raw & JPEG for Quality. If you limit the image quality to Fine, with no Raw images, you can fit about 5700 images on the card. If you reduce the Image Size setting to Small, you can store more than 10,000 images. I am unlikely ever to need more than about 300 or 400 images in any one session, unless I shoot a number of bursts, especially bursts using the highest speed. With the camera capturing images at 24 frames per second, the number of images can add up very rapidly. So, if you believe you will be shooting bursts, you should consider using a card that holds at least 64 GB of files.

If space on your memory card is not a consideration, then I recommend you use the L setting at all times. You never know when you might need the larger-sized image, so you might as well use the L setting and be safe. Your situation might be different, of course. If you were taking photos purely for a business purpose, such

as making photo identification cards, you might want to use the Small setting to store the maximum number of images on a memory card and reduce expense. For general photography, though, I rarely use any setting other than L for Image Size. (One exception could be when I want to increase the range of the optical zoom lens without losing image quality; see the discussion of Smart Zoom and related topics in Chapter 7.)

When Quality, discussed later in this chapter, is set to Raw, the Image Size option is dimmed and unavailable for selection because you cannot select an image size for Raw images; they are always at the maximum size, as is shown above on the table showing the numbers of images that can fit on a memory card.

Aspect Ratio

This second option on the Shooting menu lets you choose the shape of your still images. The choices are the default of 3:2, as well as 4:3, 16:9, and 1:1, as shown in Figure 4-9.

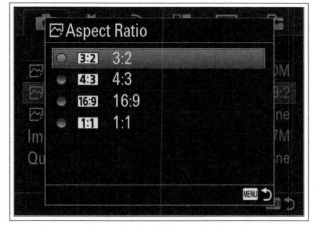

Figure 4-9. Aspect Ratio Menu Options Screen

These numbers are the ratio of units of width to units of height. For example, with the 16:9 setting, the image is 16 units wide for every nine units of height. The aspect ratio that uses all pixels on the image sensor is 3:2; with any other aspect ratio, some pixels are cropped out. So, if you want to record every possible pixel, you should use the 3:2 setting. If you shoot using the 3:2 aspect ratio, you can always alter the shape of the image later in editing software such as Photoshop by cropping away parts of the image. However, if you want to compose your images in a certain shape and don't plan to do post-processing in software, the aspect ratio settings of this menu item can help you frame your images in the camera using the appropriate aspect ratio on the display.

The RX100 V provides more options in this area than many other cameras do. For each of the aspect ratios discussed below, I am including an image I took using that setting in the same location at the same time, to give an idea of what the different aspect ratios look like.

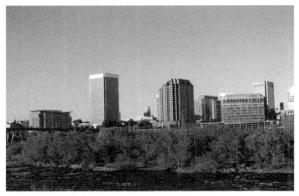

Figure 4-10. Aspect Ratio 3:2

The default 3:2 setting, used for Figure 4-10, includes the maximum number of pixels, and is the ratio used by traditional 35mm film. This aspect ratio can be used without cropping to make prints in the common U.S. size of six inches by four inches (15 cm by 10 cm).

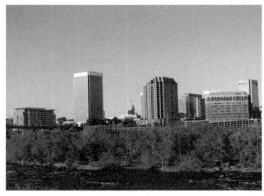

Figure 4-11. Aspect Ratio 4:3

The 4:3 setting, shown in Figure 4-11, is in the shape of a traditional (non-widescreen) computer screen, so if you want to view your images on that sort of display, this may be your preferred setting.

As I noted earlier in discussing Image Size, if you want to use the VGA setting for Image Size, the camera must be set to the 4:3 aspect ratio. With this setting, some pixels are lost at the left and right sides of the image.

The 16:9 setting, illustrated in Figure 4-12, is the "widescreen" option, like that found on many modern HD television sets. You might use this setting when you plan to show your images on an HDTV set. Or, it might be suitable for a particular composition in which the subject matter is stretched out in a horizontal arrangement. With this setting, some pixels are cropped out at the top and bottom, though none are lost at the left or right.

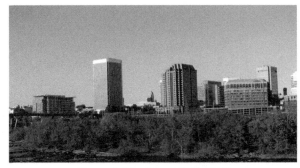

Figure 4-12. Aspect Ratio 16:9

The 1:1 ratio, illustrated in Figure 4-13, produces a square shape, which some photographers prefer because of its symmetry and because the neutrality of the shape leaves open many possibilities for composition. With the 1:1 setting, the camera crops pixels from the left and right sides of the image.

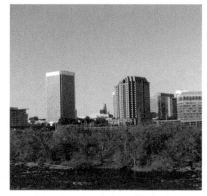

Figure 4-13. Aspect Ratio 1:1

The Aspect Ratio setting is available in all shooting modes except Sweep Panorama. However, although you can set Aspect Ratio when the camera is in Movie mode or HFR mode (Mode dial turned to movie-film icon or HFR), that setting will have no effect until you switch to a mode for taking still images, such as Program mode. When the Mode dial is set to the Movie position, you cannot take still images other than during movie recording. The aspect ratio of a still image taken while recording a movie is determined by the File Format and Record Setting menu options, not by the Aspect Ratio option. With the Mode dial at the HFR position, you cannot take still images at all.

Quality

The Quality setting, below Aspect Ratio, is one of the most important Shooting menu options for still images. The choices are Raw, Raw & JPEG, Extra Fine, Fine, and Standard, as shown in Figure 4-14.

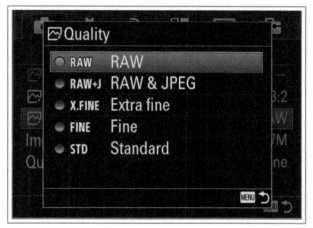

Figure 4-14. Quality Menu Options Screen

The term "quality" in this context concerns the way in which digital images are processed. In particular, JPEG (non-Raw) images are digitally "compressed" to reduce their size without losing too much information or detail from the picture. However, the more an image is compressed, the greater the loss of detail and clarity in the image.

Raw files, which are in a class by themselves, are the least compressed of all and have the greatest level of quality, though they come with some complications, as discussed below. All other (non-Raw) formats for still images used by the RX100 V (as with most similar cameras) are classified as JPEG, which is an acronym for Joint Photographic Experts Group, an industry group that created the JPEG standard. The JPEG files, in turn, come in three varieties on the RX100 V: Extra Fine, Fine, and Standard. The Extra Fine setting provides the least compression. Images captured with the Fine or Standard setting undergo increasingly more compression, resulting in smaller files with somewhat reduced quality.

Here are some guidelines for using these settings. First, you need to choose between Raw and JPEG images. Raw files are larger than other files, so they take up more space on your memory card, and on your computer, than JPEG files. But Raw files offer advantages over JPEG files. When you shoot in the Raw format, the camera records as much information as it can about the image and preserves that information in the file it saves to the memory card. When you open the Raw file later on your computer, your software can process that information in various ways. For example, you can change the exposure or white balance of the image when you edit it on the computer, just as if you had changed your settings while shooting. In effect, the Raw format gives you what almost amounts to a chance to travel back in time to improve some of the settings that you didn't get quite right when you pressed the shutter button.

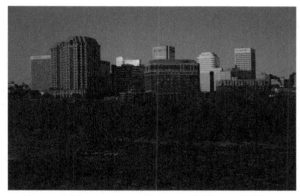

Figure 4-15. Raw Image Taken with Wrong Settings

For example, Figure 4-15 is an image I took with the RX100 V using the Raw format, with the exposure purposely set too dark and the white balance set to Incandescent, even though I took the picture outdoors on a sunny day.

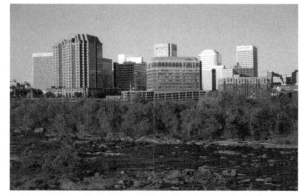

Figure 4-16. Raw Image After Corrections in Software

Figure 4-16 shows the same image after I opened it in Sony's Image Data Converter software and adjusted the settings to correct the exposure and white balance. The result was an image that looked just as it would have if I had used the correct settings when I shot it.

Raw is not a cure-all; you cannot fix bad focus or excessive exposure problems. But you can improve some exposure-related issues and white balance with Raw-processing software. You can use Sony's Image Data Converter software to view or edit Raw files, and you also can use other programs, such as Adobe Camera Raw, that have been updated to handle Raw files from this camera. Another option is Capture One Express, which is available from Sony to purchasers of this camera.

Using Raw can have disadvantages, also. The files take up a lot of storage space; Raw images taken with the RX100 V are about 20 MB in size, while Large JPEG images I have taken are between about four and 14 MB, depending on the settings used. Also, Raw files have to be processed on a computer; you can't take a Raw image and immediately share it through social media or print it; you first have to use software to convert it to JPEG, TIFF, or some other standard format for manipulating digital photographs. If you are pressed for time, you may not want to take that extra step. Finally, some features of the RX100 V are not available when you are using the Raw format, such as the Auto HDR, Picture Effect, and Digital Zoom menu options.

If you're undecided as to whether to use Raw or JPEG, you have the option of selecting Raw & JPEG, the second choice for the Quality menu item. With that setting, the camera records both a Raw and a JPEG image when you press the shutter button.

The advantage with that approach is that you have a Raw image with maximum quality and the ability to do extensive post-processing, and you also have a JPEG image that you can use for viewing, sharing, printing, and the like. Of course, this setting consumes storage space more quickly than saving your images in just Raw or JPEG format, and it can take the camera longer to store the images, so there may be a slowdown in the rate of continuous shooting, if you are using that feature. You also cannot use some menu options that conflict with the Raw setting.

When you choose Raw & JPEG, you can select an Image Size setting that will apply only to the JPEG image; the Raw image, as noted earlier, is always at the maximum size. You cannot select a Quality setting for the JPEG image with the Raw & JPEG selection; the JPEG image will be fixed at the Fine setting.

The best bet for preserving the quality of your images and your options for post-processing and fixing exposure mistakes later is to choose Raw files. However, if you want to use features such as Sweep Panorama mode, some Scene mode types such as Anti Motion Blur, the Picture Effect menu option, and others, which are not available with Raw files, then choose JPEG. If you do choose JPEG, I strongly recommend that you choose the Large size and Extra Fine quality, unless you have an urgent need to conserve storage space on your memory card or on your computer. If you want Raw quality and are not concerned about storage space or speed of shooting, choose Raw & JPEG. However, you will still not be able to use Picture Effect and some other options.

Image Size (Dual Recording)

This next command on the Shooting menu sets the size of still images that are captured during video recording. When you have started recording a video, you can press the shutter button at any time to capture a still image. You also can use the Auto Dual Recording option, on screen 7 of the Shooting menu, to set the camera to capture still images automatically during video recording. There are some limitations on these capabilities, which are discussed in Chapter 8.

The choices for Image Size are L:17M, M:7.5M, and S:4.2M, for Large, Medium, and Small.

Quality (Dual Recording)

Like the previous command, this one affects still images that are captured while a video is being recorded. The three options available for this setting are Extra Fine, Fine, and Standard. The Raw setting is not available.

The next settings to be discussed are on screen 2 of the Shooting menu, shown in Figure 4-17.

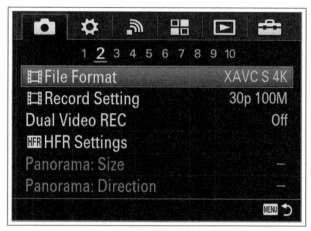

Figure 4-17. Screen 2 of Shooting Menu

File Format

This first option on screen 2 of the Shooting menu is preceded by a movie-film icon, meaning it applies only for movies. I will discuss this option in Chapter 8. For now, you should know that XAVC S (4K or HD) gives the highest quality but is available only if you use an SD card rated in Speed Class 10 or UHS Speed Class 1 (UHS Speed Class 3 for some settings). The AVCHD option yields very high quality and MP4 gives somewhat lower quality but can be easier to work with for editing. The choice you make for this setting depends to a large extent on the type of video you are recording, as discussed in Chapter 8.

Record Setting

This next option on screen 2 of the Shooting menu is related to the File Format option, discussed above. The available options for Record Setting will change, depending on what you select for File Format. I will discuss the details of this option in Chapter 8. For now, if you want the highest quality for MP4 video, choose the top option, 1920 x 1080 60p 28M. These options will be different if you choose XAVC S 4K, XAVC S HD, or MP4 for File Format. They also will be different if you have set the NTSC/PAL selector, on screen 3 of the Setup menu, to PAL, the TV system used in much of Europe and some other locations. For example, the top option for MP4 in that case is 1920 x 1080 50p 28M. In this book, I will discuss the video options that are applicable for the NTSC system, as used in the United States, Japan, and elsewhere.

Dual Video Recording

This option is somewhat like a video version of the Raw & JPEG setting for still images. When it is turned on and File Format is set to XAVC S 4K, XAVC S HD, or AVCHD, the camera also records the video in the MP4 format, giving you a second video file that is easier to edit and share. I recommend leaving this option turned off unless you have a specific reason to use it. I will discuss it further in Chapter 8. There are some limitations on this setting, which I will also discuss in Chapter 8.

HFR Settings

This menu option controls the settings for HFR, or high frame rate video recording, when the Mode dial is set to the HFR position. I will discuss this option and other aspects of HFR recording in Chapter 8.

Panorama Size and Panorama Direction

The last two commands on this screen of the Shooting menu are available only when the Mode dial is set to Sweep Panorama mode. I discussed these settings in Chapter 3, in connection with that shooting mode. When the Control ring is set to its Standard setting through the Custom Key (Shooting) option on screen 5 of the Custom menu, you can set the panorama direction by turning that ring (unless you are using manual focus or DMF, which take over the use of the ring). You also can change the direction by turning the Control wheel, regardless of the setting for the Control ring.

The next menu options are on screen 3 of the Shooting menu, shown in Figure 4-18.

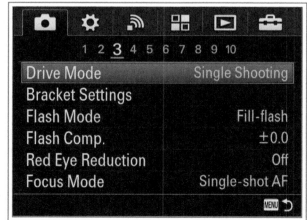

Figure 4-18. Screen 3 of Shooting Menu

Drive Mode

This first option on screen 3 of the menu gives access to continuous shooting and related features of the RX100 V, for shooting bursts of images, bracketing exposures, and using the self-timer. You can also get access to this menu option by pressing the Drive Mode button (Left button), as discussed in Chapter 5, unless that button has been assigned to a different function using the Custom Key (Shooting) option on screen 5 of the Custom menu. Or, you can get access to these options through the Function menu or the Quick Navi system, as also discussed in Chapter 5.

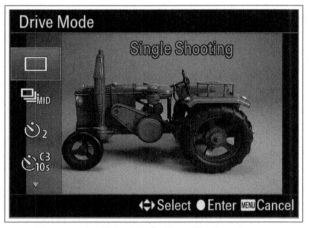

Figure 4-19. Drive Mode Menu Options Screen

When you highlight the Drive Mode option and press the Center button, the menu in Figure 4-19 appears, with eight choices: Single Shooting, Continuous Shooting, Self-timer, Self-timer (Continuous), Continuous Exposure Bracketing, Single Exposure Bracketing, White Balance Bracketing, and DRO Bracketing. (You have to scroll down for the last four choices.)

Details for each of these Drive Mode settings are discussed below.

SINGLE SHOOTING

This is the normal mode for shooting still images. Select this top choice on the Drive Mode menu to turn off all continuous shooting. In some cases, having one of the continuous-shooting options selected makes it impossible to use other settings, such as Soft Skin Effect or Long Exposure Noise Reduction. If you find you cannot make a certain setting, select single shooting to see if that removes the conflict and fixes the problem.

As noted earlier, this option is not available with the Sports Action setting of Scene mode.

CONTINUOUS SHOOTING

Continuous shooting, sometimes called burst shooting, is useful in many contexts, from shooting an action sequence at a sporting event to taking a series of shots of a person in order to capture changing facial expressions. I often use this setting for street photography to increase my chances of catching an interesting shot.

The RX100 V has a particularly strong set of features for burst shooting, thanks to its newly enhanced autofocus system with 315 phase detection focus points, which allow the camera to focus more rapidly than previous models. In addition, the camera uses an LSI (large scale integration) chip, which works with the image sensor and image processor to increase the size of the buffer that stores images as a burst is being shot. As a result, the camera can shoot rapidly for a longer burst than with other cameras, and you can view the images as soon as they have been captured, without having to wait for the camera to "digest" the burst of shots. Also, the RX100 V can carry out this rapid shooting while still using its autofocus and autoexposure mechanisms for each shot.

To use burst shooting, use the Down button or the Control wheel to move the highlight to the second icon on the Drive menu, for continuous shooting, as shown in Figure 4-20. Then use the Left and Right buttons to select either Hi, Mid, or Lo for the speed of continuous shooting. Once the desired speed is highlighted, press the Center button to confirm the selection and the camera will return to the shooting screen.

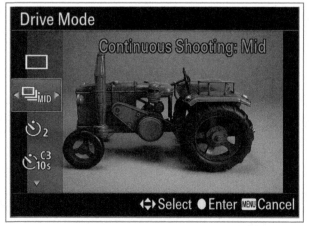

Figure 4-20. Continuous Shooting Icon Highlighted on Menu

With the Hi setting, the camera will shoot at a rate of up to 24 frames per second; with Mid, at up to 10 frames per second; and with Lo, at up to 3.5 frames per second.

If you have Focus Mode set to single autofocus, the camera will not adjust its focus during the burst of shots. But, if you set the focus mode to AF-C for continuous autofocus or AF-A for automatic autofocus, the camera will adjust focus for each shot. The speed of shooting slows down somewhat to allow for the focusing operations.

If you want the camera to adjust its exposure during the series of continuous shots, you need to go to screen 4 of the Custom menu and check the setting of the AEL w/ Shutter menu item. If that item is set to On, the camera will lock exposure when you press the shutter button, and exposure will be locked throughout the burst as it was set for the first image, even if lighting changes dramatically. However, if you set AEL w/Shutter to Off, then the camera will adjust its exposure as needed during the burst of shots.

If you set AEL w/Shutter to Auto, then the camera will adjust exposure during continuous shooting if Focus Mode is set to continuous autofocus or automatic autofocus. If it is set to single autofocus, then the camera will keep the exposure locked. (Of course, if you want the camera to adjust exposure automatically, you have to use an exposure mode in which the camera normally controls exposure. If you use Manual mode with a fixed ISO value, the exposure will not change.)

Depending on conditions such as image size and quality, lighting, settings for autofocus and autoexposure lock, and the speed of the memory card, the rate of burst shooting can vary considerably. In addition, the camera's memory buffer eventually fills up, causing a noticeable slowdown in burst shooting. When shooting at Hi speed with Quality set to Extra Fine, I found that the shooting speed slowed down after about 160 shots. With Quality set to Raw & JPEG, shooting slowed after only about 65 shots. With the slower speeds for continuous shooting, the buffer was able to hold more shots before shooting slowed. For example, the camera managed to fire off 185 shots before slowing down when using the Mid speed, with Quality set to Extra Fine. In all of the cases mentioned

here, I had the camera set to adjust focus and exposure during the burst shooting.

Although you can turn on the flash when the continuous shooting option is selected, and the camera will take a series of shots with flash as you hold down the shutter button, the time between shots may be several seconds because the flash cannot recycle quickly enough to take a rapid series of shots.

After taking a burst of shots, it can take the camera a while to save them to the memory card. You can't use the menu system until the data has been saved, although you can take additional shots and view the shots that have been saved to the card. While the shots stored in the memory buffer are being saved, the camera displays a moving bar of small lines in the upper left corner of the screen in playback mode, showing how many shots are still being stored to the memory card, as shown in Figure 4-21.

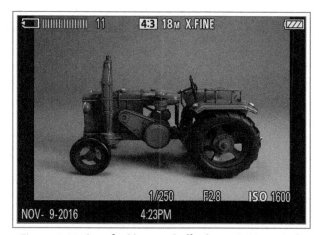

Figure 4-21. Icon for Memory Buffer Status in Upper Left

There also is an access lamp that lights up in red while the camera is writing to the card, but you cannot readily see it. It is inside the battery compartment near the edge of the camera, as shown in Figure 2-8, back in Chapter 2. While that light is illuminated, be sure not to remove the battery or the memory card.

Figure 4-22 is an image I took using high-speed continuous shooting. I attached the RX100 V to a spotting scope, as discussed in Chapter 9, and waited for birds to visit the bird feeder. After taking hundreds of rapid-fire shots, I managed to catch this one of a bird in flight approaching the bird feeder. I used a shutter speed of 1/1250 second in Shutter Priority mode to freeze the action without too much motion blur.

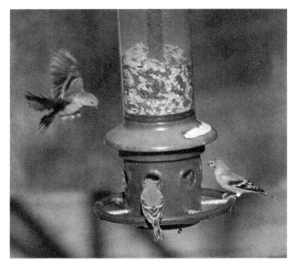

Figure 4-22. Continuous Shooting Example

The continuous shooting options are not available with Sweep Panorama mode or with any settings in Scene mode other than Sports Action. They also are not available with certain Picture Effect settings: Soft Focus, HDR Painting, Rich-tone Monochrome, Miniature, Watercolor, and Illustration; with the Multi Frame Noise Reduction setting for ISO; or when the Smile Shutter is being used.

SELF-TIMER

The next icon down on the menu of Drive Mode options represents the self-timer, as shown in Figure 4-23. The self-timer is useful when you need to participate in a group photograph. You can place the RX100 V on a tripod, set the timer for five or 10 seconds, and insert yourself into the group before the shutter clicks. The self-timer also is helpful when you don't want to cause blur by jiggling the camera as you press the shutter button.

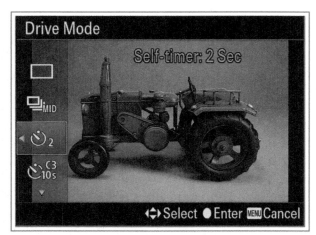

Figure 4-23. Self-timer Icon Highlighted on Menu

For example, when you're taking a macro shot very close to the subject, focusing can be critical, and any bump to the camera could cause motion blur. Using the self-timer gives the camera a chance to settle down after the shutter button is pressed, before the image is recorded.

The self-timer option presents you with three choices: 10 seconds, five seconds, and two seconds. When the self-timer icon is highlighted, press the Left or Right button on the Control wheel to choose one of these options by highlighting it and pressing the Center button to select it. After you make this selection, the self-timer icon will appear in the upper left corner of the display with the chosen number of seconds (10, 5, or 2) displayed next to the icon, as shown in Figure 4-24. (If you don't see the icon, press the Display button until the screen with the various shooting icons appears.)

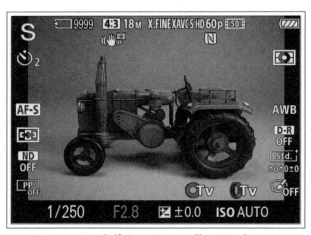

Figure 4-24. Self-timer Icon on Shooting Screen

Once the self-timer is set, when you press the shutter button, the timer will count down for the specified number of seconds and then take the picture. The reddish lamp on the front of the camera will blink, and the camera will beep during the countdown.

The self-timer is not available in Sweep Panorama mode or for recording a movie with the Movie button.

SELF-TIMER (CONTINUOUS)

The next item down on the Drive Mode menu, shown in Figure 4-25, is another variation on the self-timer. With this option, the camera takes multiple shots after the countdown ends. You can choose any of the three time intervals, and you can set the camera to take either three or five shots after the delay. When you highlight this option, you will see a horizontal triangle indicating that, using the Left and Right buttons, you can select one of six combinations of the number of shots and the timer interval. For example, the option designated as C3/2S sets the camera to take three shots after the timer counts down for two seconds; C5/10S sets it for five shots after a 10-second delay.

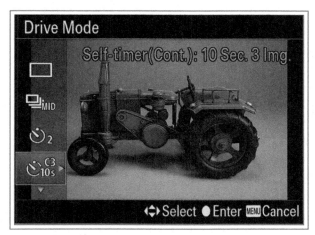

Figure 4-25. Self-timer (Continuous) Icon Highlighted on Menu

This option is useful for group photos; when a series of shots is taken, you increase your chances of getting at least one shot in which everyone is looking at the camera and smiling. You can choose any settings you want for Image Size and Quality, including Raw & JPEG, and you will still get three or five rapidly fired shots, though the speed of the shooting will decrease slightly at the highest Quality settings. You cannot use the continuous AF setting for Focus Mode with this option.

CONTINUOUS EXPOSURE BRACKETING

This next option on the Drive Mode menu, shown in Figure 4-26, sets the camera to take three, five, or nine images with one press of the shutter button but with a different exposure level for each image, giving you a greater chance of having one image that is properly exposed.

When you highlight this option, you will see a horizontal triangle meaning that you can use the Left and Right buttons to select one of 13 combinations of the difference in exposure value and the number of images in the bracket. The first nine choices include exposure value (EV) intervals of 0.3, 0.7, or 1.0, each with a bracket of three, five or nine exposures. The other four choices are for EV intervals of 2.0 or 3.0 EV, each with a bracket of three or five exposures.

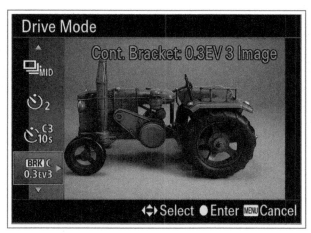

Figure 4-26. Continuous Exposure Bracketing Icon Highlighted on Menu

The decimal numbers represent the difference in EV among the multiple (three, five or nine) exposures that the camera will take. (Note that, with the larger EV intervals of 2.0 or 3.0 EV, the available numbers of shots are three or five; there is no option for choosing nine shots, because the overall exposure range would be too great, given the larger EV interval and the large number of shots.)

For example, if you select 0.7 EV as the interval for three exposures, the camera will take three shots— one at the metered exposure level; one at a level 0.7 EV (or f-stop) below that, resulting in a darker image; and one at a level 0.7 EV above that, resulting in a brighter image. If you want the maximum exposure difference among the shots, select 3.0 EV as the interval for the three or five shots.

Once you have set this option as you want it and composed your scene, press and hold the shutter button and the camera will take the three, five or nine shots in rapid succession while you hold down the button.

If you set this option for three exposures, the first one will be at the metered value, the second one underexposed by the selected interval, and the third one overexposed to the same extent. If you set it for five exposures, the first three shots will have the values noted above, the fourth will have the most negative EV, and the fifth will have the most positive EV. With nine exposures, the pattern will be similar, with the final two exposures having the most negative and positive EV settings, respectively. (You can change this order using the Bracket Settings menu option, discussed later in this chapter.)

You can use exposure compensation, in which case the camera will use the image with exposure compensation as the base level, and then take exposures that deviate under and over the exposure of the image with exposure compensation.

If you pop up the flash and set it to fire, using the Fill-flash setting for example, the flash will fire for each of the bracketed shots and the exposure will be varied, but you have to press the shutter button for each shot, after the flash has recycled. (The orange dot to the right of the flash icon on the screen shows when the flash is ready to fire again.) With this approach, the camera will vary the output of the flash unit rather than the exposure value of the images themselves.

When using Manual exposure mode with ISO set to Auto, the camera adjusts the ISO setting to achieve the different exposure levels for the multiple images. If ISO is set to a specific value, the camera varies the shutter speeds for the multiple shots.

SINGLE EXPOSURE BRACKETING

The next option is similar to the previous one, except that, with this selection, you have to press the shutter button for each shot; the camera will not take multiple shots while you hold down the shutter button. You have the same 13 choices for combinations of EV intervals and numbers of exposures. You might want to choose this option when you need to pause between shots for some reason, such as if you are using a model who needs to have some costume or makeup adjustments for each exposure. It also could be useful if you want to look at the resulting image after each shot to see if you need to make further adjustments to your settings.

Apart from using individual shutter presses, this option works the same as continuous exposure bracketing. For example, you can use flash and you can change the order of the exposures using the Bracket Settings menu option.

None of the bracketing options—exposure, white balance, or DRO—is available in the Auto, Scene, or Sweep Panorama shooting mode.

WHITE BALANCE BRACKETING

The next option on the Drive Mode menu, White Balance Bracket, whose icon is highlighted in Figure

4-27, is similar to Continuous Exposure Bracketing, except that only three images can be taken and the value that is varied for the three shots is white balance rather than exposure.

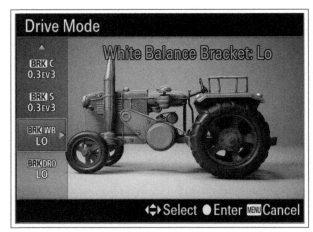

Figure 4-27. White Balance Bracketing Icon Highlighted on Menu

Using the Left and Right buttons, select either Lo or Hi for the amount of deviation from the normal white balance setting. Then, when you press the shutter button (you don't have to hold it down), the camera will take a series of three shots—one at the normal setting; the next one with a lower color temperature, resulting in a "cooler," more bluish image; and the last one with a higher color temperature, resulting in a "warmer," more reddish image. When you use this form of bracketing, unlike exposure bracketing, you will hear only one shutter sound because the camera takes just one image, with one quick shutter press, and then electronically creates the other two exposures with the different white balance values.

You can change the order of the exposures using the Bracket Settings menu option, discussed later in this chapter.

DRO BRACKETING

This final option on the Drive Mode menu, whose icon is shown in Figure 4-28, sets the RX100 V to take a series of three shots at different settings of the DRO (dynamic range optimizer) option.

I'll discuss DRO later in this chapter. Essentially, DRO alters the RX100 V's image processing to even out the contrast between shadowed and bright areas. It can be difficult to decide how much DRO processing to use, and this option gives you a way to experiment with several different settings before you decide on the amount of DRO for your final image.

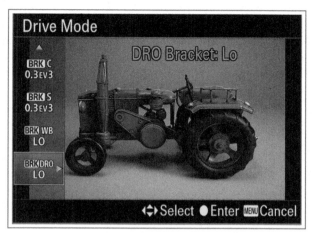

Figure 4-28. DRO Bracketing Icon HIghlighted on Menu

As with White Balance Bracket, you can select Hi or Lo for the DRO interval. Also, as with White Balance Bracket, you only need to press the shutter button once, briefly; the camera will record the three different exposures electronically. The order of these exposures is not affected by the Bracket Order menu option.

Bracket Settings

The second option on this menu screen lets you adjust two settings for how bracketed exposures are taken. When you select Bracket Settings, you will see two sub-options: Self-timer During Bracket, and Bracket Order.

The first choice, Self-timer During Bracket, lets you use the self-timer with bracket shooting. Without this option you could not use bracketing and the self-timer at the same time, because they are selected by different options on the Drive Mode menu. With this menu option, you can have the self-timer set for two, five, or 10 seconds before the first bracket shot is triggered, or you can leave the self-timer turned off. This setting turns on the self-timer for any type of bracket shooting you choose—exposure, white balance, or DRO.

The second sub-option, Bracket Order, lets you alter the sequence of the bracketed shots. As shown in Figure 4-29, there are two choices. The first one is the default setting, with which the first shot is at the normal setting, the next is more negative (or with lower color temperature), the one after that is more positive (or with higher color temperature), and so on, ending with the most negative setting and, finally, the most positive

setting. If you choose the second option, the images are shot in a strictly ascending series, moving from the most negative setting to the most positive setting.

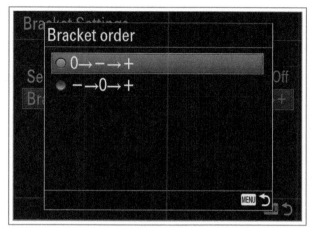

Figure 4-29. Bracket Order Menu Options Screen

The Bracket Order option affects the order for exposure bracketing and white balance bracketing, but not for DRO bracketing.

Flash Mode

In Chapter 2, I discussed the use of the RX100 V's built-in flash, which is controlled with the Flash Mode menu option. As I discussed earlier, that option can be reached by pressing the Flash button, which is the Right button on the Control wheel. Flash Mode also is this third option on screen 3 of the Shooting menu.

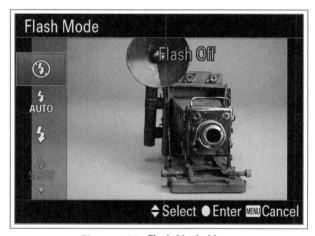

Figure 4-30. Flash Mode Menu

There are five options on the Flash Mode menu—Flash Off, Autoflash, Fill-flash, Slow Sync, and Rear Sync—the first four of which are shown in Figure 4-30. The Slow Sync option is dimmed on this screen, because that setting is not available for selection in the shooting mode illustrated here. There is no shooting mode in which all five options are available. Here is a brief summary of the options I discussed in Chapter 2, followed by a discussion of the ones I did not discuss there.

FLASH OFF

To make sure the flash will not fire, choose Flash Off. This is a good choice when you are in a museum or other place where you don't want the flash to fire, or if you know you will not be using flash. It also can be helpful to avoid depleting a battery that is running low. This option is available in Auto mode and with the Portrait, Sports Action, Macro, Landscape, Sunset, Pet, and Gourmet settings of Scene mode. Of course, with the RX100 V you also have the option of just not raising the flash with the flash pop-up switch, which will have the same effect as using this Flash Mode option.

AUTOFLASH

With Autoflash, you leave it up to the camera to decide whether to fire the flash. The camera will analyze the lighting and other aspects of the scene and decide whether to use flash without further input from you. This selection is available only in Auto mode and with the Portrait and Macro settings of Scene mode.

FILL-FLASH

With Fill-flash, you are making a decision to use flash no matter what the lighting conditions are. If you choose this option, the flash will fire every time you press the shutter button, if the flash is popped up. This is the setting to use when the sun is shining and you need to soften shadows on a subject's face, or when you need to correct the lighting when a subject is backlit.

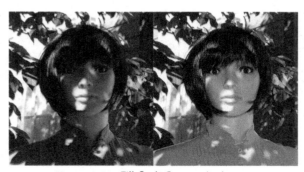

Figure 4-31. Fill-flash Composite Image

For example, for Figure 4-31, I took two shots of a mannequin outdoors on a sunny day, with the

mannequin's head covered with several shadows from a tree. For the left image I left the flash turned off, and for the right one I used Fill-flash. I used the Flash Compensation menu option to increase the flash's output by 3.0 EV, because the flash was not powerful enough to overcome the shadows on such a bright day. With that setting, the flash did manage to make the face much more visible than it was without flash.

With this option, the camera uses what could be called "Front Sync," as opposed to Rear Sync, the last option on the Flash Mode menu, discussed later in this section. Fill-flash is available with all shooting modes except Movie, HFR, and Sweep Panorama, and these Scene mode settings: Night Scene, Hand-held Twilight, Night Portrait, Anti Motion Blur, Fireworks, and High Sensitivity.

SLOW SYNC

Slow Sync is one of the settings I did not discuss in detail in Chapter 2. This option is designed for use when you are taking a flash photograph of a subject at night or in dim lighting. With this setting, the camera uses a relatively slow shutter speed so the ambient (natural) lighting will have time to register on the image. In other words, if you're in a fairly dark environment and fire the flash normally, it will likely light up the subject (such as a person), but because the exposure time is short, the surrounding scene may be black. If you use the Slow Sync setting, the slower shutter speed allows the surrounding scene to be visible also.

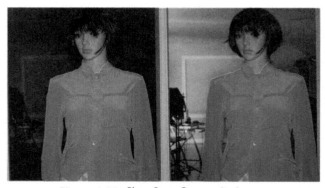

Figure 4-32. Slow Sync Composite Image

I took the two images in Figure 4-32 with identical lighting and camera settings, except that I took the left image with the flash set to Fill-flash and shutter speed at 1/30 second, and I took the right image with the flash set to Slow Sync, resulting in a longer shutter speed of 3/10 second. In the left image, the flash illuminated the mannequin in the foreground, but the background is dark. In the right image, the room beyond the mannequin is illuminated by ambient light because of the slower shutter speed.

When you use Slow Sync, you should use a tripod because the camera may choose a slow shutter speed, such as three seconds or longer. Note that you can choose Slow Sync even in Shutter Priority mode. If you do so, you should select a slow shutter speed because the point is to use a slow shutter speed to light the background with ambient light. With Shutter Priority mode you can choose the shutter speed, but it would not make sense to select a relatively fast one, such as, say, 1/30 second. The same consideration applies for Manual exposure mode, in which you also can select Slow Sync.

Slow Sync is available only in the Program, Aperture Priority, Shutter Priority, and Manual exposure modes. With the Night Portrait setting of Scene mode, Slow Sync is set by the camera and cannot be changed.

REAR SYNC

The last setting for Flash Mode is Rear Sync. You should not need this option unless you encounter the situation it is designed for. If you don't activate this setting (that is, if you select any other flash mode in which the flash fires), the camera uses the unnamed default setting, which could be called "Front Sync." In that case, the flash fires very soon after the shutter opens to expose the image. If you choose the Rear Sync setting instead, the flash fires later—just before the shutter closes.

Rear Sync helps avoid a strange-looking result in some situations. This issue arises, for example, with a relatively long exposure, say one-half second, of a subject with lights, such as a car or motorcycle at night, moving across your field of view. With normal (Front) sync, the flash will fire early in the process, freezing the vehicle in a clear image. However, as the shutter remains open while the vehicle keeps going, the camera will capture the moving lights in a stream extending in front of the vehicle. If, instead, you use Rear Sync, the initial part of the exposure will capture the lights in a trail that appears behind the vehicle, while the vehicle itself is not frozen by the flash until later in the exposure. With Rear Sync in this particular situation, if the lights in question are taillights that look more natural behind the vehicle, the final image is likely to

look more natural than with the Front Sync (default) setting.

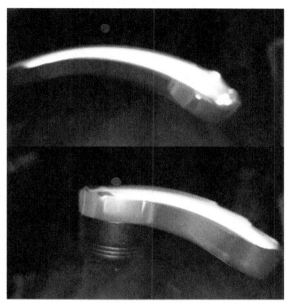

Figure 4-33. Rear Sync Composite Image

The images in Figure 4-33 illustrate this concept using a flashlight. I took both pictures using the built-in flash, with a shutter speed of 1/4 second. For each shot, I waved the flashlight from right to left. In the top image, using the normal (Fill-flash) setting, the flash fired quickly, making a clear image of the flashlight at the right of the image, and the light beam continued on to the left during the long exposure to make a light trail in front of the flashlight's path of movement.

In the bottom image, using Rear Sync, the flash did not fire until the flashlight had traveled all the way to the left, and the trail of light from its beam appeared behind the flashlight's path of motion. If you are trying to convey a sense of natural movement, the Rear Sync setting, as seen here, is likely to give you better results than the default setting.

A good general rule is to use Rear Sync only when you have a definite need for it. Using this option makes it harder to compose and set up the shot, because you have to anticipate where the main subject will be when the flash finally fires late in the exposure process. But, in the relatively rare situations when it is useful, Rear Sync can make a dramatic difference. Rear Sync is available in the more advanced shooting modes: Program, Aperture Priority, Shutter Priority, and Manual exposure.

Here is one more note about using flash: The built-in flash unit can synchronize with the shutter at any speed up to 1/2000 second when Shutter Type is set to Auto or Mechanical. However, when the electronic shutter is in use, the fastest speed at which the flash can synchronize is 1/100 second. So, if you need to use the flash with a shutter speed faster than 1/100 second, you have to use the mechanical shutter.

Flash Compensation

This menu item lets you control the output of the camera's built-in flash unit. This function works similarly to exposure compensation, which is available by pressing the Down button in the more advanced shooting modes. (Exposure compensation is discussed in Chapter 5.) The difference between the two options is that flash compensation varies only the brightness of the light emitted by the flash, while exposure compensation varies the overall exposure of a given shot, whether or not flash is used.

Flash compensation is useful when you are using flash but don't want the subject overwhelmed with light. I often use this setting when I am shooting a portrait outdoors with the Fill-flash setting to reduce shadows on the subject. With a bit of negative flash compensation, I can keep the flash from overexposing the image or casting a harsh light on the subject's face. On a very bright day, I can use positive flash compensation to help the flash overcome harsh shadows, as shown earlier in Figure 4-31.

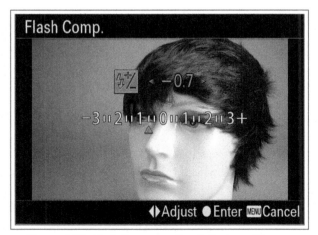

Figure 4-34. Flash Compensation Adjustment Screen

To use this option, highlight it on the menu screen and press the Center button, then, on the next screen,

shown in Figure 4-34, press the Left and Right buttons or turn the Control wheel to set the amount of positive or negative compensation you want.

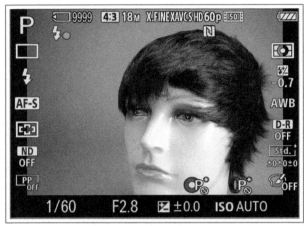

Figure 4-35. Flash Compensation Icon on Shooting Screen

Whenever the flash unit is popped up, an icon will appear in the upper right corner of the display showing the amount of flash compensation in effect, even if it is zero, as shown in Figure 4-35. Be careful to set the value back to zero when you are done with the setting, because any setting you make will stay in place even after the camera has been powered off and back on again.

Note, also, that the Flash Compensation option is not available for selection on the menu in the Auto, Scene, or Sweep Panorama modes.

Red Eye Reduction

This next option is designed to combat "red eye"—the eerie red glow in human eyes that appears in images when on-camera flash lights up the blood vessels on the retinas. This menu item can be set to either On or Off. If it is turned on, then, whenever the flash is used, it fires a few times before the actual flash that illuminates the image. The pre-flashes cause the subject's pupils to narrow, reducing the ability of the later, full flash to bounce off the retinas and produce the unwanted red glow in the eyes.

I prefer to leave this option turned off and deal with any red eye effects using editing software. However, if you will be taking flash photos at a party, you may want to use this menu option to minimize the occurrence of red eye effects in the first place.

Focus Mode

The Focus Mode option gives you five choices for the method the camera uses for focusing. This is one of the more important choices you can make for your photography. Following are details about each of the five selections, the first four of which are shown in Figure 4-36. You have to scroll down through the menu to see the last option, manual focus.

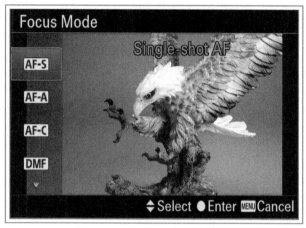

Figure 4-36. Focus Mode Menu

SINGLE-SHOT AF

The first Focus Mode option is single-shot AF, indicated by the AF-S icon. With this option, the camera tries to focus on the scene using the focus area that is selected using the Focus Area menu option, discussed below. If the Pre-AF option on screen 3 of the Custom menu is turned on, the camera will continuously adjust focus, even before you press the shutter button halfway down. When you do press the button halfway down, the camera will lock in the focus and keep it locked as long as you keep the button pressed halfway.

If the Pre-AF menu option is not turned on, then the camera will not make any attempt to adjust focus until you press the shutter button halfway down.

Once you press the shutter button halfway down, you will see one or more green focus brackets on the screen indicating the point or points where the camera achieved sharp focus, as shown in Figure 4-37, and you will hear a beep (unless beeps have been turned off through the Setup menu, as discussed in Chapter 7).

In addition, a green disc in the lower left corner of the display will light up steadily indicating that focus is confirmed. If focus cannot be achieved, the green disc will blink and no focus brackets will appear on the screen.

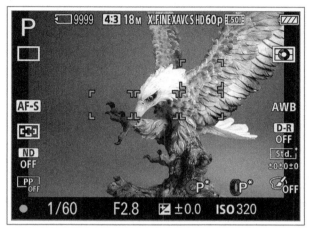

Figure 4-37. Green Focus Brackets with Single-shot AF

Once you have pressed the shutter button halfway to lock focus, you can use the locked focus on a different subject that is at the same distance as the one the camera originally locked its focus on. For example, if you have focused on a person at a distance of 15 feet (4.6 m), and then you decide you want to include another person or object in the scene, once you have locked the focus on the first person by pressing the shutter button halfway down, you can move the camera to include the other person or object in the scene as long as you keep the camera at about the same distance from the subject. The focus will remain locked at that distance until you press the shutter button the rest of the way down to take the picture.

AUTOMATIC AF

The second option for Focus Mode, automatic AF, designated by the AF-A icon, is a mixture of the first and third options, single AF and continuous AF. With automatic AF, the camera locks focus on the subject as with single AF, but, if the subject or camera then moves in a way that changes the focus point, the camera will continue to adjust focus, as with continuous AF. I generally prefer to use either single AF or continuous AF, so I will know whether the camera is going to be adjusting focus, rather than relying on its electronic judgment as to whether focus needs to be changed. But, in a case where the subject initially is stationary but may be moving, this mode could be useful.

CONTINUOUS AF

The next option for Focus Mode, continuous AF, is designated by the AF-C icon on the menu. With this option, as with single-shot AF, the RX100 V focuses continuously before you press the shutter button if the Pre-AF menu option is turned on. If that option is turned off, the camera does not adjust focus until you press the shutter button halfway.

The difference with this mode is that the camera does not lock in the focus when you press the shutter button halfway. Instead, the focus will continue to be adjusted if the subject moves or the distance to the subject changes through camera motion. You will not hear a beep or see any focus brackets to confirm focus. Instead, the green disc in the lower left corner of the display will change its appearance to show the focus status.

If the green disc is surrounded by curved lines, as shown in Figure 4-38, that means focus is currently sharp but is subject to adjustment if needed.

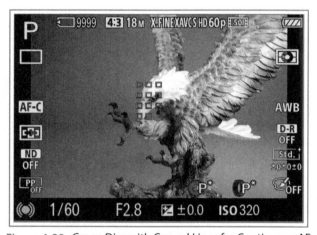

Figure 4-38. Green Disc with Curved Lines for Continuous AF

If only the curved lines appear, that means the camera is still trying to achieve focus. If the green disc flashes, that means the camera is having trouble focusing.

This focusing mode can be useful when you are shooting a moving subject. With this option, you can get the RX100 V to fix its focus on the subject, but you don't have to let up the shutter button to refocus; instead, you can hold the button down halfway until the instant when you take the picture. In this way, you may save some time, rather than having to keep starting the focus and exposure process over by pressing the shutter

button halfway again. Continuous AF is the only autofocus option available for recording movies.

DMF

The third option for Focus Mode is DMF, which stands for direct manual focus. This feature lets you use a combination of autofocus and manual focus. DMF can be helpful if you are shooting an extreme closeup of a small object, when focus can be critical and hard to achieve. With the DMF option, you can start the focusing process by pressing the shutter button halfway down. The camera will make its best attempt to focus sharply using the autofocus mechanism. Then you can use the camera's manual focusing mechanism (turning the Control ring, as discussed below in this section) to fine-tune the focus, concentrating on the parts of the subject that you want to be most sharply focused.

Another time DMF can be useful is when you are shooting a scene with objects at varying distances and you want to focus on one of the more distant ones. In that case, you can start out using manual focus, adjusting it for the most important object, to let the camera know which item to focus on. Then you can press the shutter button halfway to let the camera take over and use autofocus to improve the sharpness of the focus.

When DMF is activated, you can turn on the Peaking Level feature on the Custom menu, as discussed below, and it will function for autofocus as well as for manual focus. In addition, you can use the MF Assist feature with DMF. That feature is discussed below in connection with manual focus. If you use MF Assist with DMF, you have to hold the shutter button halfway down while turning the Control ring to focus, in order for the screen to be enlarged. If you turn the Control ring without holding the shutter button halfway, the focus will be adjusted, but without the enlargement of the screen.

MANUAL FOCUS

The final selection on the Focus Mode menu is Manual Focus. As I indicated in the discussion of DMF, there are various situations in which you may achieve sharper focus by adjusting it on your own rather than by relying on the camera's autofocus system. Those situations include shooting extreme closeups; shooting a group of objects at differing distances; or shooting through a barrier such as glass or a wire fence.

Also, manual focus gives you the freedom to use a soft focus effect purposely. As I will discuss later in this chapter, the RX100 V includes a setting on the Picture Effect menu called "Soft Focus," which adds a pleasing softness to your image. If you would rather create this effect on your own by controlling the focus directly, you can set the camera for manual focus and defocus all or part of the subject in precisely the way you want.

Using manual focus with the RX100 V is a pleasure because of the way the controls are set up. All you have to do is turn the Control ring—the large ring around the lens, next to the camera's body. This action is intuitive, and it is similar to the way most lenses were focused in the days before autofocus existed.

In addition, there are several functions available to assist with your manual focusing. I will discuss those menu options in Chapter 7, but I will briefly describe them here so you can get started with manual focus.

The first option, MF Assist, is turned on or off through the second option on screen 1 of the Custom menu. With MF Assist turned on, whenever you start turning the Control ring to adjust focus in manual focus mode, the image on the display is magnified 5.3 times, as shown in Figure 4-39, so you can more clearly check the focus.

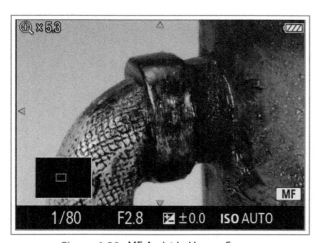

Figure 4-39. MF Assist in Use on Screen

Once the magnified image is displayed, if you press the Center button, the image is magnified further to 10.7 times normal. Press the Center button again to return to the 5.3-times view and press the shutter button halfway to return the display to normal size. You can adjust how long the magnified display stays on the screen using the Focus Magnification Time option, which is directly below MF Assist on the Custom

menu. I prefer to set the time to No Limit, so the magnification does not disappear just as I am getting the focus adjusted as I want it. With the No Limit setting, the magnification remains on the screen until you dismiss it by pressing the shutter button halfway.

If you don't want the camera to enlarge the image as soon as you start focusing, you can use the Focus Magnifier option instead of MF Assist. You can activate Focus Magnifier through screen 6 of the Shooting menu, or you can assign it to a control button using the Custom Key (Shooting) option on screen 5 of the Custom menu. You can set the Custom, Center, Left, or Right button to activate the Focus Magnifier option.

Once Focus Magnifier is activated, a small orange frame appears on the screen, as shown in Figure 4-40.

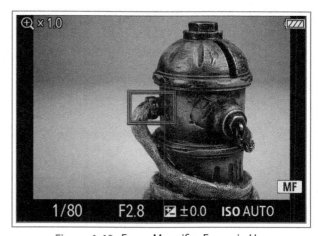

Figure 4-40. Focus Magnifier Frame in Use

You can move that frame around the screen with the Control wheel or the direction buttons. The frame represents the area that will be magnified when you press the Center button. By pressing the Center button, you can switch magnification to various levels.

You can use both MF Assist and Focus Magnifier, though I see no need to do so. My preference is to use only the MF Assist option. I prefer not to go through the steps to turn on the Focus Magnifier option, which does not add that much to the focusing options. However, when I am faced with a challenging task such as shooting in dim lighting, I sometimes use the Focus Magnifier option because it is easier to deal with that situation by being able to see the subject clearly at its normal size and selecting the focus point before using magnification and starting to focus.

The RX100 V provides one more aid to manual focusing, called Peaking Level, the next-to-last item on screen 2 of the Custom menu. That option can be turned off, or it can be set to Low, Mid, or High. When Peaking Level is turned on to any of those levels, then, when you are using manual focus or DMF, the camera places bright pixels around the areas of the image that it judges to be in focus, as shown in Figure 4-41 (without Peaking) and Figure 4-42 (with Peaking Level set to High).

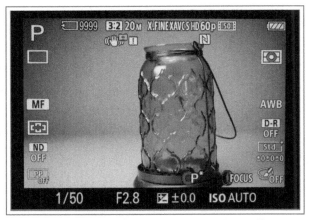

Figure 4-41. Peaking Example: Peaking Off

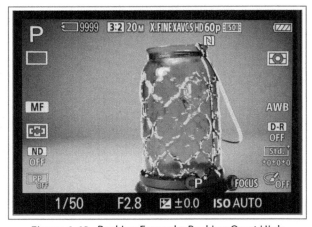

Figure 4-42. Peaking Example: Peaking On at High

Besides setting the intensity of this display, you can set its color—white, red, or yellow—using the Peaking Color option on the Custom menu. I find Peaking to be especially useful in dark conditions because the Peaking effect contrasts with the dark display. Also, as noted above, Peaking works with both the autofocus and manual focus aspects of the DMF option. I will discuss Peaking further in Chapter 7.

Finally, there is another way to customize the use of manual focus with the RX100 V. On screen 5 of the Custom menu, as noted above, you can use the Custom

Key (Shooting) menu option to assign the Custom, Center, Left, or Right button to control any one of a long list of functions. One of those functions, called AF/MF Control Toggle, is useful if you need to switch back and forth between autofocus and manual focus on frequent occasions. When this function is assigned to a button, you can press the button to switch instantly between these two focus modes. This is so much more convenient than going back to the Shooting menu and using the Focus Mode menu option, that it may be worthwhile dedicating a button to this use.

Screen 4 of the Shooting menu is shown in Figure 4-43.

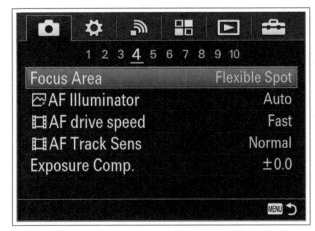

Figure 4-43. Screen 4 of Shooting Menu

Focus Area

The first option on this menu screen, Focus Area, lets you choose what area the camera focuses on when using autofocus. This option is applicable when the camera uses single AF, automatic AF, continuous AF, or direct manual focus.

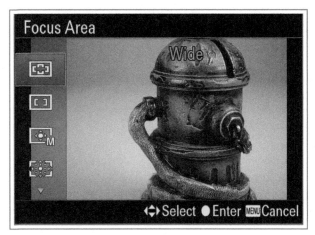

Figure 4-44. Focus Area Menu Options Screen

The choices for Focus Area are Wide, Center, Flexible Spot, Expand Flexible Spot, and Lock-on AF. Figure 4-44 shows the first four of these, from top to bottom; you have to scroll down to see the last option, Lock-on AF.

The ways these selections operate vary somewhat depending on whether you select single AF or continuous AF for the Focus Mode option. If you select direct manual focus, you can use autofocus in the same way as with single AF, so DMF is the same as single AF with respect to Focus Area. If you select automatic AF, the focus mechanism changes its operation depending on whether the subject moves, so Automatic is the same as single AF at some times and the same as continuous AF at other times.

I will discuss the following options assuming at first that you are using single AF or DMF as your focus mode.

WIDE

With Wide, the RX100 V uses multiple focus zones and tries to detect one or more items within the scene to focus on based on their locations. When it has achieved sharp focus on one or more items, the camera displays a green frame indicating the focus point. You may see one or several green frames, depending on how many focus points are detected at the same distance. An example with multiple frames is shown in Figure 4-45.

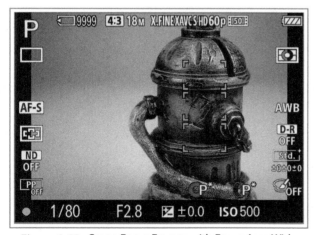

Figure 4-45. Green Focus Frames with Focus Area Wide

If the camera has difficulty picking out a subject to focus on, it will display a large, dotted frame around the whole image, as shown in Figure 4-46. The camera also uses this type of frame when it is using Clear Image Zoom or Digital Zoom.

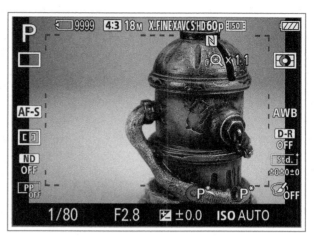

Figure 4-46. Large, Dotted Focus Frame

When you are using single autofocus, the Wide option is excellent for shots of landscapes, buildings, and the like. In continuous autofocus mode, the RX100 V does not display any focus frame with the Wide setting. The camera tries to focus on the subjects that appear to be the main ones. However, if you turn on the Display Continuous AF Area option on screen 3 of the Custom menu, the camera displays the small green squares that indicate phase detection focus points, as the autofocus system continues to adjust focus.

I don't recommend using Wide for Focus Area with continuous autofocus unless you are focusing on a single, clearly defined subject, so the camera will be able to maintain focus on the proper area.

CENTER

If you select Center for the Focus Area setting, the camera places a black focus frame in the center of the display, as shown in Figure 4-47, and focuses on whatever it finds within that frame.

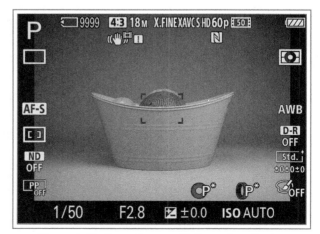

Figure 4-47. Focus Frame with Focus Area Center

When you press the shutter halfway, if the camera can focus it will beep and the frame will turn green. This option is useful for an object in the center of the scene.

Even if you need to focus on an off-center object, you can use this setting. To focus on an object at the right, center that object in the focus frame and press the shutter button halfway to lock focus. Keeping the button pressed halfway, move the camera so the object is on the right, and press the button to take the picture.

If you turn on continuous autofocus with the Center setting, the camera still will display a black focus frame. When you press the shutter button halfway, the frame will turn green when focus is sharp. As the camera or subject moves, the camera will continue to re-focus as you hold the shutter button halfway. You can use this technique to carry out your own focus tracking, by moving the camera to keep the center frame targeted on a moving subject.

FLEXIBLE SPOT

The Flexible Spot option gives you more control over the focus area, with a frame you can move around the screen and resize. When you highlight this option on the Shooting menu, the camera displays the screen shown in Figure 4-48.

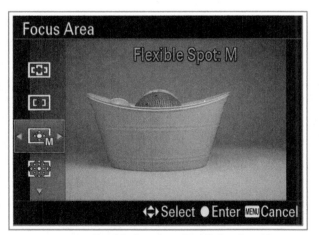

Figure 4-48. Flexible Spot Icon Highlighted on Menu

On this screen, press the Right or Left button to select the size of the Flexible Spot focus frame: L, M, or S, for Large, Medium, or Small. After choosing a size, press the Center button and you will see a screen like that in Figure 4-49, with a white focus frame of that size with arrows pointing to the four edges of the display.

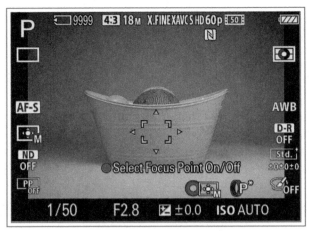

Figure 4-49. Flexible Spot Focus Frame Ready to Move

Use the four direction buttons to move the frame around the display, and turn the Control wheel to change the frame's size. When the frame is located and sized as you want it, press the Center button to fix it in place. The camera will display a black frame of the chosen size in the chosen location. When you press the shutter button halfway to focus, the focus frame will turn green when focus is sharp.

This frame operates the same way as the frame for the Center option, except for the ability to change the location and size. To return the frame quickly to the center of the screen, press the Custom (Delete) button while the frame is activated for moving, and it will move back to the center of the display.

This option is useful for focusing on a particular point, such as an object at the far right, without having to move the camera to place a focus frame over that object. This might help if you are using a tripod, for example, and need to set up the shot with precision, focusing on an off-center subject. If the subject is small, using the smallest focus frame can make the process even easier.

If you use continuous AF, the Flexible Spot option works the same way as the Center option, discussed above, but with the added ability to change the size and location of the frame.

One problem with the Flexible Spot menu option is that it can be cumbersome to move the frame again once you have fixed it in place. One way to do this is to select the Focus Area menu option and repeat all of the steps discussed above. There are a couple of quicker ways to move the frame, though.

The easiest way to do this is to go to screen 5 of the Custom menu and select the Custom Key (Shooting) option. On the next screen, select Center Button, and assign the Focus Standard setting to that button. Then, whenever Flexible Spot is in effect, just press the Center button on the shooting screen, and the screen for moving the focus frame will appear. You can quickly use the direction buttons to move the frame where you want it, or you can press the Custom (Delete) button to center it. You also can turn the Control wheel to change the size of the focus frame.

If you want to use the Center button for some other operation, you can assign Focus Standard to the Custom button using the Custom Key (Shooting) menu option. Or, you can assign the Focus Area menu option to the Custom, Left, or Right button using that option. Then, when you press the assigned button, the camera displays the menu for choosing the size of the Flexible Spot frame. Or, you can assign Focus Area to the Function menu, which is called up by pressing the Function button. I will discuss that menu in Chapter 7.

My preference is to assign the Focus Standard setting to the Center button. Then, to move the focus frame, I just press that button and it is an easy matter to adjust the frame's location and size. I will discuss the Custom Key (Shooting) options further in Chapter 7.

EXPAND FLEXIBLE SPOT

This next option is a variation on the previous one, Flexible Spot. It operates the same way, with a couple of differences. First, the frame is small and cannot be resized. Second, because the Control wheel is not needed to resize the frame, it can move the frame around the screen. (You also can use the direction buttons to move the frame.)

When you use this frame to fix the focus for your shot, the camera will first try to focus on a subject within the frame. If it cannot find a subject to focus on in that small area, it will expand its scope and try to focus on a subject within the area immediately surrounding the frame. That area is outlined by four small brackets outside the corners of the focus frame, as shown in Figure 4-50.

This option can be of use when you want to focus on a small area, but don't want the focusing to fail if focus can't be achieved in that exact spot.

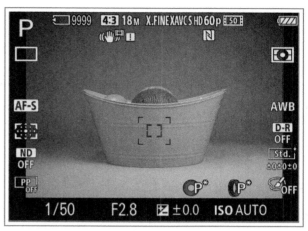

Figure 4-50. Expand Flexible Spot Focus Frame in Use

LOCK-ON AF

The final option for Focus Area is Lock-on AF, which sets up the camera to track a moving object. This option is available for selection only when Focus Mode is set to continuous AF. When you highlight this option on the menu, as shown in Figure 4-51, the camera gives you six choices for the Lock-on AF focus frame: Wide, Center, Flexible Spot Small, Flexible Spot Medium, Flexible Spot Large, or Lock-on AF: Expand Flexible Spot. These frames correspond to the other choices for Focus Area, discussed above, and each one also includes the Lock-on frame's ability to "lock on" to a subject and track it as it moves.

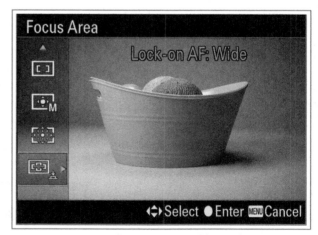

Figure 4-51. Lock-on AF Icon Highlighted on Menu

After choosing one of these six frames, aim the camera at the subject, place the focus frame over it, and press the shutter button halfway. The camera will make an attempt to keep the subject in focus as it moves. The camera will not display any special focus frame, apart from the initial frame that appears if you have selected Center, Flexible Spot, or Expand Flexible Spot as part of the Lock-on

AF setting. When you press the shutter button halfway down, the initial focus frame (if any) will disappear and the camera will attempt to maintain focus on the subject that started out within the frame. If you have turned on Display Continuous AF Area on screen 3 of the Custom menu, small green focus blocks will appear in the area where the camera is directing its focus.

When you are ready to take the picture, press the shutter button all the way. If the autofocus system worked as expected, the image should be in focus.

When you are deciding which of the six sub-options for Lock-on AF to choose, consider the subject that you want the camera to lock onto, and choose accordingly. For example, if the subject is an automobile that is not too far away, you can probably choose Wide. If the subject is a person some distance away, you may want to choose Flexible Spot Small or Medium.

The Lock-on AF option will not give good results if the subject moves too rapidly or erratically, or moves completely out of the frame. But, for subjects that are moving moderately in stable patterns, the Lock-on AF system is worth trying.

If this feature does not produce the results you want, you should consider using the Center Lock-on AF option, found on screen 7 of the Shooting menu, discussed later in this chapter.

AF Illuminator

The AF Illuminator menu item gives you the option of disabling the use of the reddish lamp on the front of the camera for autofocusing for still images. By default, this option is set to Auto, which means that when you are shooting in a dim area, the camera will turn on the lamp briefly if needed to light up the subject and assist the autofocus mechanism in gauging the distance to the subject. If you would rather make sure the light never comes on for that purpose—to avoid causing distractions in a museum or other sensitive area, or to avoid alerting a subject of candid photography—you can set this option to Off. In that case, the lamp will never light up for focusing assistance, though it will still illuminate if the self-timer is activated.

AF Drive Speed

This setting is applicable only for shooting movies. I will discuss it in Chapter 8.

AF Tracking Sensitivity

This option, like the previous one, applies only for shooting movies. I will discuss it in Chapter 8 also.

Exposure Compensation

This last option on screen 4 of the Shooting menu gives you a second way to adjust exposure compensation. As I discuss in Chapters 2 and 5, the primary way to adjust this option is by pressing the Down button, labeled with the exposure compensation icon, with its plus and minus signs. However, when the camera is set to Manual exposure mode, the Down button is used to toggle the function of the Control wheel between adjusting aperture and adjusting shutter speed. Therefore, in that shooting mode, the Down button is not available for setting exposure compensation, and this menu option can be used for that purpose. (Another option when using Manual mode is to assign exposure compensation to the Control ring or to a control button using the Custom Key (Shooting) menu option, or to use the Function menu, as discussed in Chapter 7.) Note, though, that exposure compensation cannot be adjusted in Manual mode by any method unless ISO is set to Auto ISO.

When you use the Exposure Compensation menu option, there is no difference from the procedure when you press the Down button. Once the EV scale appears on the display, use the Left and Right buttons or the Control wheel to set the amount of positive or negative compensation, to make the image brighter or darker than it would be otherwise. Exposure compensation can be adjusted up to 3.0 EV in a positive or negative amount for still images, but only up to 2.0 EV in either direction for movies.

Screen 5 of the Shooting menu is shown in Figure 4-52.

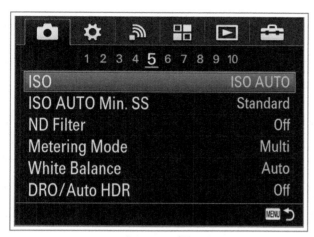

Figure 4-52. Screen 5 of Shooting Menu

ISO

ISO is a measure of the sensor's sensitivity to light. When ISO is set to higher values, the camera's sensor needs less light to capture an image and the camera can use faster shutter speeds and narrower apertures. The problem with higher values is that their use produces visual "noise" that can reduce the clarity and detail in your images, adding a grainy, textured appearance.

In practical terms, you should shoot with low ISO settings (around 125) when possible; shoot with high ISO settings (800 or higher) when necessary to allow a fast shutter speed to stop action and avoid motion blur, or when desired to achieve a creative effect with graininess.

With that background, here is how to set ISO on this camera. As is discussed in Chapters 5 and 7, with the RX100 V you can get quick access to certain important settings, such as ISO, using the Function menu, the Quick Navi system, or, if you want, using the Custom, Center, Left, or Right button or the Control ring. However, you can also set ISO from the Shooting menu, and you can get access to some additional ISO settings only from this menu. So, it's important to know how to use this menu item.

ISO is the first item on screen 5 of the Shooting menu. After you highlight it, press the Center button to bring up the vertical ISO menu at the left of the screen, as seen in Figure 4-53. Scroll through the options by turning the Control wheel or by pressing the Up and Down buttons to select a value ranging from one of the top two options—Multi Frame Noise Reduction and

Auto ISO—through 80, 100, 125, 160, 200, and other specific values, to a maximum of 12800 at the bottom of the scale.

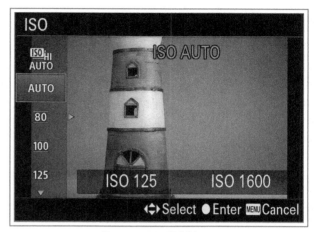

Figure 4-53. ISO Menu

(If you want to use an ISO value higher than 12800, you need to use the Multi Frame Noise Reduction feature, discussed below, or the High Sensitivity setting of Scene mode, discussed in Chapter 3.)

If you choose Auto ISO (the second option on the menu, highlighted in Figure 4-53), the camera will select a numerical value automatically depending on the lighting conditions and other camera settings. You can select both the minimum and maximum levels for Auto ISO. In other words, you can set the camera to choose the ISO value automatically within a defined range such as, say, ISO 200 to ISO 1600. In that way, you can be assured that the camera will not select a value outside that range, but you will still leave some flexibility for the setting.

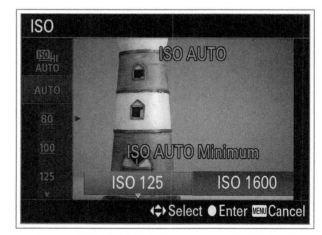

Figure 4-54. ISO Auto Minimum Value Highlighted

To set minimum and maximum values, while the orange highlight is on the Auto ISO option, press the

Right button to move the highlight to the right side of the screen, where there are two rectangles that are labeled (when highlighted) ISO Auto Minimum and ISO Auto Maximum, as shown in Figure 4-54.

Move the highlight to each of these blocks in turn using the Right button and change the value as you wish, by pressing the Up and Down buttons or turning the Control wheel. You can set both the minimum and the maximum to values from 125 to 12800. When both values have been set, press the Center button to move to the shooting screen.

Once those values are set, the camera will keep the ISO level within the range you have specified whenever you select Auto ISO or the Auto setting for Multi Frame Noise Reduction, discussed below. Of course, you can always set a specific ISO value at any other level by selecting it from the ISO menu. In that case, the ISO Auto Minimum and Maximum settings have no effect.

MULTI FRAME NOISE REDUCTION

The top item on the ISO menu, whose icon includes the ISO label and a stack of frames, as shown in Figure 4-55, is Multi Frame Noise Reduction (MFNR).

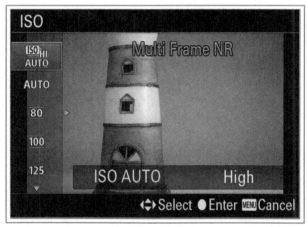

Figure 4-55. Multi Frame Noise Reduction Icon Highlighted

This setting lets you set an ISO value as high as 25600, twice as high as the maximum value on the standard ISO menu. When you use MFNR, the camera takes multiple shots in a rapid burst and creates a composite image with reduced noise. The camera also attempts to select frames with minimal motion blur.

After you have selected MFNR, use the Right button to move the highlight to the first orange block on the right

side of the screen, to choose the ISO setting to be used, as shown in Figure 4-56.

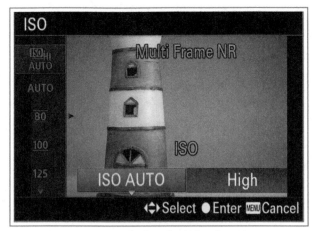

Figure 4-56. Block to Set Value for MFNR

Use the Up and Down buttons or turn the Control wheel to select a value, which can be Auto or a specific value from 200 all the way up to 25600. If you choose Auto, the camera will select an ISO value within the limits set for ISO Auto Minimum and Maximum, and it will take multiple shots using that value.

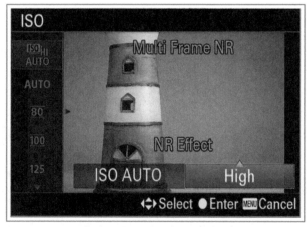

Figure 4-57. Block to Set Value for Noise Reduction Effect

After setting the ISO value to be used with MFNR, you can press the Right button to move to the second selection block on the right side of the screen, as shown in Figure 4-57. In that block, using the Up and Down buttons or the Control wheel, you can set the Noise Reduction Effect to Standard or High. With the Standard setting, the camera shoots four images and combines them internally. With the High setting, the camera shoots 12 images, resulting in a greater likelihood that the final composite image will be of high quality with low noise, but it will take longer for the camera to carry out the shooting and processing operations. If you are shooting a subject that is not likely to move while 12 exposures are quickly captured, and you want to maximize quality, choose High. Otherwise, Standard yields good results.

You cannot use the flash, DRO, or Auto HDR when MFNR is in effect. Also, you cannot use Raw quality or continuous shooting with this setting, and MFNR is not compatible with the use of any Picture Profile or Picture Effect settings.

Using the MFNR setting is the only way to directly set the RX100 V to an ISO level above 12800. (You can, however, use the High Sensitivity setting of Scene mode, in which case the camera may use the ISO 25600 setting if it finds it necessary.) If you are faced with the prospect of taking pictures in an unusually dark environment, consider using the specialized MFNR setting, which really is more akin to a shooting mode than to an ISO setting.

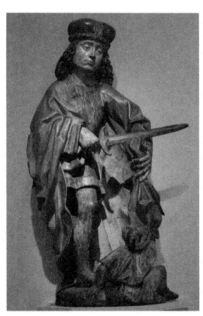

Figure 4-58. MFNR Example

In Figure 4-58, I used the Auto setting of MFNR, with Noise Reduction Effect set to High, to capture a view of a figure in a dimly lighted museum display. The RX100 V set the ISO to 1600 and used a shutter speed of 1/30 second.

Here are some more notes on ISO. As I discussed in Chapter 3, with the RX100 V, unlike many other cameras, you can select Auto ISO in Manual exposure mode. In that way, you can set both the shutter speed

and aperture, and still have the camera set the exposure automatically by varying the ISO level. In the Auto shooting modes, Scene mode, and Sweep Panorama mode, Auto ISO is automatically set, and you cannot adjust the ISO setting. The available ISO settings for movie recording are different from those for stills; I will discuss that point in Chapter 8.

Also, note that the settings for ISO 80 and 100 are surrounded by lines on the menu, as shown in Figure 4-53. The lines indicate that those two settings are not "native" to the RX100 V's sensor, whose base ISO is 125. So, although using the two lower settings reduces the sensor's sensitivity to light and darkens the exposure, it does not improve dynamic range or reduce noise in your images significantly.

My recommendation is to use Auto ISO for general snapshots when the main consideration is to have a properly exposed image. When you know you will need a fast shutter speed, select a high ISO setting as necessary. When you need to use a wide aperture to blur the background or a slow shutter speed to smooth out the appearance of flowing water, use a low ISO setting. When you are shooting in unusually dark conditions, consider using the MFNR setting with a high upper limit for ISO, even as high as 25600 in extreme cases.

ISO Auto Minimum Shutter Speed

The second option on screen 5 of the Shooting menu lets you set a minimum shutter speed, or shutter speed range, for the camera to use when ISO is set to Auto ISO. This option is available for selection only when the shooting mode is set to Program or Aperture Priority, the only two advanced shooting modes in which the camera chooses the shutter speed. The purpose of this setting is to give you a way to ensure that the camera uses a shutter speed fast enough to stop the action for the scene you are shooting.

For example, if you are shooting images of children at play with the camera set to Program mode and Auto ISO in effect with a range from 200 minimum to 1600 maximum, the camera ordinarily may choose a relatively low ISO setting in order to maintain high image quality and low noise. However, using that setting may result in the use of a fairly slow shutter speed, such as 1/30 second, in order to provide enough light for the exposure. With the ISO Auto Minimum Shutter Speed setting, you can set the minimum shutter speed you want the camera to use, such as, say, 1/125 second, to avoid motion blur. You also can specify a more general range of shutter speeds, using several categories, as discussed below.

To use this option, make sure the shooting mode is set to Program or Aperture Priority and that ISO is set to Auto ISO, or to Multi Frame Noise Reduction, with Auto ISO in effect for that setting. Then, highlight this option and press the Center button. You will see the menu shown in Figure 4-59, which includes numerous options as you scroll down through several screens.

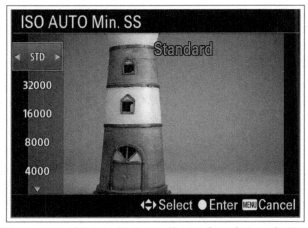

Figure 4-59. ISO Auto Minimum Shutter Speed Menu Option

Most of the options are specific shutter speeds, ranging from 1/32000 second to 30 seconds. If you select one of those values, the camera will attempt to use a shutter speed at least that fast for every shot while maintaining the minimum ISO setting. Once the camera has found it necessary to lower the shutter speed to the minimum value, it will start raising the ISO level as needed. If the camera has set the ISO value to the upper range specified for Maximum ISO and still cannot expose the image properly at the ISO Auto Minimum Shutter Speed, the camera will then set a shutter speed slower than the minimum value, in order to achieve a proper exposure.

For example, in the situation discussed above, using Auto ISO with a range from 200 to 1600, if there is plenty of light, the camera may select shutter speeds such as 1/250 second or 1/500 second. It will maintain the ISO at 200 if possible, and it will never select a shutter speed slower than 1/125 second. If the lighting conditions become such that the camera needs to lower the shutter speed all the way to the minimum setting of

1/125 second, the camera will raise the ISO as needed. If the light becomes too dim, the camera may set the ISO to the top of its Auto ISO range at 1600 but still find it impossible to get a good exposure using 1/125 second for the shutter speed. In that case, the camera will use a slower setting, such as 1/60 second or 1/30 second, as needed.

The item at the top of the menu for this option lists settings that are not specific shutter speeds: Standard, Fast, Faster, Slower, and Slow. You can use one of these if you don't need to specify a particular shutter speed but just want to set general guidance for the camera to use. If you choose Standard, the camera tries to maintain a normal shutter speed based on its programming, taking into account the current focal length of the lens. So, if the lens is at its 24mm wide-angle setting, the camera will try to maintain a shutter speed faster than 1/24 second. If it is zoomed in to 70mm, it will try to use a speed faster than 1/70 second. If you choose Fast or Faster, the camera attempts to maintain a faster shutter speed than with Standard; Slow or Slower has the opposite effect.

ND Filter

With the ND Filter option, you can use the camera's built-in neutral density filter to reduce the amount of light entering the lens, so you will have more flexibility in setting shutter speed and aperture.

The main use for this feature is when the light is bright and you need to use a slow shutter speed or wide aperture. You may need a slow shutter speed to blur the appearance of a waterfall or a wide aperture to blur the background for a portrait. If conditions are bright, it may not be possible to make the setting you need.

For example, I took the photo in Figure 4-60 on a bright day when I wanted to use a slow shutter speed to smooth out the flow of water in a decorative fountain. For this image, I set the shutter speed to 1/10 second. Even with its narrowest aperture and lowest ISO setting, the camera was not able to expose the image properly using that shutter speed. As a result, the image was overexposed and unusable.

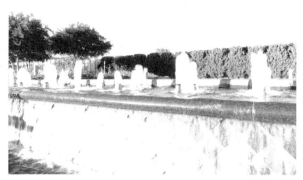

Figure 4-60. ND Filter Example: ND Filter Off

For Figure 4-61, I turned on the ND Filter option, which reduced the exposure setting by three EV. With this option enabled, I was able to use the same settings, and this time the image was exposed normally because of the reduced amount of light striking the image sensor.

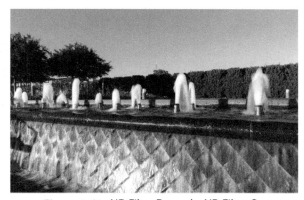

Figure 4-61. ND Filter Example: ND Filter On

This menu option has three possible settings—Auto, On, and Off. The second two are self-explanatory: The ND Filter is either used or not used. With Auto, the camera will activate the ND Filter if it detects a need to reduce the light. I prefer not to use that setting, because I like to make my own decisions about settings. In the Auto, Scene, and Sweep Panorama modes, you can't adjust this setting; the camera automatically uses the Auto option. In Manual exposure mode, you can't select the Auto option for ND Filter— only On or Off.

If you're using one of the advanced shooting modes (Program, Aperture Priority, or Shutter Priority) and taking casual shots, you might want to set ND Filter to Auto to give you more leeway in the settings you use for aperture and shutter speed without having to dig through the menu to turn on that feature. However, it might be a better idea to assign ND Filter to one of the camera's control buttons, as discussed in Chapter

7. If you do that, then it's an easy matter to press that button to call up the ND Filter menu screen and turn the filter on or off whenever you need to.

You also can control the ND Filter setting through the Quick Navi system, or through the Function menu if you have assigned the ND Filter option to that menu, as discussed in Chapter 7.

Metering Mode

This option lets you choose among the three patterns of exposure metering offered by the RX100 V—Multi, Center, and Spot—as shown in Figure 4-62.

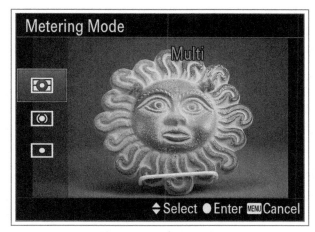

Figure 4-62. Metering Mode Menu Options Screen

This choice tells the camera's automatic exposure system what part of the scene to consider when setting the exposure. With Multi, the camera uses the entire scene that is visible on the display. With Center, the camera still measures all of the light from the scene, but it gives additional weight to the center portion of the image on the theory that your main subject is in or near the center. Finally, with Spot, the camera evaluates only the light that is found within the spot metering zone.

In Spot mode, the camera places a small circle in the center of the screen indicating the metered area, as seen in Figure 4-63.

With the Spot setting, you can see the effects of the exposure system clearly by selecting the Program exposure mode and aiming the small circle at various points, some bright and some dark, and seeing how sharply the brightness of the scene on the camera's display changes. If you try the same experiment using

Multi or Center mode, you will see more subtle and gradual changes.

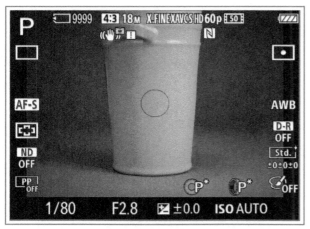

Figure 4-63. Spot Metering in Use

If you choose Spot metering, the circle you will see is different from the rectangular frames the camera uses to indicate the Center or Flexible Spot Focus Area settings. If you make either of those Focus Area settings at the same time as the Spot metering setting, you will see both a spot-metering circle and an autofocus frame in the center of the LCD screen, as in Figure 4-64, which shows the screen with the Spot metering and Center Focus Area settings in effect.

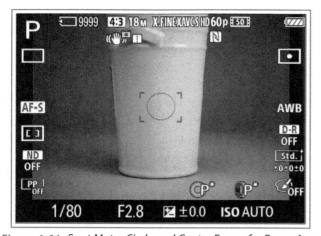

Figure 4-64. Spot Meter Circle and Center Frame for Focus Area

Be aware which one of these settings is in effect, if a circle or a frame is visible in the center of the screen. Remember that the circle is for spot metering, and the rectangular bracket is for Center or Flexible Spot autofocus (or an equivalent Lock-on AF setting).

In the two Auto modes and all varieties of Scene mode, the only metering method available is Multi. That method also is the only one available when Clear Image

Zoom or Digital Zoom is in use. (The conflict arises only when the lens is actually zoomed beyond the limit of optical zoom; at that point, the camera will change the metering method to Multi, and will change it back when the lens is zoomed back within the optical zoom limit.)

The Multi setting is best for scenes with relatively even contrast, such as landscapes, and for action shots, when the location of the main subject may move through different parts of the frame. The Center setting is good for sunrise and sunset scenes, and other situations with a large, central subject that exhibits considerable contrast with the rest of the scene. The Spot setting is good for portraits, macro shots, and other images in which there is a relatively small part of the scene whose exposure is critical. Spot metering also is useful when lighting is intense in one portion of a scene, such as when a concert performer is lit by a spotlight.

White Balance

The White Balance setting is needed because cameras record colors of objects differently according to the color temperature of the light source illuminating those objects. Color temperature is a value expressed in Kelvin (K) units. A light source with a lower K rating produces a "warmer," or more reddish light. A source with a higher rating produces a "cooler," or more bluish light. Candlelight is rated about 1,800 K, indoor tungsten light (ordinary light bulb) is rated about 3,000 K, outdoor sunlight and electronic flash are rated about 5,500 K, and outdoor shade is rated about 7,000 K. If the camera is using a white balance setting that is not designed for the light source that illuminates the scene, the colors of the recorded image are likely to be inaccurate.

The RX100 V, like most cameras, has an Auto White Balance setting that chooses the proper color correction for any given light source. The Auto White Balance setting works well, and it will produce good results in many situations, especially if you are taking snapshots whose colors are not critical.

If you need more precision in the white balance of your shots, the RX100 V has settings for common light sources, as well as options for setting white balance by color temperature and for setting a custom white balance based on the existing light source.

Once you have highlighted this menu option, press the Center button to bring up the vertical menu at the left of the screen, as shown in Figure 4-65.

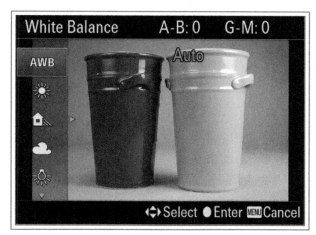

Figure 4-65. White Balance Menu

Press the Up and Down buttons or turn the Control wheel to scroll through the choices on the first screen: Auto White Balance (AWB), Daylight (sun icon), Shade (house icon), Cloudy (cloud icon), and Incandescent (round light bulb icon).

The second screen includes Fluorescent Warm White (bulb icon with -1), Fluorescent Cool White (same, with 0), Fluorescent Day White (same, with +1), Fluorescent Daylight (same, with +2), and Flash (WB with lightning icon).

The choices on the third screen are Color Temperature/ Filter (K and filter icon) and three numbered Custom choices. Below the three Custom icons is an icon with the word "SET," which represents the option for setting a Custom value.

To select a setting, highlight it and press the Center button. Most of the settings describe a light source in common use. There are four settings for fluorescent bulbs, so you should be able to find a good setting for any fluorescent light, though you may need to experiment to find the best setting for a given bulb. For settings such as Daylight, Shade, Cloudy, and Incandescent, select the setting that matches the dominant light in your location. If you are indoors and using only incandescent lights, this decision will be easy. If you have a variety of lights turned on and sunlight coming in the windows, you may want to use either the Color Temperature/Filter setting or the Custom option.

The Color Temperature/Filter option lets you set the camera's white balance according to the color temperature of the light source. One way to determine that value is with a device like the Sekonic C-700 color meter shown in Figure 4-66.

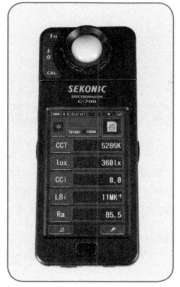

Figure 4-66. Sekonic C-700 Color Meter

That meter works well when you need extra accuracy in your white balance settings. If you don't want to use a meter, you can still use the Color Temperature/ Filter option, but you will have to do some guesswork or use your own sense of color. For example, if you are shooting under lighting that is largely incandescent, you can use the value of 3,000 K as a starting point, because, as noted earlier in this discussion, that is an approximate value for the color temperature of that light source. Then you can try setting the color temperature figure higher or lower, and watch the camera's display to see how natural the colors look.

As you lower the color temperature setting, the image will become more "cool," or bluish; as you raise it, the image will appear more "warm," or reddish. Once you find the best setting, leave it in place and take your shots. (The Live View Display option on screen 3 of the Custom menu must be set to Setting Effect On for these changes to appear on the display, as discussed in Chapter 7.)

To make this setting, after you highlight the icon for Color Temperature/Filter, press the Right button to move the orange highlight to the right side of the camera's screen, so that it highlights the color temperature value bar, as shown in Figure 4-67.

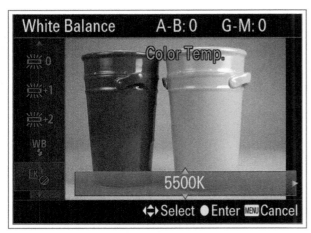

Figure 4-67. Block to Select Color Temperature Value

Raise or lower that number by pressing the Up and Down buttons or by turning the Control wheel, and press the Center button to select that value.

If you don't want to work with color temperatures, you can set a Custom White Balance. This process can be confusing, because the Custom setting has several icons on the White Balance menu. The first three Custom icons, just below the Color Temperature/Filter icon, are used to set the camera to one of three currently stored Custom White Balance settings. The fourth icon, with the word "SET", is the one to use to get a new reading for one of the Custom settings using the camera's special procedure for setting that value. Before you can use any of the three upper Custom icons, you need to use the lowest Custom icon to set the Custom White Balance value as you want it.

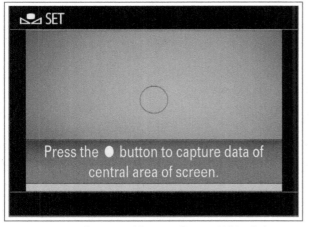

Figure 4-68. Screen to Measure Custom White Balance

To set and store a Custom White Balance, highlight the SET icon at the bottom of the White Balance menu. Press the Center button to select this option, and the

camera will display a message saying "Press the [Center] button to capture data of central area of screen," as shown in Figure 4-68. Aim the camera at a gray or white surface, lit by the light source you are measuring, that fills the circle on the screen. Press the Center button, and the camera will set the white balance.

The lower area of the screen will show the measured color temperature along with letters and numbers indicating variations along two color axes. If there is some variation, you will see an indication such as G-M: G7, meaning 7 units of variation toward green along the green-magenta axis, as shown in Figure 4-69.

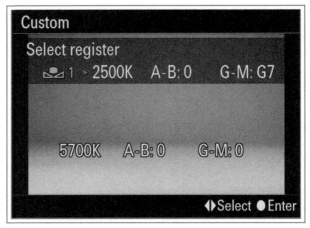

Figure 4-69. Results Screen After Measuring Custom White Balance

Press the Right and Left buttons or turn the Control wheel to select Register 1, 2, or 3. Press the Center button to store the new setting to that register, replacing the existing setting. To use the Custom White Balance setting you saved, select the 1, 2, or 3 Custom icon on the White Balance menu, depending on the slot you used to save the setting. You can change any of the Custom settings whenever you want to, if you are shooting under different lighting conditions.

There is one more way to adjust the white balance setting by taking advantage of the two color axes discussed above. If you want to tweak the white balance setting to the nth degree, when you have highlighted your desired setting (whether a preset or the Custom setting), press the Right button, and you will see a screen for fine adjustments, as shown in Figure 4-70.

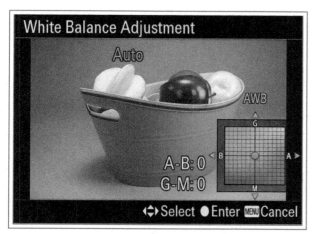

Figure 4-70. Color Axes for Adjusting White Balance

This screen has a pair of axes that intersect at a zero point marked by an orange dot. The axes are labeled G, B, M, and A for green, blue, magenta, and amber. You can now use all four direction buttons to move the orange dot along any of the axes to adjust these four values until you have the color balance exactly how you want it. Press the Center button to confirm the setting.

If you prefer, you can turn the Control wheel to adjust the G-M axis, but you still need to press the Left and Right buttons to adjust the B-A axis. Be careful to undo any adjustments using these axes when they are no longer needed; otherwise, the adjustments will alter the colors of all of your images that are shot with this white balance setting in a shooting mode for which white balance can be adjusted, even after the camera has been powered off and then back on.

Some final notes about white balance: First, if you shoot using Raw quality, you can always correct the white balance after the fact in your Raw software. So, if you are using Raw, you don't have to worry so much about what setting you are using for white balance. Still, it's a good idea always to check the setting before shooting to avoid getting caught with incorrect white balance when you are not using the Raw format.

Second, before you decide to use the "correct" white balance in every situation, consider whether that is the best course of action to get the results you want. For example, I know of one photographer who generally keeps his camera set for Daylight white balance even when shooting indoors because he likes the "warmer" appearance that comes from using that setting. I don't necessarily recommend that approach, but it's not a

bad idea to give some thought to straying from a strict approach to white balance, at least on occasion.

The White Balance menu setting is fixed to Auto White Balance in the Auto and Scene modes.

Before I leave this topic, I am including a chart in Figure 4-71 that shows how white balance settings affect images taken by the RX100 V. I took the photos in the chart under daylight-balanced light using each available white balance setting, as indicated on the chart. Most of the settings yielded acceptable results. The only ones that clearly look incorrect for this light source are the Incandescent, Fluorescent Warm White, and Fluorescent Cool White settings. The other settings produced variations that might be appropriate, depending on how you plan to use the images.

White Balance Chart for Sony RX100 V

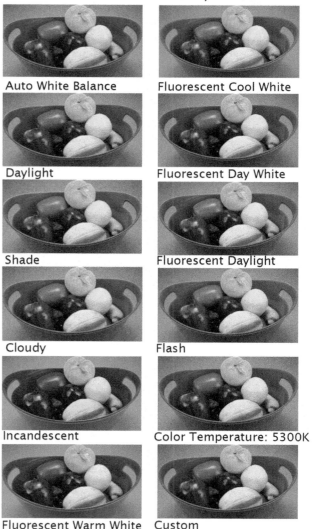

Figure 4-71. White Balance Comparison Chart

DRO/Auto HDR

The next option on the Shooting menu lets you control the dynamic range of your shots using the DRO/HDR processing of the RX100 V. These settings can help avoid problems with excessive contrast in your images. Such issues arise because digital cameras cannot easily process a wide range of dark and light areas in the same image—that is, their "dynamic range" is limited. So, if you are taking a picture in an area that is partly lit by bright sunlight and partly in deep shade, the resulting image is likely to have some dark areas in which details are lost in the shadows, or some areas in which highlights, or bright areas, are excessively bright, or "blown out," so, again, the details of the image are lost.

One way to deal with this situation is to use high dynamic range, or HDR techniques, in which multiple photographs of the same scene with different exposures are combined into a composite image that has clearly visible details throughout the entire scene. The RX100 V can take HDR shots on its own, or you can take separate exposures yourself and combine them in software on your computer into a composite HDR image. I will discuss the details of those HDR techniques later in this chapter.

The RX100 V's DRO (dynamic range optimizer) setting gives you another way to deal with the problem of uneven lighting, with special processing in the camera that can boost details in dark areas and reduce overexposure in bright areas at the same time, resulting in a single image with better-balanced exposure than would be possible otherwise. To do this, the DRO setting uses digital processing to reduce highlight blowout and pull details out of the shadows.

To use the DRO feature, press the Menu button and highlight this option, then press the Center button to bring the DRO/Auto HDR menu up on the camera's display, as shown in Figure 4-72. Scroll through the options on that menu using the Up and Down buttons or by turning the Control wheel.

With DRO Off, no special processing is used. With the second choice, press the Right and Left buttons to move through the DRO choices: Auto, or Level 1 through Level 5. With the Auto setting, the camera analyzes the scene to pick an appropriate amount of DRO processing. Otherwise, you can pick the level; the

higher the number, the greater the processing to even out contrast between light and dark areas.

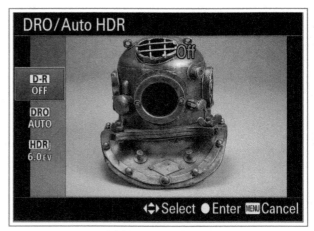

Figure 4-72. DRO/Auto HDR Menu Options Screen

Figures 4-73 through 4-75 are examples of the various levels of DRO processing, ranging from Off to Level 5.

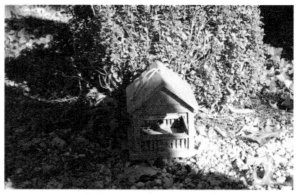

Figure 4-73. DRO Turned Off

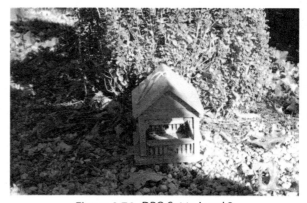

Figure 4-74. DRO Set to Level 3

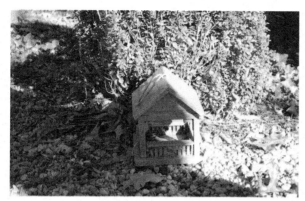

Figure 4-75. DRO Set to Level 5

As you can see, the greater the level of DRO used, the more evenly the RX100 V processed the lighting in the scene, primarily by selectively enhancing details in the shadowy areas at the left. There is some risk of increasing visual noise in the dark areas with this sort of processing, but the RX100 V does not seem to do badly in this respect; I have not seen increased noise levels in images processed with the DRO feature.

The final option for this item, HDR, involves in-camera HDR processing. With traditional HDR processing, the photographer takes two or more shots of a scene with contrasting lighting, some underexposed and others overexposed, and merges them using Photoshop or HDR software to blend differently exposed portions from all of the images. The end result is a composite HDR image with clear details throughout all parts of the image.

Because of the popularity of HDR, many makers have incorporated some degree of HDR processing into their cameras in an attempt to help the cameras even out areas of excessive brightness and darkness to preserve details. With the RX100 V, as with many modern cameras, Sony has provided an automatic method for taking multiple shots that the camera combines internally to achieve one HDR composite image. To use this feature, highlight the bottom option on the DRO/ Auto HDR menu, as shown in Figure 4-76.

Press the Right and Left buttons to scroll through the various options for the HDR setting until you have highlighted the one you want, then press the Center button to select that option and exit to the shooting screen. The available options are Auto HDR and HDR with EV settings from 1.0 through 6.0.

If you select Auto HDR, the camera will analyze the scene and the lighting conditions and select a level of

exposure difference on its own. If you select a specific level from 1.0 to 6.0, the camera will use that level as the overall difference among the three shots it takes.

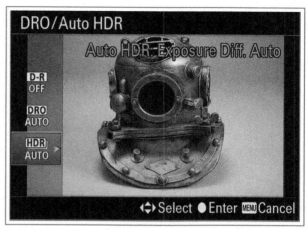

Figure 4-76. HDR Option Highlighted on Menu

For example, if you select 1.0 EV for the exposure difference, the camera will take three shots, each 0.5 EV level (f-stop) different in exposure from the next— one shot at the metered EV level, one shot at 0.5 EV lower, and one shot at 0.5 EV higher. If you choose the maximum exposure difference of 6.0 EV, then the shots will be 3.0 EV apart in their brightness levels.

When you press the shutter button, the camera will take three shots in a quick burst; you should either use a tripod or hold the camera very steady. When it has finished processing the shots, the camera will save the composite image as well as the single image that was taken at the metered exposure.

For Figures 4-77 through 4-80, I took shots of a model truck in an area with both sunlight and shadows, to illustrate the effects of the HDR settings. For Figure 4-77, HDR was turned off; for Figure 4-78, HDR was set at 3.0EV; for Figure 4-79, HDR was set to its highest value, 6.0EV. The image with HDR at 6.0EV gave the best results in terms of pulling details out of the shadows.

For comparison, I took several shots of the subject using a range of exposure levels in Manual exposure mode. I merged those images together in Photomatix Pro software and tweaked the result until I got what seemed to be the optimal dynamic range.

In my opinion, the HDR image done in software, shown in Figure 4-80, did a better job of evening out the contrast than the Auto HDR images processed in the camera. However, these images were taken under fairly extreme conditions. The in-camera HDR option is an excellent option for subjects that are partly shaded and partly in sunlight, when you don't have the time or inclination to take multiple pictures and combine them later with HDR software into a composite image.

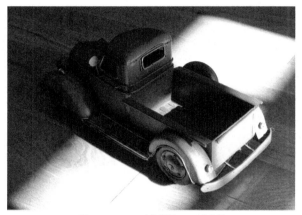

Figure 4-77. HDR Turned Off

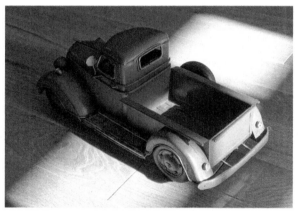

Figure 4-78. HDR Set to EV 3.0

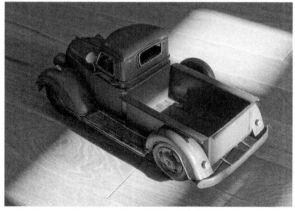

Figure 4-79. HDR Set to EV 6.0

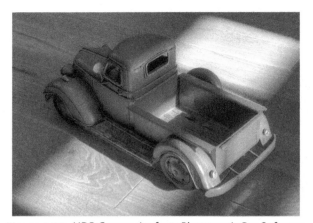

Figure 4-80. HDR Composite from Photomatix Pro Software

My recommendation is to leave the DRO Auto setting turned on for general shooting, especially if you don't plan to do post-processing. If the contrast in lighting for a given scene is extreme, then try at least some shots using the Auto HDR feature.

If you plan to do post-processing, you may want to use the Raw Quality setting so you can work with the shots using software to achieve evenly exposed final images. You also could use Manual exposure mode or exposure bracketing to take shots at different exposures and merge them with Photoshop, Photomatix, or other HDR software. The RX100 V provides high levels of dynamic range in its Raw files, particularly if you shoot with low ISO settings. Therefore, you may be able to bring details out of the shadows and reduce overexposure in bright areas using your Raw processing software.

The Auto HDR setting cannot be used if you are using the Raw format for your images. The other DRO settings do work with Raw images, but they will have no effect on the Raw images unless you process them with Sony's Image Data Converter software or some other software that has been programmed to recognize the DRO settings embedded in the Raw files.

You cannot adjust DRO and Auto HDR settings in the Auto, Scene, and Sweep Panorama modes. With the Sunset, Night Scene, Night Portrait, Hand-held Twilight, Anti Motion Blur, and Fireworks settings, DRO/Auto HDR is turned off. With other scene types, DRO is turned on. DRO/HDR cannot be used when Multi Frame NR, Picture Effect, or Picture Profile is active. You can use flash with these settings, but it will fire only for the first HDR shot, and it defeats the purpose of the settings to use flash, so you probably should not do so.

Screen 6 of the Shooting menu is shown in Figure 4-81.

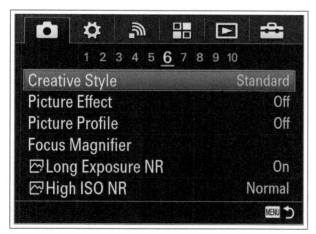

Figure 4-81. Screen 6 of Shooting Menu

Creative Style

The Creative Style setting provides options for altering the appearance of your images with in-camera adjustments to their contrast, saturation (color intensity), and sharpness. Using these settings, you can add or subtract intensity of color or make subtle changes to the look of your images, as well as shooting in monochrome. Of course, if you plan to edit your images with software such as Photoshop, you can duplicate these effects at that stage. But, if you don't want to spend time processing images in that way, being able to alter the look of your shots using this menu option can be a useful option.

To use this feature, Highlight Creative Style, the first item on screen 6 of the Shooting menu, and press the Center button to go to the next screen, as shown in Figure 4-82.

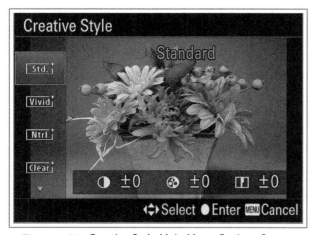

Figure 4-82. Creative Style Main Menu Options Screen

Using the Up and Down buttons or turning the Control wheel, scroll through the 13 main settings: Standard, Vivid, Neutral, Clear, Deep, Light, Portrait, Landscape, Sunset, Night Scene, Autumn Leaves, Black and White, and Sepia. If you want to choose one of these settings with no further adjustment, just press the Center button when your chosen option is highlighted.

If you select an option other than Standard, you may see a change on the camera's display in shooting mode. For example, if you choose Sepia or Black and White, the screen will have that coloration. This effect will be visible, though, only if the Live View Display option on screen 3 of the Custom menu is set to Setting Effect On. If that menu option is set to Setting Effect Off, the display will not show any change from the Creative Style setting. You will still see an icon showing which setting is in effect, in the lower right of the screen. For example, Figure 4-83 shows the display when the Sepia setting is active but Setting Effect is off. (The VIEW indicator on the display indicates that Setting Effect is turned off.)

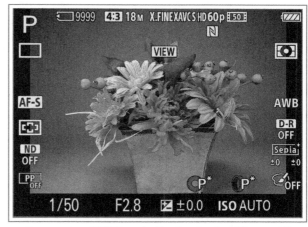

Figure 4-83. VIEW Icon Indicating Setting Effect is Off

ADJUSTING CONTRAST, SATURATION, AND SHARPNESS

To fine-tune contrast, saturation, or sharpness for a Creative Style setting, move the highlight bar to the setting, such as Vivid or Portrait, and press the Right button to put a new bar in the right side of the screen. You will see a label above a line of three icons with numbers at the bottom of the screen, as shown in Figure 4-84.

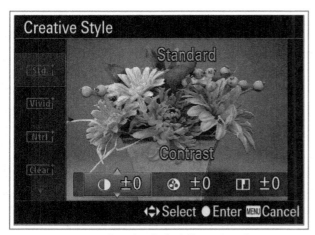

Figure 4-84. Creative Style Adjustments Screen

As you move the highlight over each icon with the Left and Right buttons, the label will change to show which value is active and ready to be adjusted. When the chosen value (contrast, saturation, or sharpness) is highlighted, use the Up and Down buttons or turn the Control wheel to adjust the value upward or downward by up to three units. When the Black and White or Sepia setting is active, there are only two adjustments available—contrast and sharpness. Saturation is not available because it adjusts the intensity of colors and there are no colors to adjust for those two settings.

By varying the amounts of these three parameters, you can achieve a considerable range of different appearances for your images. For example, by increasing saturation, you can add punch and make colors stand out. By adding contrast and/or sharpness, you can impose a "harder" appearance on your images, making them look grittier and more realistic.

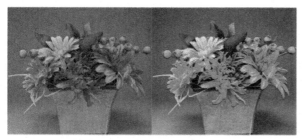

Figure 4-85. Creative Style Adjustments Comparison

Figure 4-85 is a composite image in which the left shot was taken with the Standard setting with all three parameters adjusted to their minimums, and the right shot was taken with the same setting, but with the contrast, sharpness, and saturation all adjusted to their maximum levels of +3 units. As you can see, the right

image is noticeably brighter, with a crisper look than the left one.

If you want to save adjusted settings for future use, you can create and save six different custom versions, using any of the 13 basic settings with whatever adjustments you want. To do this, scroll down on the Creative Style menu to the numbered items, starting just below the Sepia item, as shown in Figure 4-86.

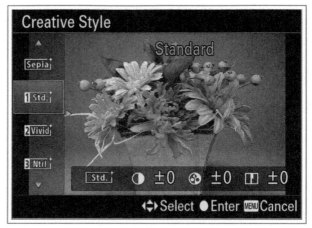

Figure 4-86. Highlight on First Numbered Slot for Custom Creative Style Setting

There are six numbered icons, of which three are visible on the screen shown here. They all work in the same way. Highlight a numbered icon, then, using the Right button, move the highlight to the right side of the screen, on the name of the setting (Vivid, Neutral, Deep, etc.). Use the Control wheel or the Up and Down buttons to select any one of the 13 basic Creative Style settings. Then, scroll to the right and adjust contrast, saturation, and sharpness as you want them. When all the adjustments are made, press the Center button to accept them. Then, whenever you want to recall that customized setting for use, call up the Creative Style menu and scroll to the numbered icon for the style you adjusted.

The Creative Style option works with all shooting modes except Auto mode and Scene mode. You can use it with the Raw format, but the results will vary depending on the Raw-conversion software you use. For example, when I shot a Raw image in Program mode using the Black and White setting, the image showed up in black and white on the camera's screen. However, when I opened the image in Capture One Express for Sony, the image was in color; that software ignored the information in the image's data about the

Creative Style setting. The same thing happened with Adobe Camera Raw and Photoshop.

When I opened the image using Sony's Image Data Converter software, though, the image appeared in black and white, because Sony's software recognized the Creative Style information. So, if you want to use this menu option with Raw files, be aware that not all software will use that data when processing the images.

The Creative Style menu option cannot be used when the Picture Effect or Picture Profile option is in use.

Figures 4-87 and 4-88 include comparison photos showing each Creative Style setting as applied to the same subject under the same lighting conditions to illustrate the different effects you can achieve with each variation. General descriptions of these effects are provided after the comparison charts.

Creative Styles Chart - Part 1

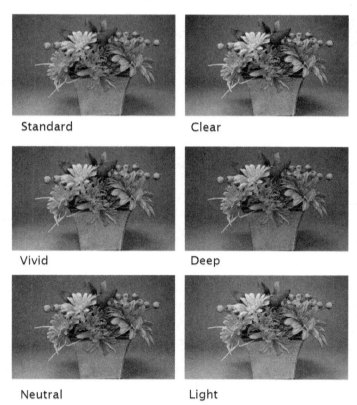

Standard   Clear

Vivid   Deep

Neutral   Light

Figure 4-87. Creative Style Comparison Chart 1

Creative Styles Chart - Part 2

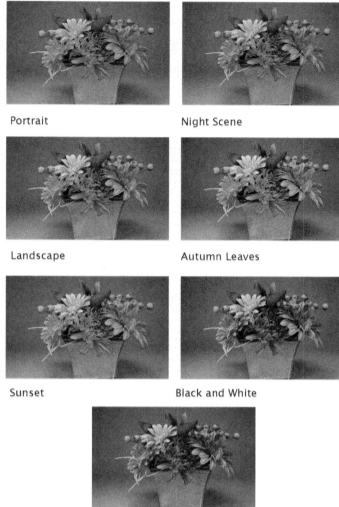

Portrait   Night Scene

Landscape   Autumn Leaves

Sunset   Black and White

Sepia

Figure 4-88. Creative Style Comparison Chart 2

STANDARD

The Standard setting uses what Sony considers to be appropriate processing to give a pleasing overall appearance for everyday photographs, with some enhancements to make color photographs appear bright and sharp. This option is intended to be a good default setting for general purposes.

VIVID

The Vivid setting increases the saturation, or intensity, of all colors in the image. As you can see from the samples, it calls attention to the scene, though it does not produce very dramatic effects. The Vivid setting might work well if you want to emphasize the colors in images taken at a birthday party or at a carnival.

NEUTRAL

With the Neutral setting, the RX100 V leaves images with reduced saturation and sharpness, so you can process them to your own taste using software.

CLEAR

Clear, according to Sony, emphasizes the highlighted areas in the image, giving them added intensity. Some users feel this setting yields images with more intensity than the Vivid setting.

DEEP

Sony says that this setting is intended to show the "solid presence" of the subject. In effect, it emphasizes the shadow tones and lowers the overall brightness of the image.

LIGHT

This setting is the opposite of Deep; it emphasizes the highlight tones and results in a brighter, lighter appearance.

PORTRAIT

The main feature of the Portrait setting is a reduction in the saturation and sharpness of colors to soften the appearance of skin tones. You might want to use this setting to take portraits that are flattering rather than harsh and realistic. Because this setting provides mid-range values for the colors and contrast, some photographers find this to be their favored Creative Style setting for general photography.

LANDSCAPE

With the Landscape setting, the RX100 V increases all three values—contrast, saturation, and sharpness— to make the features of a landscape, such as trees and mountains, stand out with clear, sharp outlines. It is similar to Portrait in its processing of colors, but the sharper outlines and contrast might be too strong for portraits.

SUNSET

With the Sunset option, the camera increases the saturation to emphasize the red hues of the sunset. In my opinion, this setting produces more changes in color images than any of the others.

NIGHT SCENE

Night Scene lowers contrast in an attempt to soften the harsh effect that may result from shots taken in dark surroundings, without affecting the saturation or hues of the colors.

AUTUMN LEAVES

This setting, designed for enhancing shots of fall foliage, increases the intensity of existing red and yellow tones in the image, but does not alter the color balance or introduce new reddish shades, as the Sunset setting does.

B/W

This setting removes all color, converting the scene to black and white. Some photographers use this setting to achieve a realistic look for their street photography.

SEPIA

This second monochrome setting also removes the color from the image, but adds a sepia tone that gives an old-fashioned appearance to the shot.

The RX100 V also has settings for Portrait, Landscape, and Sunset in Scene mode, discussed in Chapter 3. However, the similar settings of the Creative Style option are available in the more advanced shooting modes, including Program, Aperture Priority, Shutter Priority, and Manual exposure, so you have access to settings such as ISO, Metering Mode, and others. And, as noted above, you can tweak Creative Style settings by fine-tuning contrast, saturation, and sharpness.

I don't often use the Creative Style settings, because I prefer to shoot with the Raw format and process my images in software such as Photoshop. I occasionally use the Sunset setting to enhance an evening view. The Creative Style settings are of value to a photographer who needs to take numerous photographs with a certain appearance and process them quickly. For example, a wedding or sports photographer may not have time to process images in software; he or she may need to capture hundreds of images in a particular visual style and have them ready for a client or a publication without delay. For this type of application, the Creative Style settings are invaluable. The settings also are useful for any photographer who wants to maintain a consistent appearance of his or her images and is not satisfied with how the JPEG files look when captured with the factory-standard settings.

Picture Effect

The Picture Effect menu option includes a rich array of settings for shooting images with in-camera special effects. The Sony RX100 V gives you a variety of ways to add creative touches to your shots, and the Picture Effect settings are probably my favorites.

The Picture Effect settings do not work with Raw images. If you set a Picture Effect option and then select Raw (or Raw & JPEG) for Quality, the Picture Effect setting will be canceled. However, with a Picture Effect setting turned on, you still have control over many of the most important settings, including Image Size, White Balance, ISO, and even, in most cases, Drive Mode. So, unlike the situation with the Scene mode settings, when you select a Picture Effect option, you are still free to control the means of taking your images as well as other aspects of their appearance.

To use these effects, select the Picture Effect menu option as seen in Figure 4-89, and scroll through the choices at the left using the Control wheel or the Up and Down buttons.

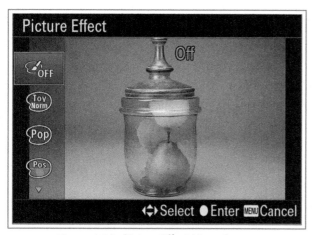

Figure 4-89. Picture Effect Menu Screen

Some selections have no other options, and some have sub-settings that you can choose by pressing the Left and Right buttons.

I will discuss each option in turn. In Figures 4-90 and 4-91, I provide charts with example images taken with each effect, all showing the same scene, for the purpose of comparison. Despite the fact that some settings are intended for other types of scenes, I believe the charts are useful to show how the various settings affect the same scene. After the charts, I will discuss each of the settings and provide a more individualized example image for each one.

Picture Effect Chart - Part 1

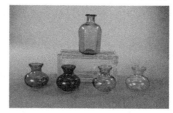

Off

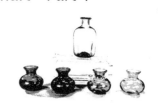

Posterization

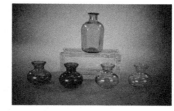

Toy Camera - Normal

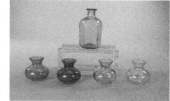

Retro Photo

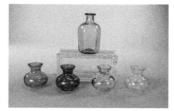

Pop Color

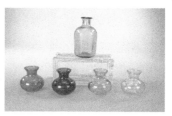

Soft High-key

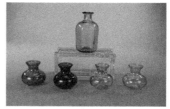

Partial Color - Green

Figure 4-90. Picture Effect Comparison Chart 1

Picture Effect Chart - Part 2

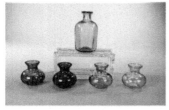
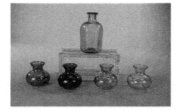

High Contrast Monochrome   Rich-tone Monochrome

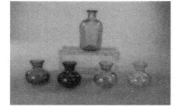
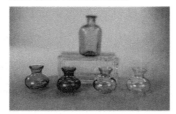

Soft Focus - Mid   Miniature

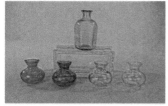
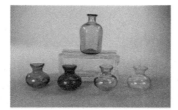

HDR Painting - Mid   Watercolor

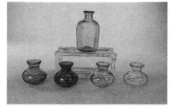

Illustration - Mid

Figure 4-91. Picture Effect Comparison Chart 2

Following are details about each of the settings.

OFF

The top setting on the Picture Effect menu is used to cancel all Picture Effect settings. When you are engaged in ordinary picture-taking or video shooting, you should make sure the Off setting is selected so that no unwanted special effects interfere with your images.

TOY CAMERA

The Toy Camera option is an alternative to using one of the "toy" film cameras such as the Holga, Diana, or Lomo, which are popular with hobbyists and artists who use them to take photos with grainy, low-resolution appearances. With all of the Toy Camera settings, the RX100 V processes the image so it looks

as if it were taken by a camera with a cheap lens: The image is dark at the corners and somewhat blurry.

The several sub-settings for Toy Camera, reached by pressing the Right and Left buttons, act as follows:

Normal: No additional processing.

Cool: Adjusts color to the "cool" side, resulting in a bluish tint.

Warm: Uses a "warm" white balance, giving a reddish hue.

Green: Adds a green tint, similar to dialing in an adjustment on the green axis for white balance.

Magenta: Similar to the Green setting, but adjustment is along the magenta axis.

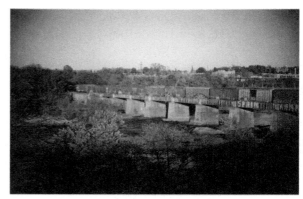

Figure 4-92. Toy Camera Example

Figure 4-92 was taken with the Toy Camera option using its Normal setting. I wanted to make this shot of railroad cars at the river look as if it came from an old-fashioned postcard, with vignetting.

POP COLOR

This setting, according to Sony, is meant to give a "pop art" feel through emphasis on bright colors. As you can see in Figure 4-93, in which I used this setting for a colorful planter packed with flowers, what you get with this setting is another way to add "punch" and intensity, along with added brightness, to your color images.

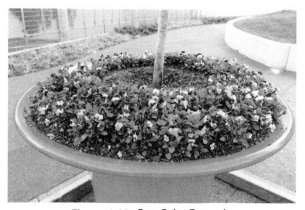

Figure 4-93. Pop Color Example

POSTERIZATION

This is a dramatic effect. Using the Right and Left buttons, you can choose to apply this effect in color or in black and white. In either case, the camera places extra emphasis on colors (or dark and light areas if you select black and white) and uses a high-contrast, pastel-like look. It is somewhat like an exotic type of HDR processing. The number of different colors (or shades of gray) used in the image is decreased to make it look as if the image were created from just a few poster paints; the result has an unrealistic but dramatic effect, as you can see in Figure 4-94, with its view of the city skyline across the river.

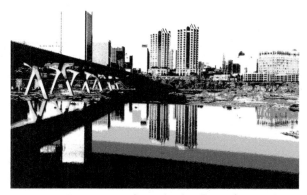

Figure 4-94. Posterization Example

Remember that with all Picture Effect settings, you can adjust other settings, including white balance, exposure compensation, and others. With Posterization, you might use exposure compensation, which can change the appearance of this effect dramatically. I have found the results with this setting often are improved by using negative exposure compensation to avoid excessive brightness. I used a negative 0.3 EV setting for Figure 4-94. I recommend using Posterization to

achieve a striking effect, perhaps for a distinctive-looking poster or greeting card.

RETRO PHOTO

With this setting, the RX100 V uses sepia tint and reduced contrast to mimic the appearance of an aging photo. This effect is not as pronounced as the sepia effects I have seen on other cameras; with the RX100 V, a good deal of the image's original color still shows up, but there is subtle softening of the image with the sepia coloration.

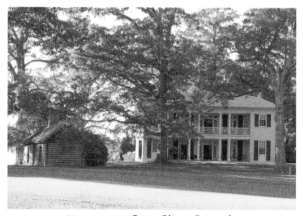

Figure 4-95. Retro Photo Example

In Figure 4-95 I used this effect for a shot of an historic house, to add a somewhat old-fashioned atmosphere.

SOFT HIGH-KEY

"High key" is a technique that uses bright lighting throughout a scene for an overall look with light colors and few shadows. With the RX100 V, Sony has added softness to give the image a light appearance without the harshness that might otherwise result from the unusually bright exposure.

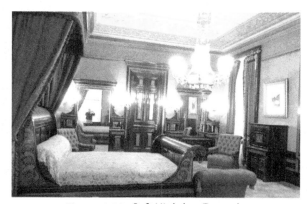

Figure 4-96. Soft High-key Example

In Figure 4-96, I used this setting to brighten and soften an image of a model 19th Century bedroom in the art museum. Without this setting, the room would have looked rather dark and muddy, so I was glad to have this way to brighten it up with just one setting.

PARTIAL COLOR

The Partial Color effect lets you choose a single color to retain in an image; the camera reduces the saturation of all other colors to monochrome, so that only objects of that single hue remain in color in the image. I really enjoy this setting, which can be used to isolate a particular object with dramatic effect. In Figure 4-97, I used this setting to single out the orange chairs in the art museum's lobby.

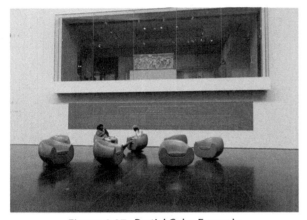

Figure 4-97. Partial Color Example

The choices for the color to be retained are red, green, blue, and yellow; use the Left and Right buttons to select one of those colors. When you aim the camera at your subject, you will see on the display what objects will show up in color, if the Live View Display menu option is set to Setting Effect On.

There is no direct way to adjust the color tolerance of this setting, so you cannot, for example, set the camera to accept a broad range of reds to be retained in the image. However, if you change the white balance setting, the camera will perceive colors differently.

So, if there is a particular object that you want to depict in color, but the camera does not "see" it as red, green, blue, or yellow, you can try selecting a different white balance setting and see if the color will be retained. You also can fine-tune the white balance using the color axes to add or subtract these hues if you want to bring a

particular object within the range of the color that will be retained.

By choosing a color that does not appear in the scene at all, you can take a straight monochrome photograph.

HIGH CONTRAST MONOCHROME

This setting lets you take black and white photographs with a stark, high-contrast appearance. You might want to consider this setting for street photography or any other situation in which you are not looking for a soft or flattering appearance.

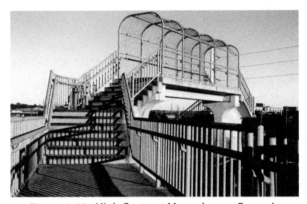

Figure 4-98. High Contrast Monochrome Example

I used this setting for Figure 4-98, an image of concrete steps enclosed by a stark-looking fence on a walkway by the river. I felt that this setting was good for emphasizing the geometric structure of the stairs and the light patterns from the late afternoon sun.

SOFT FOCUS

The Soft Focus effect is another setting that is variable; you can select either Lo, Mid, or Hi by pressing the Right and Left buttons to scroll through those options. This effect is quite straightforward; the camera blurs the focus to achieve a dreamlike aura. Note that this is the first of several Picture Effect settings that cannot be previewed on the screen; you have to take the picture and then play it back to see the results of the Soft Focus setting. As I noted earlier in this chapter, you also have the option of setting Focus Mode to manual focus and defocusing the image to your own taste to achieve a similar effect.

For Figure 4-99, I used this effect at its Mid level for an image of a couple walking along a path near the river. I find that this effect is good for adding an air of peacefulness to a scene.

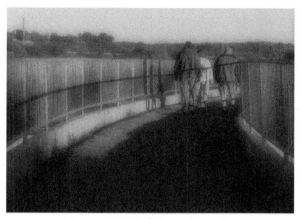

Figure 4-99. Soft Focus Example

HDR Painting

The HDR Painting setting is similar to the HDR setting of the DRO/Auto HDR menu option. With this option, the camera takes a burst of three shots at different exposure settings and combines them internally into a single image to achieve even exposure over a range of areas with differing brightness. Unlike the more standard HDR setting, this one does not let you select the specific exposure differential for the three shots, but it lets you choose Lo, Mid, or Hi for the intensity of the effect. Also, it adds stylized processing to give the final image a painterly appearance.

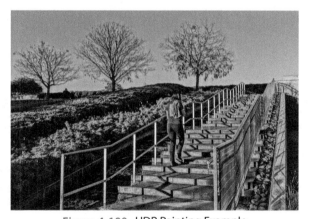

Figure 4-100. HDR Painting Example

I have often had good results with this setting when I shoot from an indoor area through a window on a sunny day, especially when there is a variety of colorful items outside. For Figure 4-100, though, I chose an outdoor scene, with the effect set at its Mid level to avoid an overly harsh result. Because the camera takes multiple images with this effect, you can't preview the results on the screen before taking the picture. Using a tripod is advisable to avoid blur from camera motion

while the three shots are being taken. Figure 4-100 was taken without a tripod, though.

Rich-Tone Monochrome

The Rich-tone Monochrome setting can be considered as a black and white version of the HDR Painting setting. With this option, like that one, the RX100 V takes a triple burst of shots at different exposures and combines them digitally into a single composite photo with a broader dynamic range than would otherwise be possible. Unlike the color setting, though, this one does not let you select the intensity of the effect. I used it in Figure 4-101 for a photo of a Civil War-era cannon outside a museum.

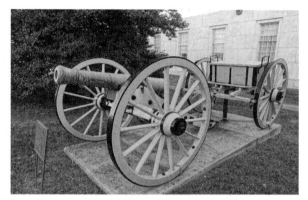

Figure 4-101. Rich-tone Monochrome Example

Miniature Effect

With the Miniature Effect option, the camera adds blurring at one or more sides or the top or bottom of an image to simulate the look of a photograph of a tabletop model or miniature. Such images often appear hazy in one or more areas, either because of the narrow depth of field of these closeup photos, or because of the use of a tilt-and-shift lens, which causes blurring at the edges.

For this feature to work well, you need an appropriate subject. I have found that this effect looks interesting when applied to something like a street scene or a train, which might actually be reproduced in a tabletop model. For example, if you are able to get a high vantage point above a road intersection or a railroad, you may be able to use this processing to make it look as if you had photographed a high-quality tabletop display.

After highlighting this option on the Shooting menu, press the Right and Left buttons to choose either Top, Middle (Horizontal), Bottom, Right, Middle (Vertical),

Left, or Auto for the configuration of the effect. If you choose a specific area, that area will remain sharp. For example, if you choose Top, then, after you take the picture, the top area (roughly one-third) will remain sharp, and the rest of the image below that area will appear blurred. If you choose Auto, the camera will select the area to remain sharp based on the area that was focused on by the autofocus system and by the camera's sensing how you are holding the camera.

You will not see how the effect will alter the image while viewing the scene, though the camera will place gray areas on the parts of the image that will ultimately be blurred to give an idea of how the final product will look. In Figure 4-102, I used this setting for a view of trucks from a fairly high point on a pedestrian bridge.

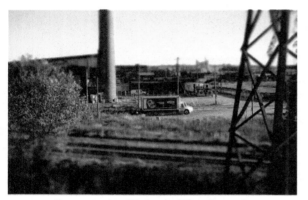

Figure 4-102. Miniature Effect Example

This effect can provide a lot of fun if you experiment with it; it can take some work to find the right subject and the best arrangement of sharp and blurry areas to achieve a satisfying result.

WATERCOLOR

The Watercolor effect blurs the colors of an image to make it look as if it were painted with watercolors that are bleeding together. You need to choose a subject that lends itself to this sort of distortion. For example, I have found that the faces of dolls and other figures can be pleasantly altered to have an impressionistic appearance; larger objects may not be affected significantly by this somewhat subtle effect. I have also had some pleasing results with plants and trees. In Figure 4-103, I thought this effect worked well for a view of the Richmond, Virginia, skyline across the river.

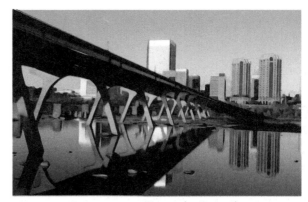

Figure 4-103. Watercolor Example

ILLUSTRATION

This final option for the Picture Effect setting is one of my favorites. This effect finds edges of objects in the scene and adds contrast to them, making the image seem like a pen-and-ink illustration that has been colored in. You can set the intensity of the effect to Lo, Mid, or Hi using the Right and Left buttons. If you choose a subject with edges that can be outlined and a repeating pattern, you can achieve a pleasing result. This is another effect whose final result you cannot judge while viewing the live scene; you need to see the recorded image to know what the actual effect will look like.

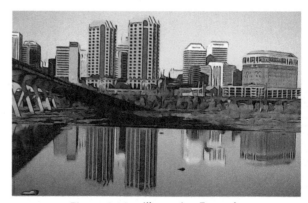

Figure 4-104. Illustration Example

As you can see in Figure 4-104, taken with Illustration set to Mid, this effect can transform an ordinary view into a stylized image while leaving the scene recognizable. The images produced with this effect may be more suited as decorative items than as depictions of actual objects or locations, but their appearance can be very striking and unusual. I have found that this setting often produces good results when people are included in the scene, especially if they are wearing clothes with bright colors. Here, though, I used it for a view of the city skyline.

Here are some more notes about the Picture Effect settings. First, several of the options are not available for shooting movies. Those settings are Soft Focus, HDR Painting, Rich-tone Monochrome, Miniature Effect, Watercolor, and Illustration. If one of those effects is turned on when you press the Movie button, the camera will turn off the effect while the movie is being recorded, and turn it back on after the recording has ended. You also cannot use Drive Mode with any of those six effects. Note that you can activate several of the Picture Effects settings with the Photo Creativity feature in the Auto shooting mode, as discussed in Chapter 2.

Picture Profile

The Picture Profile option, the third item on the sixth screen of the Shooting menu, provides powerful tools for adjusting the appearance of your files, particularly your video footage. This option is similar in some ways to the Creative Style option, which provides a separate set of preset adjustments that affect image processing, as discussed earlier in this chapter. Like Creative Style, the Picture Profile option includes several presets from which you can easily choose the one that best suits your current needs and instantly apply it to all of the videos and images you record using that setting. You also can make adjustments to several parameters within any of the Picture Profile settings, just as you can with the Creative Style settings, and you can save the adjusted settings for future use.

However, apart from those similarities, the Picture Profile option is considerably different from the Creative Style feature. Creative Style is straightforward in the adjustments it provides, both in its 13 preset options (Standard, Vivid, Neutral, etc.) and in the adjustments you can make to those settings (contrast, saturation, and sharpness). It is easy to understand what is being adjusted for the presets and to see the resulting differences in the appearance of your images and videos.

The Picture Profile option does not provide such easily categorized adjustments. These adjustments are more technical ones that are intended for use by professional videographers, to provide footage that is ready for post-processing, or that matches footage from other cameras using the same profile. In this section, I will explain how to apply a Picture Profile setting and how to adjust one, and I will provide a basic discussion of the parameters

that can be tweaked for each profile. I will not give a detailed explanation of all possible adjustments for the various settings involved, such as gamma, knee, and detail.

To use this setting, highlight Picture Profile on the menu screen and press the Center button to display the vertical menu of settings, as shown in Figure 4-105.

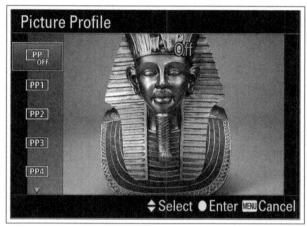

Figure 4-105. Picture Profile Menu

Use the Control wheel or the Up and Down buttons to scroll through the eight available settings, including PP Off and PP1 through PP7. If you don't need or want to bother with setting a profile, just leave this item set to PP Off and you won't have to deal with it further. If you know that you want to use one of the seven preset profiles, scroll to that setting and press the Center button to select it when it is highlighted. The selected profile will then be displayed in an icon in the lower left corner of the detailed shooting screen, as shown in Figure 4-106.

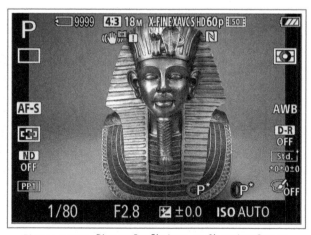

Figure 4-106. Picture Profile Icon on Shooting Screen

The basic characteristics of the seven preset profiles that come with the camera are as follows:

PICTURE PROFILE SETTINGS

PP1   Uses the standard gamma curve for movies.

PP2   Uses the standard gamma curve for still images.

PP3   Uses ITU709 gamma curve for natural color tone. The ITU709 standard is the normal set of specifications for HD television. This is a good profile to use for shooting that won't need extensive post-processing. This is also good for matching footage with that of other cameras.

PP4   Uses the ITU709 standard for color tone. Should not need much post-processing for color tone.

PP5   Uses Cine1 gamma curve to reduce contrast in dark areas and modify bright areas to produce a "relaxed" color effect. Good for sunny days and conditions with high contrast.

PP6   Uses Cine2 gamma curve, optimized for editing with up to 100% video signal; generally similar to Cine1, for use with less need for post-processing to avoid clipping highlights.

PP7   Uses S-Log2 gamma curve, designed to yield the greatest dynamic range, for footage that will be adjusted with post-processing software.

You should be able to get good results for general footage with any of the first four Picture Profile settings. On a particularly bright day or in contrasty conditions, you might try PP5, which uses the Cine1 gamma, designed to compress the dynamic range to avoid clipping highlights, or PP6, which uses the Cine2 gamma, which compresses the range even more.

If you will be doing post-processing to correct the color of your footage, you may want to use PP7, which uses the S-Log2 gamma curve setting. With this option, your footage will look dull and somewhat dark as shot, but its dynamic range will be considerably greater than normal, so you will have excellent options for producing good-looking footage with your post-processing software. However, because of the way this setting expands dynamic range, it requires the use of an ISO setting of 1600 or greater. So, if you use PP7 or any profile that includes S-Log2 gamma, the camera will not set the ISO any lower than 1600.

The chart in Figure 4-107 shows the effects of the seven preset Picture Profile settings, as well as the same image with no Picture Profile in place, to give a general idea of how these settings affect an image.

Picture Profiles Comparison

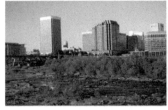
Off

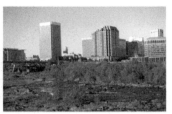
Picture Profile 4

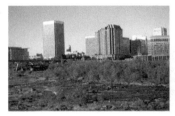
Picture Profile 1

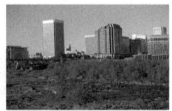
Picture Profile 5

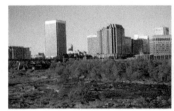
Picture Profile 2

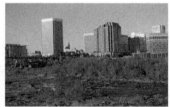
Picture Profile 6

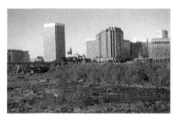
Picture Profile 3

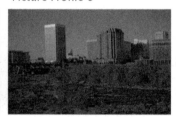
Picture Profile 7

Figure 4-107. Picture Profile Comparison Chart

If you are serious about video production, you may not be content with any of the seven pre-packaged Picture Profile settings. You can readily modify any of them in the camera. I don't recommend that you do this unless you are quite experienced and knowledgeable about video production, but the option for extensive tweaking is available. I will discuss the mechanics of how to adjust the various parameters for the Picture Profile settings, but I will not engage in a technical discussion of when and why to adjust them. (Appendix C has links to resources with further information.)

To adjust a Picture Profile setting, highlight the Picture Profile menu option and press the Center button to display the menu of Picture Profile options, as shown in Figure 4-105. Scroll to the one you want to adjust and press the Right button. You will then see a screen like that in Figure 4-108, listing the first six parameters that can be adjusted: black level, gamma, black gamma, knee, color mode, and saturation.

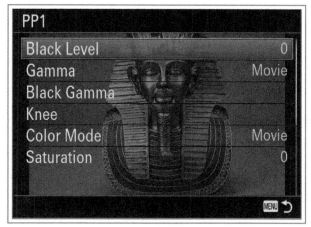

Figure 4-108. Picture Profile Adjustments Screen

Turn the Control wheel or press the Up and Down buttons to scroll through this list and on to the remaining parameters: color phase, color depth, and detail. The last two options, copy and reset, are for copying the settings or restoring the default settings.

When you have highlighted a parameter to adjust, such as gamma, press the Right button to bring up the adjustment screen, as shown in Figure 4-109.

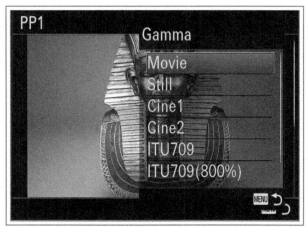

Figure 4-109. Adjustment Screen for Picture Profile Parameter

Use the Control wheel or the Up and Down buttons to choose the value to set, and press the Center button to set the value and return to the previous screen.

Continue scrolling through the parameters to set each as you want it. Once you have made the adjustments, the Picture Profile number you adjusted will retain those changes, even if the camera is turned off and back on.

If you want to copy the settings from one Picture Profile slot to another, use the copy item near the bottom of the list of parameters. Use the reset option to restore the Picture Profile setting to its default values.

Following are general descriptions of the nine parameters that you can adjust for each Picture Profile setting:

Black Level. Default 0; adjustment from -15 to +15. Adjusting in the negative direction strengthens the black color in the image; adjusting in the positive direction fades or weakens it.

Gamma. No default. Choices are Movie, Still, Cine1, Cine2, ITU709, ITU709 (800%), or S-Log2. The gamma curve is an adjustment to the video signal to account for the difference between recorded video and the output characteristics of various display devices, such as cathode ray tubes, HDTVs, etc. The first two choices are self-explanatory. Cine1 has the signal compressed to avoid clipping of highlights; Cine2 is compressed further for the same purpose. The ITU709 setting is a standard one for HDTV. The ITU709 (800%) option provides greater dynamic range than ITU709. It applies standard contrast and color levels to the video signal and turns off the knee circuit. It can be used as the finished product for video production. You may need to use this standard or S-Log2 when recording to certain external recorders, such as Odyssey7 models from Convergent Design. Finally, the S-Log2 standard, which provides the greatest possible dynamic range, produces a flat, somewhat dark signal. This standard is for use only when you are going to be correcting the appearance of the video file with post-processing software.

Black Gamma. Range default is Middle; can be set to Wide or Narrow. Level default is 0; can be set from -7 to +7. Increasing Level brightens the image and decreasing Level darkens it. Adjusting Range determines whether the Level adjustment affects only blacks (Narrow) or a wider range of grays.

Knee. The Knee adjustment sets a curve for compressing the signal in the brightest parts of the video image to avoid clipping or washing out of highlights. The Mode can be set to Auto or Manual. If you select Auto, then you need to use the Auto Set option to choose the Max Point and Sensitivity. If you choose Manual, you need to use the Manual Set option to set the Point and Slope.

Color Mode. No default. Can be set to Movie, Still, Cinema, Pro, ITU709 Matrix, Black & White, or S-Gamut. Movie is designed for use with the Movie setting for Gamma; Still for the Still setting; Cinema for the Cine1 setting; Pro for the gamma curve of Sony professional video cameras; ITU709 Matrix for use with the ITU709 gamma curve; Black & White for shooting in monochrome; and S-Gamut for shooting with the S-Log2 gamma curve. If you select the Black & White setting, the video will be shot in black and white.

Saturation. Default 0. Can be set from -32 to +32. This adjustment is similar to the saturation adjustment available with the Creative Style menu option. A negative setting lowers the intensity of colors, reducing them almost completely to black and white at the -32 level, while a positive value increases their intensity.

Color Phase. Default 0. Can be set from -7 to +7. Adjusting in the negative or positive direction makes the colors shift their hues. You can use this setting to match the color output of the RX100 V to that of another camera you are using for video production.

Color Depth. Default 0. Can be set from -7 to +7 for each of six colors: red, green, blue, cyan, magenta, and yellow. A higher number makes the color darker and richer; a lower number makes it brighter and paler.

Detail. There are two main settings: Level and Adjust. Level has a default of 0 and can be adjusted from -7 to +7. This setting affects the sharpness of edges in the image. A lower number softens the image and a higher number gives it sharper contrast. The other main setting, Adjust, has several settings, starting with Mode, which can be set to Auto or Manual. If you set Mode to Auto, you can ignore the other settings. If you set it to Manual, you can adjust V/H Balance, B/W Balance, Limit, Crispening (misspelled on the camera's menu), and Hi-Light Detail. Sony's user's guide recommends changing only the Level setting, at least at first, but the guide provides details on the other settings. You can see those details at Sony's website, http://helpguide.sony.net/di/pp/v1/en/contents/TP0000909112.html. If you are planning to use

software to process your video, you may want to reduce Level to -7 so you can determine the proper amount of sharpening on your own.

The good news about the Picture Profile setting is that you do not need to worry about it if you don't want to. If you are shooting primarily still images or videos for your own use, you don't have to select any Picture Profile setting. However, if you are using the RX100 V for professional video production, perhaps as a second camera, you may need to set the Picture Profile so the camera's output will match that of your other cameras.

Picture Profile cannot be used when DRO/HDR, Creative Style, or Picture Effect is in use. Picture Profile settings affect Raw files, but the black level, black gamma, knee, and color depth settings are not reflected in Raw images.

If you want to explore Picture Profile in greater detail, check out the resources listed in Appendix C.

Focus Magnifier

The Focus Magnifier option gives you a way to magnify a part of the shooting screen so you can evaluate the focus before capturing an image. (It works somewhat differently for movies, as discussed below.) This option is similar to the MF Assist option on screen 1 of the Custom menu, which lets you enlarge the screen when using manual focus. However, the Focus Magnifier option is available with any focus mode, not just manual focus. It also has some other differences from MF Assist, as discussed below.

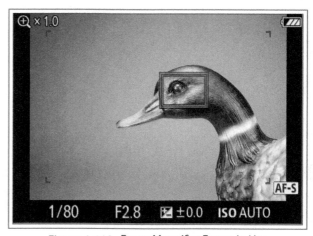

Figure 4-110. Focus Magnifier Frame in Use

When you select this menu option, the camera places an orange frame on the display, as seen in Figure 4-110. You can move the frame to any position on the display using the direction buttons or the Control wheel. When the frame is over the area where you want to check focus, press the Center button. The camera will enlarge the area within the frame to 5.3 times normal, as shown in Figure 4-111.

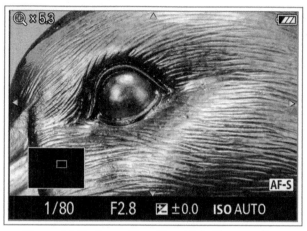

Figure 4-111. Focus Magnifier at 5.3x Magnification

An inset square will show the position of the Focus Magnifier frame. You can move the frame around the display while the display is enlarged and recall the frame to the center of the display by pressing the Custom button. Press the Center button again, and the focus area will be magnified to 10.7 times normal. A final press will restore the display to normal size. Once you press the shutter button halfway, the magnifier frame will disappear. You can call it up again using this menu option if you want to.

As noted above, Focus Magnifier acts in a similar way to MF Assist. As I discussed earlier in this chapter and will discuss in Chapter 7, when you turn on MF Assist with manual focus in effect, the focus area is enlarged to 5.3 times normal as soon as you start turning the Control ring to adjust the focus. Then, once the focus area is enlarged with that option, pressing the Center button will magnify the focus area to 10.7 times normal. You can toggle between the 5.3 and 10.7 magnifications using the Center button, and exit to the shooting screen by half-pressing the shutter button.

In other words, if the MF Assist menu option is active, the Center button always acts to magnify the focus area once you have started to adjust focus in manual focus mode. With Focus Magnifier, pressing the Center

button magnifies the display immediately, before you start focusing (if you are using manual focus). If you use the MF Assist option, the camera will enlarge the display as soon as you start turning the Control ring to adjust focus, and you will not be able to choose the location of the enlarged focus area until the display is already enlarged.

Another difference from MF Assist is that Focus Magnifier works with any focus mode, including the autofocus modes, so you can evaluate how well the camera adjusted focus on its own. You cannot cause the camera to refocus using autofocus with the Focus Magnifier, however, because, when you press the shutter button halfway down to refocus, the Focus Magnifier frame disappears. You can refocus with autofocus and then call up the Focus Magnifier frame again to check the focus, if you want.

The Focus Magnifier feature is easier to use if you assign it to one of the control buttons. For example, you can use the Custom Key (Shooting) option on screen 5 of the Custom menu to assign Focus Magnifier to the Left button. Then you can press that button to bring the enlargement frame up on the display at any time. You can quickly adjust the position of the frame, press the Center button once or twice to enlarge that area, and then evaluate the focus and take the picture.

You can set the length of time the Focus Magnifier frame remains on the display using the Focus Magnification Time item on screen 1 of the Custom menu, as discussed in Chapter 7. The time can be two seconds, five seconds, or No Limit. You also can change the setting for the initial enlargement factor of the frame, using the Initial Focus Magnification option, also on screen 1 of the Custom menu. By default, the frame initially does not magnify the display; it uses the 5.3x magnification only when you press the Center button. Using that menu option, you can change this setting so the frame magnifies the display to the 5.3x level as soon as the frame appears on the display.

As noted above, Focus Magnifier works differently for movies. The only magnification factor when shooting movies is 4.0x, rather than 5.3x and 10.7x, the factors when shooting still images.

Long Exposure Noise Reduction

This option uses processing to reduce the "noise" that affects images during exposures of 1/3 second or longer. This option is turned on by default. When it is turned on, the camera processes your shot for a time equal to the time of the exposure. So, if your exposure is for two seconds, the camera will process the shot for an additional two seconds, creating a delay before you can shoot again.

In some cases, this processing may remove details from your image. In addition, in certain situations you may prefer to leave the noise in the image because the graininess can be pleasing in some cases. Or, you may prefer to remove the noise using post-processing software. If you want to turn off this option, use this menu item to do so.

This option is not available for adjustment when the camera is set for continuous shooting, Multi Frame Noise Reduction, exposure bracketing, or in the Auto, Sweep Panorama, or Scene modes. The camera will select a setting for Long Exposure Noise Reduction in those cases. For example, the camera will turn this option off with the Sports Action, Hand-held Twilight, and Anti Motion Blur Scene mode settings, but turn it on with the Portrait and Macro settings.

I recommend you make this setting based on the type of shooting you are doing. If you're taking casual shots or don't want to do post-processing, I suggest you leave this option turned on. But, if you are shooting with Raw quality and want to do processing with software, I recommend turning it off.

High ISO Noise Reduction

This last entry on screen 6 of the Shooting menu has three settings: Normal, Low, or Off; the default is Normal. This option removes noise caused by the use of a high ISO level. One problem with this sort of noise reduction is that it takes time to process your images after they are captured. You may want to set this option to Low or Off to minimize the delay before you can take another picture. If Quality is set to Raw, this option will be unavailable on the menu because this processing is not available for Raw images. It also is not available in the Auto, Scene, or Sweep Panorama modes.

Screen 7 of the Shooting menu is shown in Figure 4-112.

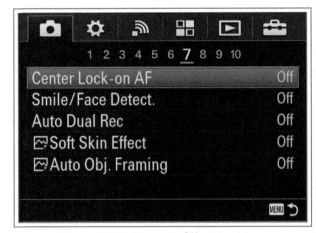

Figure 4-112. Screen 7 of Shooting Menu

Center Lock-on AF

This first option on screen 7 of the menu is similar to the Lock-on AF option discussed earlier in this chapter, but there are differences. Lock-on AF is a setting that is available for Focus Area on screen 4 of the Shooting menu. That option is available only with continuous autofocus. When it is activated, the camera uses the focus method of your choice. When you focus on your subject using that method and half-press the shutter button, the camera will try to keep the subject in focus as it moves.

The option being discussed here, Center Lock-on AF, is a separate menu option. It is not available when the Lock-on AF option has been selected for Focus Area. However, unlike the other option, Center Lock-on AF is available with both single autofocus and continuous autofocus.

To use Center Lock-on AF, select this menu option and turn it on. The camera will display a message saying it will track the subject nearest to the screen center when you press the Center button. Then, from the shooting screen, locate the subject you want to focus on in the center of the screen and press the Center button. The camera will display a double-bordered frame that will move around the display and expand as needed to keep the subject inside the frame and in focus. When you are ready to take the picture, press the shutter button. To cancel the tracking, press the Center button. To start it again, press the Center button to reactivate the feature.

This option can be more convenient to use than the Lock-on AF option, because you can use it with either single or continuous autofocus and you don't have to select a particular focus mode. You can just press the Center button and the tracking function will start.

This option does not work with Sweep Panorama mode or with the Hand-held Twilight or Anti Motion Blur settings of Scene mode. It also does not work with digital zoom, in Movie mode when SteadyShot (Movies) is set to Intelligent Active, or when Record Setting is set to 120p (100p for PAL systems).

Smile/Face Detection

This option gives you access to two functions with fairly different features. There are four separate entries on the vertical menu that pops up when this menu item is selected, shown in Figure 4-113.

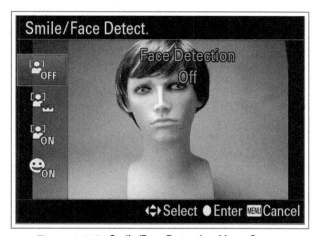

Figure 4-113. Smile/Face Detection Menu Screen

You can select the top setting, Off, which leaves all options turned off, or you can select one of the other three, which operate as follows:

FACE DETECTION ON (REGISTERED FACES)

This option is designated on the menu screen by an icon of a person's head and a crown. When you select this choice, the camera searches for faces that you have previously registered using the Face Registration option on screen 5 of the Custom menu, as discussed in Chapter 7.

If the camera detects a registered face, it should consider that face to have priority, in which case it will place a white frame on the face and adjust the Focus Area, Flash Mode, exposure compensation, white balance, and Red Eye Reduction values automatically to produce optimum exposure for that particular face. If there are multiple faces, some of which are registered, the camera should place a white frame over the one with the highest priority and purple frames over registered faces with lower priorities.

In daily shooting, I do not use this feature. It could be useful if you are taking pictures of children in a group setting and you want to make sure your own child is in focus and has his or her face properly exposed. I tested this option by registering one face and then aiming the camera at that face along with some unregistered faces. I found that the camera did a good job of distinguishing the registered face from the unregistered ones, though results undoubtedly will vary. This feature is certainly worth trying if it would be of use to you.

FACE DETECTION ON

This setting is similar to the previous one, except that it does not involve registered faces. As shown in Figure 4-114, the camera will detect any human faces, up to eight in total, and select one as the main face to concentrate its settings on.

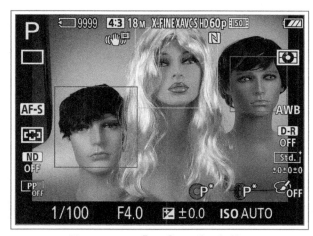

Figure 4-114. Face Detection in Use

Before you press the shutter button, the camera will display white or gray frames around any faces it finds. When you press the shutter button halfway to lock focus and exposure, the frame over the face the camera has selected as the main face will turn green. The camera may place multiple green frames if there are multiple faces at the same distance from the camera.

SMILE SHUTTER

The final option for this menu item is the Smile Shutter, which is a sort of self-timer that is activated when the subject smiles.

After highlighting this option, use the Left and Right buttons to choose the level of smile that is needed to trigger the camera—Slight Smile, Normal Smile, or Big Smile. Then press the Center button to exit back to the shooting screen, and aim the camera at the subject or subjects. (You can, of course, put the camera on a tripod and aim it at yourself, if you want.)

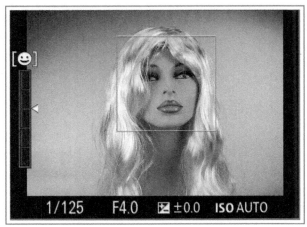

Figure 4-115. Smile Shutter Meter on Shooting Screen

As shown in Figure 4-115, the camera will show a meter on the left of the screen with a pointer to indicate how large a smile is needed to trigger a shot. As soon as the camera detects a big enough smile from any person, the shutter will fire. If a person smiles again, the camera will be triggered again, with no limit on the number of shots that can be taken. In effect, this feature acts as a limited kind of remote control with one specific function. I consider this option to be something of a novelty, which can be entertaining but is not necessary for everyday photography.

Auto Dual Recording

This menu option lets you set the camera to capture still images automatically during a video recording, when the camera detects what it considers to be "impressive compositions, including people." If this feature is turned on, when you record a video sequence, the camera may, from time to time, snap a still image during the recording, if the camera believes a particular scene with human faces is worthy of a still photo.

When you highlight the icon for turning this option on, you can press the Left and Right buttons to select a shooting frequency of Low, Standard, or High. This setting controls how often the camera is likely to capture a still image. When the camera does take a still photo, the word CAPTURE appears in green letters at the top of the display screen.

The size and quality of the still images captured with this feature are controlled by the Image Size (Dual Rec) and Quality (Dual Rec) items on screen 1 of the Shooting menu. The choices for Image Size are L:17M, M:7.5M, and S:4.2M. The options for Quality are Extra Fine, Fine, and Standard. If you are going to use this feature, I recommend using the L:17M and Extra Fine settings, for the best results. I also recommend using the High setting for frequency, unless you find the camera takes too many still images with that option.

I cannot imagine many situations in which I would want to use this feature, because it provides you with very little control over what the camera does. If you want to capture still images while recording video, you can press the shutter button to do so at any time you choose. However, if you have placed the camera unattended on a tripod to record an event, such as a family gathering or a wedding, it might be useful to use this feature to set the camera to take some still photos if it detects a good composition with family members or guests.

Soft Skin Effect

This menu option softens skin tones in the faces of your subjects for still images. The option is dimmed and unavailable in some situations, such as when one of the continuous shooting options or the Raw setting for Quality is selected. After you select it and turn it on, you can use the Right and Left buttons to set the level at Lo, Mid, or Hi, as shown in Figure 4-116. However, even if you turn the Soft Skin Effect option on, it will not produce any changes in your images unless you also have Face Detection turned on in the menu system and the RX100 V has detected a face.

When it works, this setting reduces sharpness and contrast in areas that the camera perceives as skin tones. It can do a good job of smoothing out wrinkles. Figure 4-117 shows the results of a test I made. The image on the left was taken with the effect turned off; the image on the right had the setting at its Hi level.

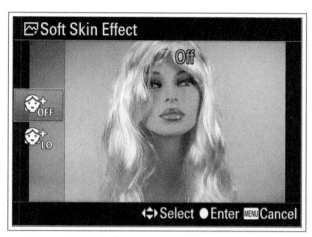

Figure 4-116. Soft Skin Effect Menu Options Screen

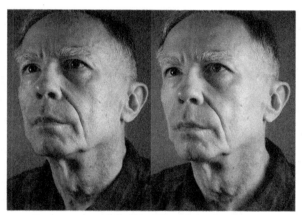

Figure 4-117. Soft Skin Effect Composite Image

This can be a useful option for doing some basic retouching of your JPEG portraits in the camera.

Auto Object Framing

This menu option provides a somewhat unusual function: It rearranges the composition of your shot based on the camera's electronic judgment. To activate it, set it to Auto on the menu. Then, when you capture your image, the camera will display a large white frame around what it believes to be the subject if it finds that the image can benefit by being trimmed to fit the subject better. For this feature to work with faces, you need to have Face Detection turned on with the Smile/ Face Detection menu option discussed above. Besides faces, Sony says that the feature will work with macro shots and objects tracked with Lock-on AF.

When you take a picture of the face or other subject, the camera may, if it finds it possible, crop the image and produce a new version of the image with the frame trimmed and resized to emphasize the subject

in a more pleasing way. An example is shown in Figure 4-118 and Figure 4-119, which show the uncropped and cropped versions, respectively, of a mannequin head I photographed with Face Detection activated.

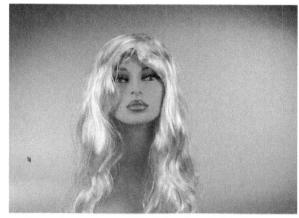

Figure 4-118. Auto Object Framing: Original Image

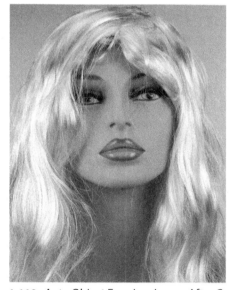

Figure 4-119. Auto Object Framing: Image After Cropping

The camera's cropping looks appropriate, but I would rather do the cropping myself in Photoshop or just compose the image in this way to begin with.

The camera saves both versions, so there is no harm in using this feature. It could be useful if you are pressed for time or are unable to get into position to take the shot you want. If you need a more nicely cropped version of the image quickly for a slide show, perhaps, this could be a good way to fill that need.

This feature is available for selection only if the camera is set for autofocus with Quality set to Extra Fine, Fine, or Standard. This option does not work with Raw images or when the lens is zoomed beyond the full optical zoom range.

Screen 8 of the Shooting menu is shown in Figure 4-120.

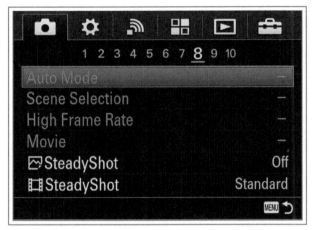

Figure 4-120. Screen 8 of Shooting Menu

Auto Mode

This first option on screen 8 of the Shooting menu is available for selection only when the Mode dial is set to the AUTO position. This menu item lets you choose either Intelligent Auto or Superior Auto for the shooting mode, as discussed in Chapter 3. If the Mode Dial Guide option is turned on through screen 2 of the Setup menu, the screen for choosing between these two modes is automatically displayed whenever you turn the Mode dial to the AUTO position and press the Center button after the Mode Dial Guide appears. If that option is not turned on, you can use the Auto Mode option to choose one or the other of the Auto modes.

Scene Selection

As discussed in Chapter 3, this option is used only when the camera is set to Scene mode; you use this menu item to select one of the settings in that shooting mode, including Portrait, Anti Motion Blur, Sunset, and others. Note that you also can use the Control ring to change scene types, as long as the Control Ring function is set to Standard through the Custom Key (Shooting) option on the Custom menu and you are not using manual focus or DMF. You also can turn the Control wheel to change scene types from the shooting screen. In addition, the Scene Selection menu screen appears automatically when you turn the Mode dial to

the SCN position and press the Center button, if the Mode Dial Guide option on screen 2 of the Setup menu is turned on.

High Frame Rate

This is another mode-specific option. It is available for selection only when the Mode dial is set to the HFR position, for high frame rate movie recording. This option lets you choose one of the four shooting modes for recording super-slow-motion movies: Program, Aperture Priority, Shutter Priority, or Manual. I will discuss those modes, as well as other aspects of HFR recording, in Chapter 8.

Movie

This menu item is available for selection only when the Mode dial is set to Movie mode (the position marked by a movie-film icon). Like the High Frame Rate option discussed above, it lets you select one of the four available exposure settings for recording movies in that mode. The Movie mode is for recording movies at normal speeds, as opposed to the high frame rates used for slow-motion movies recorded in the HFR mode. I will discuss this option in Chapter 8.

SteadyShot (Still Images)

SteadyShot is Sony's optical image stabilization system, which compensates for small movements of the camera to avoid motion blur, especially during exposures of longer than about 1/30 second. This setting is turned on by default, and I recommend leaving it on at all times, except when the camera is on a tripod. In that case, SteadyShot is not needed, and there is some chance it can "fool" the camera and cause it to try to correct for motion that does not exist, resulting in image blur.

SteadyShot (Movies)

This next option is a separate SteadyShot setting, for movies only. This menu item has a movie film icon in front of its name, whereas the previous one, for still images, has a mountain-landscape icon in front of its name. I will discuss this video-oriented SteadyShot option in Chapter 8.

Screen 9 of the Shooting menu is shown in Figure 4-121.

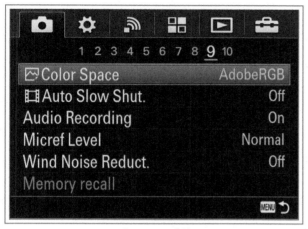

Figure 4-121. Screen 9 of Shooting Menu

Color Space

With this first option on screen 9 of the Shooting menu, you can choose to record your still images using the sRGB "color space," the more common choice and the default, or the Adobe RGB color space. The sRGB color space has fewer colors than Adobe RGB; therefore, it is more suitable for producing images for the web and other forms of digital display than for printing. If your images are likely to be printed commercially in a book or magazine or it is critical that you be able to match a great many different color variations, you might want to consider using the Adobe RGB color space. I always leave the color space set to sRGB, and I recommend that you do so as well unless you have a specific need to use Adobe RGB, such as a requirement from a printing company that you are using to print your images.

If you are shooting images with the Raw format, you don't need to worry so much about color space, because you can set it later using your Raw-processing software.

Auto Slow Shutter

This menu item is preceded by a movie film icon, indicating that it is used only for recording movies. This option lets the camera automatically set a slower shutter speed than normal when shooting a movie, in order to compensate for dim lighting. I will discuss this option in Chapter 8.

Audio Recording, Micref Level, and Wind Noise Reduction

I will discuss the Audio Recording, Micref Level, and Wind Noise Reduction menu options in Chapter 8, because they all are concerned with video recording.

Memory Recall

The final option on screen 9 of the Shooting menu, Memory Recall, is used only when the Mode dial is set to MR, for Memory Recall mode. Using this option, you can recall the shooting settings that you stored to one of the seven slots for this mode, as discussed in Chapter 3.

When the Mode dial is first turned to the MR position, this option's main screen appears automatically on the camera's display with one of the seven designations at the upper right highlighted, as shown in Figure 4-122.

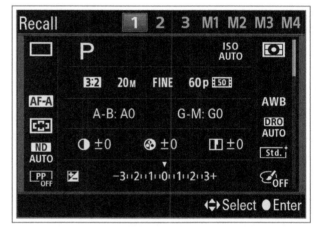

Figure 4-122. Memory Recall Settings Screen

(If the Mode Dial Guide option is turned on through screen 2 of the Setup menu, the Mode Dial Guide screen will appear first; you then have to press the Center button to make this screen appear.)

If the camera is already set to Memory Recall mode and you want to change to one of the other memory registers, you can use the menu system to call up this option. Once the Memory Recall screen is displayed, either by turning the Mode dial to MR or by using this menu option, use the direction buttons or turn the Control wheel to select register 1, 2, 3, M1, M2, M3, or M4 at the upper right of the screen. Then press the Center button, and the new set of shooting settings that were stored to that register will take effect. The M1 through M4 registers are stored on the memory card inserted in the camera, while the first three registers are stored to the camera's internal memory.

The tenth and final screen of the Shooting menu is shown in Figure 4-123

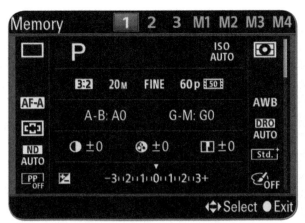

Figure 4-124. Memory Settings Screen

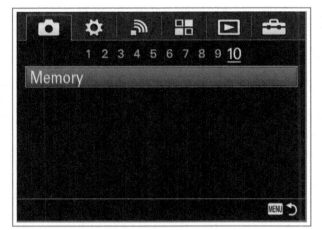

Figure 4-123. Screen 10 of Shooting Menu

Memory

The only option on the last screen of the Shooting menu, Memory, was discussed in Chapter 3 in connection with the Memory Recall shooting mode. Once you have set up the RX100 V with the menu options and other settings you want to store to a register of the Memory Recall shooting mode, you select the Memory menu option and choose one of the seven numbered registers, as shown in Figure 4-124.

Press the Center button, and all of the current settings will be stored to that register for the Memory Recall mode. You can recall those settings at any time by turning the Mode dial to the MR position (or selecting the Memory Recall menu option if the Mode dial is already at that position) and selecting register 1, 2, or 3 from the camera's internal memory, or register M1 through M4, which are stored on the memory card currently in the camera.

With either the Memory Recall or Memory option, you can scroll to additional screens using the Down button to see other settings currently in effect, such as ISO Auto Maximum and Minimum, Red Eye Reduction, High ISO NR, Center Lock-on AF, and several others.

CHAPTER 5: PHYSICAL CONTROLS

The Sony RX100 V, like other compact cameras, does not have very many physical controls. It relies largely on its menus for changing settings. But the RX100 V is a high-quality compact camera, and one aspect of its quality is that its controls can be configured to adjust many settings on the camera. In this chapter, I'll discuss each of the camera's physical controls and how they can be used to best advantage, starting with the controls on top of the camera, shown in Figure 5-1.

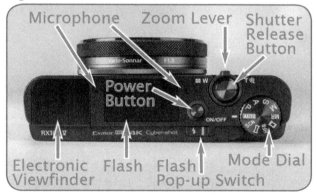

Figure 5-1. Controls on Top of Camera

Mode Dial

The Mode dial has just one function—to select a shooting mode. I discussed the shooting modes in Chapter 3. To take a quick still picture, turn this dial to the AUTO position, select either Intelligent Auto or Superior Auto for the shooting mode, and fire away. To record a video sequence, turn the dial to that same position and press the red Movie button, just below the Mode dial at the top of the camera's back. It is important to remember that you can record a movie with the Mode dial set to any position. There are two movie-oriented modes on this dial, one marked by a movie-film icon and one marked by HFR for high frame rate, but you do not have to select either of those icons to record movies.

Note, though, that screen 6 of the Custom menu has an option called Movie Button for locking out the use of the Movie button unless the camera is in Movie mode. If the Mode dial is set to any position other than Movie, the Movie button will not start a movie recording if the Movie Button menu option is set to Movie Mode Only. (To record high frame rate movies, a different procedure is used, as discussed in Chapter 8.)

Shutter Release Button

When you press the shutter button halfway, the camera evaluates and locks focus and exposure if you're using standard settings, including single autofocus. You can change this behavior in various ways. For example, as discussed in Chapter 4, you can use manual focus and adjust the focus yourself, or you can use continuous autofocus, which does not lock focus when you press the shutter button halfway. You also can go to screen 4 of the Custom menu and set the AEL w/Shutter option to Off, in which case the camera will never lock exposure when you press the shutter button halfway. I will discuss that option in Chapter 7.

In Manual exposure mode, the camera still evaluates exposure when you press the shutter button, but it does not change the aperture or shutter speed settings you have made. If Auto ISO is in effect, the camera will adjust the ISO to achieve a normal exposure if possible, and you can lock that exposure by half-pressing the shutter button, assuming AEL w/Shutter is turned on.

Once you are satisfied with the settings, press the button all the way to take the picture. When the camera is set for continuous shooting, you hold this button down to cause the camera to fire repeatedly. You also can press this button halfway to exit to the live view from playback mode, menu screens, and help screens. You can press the shutter button during video recording to take still images, with some limitations, as discussed in Chapter 8.

Zoom Lever

The zoom lever is a small ring with a short handle surrounding the shutter button. Its primary function is to vary the focal length of the lens between its wide-angle setting of 24mm and its telephoto setting of 70mm. If you have the camera set for Clear Image Zoom or Digital Zoom through the Zoom Setting item on screen 4 of the Custom menu, the lever will take the zoom to higher levels, as discussed in Chapter 7.

You can also zoom using the Control ring, if you assign the zoom function to the Control ring using the Custom Key (Shooting) option on screen 5 of the Custom menu. And, you can set the Control ring to use the Step Zoom function, which causes the lens to zoom in a predefined step each time you turn the ring. (That function is controlled by the Zoom Function on Ring option on screen 6 of the Custom menu.) The Step Zoom function does not work with the zoom lever, though. When you use the zoom lever, the lens zooms continuously, even if Step Zoom is turned on for the Control ring. You adjust the speed of zooming with the lever using the Zoom Speed item on screen 4 of the Custom menu.

In playback mode, moving the zoom lever to the left produces an index screen, and moving the lever to the right enlarges the current image. Those operations are discussed in Chapter 6.

Power Button

This button is used to turn the camera on and off. An orange light in the center of the button glows when the battery is being charged in the camera. A green light in the button glows when the camera is powered on. You also can turn the camera's power on by pressing the Playback button, which places the camera into playback mode, or by popping up the EVF with the Finder switch.

Built-in Flash and Flash Pop-up Switch

The camera's built-in flash unit is normally retracted and hidden in the center area of the camera's top. If you want the flash to be available for use, you first have to pop it up using the flash pop-up switch, located directly behind the power button.

Once you have popped up the flash unit, if you want it to fire, you need to make an appropriate setting using the Flash Mode menu. You can find the Flash Mode option on screen 3 of the Shooting menu. You also can bring up that menu by pressing the Flash button, which is the Right button on the Control wheel, unless that button has been assigned to a different function using the Custom Key (Shooting) option on screen 5 of the Custom menu.

Once you have popped up the flash unit and selected a flash mode, the flash may fire when you press the shutter button, depending on the settings that are in effect and the lighting conditions.

If you want the flash to be stowed away again, you need to press it gently back down into the camera until it clicks into place. If you want to use "bounce flash," which causes the flash to be reflected by the ceiling or wall to reduce its intensity, you can pull the flash unit back carefully with your finger and hold the flash so that it is aiming upward while it fires.

Electronic Viewfinder

One of the most interesting features of the Sony RX100 V is its retractable electronic viewfinder, or EVF. With this option, the camera can be used in bright conditions without having the LCD display washed out by sunlight. In addition, you can hold the camera up to your eye and keep it steady against your forehead while viewing a high-resolution image that includes the same information that is available with the LCD display.

To use the EVF, first pop it up by pressing down on the Finder switch on the left side of the camera. If the camera was not already powered on, popping up the viewfinder will turn the camera on.

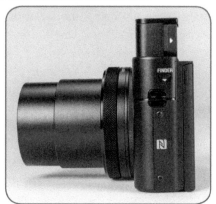

Figure 5-2. Electronic Viewfinder Popped Up

Once the EVF has popped up, as shown in Figure 5-2, you need to grasp the sides of the eyepiece, without grabbing the upper lid of the viewfinder assembly, and gently pull the eyepiece out of the assembly, as shown in Figure 5-3.

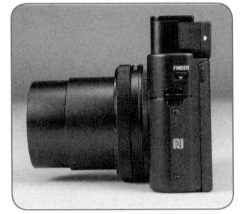

Figure 5-3. Electronic Viewfinder Eyepiece Pulled Out

Adjust the EVF for your vision using the diopter adjustment lever on top of the eyepiece, shown in Figure 5-4. How you use the EVF, of course, is a matter of personal preference. You can hold it up to either your left or right eye, depending on which feels more comfortable to you. If you wear glasses you may find it more comfortable to take them off and use the diopter adjustment lever to compensate.

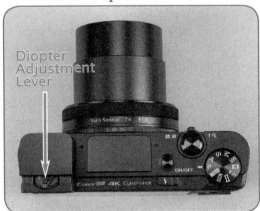

Figure 5-4. Diopter Adjustment Lever on Top of EVF

By default, the camera switches automatically between the EVF and the LCD. That is, when the EVF is popped up and your head is against the EVF, the EVF is active and the LCD is turned off. When you move your head away from the EVF, the LCD screen becomes active and the EVF is turned off. If you want the EVF to be active whenever it is popped up, regardless of the position of your head, use the Finder/Monitor option on screen 4 of the Custom menu; set that option to Viewfinder

(Manual) to keep the EVF active at all times when it is popped up. (The eye sensor that detects the presence of your head near the screen is shown in Figure 5-7.)

To adjust the brightness of the EVF, use the Viewfinder Brightness option on screen 1 of the Setup menu, as discussed in Chapter 7. The EVF does not function when the camera is being controlled by a smartphone.

The information displayed in the EVF is independent of what is displayed on the LCD screen. That is, with one exception, you can have the EVF display all of the same information that can be shown on the LCD, but you don't have to do that. (The one exception is the For Viewfinder display, which is available only on the LCD screen, as discussed in Chapter 7.)

To set the information displays for the LCD and EVF, use the Display Button option on screen 2 of the Custom menu to choose from the possible displays. Cycle from one display to another by pressing the Display button. I will discuss that menu option and the available information displays in Chapter 7.

When you have finished using the EVF, stow it inside the camera by pressing the eyepiece into the housing and then pushing the EVF down until it clicks into place. When you do that, the camera will turn off or stay powered on, depending on a menu setting. To determine what happens in that situation, go to the Function for VF Close option, the first item on screen 3 of the Setup menu. The choices are Power Off or Not Power Off. If you choose Power Off, the camera will turn off when you press the EVF down into the camera's body. If you choose Not Power Off, the camera will remain powered on when the EVF is stowed. I prefer to have the camera stay powered on, but it is good to have this choice available.

There are two items to discuss on the front of the camera, as seen in Figure 5-5, before turning to the controls on the back.

AF Illuminator/Self-Timer Lamp

The reddish light on the front of the camera near the Control ring blinks to signal the operation of the self-timer, and it turns on in dark environments to assist with autofocusing. You can control its function for helping with autofocus through the AF Illuminator item on screen 4 of the Shooting menu, as discussed in Chapter 4. If you set that menu item to Auto, the lamp will light as needed for autofocus; if you set it to Off, the lamp will never light for that purpose, though it will still illuminate for the self-timer.

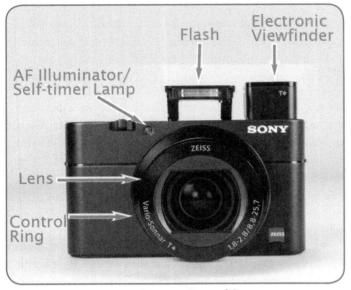

Figure 5-5. Items on Front of Camera

Control Ring

Whenever the camera is set to manual focus or DMF (direct manual focus) using the Focus Mode option on screen 3 of the Shooting menu, the Control ring adjusts focus. The ring also has other functions, depending on the settings you make.

To assign functions to the Control ring, use the Custom Key (Shooting) option on screen 5 of the Custom menu. The first sub-option for this menu item is Control Ring, whose first screen of options is shown in Figure 5-6.

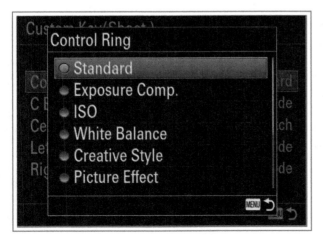

Figure 5-6. Control Ring Menu Options Screen

By default, the Control Ring item is set to Standard. When the Standard setting is in effect, the Control ring

controls just one function in any given shooting mode; the function it controls depends on which shooting mode the camera is set to. For example, if the camera is set to the Aperture Priority mode, the Control ring controls aperture; in Shutter Priority mode, the ring controls shutter speed. In the Scene shooting mode, the ring controls selection of scene types. I usually leave the Control Ring menu item set to Standard because the functions the ring controls in the various shooting modes in that case are quite useful.

However, if you want to use the ring for one dedicated function no matter what shooting mode is in effect, you can use the Control Ring menu item to choose one of the following items that will stay assigned to the ring until you make another change: Exposure Compensation, ISO, White Balance, Creative Style, Picture Effect, Zoom, Shutter Speed, or Aperture. You also can choose Not Set, in which case turning the ring will have no effect (unless you activate a function, such as manual focus, that requires use of the ring).

A function assigned to the ring only works if the context permits it. For example, if you assign Aperture to the Control ring, the ring will control aperture if the camera is set to Aperture Priority or Manual exposure mode. In any other shooting mode, turning the ring will have no effect (except for adjusting manual focus) because aperture cannot be controlled manually in other modes. Also, when you are using the Photo Creativity option in Intelligent Auto or Superior Auto mode, any function assigned to the ring through the Custom menu will not operate, because that operation could conflict with the Photo Creativity settings. Table 5-1 lists the functions that are assigned to the Control ring with the Standard setting.

Table 5-1.   **Control Ring: Standard Setting— Shooting Modes vs. Assigned Functions**

Shooting Mode	Assigned Function
Intelligent Auto	Zoom
Superior Auto	Zoom
Program	Program Shift
Aperture Priority	Aperture
Shutter Priority	Shutter Speed
Manual Exposure	Aperture
Scene	Scene Selection

Table 5-1.   **Control Ring: Standard Setting—Shooting Modes vs. Assigned Functions**

Sweep Panorama	Panorama Direction
Memory Recall	Depends on Saved Setting
Movie	Depends on Movie exposure mode setting
HFR	Depends on HFR exposure mode setting

The Control ring also is used in a few other situations regardless of how you have set its assigned function. When you press the Function button (discussed later in this chapter) in shooting mode, the camera activates a menu that shows several options—including items such as white balance, ISO, exposure compensation, etc.—depending on the settings you have chosen for that menu. Once you have pressed the Function button to display that menu, you can turn the Control ring (or the Control wheel) to select the value for the setting that is highlighted on the menu. The Control ring also is used to adjust settings using the Quick Navi system, which is also called up with the Function button.

When the camera is set to manual focus or DMF (direct manual focus), you use the Control ring to adjust focus. If the MF Assist option is turned on through screen 1 of the Custom menu, the display will be magnified to assist with focusing as soon as you start turning the Control ring. (With DMF, you have to half-press the shutter button while turning the Control ring to use MF Assist.) When the camera is set to either of those focus modes, you cannot use the Control ring for any other function.

The controls on the back of the RX100 V are seen in Figure 5-7.

Playback Button

This button to the lower left of the Control wheel, marked with a small triangle, is used to put the camera into playback mode, which allows you to view your images on the LCD screen or in the EVF. It also can be used instead of the power button to turn the camera on, placing the RX100 V immediately into playback mode with the lens retracted. When the camera is in playback mode, you can press the shutter button halfway or press the Playback button again to switch the camera into shooting mode.

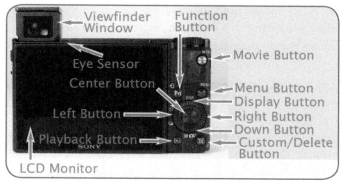

Figure 5-7. Controls on Back of Camera

Movie Button

The red button at the upper right of the camera's back has just one function—to start and stop the recording of a movie sequence. As I noted in discussing the Mode dial earlier in this chapter, you can control how the Movie button operates. If you want to be able to start recording a movie in any shooting mode (except HFR), go to the Custom menu and select the second option on screen 6, called Movie Button. If you set that menu option to Always (the default setting), then the Movie button will operate in any shooting mode except HFR. If you set the option to Movie Mode Only, then the Movie button will not start recording a movie unless the camera is set to Movie mode using the Mode dial. (Movie mode is the mode marked by a movie-film icon.)

This is a fairly important decision to make, and it depends on your preferences and likely uses of the camera. If you want to be able to start recording a video at any time without delay, leave the Movie Button option set to Always. The reason you might not want to do this is that it is easy to press the Movie button by mistake. I have done that often. When you press the button by mistake, you have to press it again to stop the recording, and wait for the camera to finish processing the movie before you can use any other controls. And, of course, the camera will have an unwanted file cluttering the memory card, until you delete it.

My preference is to limit use of the Movie button to when the camera is in Movie mode, but if I were going on a vacation and wanted to be able to start recording a movie in Auto mode without delay, I would enable the button for use in all modes.

There are differences in how the camera operates for video recording in different shooting modes. I will discuss movie making in detail in Chapter 8.

Menu Button

The Menu button, to the upper right of the Control wheel, is straightforward in its basic function. Press it to enter the menu system, and press it once more to return to whatever mode the camera was in previously (shooting mode or playback mode). The button also cancels out of sub-menus, taking you back to the previous menu screen. In playback mode, when an image has been enlarged using the zoom lever, you can press the Menu button (or the Center button) to return it to the normal-sized view.

Function Button

The button marked Fn, for Function, has different functions in shooting mode and playback mode.

SHOOTING MODE: FUNCTION MENU

When the camera is in shooting mode, the Function button gives you options for setting up the RX100 V according to your own preferences. With the Function Menu Settings option on screen 5 of the Custom menu (discussed in Chapter 7), you can assign up to 12 functions to the Function menu from 34 choices, including items such as ISO, Drive Mode, White Balance, Metering Mode, and Picture Effect. You also can choose Not Set, to leave a slot on the Function menu blank.

Scroll through the lines from Function Upper1 through Function Upper6 on the first sub-screen of this menu option and Function Lower1 through Function Lower6 on the second screen. On each line, press the Center button and then scroll through the 34 options to highlight the one you want, and press the Center button to confirm that selection.

Once you have assigned up to 12 options to this button, it is ready for action. To use an option, press the Function button when the camera is in shooting mode, and a menu will appear at the bottom of the display in two rows with six choices each, as shown in Figure 5-8.

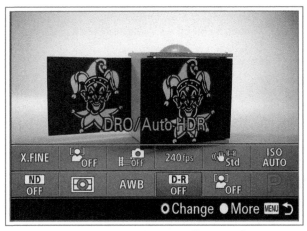

Figure 5-8. Function Menu on Shooting Screen

Use the four direction buttons to move to and highlight an option to adjust. Then turn either the Control wheel or the Control ring to change the value of that option. For example, if you have moved the orange highlight block to the Quality item, turn the Control wheel or the Control ring until the setting you want to make appears, as shown in Figure 5-9, where Fine is selected.

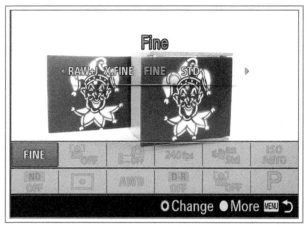

Figure 5-9. Fine Selected for Quality on Function Menu

Then, press the Function button to confirm the setting and exit from the Function menu screen. Or, if you want to make multiple settings from the Function menu options, after changing one setting you can press the Center button to go back to the Function menu and make more settings before you press the Function button to exit to the shooting screen.

If the setting you are adjusting needs to have a sub-option set, you can press the Center button to go directly to the menu screen for that setting. For example, suppose you want to set a particular color temperature for white balance. First, from the shooting screen press the Function button to bring up the Function menu, and use the four direction buttons to scroll to the White Balance block. Then, instead of choosing a value with the Control wheel or Control ring, press the Center button, and the camera will display the regular White Balance menu screen, as shown in Figure 5-10.

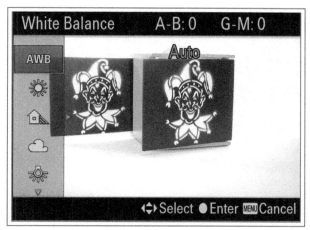

Figure 5-10. White Balance Menu Displayed from Function Menu

From that screen, you can navigate to the Color Temperature/Filter option and select the color temperature you want to set. When you have finished, press the Menu button to return to the Function menu. From there, you can press the Function button to return to the shooting screen.

There may be items on the Function menu whose icons are dimmed because the item is unavailable for selection in the current context. If you move the highlight to one of those items and then try to change the setting, the camera will display an error message.

Also, the selections I discussed above may not be available because they have not been assigned to the Function menu. If that is the case, you can use the Function Menu Settings menu option to assign them if you want to follow the examples.

I strongly recommend that you develop a group of 12 items to assign to the Function menu and make use of this speedy way to change important settings.

QUICK NAVI SYSTEM

In shooting mode, the Function button also gives you access to the Quick Navi system for changing settings rapidly. This system has similarities to the Function menu system I just discussed, but there are significant differences.

The Quick Navi system comes into play in only one situation—when you have called up the special display screen shown in Figure 5-11, which Sony calls the "For Viewfinder" display.

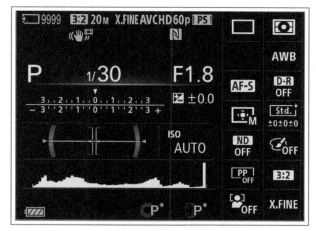

Figure 5-11. For Viewfinder Display Screen

This is the only shooting mode display that does not include the live view. It is called "For viewfinder" because this screen is designed for use when you are using the viewfinder to frame your composition, so you can see the live view through the viewfinder and see the details of your settings on this display, which appears only on the LCD screen.

The For Viewfinder display is summoned by pressing the Display button, but only if you have selected it for inclusion in the cycle of display screens.

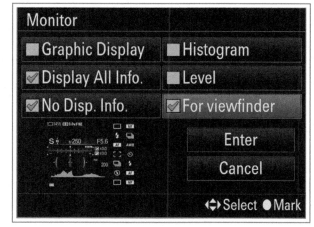

Figure 5-12. For Viewfinder Screen Selected for Display Button

You do that using the Display Button option on screen 2 of the Custom menu. From that option, select the sub-option for Monitor, then check the box for the For Viewfinder item on the next screen, as shown in Figure 5-12.

As seen in Figure 5-11, the For Viewfinder screen displays a lot of information at the right, including Drive Mode, White Balance, Focus Area, DRO, Picture Effect, Picture Profile, ND Filter, and several others.

Normally, these items are displayed for information; you cannot adjust them. But, if you press the Function button, an orange highlight appears at the right, as shown in Figure 5-13, indicating that the Quick Navi system is in use.

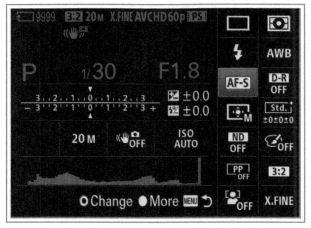

Figure 5-13. Quick Navi System Activated

Use the direction buttons to move through the settings. You can press the Left button to move the orange highlight to the left, to settings such as ISO, SteadyShot, and Image Size. When you have highlighted a setting to adjust, turn the Control wheel or the Control ring to scroll through the available values and make the adjustment quickly.

When you use the Control wheel or Control ring to adjust a setting, such as Aspect Ratio, a secondary window opens in the top part of the display, as shown in Figure 5-14, showing the options available for the setting.

After changing a setting, you can move to other settings using the direction buttons. Once you have made all of your changes, press the Function button again to exit to the static For Viewfinder display, which will now show the new settings in place.

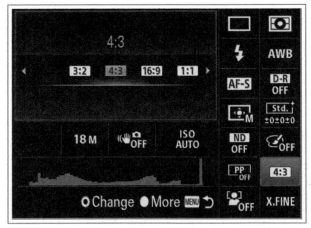

Figure 5-14. Secondary Window Open on Quick Navi Screen

If you select an option that requires a sub-setting, the steps are slightly different. For example, suppose you want to turn on HDR using the maximum setting of 6.0EV. From the Quick Navi screen, highlight the DRO option and, instead of turning the Control wheel or Control ring to change the setting, press the Center button. You will be taken to a special menu screen for the DRO option, as shown in Figure 5-15.

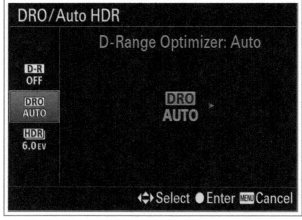

Figure 5-15. Menu Screen for DRO from Quick Navi

On that screen, you can select HDR and set it to 6.0EV. Press the Center button to select this setting and exit to the For Viewfinder display.

You also can press the Center button when an option is highlighted, even if a sub-setting is not needed, if you prefer to use a menu screen to make the adjustment. For example, when Aspect Ratio is highlighted on the Quick Navi screen, you can press the Center button to call up a menu, rather than just turning the Control wheel or Control ring.

The Quick Navi system can streamline your ability to change settings once you get used to it. I recommend you devote some time to practicing with it, if speed is important to you.

WHEEL LOCK

The Function button also can carry out one other operation in shooting mode, depending on how a Custom menu option is set. The final item on screen 6 of that menu is the Wheel Lock option. If that option is set to Lock, then, when you press and hold the Function button for several seconds when the shooting screen is displayed, the shooting-related operations that are adjusted by turning the Control wheel are locked. The wheel will still operate to navigate through menu screens and menu settings, but turning it will not set items such as ISO, shutter speed, and scene types. The buttons at the edges of the wheel will still operate. I will discuss that menu option in Chapter 7.

PLAYBACK MODE: SEND TO SMARTPHONE

When the RX100 V is in playback mode, the Function button carries out one function, which you can choose using the Custom Key (Playback) option on screen 5 of the Custom menu. By default, pressing the Function button activates the Send to Smartphone option, just as if you had chosen that menu option from the Wi-Fi menu. So, if you have taken a photo and want to transfer it to your phone for sharing with friends or posting to Facebook, you can press the Function button in playback mode and make the transfer quickly.

However, if you prefer, you can assign any one of 10 other functions to this button for use in playback mode. I will discuss the Custom Key (Playback) menu option in Chapter 7.

Custom/Delete Button

The button marked with a C, to the right of the Playback button, is called the Custom/Delete button. This button can be programmed to perform any one of 53 functions, or can be designated as Not Set. To make this choice, use the Custom Key (Shooting) option on screen 5 of the Custom menu, and then select the C Button sub-option. I will discuss that menu option in Chapter 7.

By default, the C button is assigned the In-Camera Guide function. With that option, when the camera is

displaying a menu you can press the button to display a brief help screen with guidance or tips about the menu option that is highlighted or selected. The help screen varies depending on the context.

If the camera is displaying the main page of a menu screen with the highlight on a particular feature, pressing the C button will bring up a screen with a brief message explaining the use of that feature. For example, Figure 5-16 shows the message that is displayed when the camera is displaying screen 3 of the Shooting menu, with the Drive Mode item highlighted.

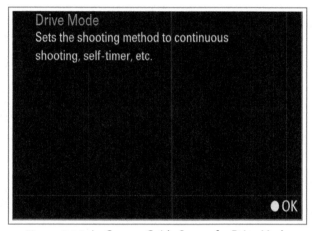

Figure 5-16. In-Camera Guide Screen for Drive Mode

If you select a sub-option for a menu item and press the C button, the camera will display a message with details about that option. For example, Figure 5-17 shows the help screen that was displayed when I pressed the C button after highlighting the Continuous Shooting option for the Drive Mode item, with the Hi option selected for speed of shooting.

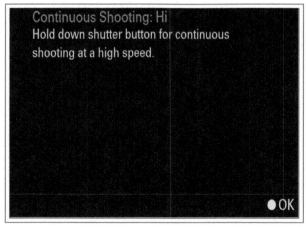

Figure 5-17. In-Camera Guide Screen for Continuous Shooting

This help system is quite detailed; for example, it provides guidance even for different ISO settings, such as ISO 100, 320, and 1600, with tips about when to use each setting. The help function operates with all of the RX100 V menu systems, including Custom, Playback, Setup, and the others, not just the Shooting menu. It also works with the Function menu and the Quick Navi system to give information about a highlighted option.

The C button has a special function when the camera is in the Intelligent Auto or Superior Auto mode, regardless of any function assigned to the button using the Custom Key (Shooting) option. When you are using the Photo Creativity option in either of those modes and you have moved the indicator along the curved scale on the screen to change a setting (such as Brightness or Color), you can press the C button to reset the option to its default value.

When the camera is in playback mode, displaying a recorded image or movie (not a menu screen), this button becomes the Delete button, as indicated by the trash can icon to the lower right of the button. If you press it, the camera displays the message shown in Figure 5-18, prompting you to select Delete or Cancel.

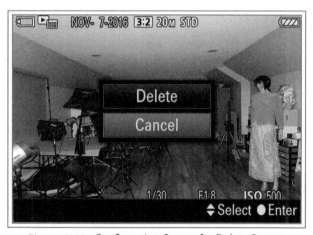

Figure 5-18. Confirmation Screen for Delete Button

If you highlight Delete and press the Center button, the camera will delete the image or video that was displayed. If you choose Cancel, the camera will return to the playback mode screen. This operation also works when an image is being displayed briefly with the Auto Review option, right after the image was captured.

How you program the C button is, of course, a matter of personal preference. The In-Camera Guide option is quite useful, especially when you are first learning the

operation of the camera. Once you are more confident with the camera's functions, you might want to use this button for an operation that is not available through the menu system, or not readily available through a menu, such as Eye AF or AF/MF Control Toggle. I will discuss all of the options in Chapter 7.

Control Wheel and Its Buttons

Several controls are within the perimeter of the Control wheel, the ridged wheel with icons around its outer edges. In the middle of the wheel is the Center button, a much-used control. The four edges of the wheel (up, down, left, and right) act as buttons. If you press the wheel's rim at any of those four points, you are, in effect, pressing a button. Each button has at least two functions—as a direction control along with one or more other specific assignments. When they act as direction controls, the buttons are used to navigate through menu options and other choices for controlling the camera's settings. The other main functions of the buttons are indicated by one or more icons at each button's position on the Control wheel. I will discuss all of these controls in turn.

CONTROL WHEEL

In many cases, to choose a menu item or a setting, you can turn this wheel. In some cases, you have the choice of using this wheel or pressing the direction buttons. One helpful feature of the RX100 V is that it places a round icon on the shooting screen representing the Control wheel when there is a value that can be adjusted at that point by the wheel. (If you don't see the icon, press the Display button until it appears.)

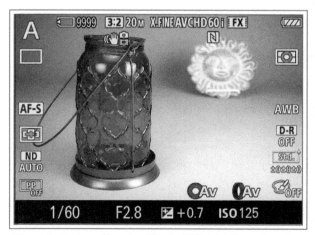

Figure 5-19. Icon Showing Control Wheel Adjusts Aperture

For example, in Figure 5-19, the icon, which looks like a gray ring lying flat on the screen in the lower right corner, is positioned next to the Av indicator, meaning the Control wheel can now control aperture. (The more three-dimensional icon to the right of that one shows that the Control ring also can control aperture.)

Figure 5-20 shows the camera in Manual exposure mode, and the icon for the Control wheel is next to the Tv indicator, standing for time value or shutter speed, indicating that you can adjust the shutter speed by turning the Control wheel. (The icon to the right shows that the Control ring now adjusts aperture.)

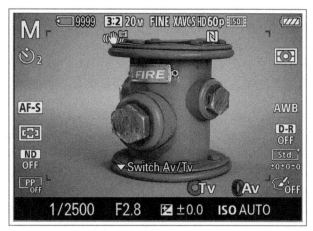

Figure 5-20. Icon Showing Control Wheel Adjusts Shutter Speed

In Aperture Priority mode, the wheel controls aperture, and in Shutter Priority mode it controls shutter speed. When the camera is in Scene mode, you can turn the Control wheel to change the scene type, such as Portrait, Landscape, and the like. In Sweep Panorama mode, turning the wheel changes the direction of the panorama. In Program mode, it controls Program Shift.

The Control wheel has several other functions. When you are viewing a menu screen, you can navigate through the lists of options by turning the wheel. When you are adjusting items using the Function menu or Quick Navi system, you can change the value for the selected setting by turning the Control wheel. When you are using manual focus and you have the Focus Magnifier option turned on, you can turn the Control wheel to vary the area of the scene that is being magnified. With the Flexible Spot setting for the Focus Area menu option, you can turn the Control wheel to adjust the size of the focus frame when the frame is activated for moving around the display.

In playback mode, you can turn the Control wheel to navigate through images. Also, when a video is being played in the camera, you can turn the Control wheel to fast-forward or rewind, or, when the video is paused, to play it slowly, frame-by-frame, either forward or in reverse.

CENTER BUTTON

This button in the center of the Control wheel has many uses. On menu screens that have additional options, such as the Image Size screen, this button takes you to the next screen to view the other options. It also acts as a selection button when you choose certain options. For example, after you select Focus Mode from screen 3 of the Shooting menu and then navigate to your desired focus option, you can press the Center button to confirm your selection and exit from the menu screen back to the shooting screen.

The Center button also has several other possible uses depending on how it is set up. Screen 5 of the Custom menu (discussed in Chapter 7) has an item called Custom Key (Shooting), with a sub-option for setting the function of the Center button. Using that option, you can set the Center button to have its normal default functions by selecting the Focus Standard option.

If you select the Focus Standard option, then, if the Focus Area is set to Flexible Spot or Expand Flexible Spot, pressing the Center button activates the screen for adjusting the location of the focus frame. If Center Lock-on AF is turned on with Focus Area set to Wide or Center, this button activates focus tracking.

When the camera is set to manual focus and MF Assist or Focus Magnifier is turned on, pressing the Center button changes the magnification factor of the display.

If you prefer not to use the Focus Standard option, you can use the Custom Key (Shooting) option to set this button to carry out one of 51 other functions or to be Not Set. I will discuss that menu option in Chapter 7.

In playback mode, you press the Center button to start playing a video whose first frame is displayed on the camera's screen. Once the video is playing, press the Center button to pause the playback and then to toggle between play and pause. When a panoramic image is displayed, press the Center button to make it scroll on the screen at a larger size using the full expanse of the display screen. When you have enlarged an image using the zoom lever, you can return it immediately to its normal size by pressing the Center button. When you are selecting images for deletion, protection, or printing using the appropriate Playback menu options, you use the Center button to mark or unmark an image for that purpose.

Direction Buttons

Each of the four edges of the Control wheel is a button you can press to get access to a setting or operation. This is not immediately obvious, and sometimes it can be tricky to press in exactly the right spot, but these four buttons are important to your control of the camera. You use them to navigate through menus and screens for settings, whether moving left and right or up and down.

You also use these buttons in playback mode to move through your images and, when you have enlarged an image using the zoom lever, to scroll around within the magnified image.

In addition to navigation, the direction buttons are used for miscellaneous functions in connection with various settings. For example, when the camera is set to Manual exposure mode, you can press the Down button to toggle the action of the Control wheel between setting aperture and setting shutter speed. And, as with the Center button, the Right and Left buttons can be assigned to carry out other functions through the Custom Key (Shooting) option on screen 5 of the Custom menu, as discussed in Chapter 7.

Finally, each of the direction buttons has its own separate identity, as indicated by the one or two icons that appear near each of the buttons, as discussed below.

Up Button: Display

The Up button, marked "DISP," switches among information displays on the LCD screen and in the viewfinder, in both shooting and playback modes. As discussed in Chapter 7, you can change the contents of the shooting mode screens using the Display Button option on screen 2 of the Custom menu. The various display screens for playback mode are discussed in Chapter 6.

The Up button cannot be reassigned using the menu system; it is permanently assigned as the Display button.

Right Button: Flash Mode

When the camera is in shooting mode, pressing the Right button brings up a menu on the left of the display showing the options for setting the behavior of the flash unit. The options are Flash Off, Autoflash, Fill-flash, Slow Sync, and Rear Sync, although not all of them are available in any one shooting mode. This menu can also be summoned from screen 3 of the Shooting menu. I discussed the use of these settings in Chapter 4.

One important point is that you have to use the flash pop-up switch to pop up the flash before it can be used, no matter what option you have selected from the Flash Mode menu.

You can reassign the function of the Right button using the Custom Key (Shooting) option on screen 5 of the Custom menu. You can choose any one of 47 options, including Flash Mode, Focus Mode, Focus Area, ISO, White Balance, and others; I will discuss that menu option in Chapter 7.

Down Button: Photo Creativity/Exposure Compensation

The Down button has two icons directly below it, indicating that it has two different functions depending on the shooting mode. In the Intelligent Auto and Superior Auto modes, pressing this button brings up the Photo Creativity options, which I discussed in Chapter 2. In the Program, Aperture Priority, Shutter Priority, Movie, HFR, and Sweep Panorama modes, this button controls exposure compensation, discussed below.

In Manual exposure mode, this button toggles the Control wheel's function between controlling aperture and controlling shutter speed. In that mode, you can use the Exposure Compensation item on screen 4 of the Shooting menu to adjust exposure compensation, or you can use the Custom Key (Shooting) menu option to assign a control button or the Control ring to adjust that setting. (Exposure compensation can be adjusted in Manual exposure mode only if ISO is set to Auto ISO.)

In Scene mode, the Down button has no function other than as a direction button. If you press it when the shooting screen is displayed in that shooting mode, you will see an error message.

Exposure Compensation

Here is an example of the use of exposure compensation to adjust for an unusual, or non-optimal, lighting situation. Figure 5-21 is a photo of a bunch of artificial grapes in front of a bright white background, taken using the Program shooting mode with Metering Mode set to Multi.

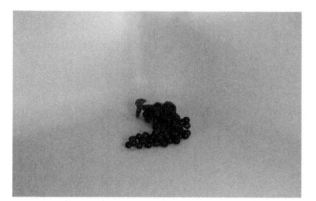

Figure 5-21. Exposure Compensation Example: Before Adjustment

The camera's metering system measured the light being reflected from the white background along with the light from the dark subject, and because of the bright background, the metering system reduced the exposure setting and underexposed the bunch of grapes.

One solution to this problem is to use exposure compensation to increase the overall exposure of the image, so the subject will not be too dark. To accomplish this with the RX100 V, press the Down button to bring the exposure compensation scale up on the display, as shown in Figure 5-22.

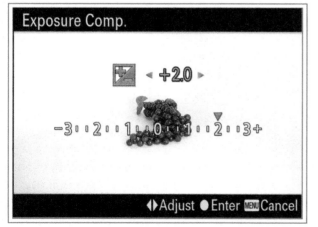

Figure 5-22. Exposure Compensation Scale on Shooting Screen

Turn the Control wheel or press the Left and Right buttons to move the orange triangle above the scale, so it points to a value to the left or right of the zero point.

As you do this, the numbers near the top of the display will change. With a negative value, the image will be darker than it otherwise would be; with a positive value, it will be brighter. The camera's display will grow brighter or darker to indicate the effect of the adjustment, if the Live View Display item on screen 3 of the Custom menu is set to Setting Effect On.

In this case, with exposure compensation increased by 2.0 EV (exposure value) units, the bunch of grapes becomes brighter and is no longer underexposed, as shown in the final image in Figure 5-23.

Figure 5-23. Exposure Compensation Example: After Adjustment

Some photographers follow the practice of generally leaving exposure compensation set at a particular amount, such as negative 0.7 EV. You might do this if you find your images generally are slightly overexposed or if you see that highlights are clipping in many cases. (You can tell if highlights are clipping by checking the histogram, as discussed in Chapter 6. If the histogram is bunched to the right, with no space between the data lines and the right side of the chart, highlights are clipping, or reaching the maximum value.) It is difficult to recover details from images whose highlights have clipped, so it can be a safety measure to underexpose images slightly to avoid that situation.

If you don't plan to leave a permanent exposure compensation setting in place, you should return the setting to the zero point when you are finished with it, so you won't inadvertently change the exposure of later images that don't need the adjustment. (The exposure compensation setting will remain in place even after the camera has been turned off and back on again.)

If you use exposure compensation often, you can assign it to the Control ring using the Custom Key (Shooting) menu option. Then you can turn the ring to adjust exposure compensation with a circular scale on the screen, as shown in Figure 5-24.

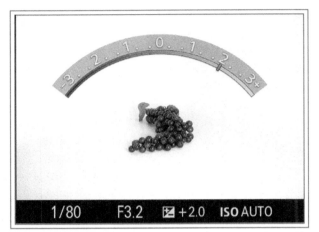

Figure 5-24. Display for Exposure Compensation Adjusted by Control Ring

(The ring will not adjust exposure compensation if the camera is set for manual focus or DMF, because the ring is used to adjust focus with those settings.)

There is one other duty performed by the Down button. In playback mode, when a movie is displayed as ready to play, you can press this button to move to a screen for adjusting the sound level for playback of movies, as shown in Figure 5-25.

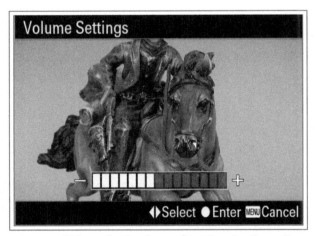

Figure 5-25. Volume Setting Screen from Pressing Down Button

This function also works when a still image is displayed, if the View Mode option on the Playback menu is set to a view that includes movies, such as Date View. When a movie is playing, you can press this button to get to the full panel of playback controls, as shown in Figure 5-26.

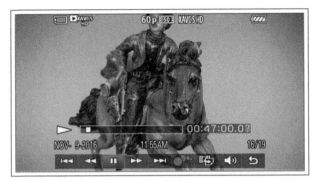

Figure 5-26. Movie Control Panel from Pressing Down Button

The Down button is permanently assigned to control exposure compensation and Photo Creativity and cannot be reassigned to other operations through the Custom Key (Shooting) menu option.

Left Button: Self-Timer/Drive Mode

The Left button is labeled with the timer dial icon for the self-timer and the stack-of-frames icon for continuous shooting. When you press this button, the camera brings up the Drive Mode menu with its options for self-timer, continuous shooting, and several types of bracketing. I discussed these options in Chapter four in connection with the Drive Mode option on the Shooting menu.

You can reassign the function of the Left button using the Custom Key (Shooting) option on screen 5 of the Custom menu. You can choose any one of 47 options, as discussed in Chapter 7.

Tilting LCD Screen

The next item to be discussed is the tilting LCD screen. This screen, even without its tilting ability, is a notable feature of the camera. It has a diagonal span of three inches (7.5 cm) and provides a resolution of 1.2 million dots using Sony's "WhiteMagic" technology, which adds a white sub-pixel to the normal red, green, and blue ones, giving a clear and sharp view of your images before and after you capture them.

The screen can tilt to assist with various types of shots. First, it can tilt downward as much as 45 degrees, as shown in Figure 5-27. You can grab the small tab sticking out at the upper left of the screen to pull it away from the camera.

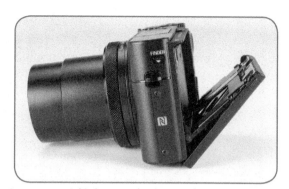

Figure 5-27. LCD Screen Tilted Down for Overhead Shots

When the LCD is tilted downward, you can hold the camera above your head and view the scene as if you were an arm's length taller or were standing on a small ladder. If you attach the camera to a monopod or other support and hold it up in the air, you can extend the height even farther and still view the LCD screen quite well. You can activate the self-timer before raising the camera up in the air to take the photo. You also can use a smartphone or tablet connected to the camera by Wi-Fi to trigger the camera by remote control while it is raised overhead, as discussed in Chapter 9, or you can use a wired remote control device, as discussed in Appendix A.

On the other hand, if you need to take images from a vantage point near ground level, you can rotate the screen so it tilts upward toward your eye, as shown in Figure 5-28, and hold the camera down as far as you need to get a mole's-eye view of the world.

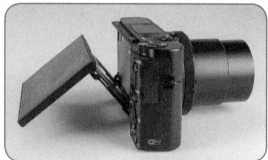

Figure 5-28. LCD Screen Tilted Up for Low-angle Shots

It can be helpful to shoot upward like this when your subject is in an area with a busy, distracting background. You can hold the camera down low and shoot with the sky as your background to reduce or eliminate the distractions. (Similarly, you may be able to shoot from a high angle to frame your subject against the ground or floor to have a less-cluttered background.)

The tilting display also is useful for street photography: You can fold the screen upward and look down at the

camera while taking photos of people without drawing undue attention to yourself.

Finally, you can rotate the screen 180 degrees so it faces in the same direction as the lens, as seen in Figure 5-29.

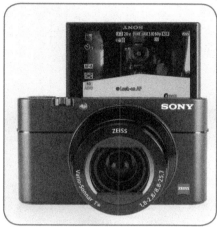

Figure 5-29. LCD Screen Rotated Forward for Self-portraits

With this orientation, you can take self-portraits. If you turn on the self-portrait timer option on screen 5 of the Custom menu, then, when the screen is in this position, the camera will count down from three to one with large numbers on the screen, as shown in Figure 5-30. This orientation also is useful if you need to see yourself as you record a video blog.

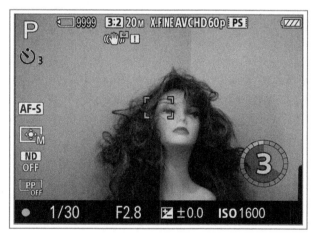

Figure 5-30. Self-portrait Timer in Use

Ports and Other Items on Right and Left Sides of Camera

There are two important connection ports on the right side of the camera. Figure 5-31 shows this side of the camera with the protective flaps over those ports opened.

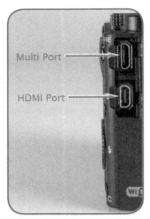

Figure 5-31. Right Side of Camera with Port Flaps Open

The top port is the Multi port. This is where you plug in the USB cable for charging the battery, powering the camera with an external power source, uploading images and videos to a computer, or connecting the camera directly to a printer to print images. You also can plug in other accessories that are compatible with this special terminal, including various models of wired remote controls, which I discuss in Appendix A.

The lower port is the HDMI port, where you plug in an optional micro HDMI cable to connect the camera to an HDTV for viewing images and videos. You also can view the shooting display from the camera through this connection, so you can connect the camera to an HDTV to act as a monitor for your shooting of still images or videos. I will discuss that process in Chapter 9. You also can set the camera to output a "clean" HDMI signal, which can be routed through an HDMI cable to an external video recorder. I will discuss that process in Chapter 8.

The left side of the camera, shown in Figure 5-32, is where the finder release switch is located. Press down on this switch to release the electronic viewfinder so it will pop up. If the camera is turned off, popping up the viewfinder will turn the camera on. Pressing the viewfinder back into the camera's body will power the camera off or leave it powered on, depending on the setting of the Function for VF Close option on screen 3 of the Setup menu.

Below the finder release switch is a decorative letter N, which marks the NFC active area for the RX100 V. This is where you touch the camera against the similar area on a compatible Android smartphone or tablet that uses the near field communication protocol. As discussed in Chapter 9, when the two devices are touched together

at their NFC active areas, they should automatically connect through a Wi-Fi network. Once the connection is established, they can share images and the phone or tablet can control the camera in some ways.

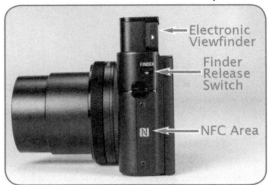

Figure 5-32. Left Side of Camera

The bottom of the RX100 V is shown in Figure 5-33.

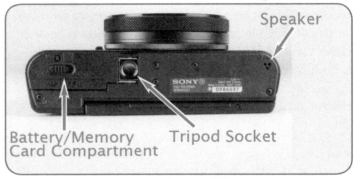

Figure 5-33. Bottom of Camera

The major items here are the tripod socket and the battery/memory card compartment. There is an access lamp inside this compartment, as seen in Figure 5-34.

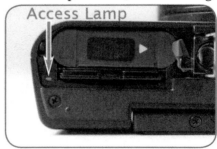

Figure 5-34. Access Lamp Inside Battery Compartment

The red access lamp lights when the camera is writing data to the memory card. When the lamp is lit, it's important not to remove the card or the battery from the compartment. Also on the bottom of the camera is the speaker, which emits the sound for movies played in the camera.

CHAPTER 6: PLAYBACK AND PRINTING

You may not spend a lot of time viewing images and videos in the camera, but it's still useful to know how the various playback functions work. You may need to examine an image closely in the camera to check focus, composition, and other aspects, or you may want to share images with friends and family. So it's worth looking at the playback functions of the RX100 V. I'll also discuss options for printing images in this chapter.

Normal Playback

First, you should be aware of the setting for Auto Review on screen 2 of the Custom menu. This setting determines whether and for how long the image stays on the screen for review when you take a new picture. If your major concern is to check images right after they are taken, this option is all you need to use. As discussed in Chapter 7, you can leave Auto Review turned off or set it to two, five, or 10 seconds.

To control how stored images and videos are viewed later on, you need to use the options available in playback mode. For plain review of images, press the Playback button, marked by a small triangle to the lower left of the Control wheel. Once you press that button, the camera is in playback mode, and you will see the most recent image or video saved to the memory card, depending on the View Mode setting on the Playback menu. To move back through older images and videos, press the Left button or turn the Control wheel to the left. To see more recent items, use the Right button or turn the wheel to the right. To speed through the items, hold down the Left or Right button.

Index View and Enlarging Images

In playback mode, you can press the zoom lever to view an index screen of images and videos or to enlarge a single image. When you are viewing an individual image or video, press the zoom lever once to the left, and you

will see a screen showing either nine or 25 items, one of which is outlined by an orange frame, as shown in Figure 6-1. (You can choose whether this screen shows nine or 25 images using the Image Index option on the Playback menu, discussed later in this chapter.)

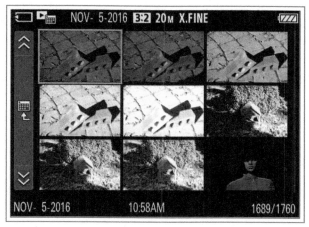

Figure 6-1. Index Screen with Nine Images

You can press the Center button to view the outlined image or video, or you can move through the items on the index screen by pressing the four direction buttons or by turning the Control wheel. If you move the orange highlight to the far left of the display, as seen in Figure 6-2, you can use the Up and Down buttons to move through the images a screen at a time.

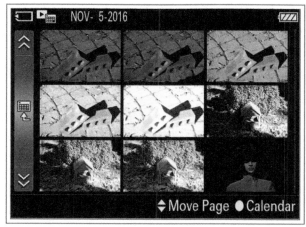

Figure 6-2. Highlight on Bar to Move a Screen at a Time

On the nine-image or 25-image index screen, one more press of the zoom lever to the left brings up another screen. For example, if View Mode, discussed later in this chapter, is set to Date View, this next screen will be a calendar display, as shown in Figure 6-3.

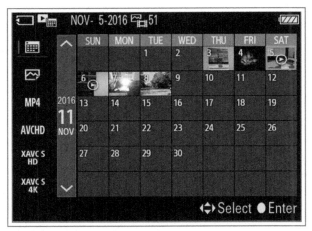

Figure 6-3. Calendar Index Screen

On that screen, you can move the orange frame to any date and press the Center button to bring up a view with all images and videos from that date. If you move the orange highlight to the narrow strip to the left of the calendar, as seen in Figure 6-4, you can move through the items by months with the Up and Down buttons.

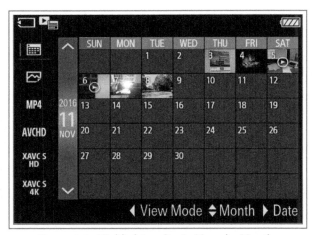

Figure 6-4. Highlight on Bar to Move by Months

If you move the highlight to the far left of the screen, as in Figure 6-5, you can use the Up and Down buttons to move through the six icons, from which you can choose the date view, still-images view, MP4 videos view, AVCHD videos view, XAVC S HD videos view, or XAVC S 4K videos view. I will discuss those options later in this chapter, in connection with the View Mode menu option on the Playback menu.

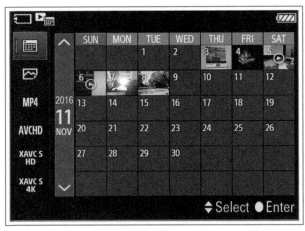

Figure 6-5. Highlight on Bar to Select View Mode Icon

When you are viewing a single still image, one press of the zoom lever to the right enlarges the image, with the enlargement centered on the point where the camera used autofocus, if it did so. (You can change that behavior using the Enlarge Initial Position option on the Playback menu, as discussed later in this chapter.) Otherwise, the camera will zoom in on the center of the image. A display in the lower left corner of the image shows a thumbnail with an inset frame that represents the portion of the image that is filling the screen in enlarged view, as shown in Figure 6-6. This feature is useful for quickly checking the focus of the image.

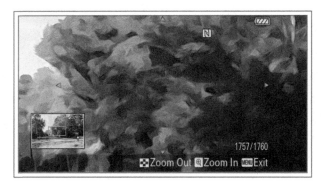

Figure 6-6. Enlarged Image in Playback Mode

If you press the zoom lever to the right repeatedly, the image will be enlarged to increasing levels. While it is magnified, you can scroll in it with the four direction buttons; you will see the inset frame move around within the thumbnail image. To reduce the image size again, press the zoom lever to the left as many times as necessary or press the Center button or the Menu button to revert immediately to normal size. You can press the Custom/Delete button to bring up the Delete screen for that image while it is enlarged. To move to other images while the display is magnified, turn the Control wheel.

Playback Screens

When you view an image in single-image mode, pressing the Display (Up) button repeatedly cycles through the three screens that are available: (1) full image with no added information; (2) full image with basic information, including date and time taken, image number, aspect ratio, aperture, shutter speed, ISO, and image size and quality, as shown in Figure 6-7; and (3) thumbnail image with detailed recording information, including exposure compensation, Picture Effect setting (if any), Metering Mode, DRO setting, shooting mode, white balance, and other data, plus a histogram, as shown in Figure 6-8.

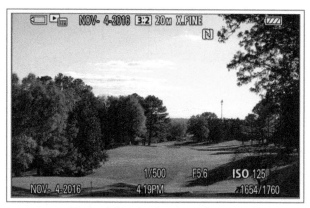

Figure 6-7. Playback Display Screen with Basic Information

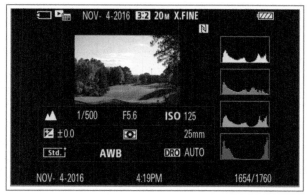

Figure 6-8. Playback Display Screen with Detailed Information

A histogram is a graph showing the distribution of dark and bright areas in the image displayed on the screen. The darkest blacks are represented by peaks on the left and the brightest whites by peaks on the right, with continuous gradations in between. With the RX100 V,

the histogram displayed in playback mode includes four boxes with information.

The top box provides information about the overall brightness of the image. The three lower boxes provide information about the brightness of the colors that make up the image: red, green, and blue. If a histogram has peaks bunched at the left, there are too many dark areas and few bright and white areas. If the graph runs into the left side of the chart, it means shadow areas are "clipped" so that details have been lost in the dark areas.

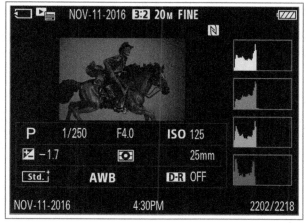

Figure 6-9. Histogram for Underexposed Image

The histogram in Figure 6-9 illustrates this degree of underexposure. A histogram with its high points bunched to the right means the opposite—too bright, as in Figure 6-10. When the graph runs into the right side of the chart, as here, that means highlights are clipped and the image has lost details in bright areas.

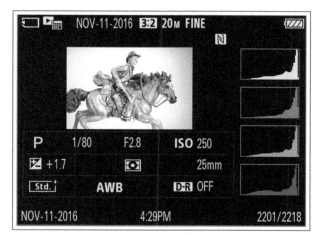

Figure 6-10. Histogram for Overexposed Image

A histogram that is "just right" has high points arranged more evenly in the middle of the chart. That pattern, as illustrated by Figure 6-11, indicates a good balance of light, dark, and medium tones.

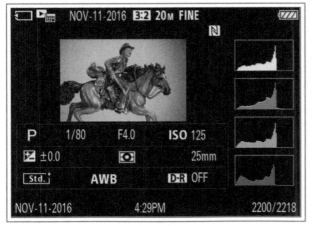

Figure 6-11. Histogram for Normally Exposed Image

When the playback histogram is displayed, areas containing highlights that are excessively bright will blink to show possible overexposure, indicating that you may need to take another shot with the exposure adjusted to correct that situation.

The histogram can give you helpful feedback about the exposure of images. Also, there may be instances in which it is appropriate to have a histogram skewed to the left or right for intentionally "low-key" (dark) or "high-key" (brightly lit) scenes.

To turn on the histogram for the live view in shooting mode, use the Display Button option on screen 2 of the Custom menu.

Deleting Images with the Delete Button

As I mentioned in Chapter 5, you can delete individual images by pressing the Delete button, also known as the Custom (C) button. If you press this button when a still image or a video is displayed, whether individually or highlighted on an index screen, the camera will display the Delete/Cancel box shown in Figure 6-12.

Highlight your choice and press the Center button to confirm. To delete multiple items, you need to use the Delete option on the Playback menu, discussed later in this chapter. You also can use the Delete button to delete an image when it is displayed immediately after it was taken, with the Auto Review option.

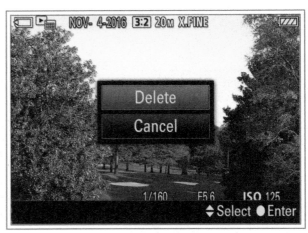

Figure 6-12. Confirmation Screen for Delete Button

Playback Menu

Other options for playback on the RX100 V appear as items on the Playback menu, whose first screen is shown in Figure 6-13.

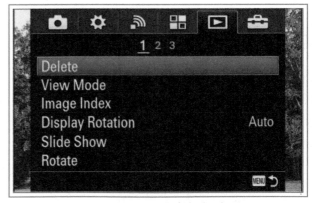

Figure 6-13. Screen 1 of Playback Menu

You get access to this menu by pressing the Menu button. The camera does not have to be in playback mode to get access to this menu, but, in playback mode, pressing the Menu button will take you directly to the Playback menu. Otherwise, you may need to navigate to this menu. You enter playback mode by pressing the Playback button when the camera is turned on in shooting mode. If the camera is turned off, you can turn it on in playback mode by pressing the Playback button instead of the power button.

Following is information about the items on the Playback menu:

DELETE

Use this option to delete multiple images or videos in one operation. (If you just want to delete one or two images or videos, it's easier to display each item on the screen, then press the Delete button and confirm the erasure.) When you select the Delete command, the menu offers you various choices, as shown in Figure 6-14.

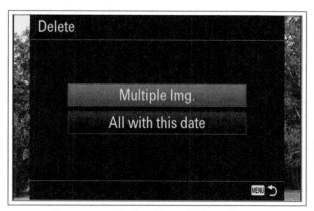

Figure 6-14. Delete Menu Options Screen

These choices may include Multiple Images, All in this Folder, or All with this Date, depending on the current setting for the View Mode option, discussed below. If the Delete command is dimmed and unavailable for selection, that means there are no items on the memory card that fall into the current View Mode category.

If you choose Multiple Images, the camera will display images or videos with a check box at the left side, if any exist on the memory card, as shown in Figure 6-15.

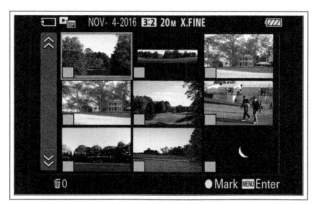

Figure 6-15. Image Selection Screen for Delete Menu Option

The images and videos may be shown individually or on an index screen, depending on current settings. You can change between full-screen and index views using the zoom lever.

Scroll through the images and videos with the Control wheel or the direction buttons. When you reach an image you want to delete, press the Center button to place a check mark in the check box on that image. Continue with this process until you have marked all images you want to delete, as shown in Figure 6-16.

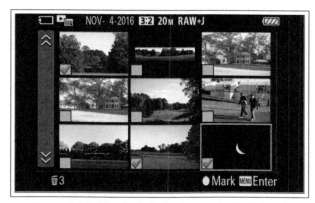

Figure 6-16. Check Marks for Images to Be Deleted

Then press the Menu button to move to the next screen, where the camera will prompt you to highlight OK or Cancel, as shown in Figure 6-17, and press the Center button to confirm. If you select OK, all of the marked images and videos will be deleted.

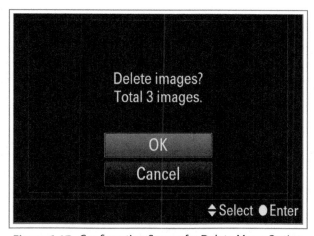

Figure 6-17. Confirmation Screen for Delete Menu Option

If, instead of Multiple Images, you choose All in Folder, the camera will display a screen asking you to confirm deletion of all files in the current folder. If you select All with this Date, you will have the opportunity to delete all images and videos from the selected date.

If any images have a key icon displayed at the top, those images are protected, and cannot be deleted using this option unless you first unprotect them, as discussed later in this chapter.

VIEW MODE

This second option on the Playback menu lets you choose which images or videos are currently viewed in playback mode. The options are Date View, Folder View (Still), Folder View (MP4), AVCHD View, XAVC S HD View, and XAVC S 4K View, as shown in Figure 6-18.

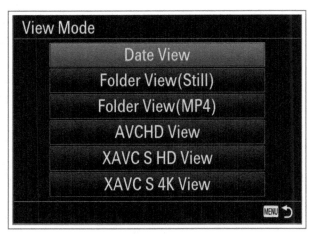

Figure 6-18. View Mode Menu Options Screen

If you select Date View, the camera will display the calendar screen shown earlier in Figure 6-3. You can navigate through that screen using the Control wheel or the direction buttons. Highlight a date and press the Center button; the camera will display all images and videos from that date. When the calendar screen is displayed, you can move to other months by highlighting the gray strip to the left of the calendar and using the Up and Down buttons.

If you select Folder View (Still), the camera will show a screen like that in Figure 6-19, which displays the folders available for selection.

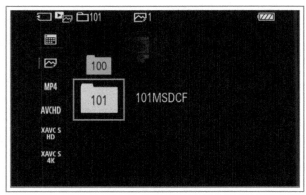

Figure 6-19. Folder View (Still) Screen

Highlight the folder you want (there may be only one) and press the Center button; the camera will display

all still images in that folder. You can navigate through the index screens for those images and select the image or images you want to view. If you select Folder View (MP4), the camera will display only the MP4 videos from the folder you select, if there are any such videos.

If you select AVCHD View, the camera will display a calendar screen with thumbnail images indicating which dates have AVCHD files associated with them. You can select any date with a thumbnail to display AVCHD videos from that date.

If you select XAVC S HD View or XAVC S 4K View, the camera will display a calendar showing the dates on which videos in that format were recorded.

My general preference is to use the Date View option, because then I can view both images and videos from a given date. However, if I want to locate a particular video, it can be quicker to choose one of the video views so I can limit my search to videos of a single format.

You can select a view option from an index screen without using the Playback menu. After moving the zoom lever to the left to call up the calendar display or folder display, move the highlight to the extreme left of the screen to the line of icons that represent the six view modes, as shown earlier in Figure 6-5, and select one of the modes from that display.

IMAGE INDEX

This menu option, shown in Figure 6-20, gives you the choice of having the camera include either nine images or 25 images when it displays an index screen.

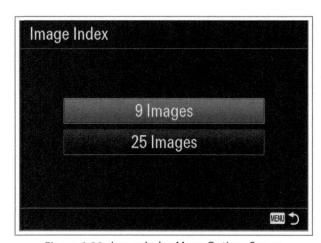

Figure 6-20. Image Index Menu Options Screen

When you make this selection, the camera displays the index screen you chose, and it will display that screen whenever you call up the index screen using the zoom lever, as discussed earlier.

Whether you choose the nine-image screen or the 25-image screen depends on your preference and other factors, including how many images and videos you have on your memory card and how easy it is to distinguish one from another by looking at the small thumbnail images.

The thumbnails on the nine-image screen are larger than those on the 25-image screen, and it may make sense to choose the nine-image screen unless you have so many images that it would be burdensome to scroll through them nine at a time.

DISPLAY ROTATION

This next item on the Playback menu controls whether images shot with the camera held vertically appear that way when you play them back on the camera's screen. By default, this option is set to Auto, meaning images taken vertically are automatically rotated so that the vertical shot appears in portrait orientation on the horizontal display, as shown in Figure 6-21.

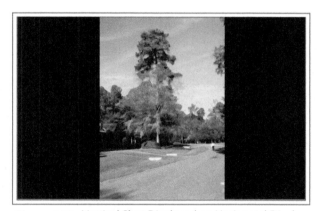

Figure 6-21. Vertical Shot Displayed on Horizontal Display

With this setting, if you tilt the camera sideways so one side is up, a vertical image will rotate to fill the screen. In this way, you get the best of both worlds: Vertical images display in proper orientation (but smaller than normal) within the horizontal display, and, when you tilt the camera in playback mode, they display at full size.

If you change the setting to Manual, a vertical image will appear vertically on the horizontal screen, in the same way as shown in Figure 6-21. The difference

with this setting from Auto is that, if you tilt the camera in playback mode, the image will not change its orientation.

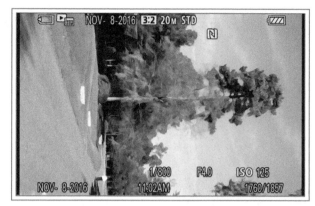

Figure 6-22. Vertical Image Displayed without Rotation

If you set this option to Off, a vertical image will display horizontally on the display at full size, as shown in Figure 6-22, so you would have to tilt the camera in playback mode to see it in its proper orientation. With all of these settings, you can use the Rotate option on the Playback menu, discussed later in this chapter, to rotate an image manually to a different orientation.

SLIDE SHOW

This feature lets you play still images and videos in sequence at an interval you specify. This option will be dimmed and unavailable if the View Mode option on the Playback menu is set to Folder View (MP4), AVCHD View, or either of the two XAVC S View settings. If that is the case, use the View Mode menu option to select either Date View or Folder View (Still). If you select Date View, the Slide Show option will display all of your movies, in all four formats, along with your still images. Each movie will play in full before the show advances to the next item, unless you interrupt it with one of the controls. If you select Folder View (Still), the Slide Show option will display only the still images from the folder you selected.

When you select the Slide Show option and press the Center button, the next screen has two options you can set: Repeat and Interval, as seen in Figure 6-23. If Repeat is turned on, the show will keep repeating; otherwise, it will play only once.

The camera will not power off automatically in this mode, so be sure to stop the show when you are done with it. The Interval setting, which controls how long each still image stays on the screen, can be set to one, three, five, 10, or 30 seconds. (The Interval setting does not apply to movies, each of which plays to its end.)

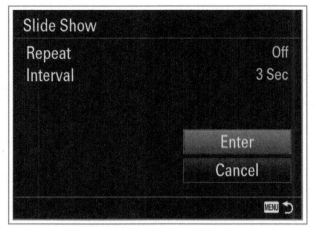

Figure 6-23. Slide Show Menu Options Screen

Once the options are set, navigate to the Enter box at the bottom of the screen using the Control wheel or the Down button, and press the Center button to start the show. You can move forward or backward through images (and videos, if included) with the Right and Left buttons. Hold the buttons down to fast-forward or fast-reverse through the images and videos.

You can stop the show by pressing the Menu button or the Playback button. There is no way to pause the show and resume it. When a movie is playing as part of the show, you can control its volume by pressing the Down button and then adjusting the sound with the Left and Right buttons or the Control wheel. Each movie plays fully before the next movie or image is displayed, but you can skip to the next movie or image using the Right button.

The Slide Show option does not provide settings such as transitions, effects, or music. You cannot select which images to play; this option just lets you play all of your still images from the selected folder, if you are using Folder View, or all still images and videos starting from the selected date, if you are using Date View.

Rotate

The Rotate option is a way to rotate a still image manually. Select this menu item, and you will see a screen like that in Figure 6-24, prompting you to press the Center button to rotate the image.

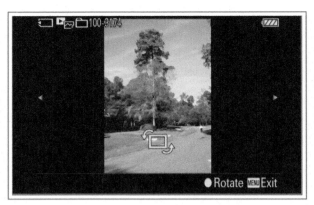

Figure 6-24. Rotate Menu Options Screen

Each time you press the button, the image will rotate 90 degrees counter-clockwise. You can use this option for images taken vertically, when Display Rotation, discussed above, is turned off. This option does not work for videos, only still images.

The second screen of the Playback menu is shown in Figure 6-25.

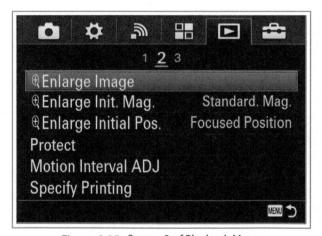

Figure 6-25. Screen 2 of Playback Menu

Enlarge Image

This option performs the same magnification for still images discussed earlier in this chapter, which you can also do with the zoom lever. When you select this option, the enlarged image will appear on the screen; you can use the zoom lever to change the enlargement factor.

Enlarge Initial Magnification

This option lets you choose either Standard Magnification or Previous Magnification, as shown in Figure 6-26.

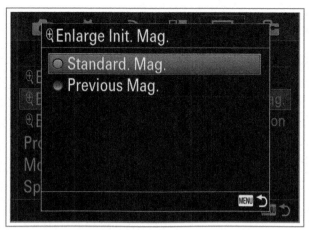

Figure 6-26. Enlarge Initial Magnification Menu Options Screen

With the Standard Magnification option, when you use the zoom lever to magnify an image, the camera uses the standard magnification factor. If you choose Previous Magnification, the camera will use whatever magnification level has been used previously for any image. So, if you like to zoom your images in with three presses of the zoom lever, you can choose Previous Magnification for this option, and, once you have enlarged one image to that degree, other images will be enlarged to that degree when you first turn the zoom lever to enlarge them.

ENLARGE INITIAL POSITION

This option lets you choose whether, when an image is enlarged, the camera centers it on the point where autofocus was achieved (if any), or on the center of the image. The menu options screen is shown in Figure 6-27.

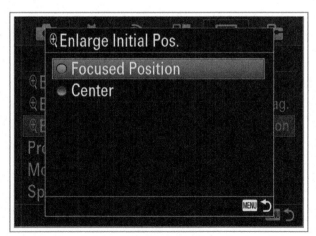

Figure 6-27. Enlarge Initial Position Menu Options Screen

If you want to check focus, it can be convenient to have the enlarged image automatically centered on the focus point when it is enlarged in playback mode. For that

option, choose Focused Position from this menu screen. Otherwise, choose Center.

PROTECT

With the Protect feature, you can "lock" selected images or videos so they cannot be erased with the normal erase functions, including using the Delete button and using the Delete option on the Playback menu, discussed above. However, if you format the memory card using the Format command, all data on the card will be erased, including protected images.

To protect images or videos using this menu item, the procedure is similar to the one for deleting images, discussed above. When you select this option, the camera will display a screen similar to that shown in Figure 6-15, with choices to select multiple images; all from the same date or folder as the current image; or to cancel protection for all images with this date or from this folder. (The current View Mode setting will determine whether the choices are for the current date or the current folder.)

If you select Multiple Images, the camera will present you with either index screens or individual images. As with the Delete option, you can scroll through your images and mark any image's check box for protection by pressing the Center button. When you have finished marking images, press the Menu button and the camera will display a confirmation screen. If you select OK to confirm, the marked images and videos will be protected. Any item that is protected will have a key icon in the upper right corner to the left of the battery icon, as shown in Figure 6-28.

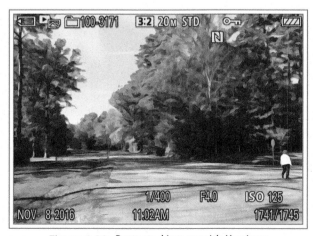

Figure 6-28. Protected Image with Key Icon

The key icon will be visible when the image is viewed with the detailed information screen or the basic information screen, but it will not appear in the image-only view.

To unprotect multiple images or videos in one operation, select the appropriate Cancel option from the Protect item on the Playback menu. That option will prompt you to Cancel All with this Date or to Cancel All in this Folder, depending on the View Mode setting.

MOTION INTERVAL ADJUSTMENT

This menu option gives you a way to adjust the length of time the camera uses for the interval between frames when it creates the Motion Shot effect in playing back a movie. The adjustment screen for this option is shown in Figure 6-29.

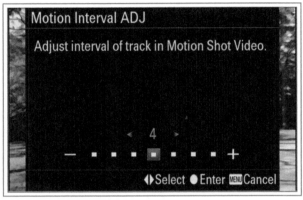

Figure 6-29. Motion Interval Adjustment Screen

The default value is four; you can set the interval to any value from one to seven. The higher the number, the greater the spacing between images in the motion shot. I will discuss this option in Chapter 8, where I discuss movie playback features.

SPECIFY PRINTING

This option lets you use the DPOF (Digital Print Order Format) function, a printing protocol built into the camera. The DPOF system lets you mark various images on your memory card to be added to a print list, which can then be sent to your own inkjet or laser printer. Or, you can take the memory card to a commercial printing company to print out the selected images.

To add images to the DPOF print list, select the Specify Printing option from the Playback menu. On the next

screen, shown in Figure 6-30, choose the option for Multiple Images.

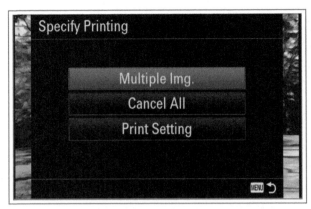

Figure 6-30. Specify Printing Menu Options Screen

The camera will display the first image with a check box at the left or an index screen with an orange frame around the currently selected image and a check box in the lower left corner of each image thumbnail, as with the Delete and Protect functions discussed earlier. You can choose to display individual images or index screens using the zoom lever. There will be a small printer icon in the lower left with a zero beside it at first, meaning no copies of any images have been set for printing yet. Use the Control wheel or direction buttons to move through the images.

When an image you want to print is displayed, press the Center button to mark it for printing or to unmark it. You can then keep browsing through images and adding them to (or removing them from) the print list. As you add images to the list, the counter in the lower left corner will show the total number of images selected for printing. You can only select JPEG images; you will see an error message if you try to select a Raw image.

When you have finished selecting images to be printed, press the Menu button to move to a screen where you can confirm your choices by selecting OK. You also can turn the Date Imprint option on or off to specify whether or not the pictures will be printed with the dates they were taken. To do this, go to the first screen of the Specify Printing menu option and select Print Setting. On the next screen, shown in Figure 6-31, you can turn on Date Imprint, to have the date printed on each image. You can take the memory card with the DPOF list to a service that prints photos using this system, or you can connect the camera to a Pictbridge-compatible printer to print the images. To cancel a

Specify Printing order, go to the Specify Printing menu item and select the Cancel All option.

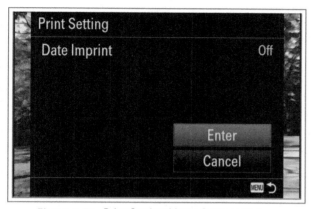

Figure 6-31. Print Setting Menu Options Screen

The third and final screen of the Playback menu is shown in Figure 6-32.

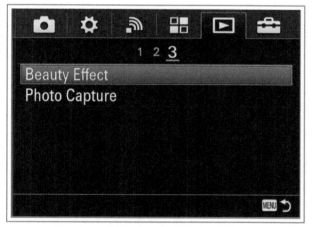

Figure 6-32. Screen 3 of Playback Menu

The menu screen in Figure 6-32 shows both items as available for selection, although it is unlikely that they both will be available at the same time. Beauty effect is available only when the image ready for playback is a still image with a face, and Photo Capture is available only when a movie is ready to be played. I have altered the menu to show both items as available for the sake of making them more visible.

Beauty Effect

This first option on the third screen of the Playback menu gives you a set of tools for retouching photographs of faces that you have previously taken. To use this feature, navigate to an image of a face in playback mode and select this option from the Playback menu. The camera will display the image with an orange

frame or a white frame around any face it detects. If the camera does not detect a face, it will display an error message. If it detects multiple faces, use the Left and Right buttons to select the one you want to retouch; the selected face will be marked with the orange frame.

After selecting the chosen face, press the Center button to move to the next screen, shown in Figure 6-33.

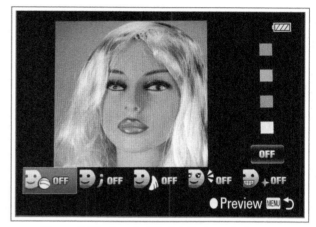

Figure 6-33. Beauty Effect Adjustments Screen

On this screen, the camera displays five controls, from left to right: Skin Toning, Skin Smoothing, Shine Removal, Eye Widening, and Teeth Whitening. Highlight an adjustment you want to make using the Left and Right buttons, and adjust each of these settings using the Up and Down buttons or the Control wheel.

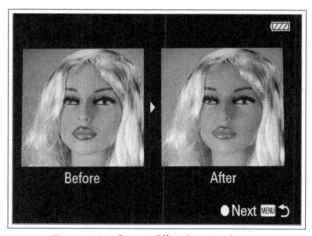

Figure 6-34. Beauty Effect Preview Screen

When they are all adjusted as you want, press the Center button to generate a preview. The camera will display Before and After images on a screen like that shown in Figure 6-34.

If you are satisfied, press the Center button, and select OK to confirm on the next screen. Then, if you need to adjust another face in the same image, select that image again and make adjustments for the next face.

PHOTO CAPTURE

This final option on the Playback menu gives you a way to save one or more still frames from a movie that was recorded with the camera. To use this option, first find the movie that you want to save a still image from. You can use the View Mode option discussed earlier in this chapter to find movies of various formats, to help narrow the search.

When you have the chosen movie displayed on the screen in playback mode, select the Photo Capture menu option, and the camera will display the movie again, but this time with a circular area with several icons at the right side of the display that represent the camera's direction buttons and Center button, as shown in Figure 6-35.

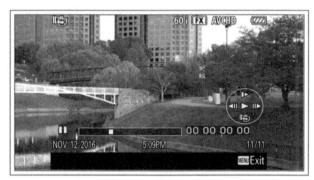

Figure 6-35. Movie with Photo Capture Controls

The top icon represents slow playback; the right one is for single-frame forward; the left one is for single-frame reverse; the center one is for play; and the bottom one is for photo capture.

Using the four direction buttons and the Center button according to that scheme, play the movie to the exact frame you want to save, and then press the Down button to capture the frame to a still image. The camera will display a Processing message briefly, and then will save a still image to the memory card. The image will have the same resolution as the movie from which it was saved. For example, if you save a frame from a 4K movie, it will have a resolution of 3840 x 2160 pixels, or about 8 megapixels.

If you want, you can start the Photo Capture process without using the menu system. To do that, start a movie playing, and press the Center button to pause it. Then press the Down button, and you will see a control panel at the bottom of the screen, as shown in Figure 6-36.

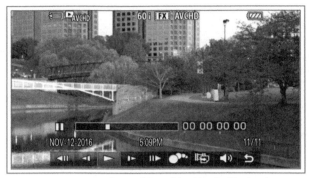

Figure 6-36. Control Panel for Movie Playback

The Photo Capture icon is the third one from the right. Use the direction buttons to navigate to that icon and select it, to start using the Photo Capture feature. Figure 6-37 is a frame that was saved from a 4K video using this feature.

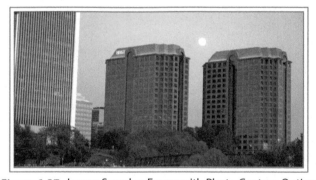

Figure 6-37. Image Saved as Frame with Photo Capture Option

Chapter 7: Custom and Setup Menus

In earlier chapters, I discussed the options available in the Shooting and Playback menu systems. The Sony RX100 V has two other menu systems—Custom and Setup—that help you set up the camera and customize its operation. In this chapter, I will discuss the options on those menus. I'll discuss menu options for Movie recording in Chapter 8 and I'll discuss the Wi-Fi and Application menus in Chapter 9.

Custom Menu

The Custom menu, whose first screen is shown in Figure 7-1, gives you control over items that affect the ways you use the camera to take pictures and videos, but that do not change photographic settings such as white balance, ISO, focus modes, and matters of that nature.

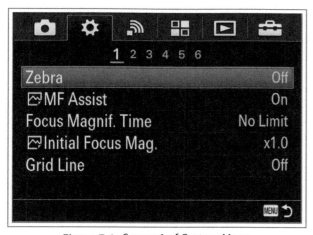

Figure 7-1. Screen 1 of Custom Menu

With this menu, the items to be adjusted are more in the categories of control and display options that help you use the major settings. Details about the options on the six screens of this menu follow.

Zebra

This first Custom menu option gives you a tool for gauging the exposure of an image or video. When you turn this menu option on, you can select a value from 70 to 100 IRE in five-unit increments, or 100+ for values greater than 100. The IRE units are a measure of relative brightness or exposure, with 0 representing black and 100 representing white.

You also can save and later use two custom values, as discussed below. Figure 7-2 shows the screen for selecting values up to 85.

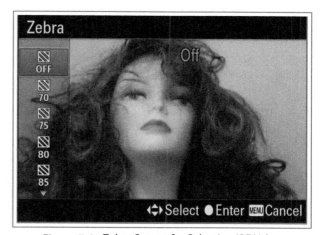

Figure 7-2. Zebra Screen for Selecting IRE Value

When you turn this option on to any level, you very likely will see, in some parts of the display, the black-and-white "zebra" stripes that give this feature its name.

Zebra stripes originally were created as a feature for professional video cameras, so the videographer could see whether the scene would be properly exposed. This tool often is used in the context of taping an interview, when proper exposure of a human face is the main concern.

There are various approaches to using these stripes. Some videographers like to set the zebra function to 90 IRE and adjust the exposure so the stripes barely appear in the brightest parts of the image. Another recommendation is to set the option to 75 IRE for a scene with Caucasian skin, and expose so that the stripes barely appear in the area of the skin.

In Figure 7-3, I set IRE to 75 and exposed to have the stripes appear clearly on the mannequin's face and neck.

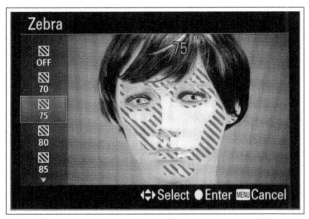

Figure 7-3. Zebra Set at IRE 75

As the brightness of the lighting increases for a subject, there may be no stripes at first, then they will gradually appear until they cover the subject, then they will seem to disappear, because the exposure is so bright that the subject is surrounded by an outline of "marching ants" rather than having stripes in its interior. The goal is to set the camera's exposure so the stripes are maximized on the subject at the chosen numerical level.

You can save customized Zebra settings to the C1 and C2 slots. A standard way to use these two values is to set C1 to a value for exposure confirmation and C2 to a value for flare confirmation.

To set C1 for exposure confirmation, scroll down to the C1 block, below the 100+ setting, and press the Right button. You will see a screen like that in Figure 7-4, with the Std+Range block highlighted in orange. (Press the Up or Down button if necessary to bring that label into the block.)

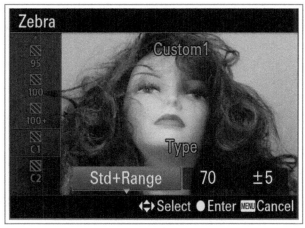

Figure 7-4. Screen to Set C1 Block

With the Std+Range block highlighted, press the Right button to move to the next block, and use the Up and Down buttons or the Control dial to set a value, which can be from zero to 109, in one-unit increments. Then press the Right button to move to the next block and select a range, which can be from ±1 to ±10.

For example, you might set the first block to 77 and the second block to ±5, so the Zebra pattern would appear when the brightness of the scene was within five units of 77, plus or minus. You could then set Zebra to C1 to confirm that the scene's exposure was within that range.

To set the C2 value for flare confirmation, scroll down to that block and press the Right button. Make sure the highlighted block contains the Lower Limit label, as shown in Figure 7-5.

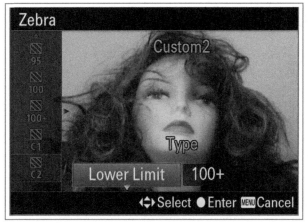

Figure 7-5. Screen to Set C2 Block

Then press the Right button to move to the second block and select a setting from 50+ to 109+ in one-unit increments. That value represents the brightness level that you don't want to exceed. You can then set Zebra to the C2 block and check the scene to make sure the lighting stays within that limit, to avoid flare. The Zebra pattern will appear if that limit is exceeded.

Zebra is a feature to consider, especially for video recording, but the RX100 V has an excellent metering system, including both live and playback histograms, so you can manage without this option if you don't want to deal with its learning curve.

MF Assist

The MF Assist option is for use with still images when manual focus or DMF is in effect. With MF Assist turned on in manual focus mode, the camera enlarges the image as soon as you start turning the Control ring to adjust focus, as shown in Figure 7-6. This feature helps show whether a particular area is in sharp focus. If you turn this option off, you can use another focusing aid, such as Focus Magnifier, discussed in Chapter 4, or Peaking Level, discussed later in this chapter. Or, you can use this option and Peaking at the same time, to provide even more assistance.

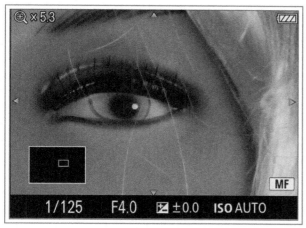

Figure 7-6. MF Assist in Use

When DMF is in effect, you have to keep the shutter button pressed halfway down while turning the Control ring to use the MF Assist enlargement feature.

I find MF Assist helpful, especially because I can set the camera to leave the enlarged screen in place indefinitely using the Focus Magnification Time option, discussed below. However, the Focus Magnifier option also is helpful, and may be preferable in one way because the screen does not become magnified until you press the Center button, select the area to be magnified using the orange frame, and then magnify the screen.

In some cases, if a subject (like the moon viewed through a telescope, as discussed in Chapter 9) does not have edges or other features to focus on, enlarging the view may not be very helpful. In those situations, Peaking Level may be more useful. Or, you may find that using Peaking Level in conjunction with MF Assist is the most useful approach of all. You should experiment with the various options to find what works best for you.

Focus Magnification Time

This option controls how long the display stays magnified with the MF Assist option, discussed above,

or the Focus Magnifier option, discussed in Chapter 4. The choices are two or five seconds or No Limit, as seen in Figure 7-7. The default is two seconds.

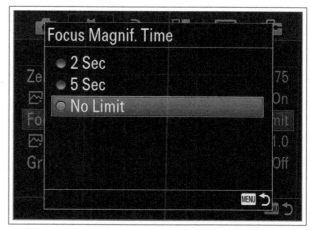

Figure 7-7. Focus Magnification Time Menu Options Screen

If you select No Limit, the image will stay magnified until you press the shutter button all the way to take the picture or press it halfway to dismiss the enlarged view. My preference is to use No Limit so I can take my time to adjust manual focus precisely.

Note, though, that with the No Limit option, whenever you turn the Control ring when using MF Assist, the image will be enlarged, and you may want to be able to keep adjusting focus with a view of the unenlarged subject. If that is the case, select one of the options with a time limit or use the Focus Magnifier option.

Initial Focus Magnification

This menu option lets you select either 1.0x or 5.3x as the initial magnification factor for the Focus Magnifier frame when it first appears on the screen. The Focus Magnifier option was discussed in Chapter 4; it is found on screen 6 of the Shooting menu, and it can be assigned to one of the camera's control buttons through the Custom Key (Shooting) option on screen 5 of the Custom menu.

If you select the default of 1.0x for this menu option, the Focus Magnifier frame will appear on the display with no magnification until you press the Center button. The area within the frame is then magnified to 5.3 times, and a second press magnifies it to 10.7 times; a third press removes the frame from the display. If you select 5.3x for this option, the frame will appear with the 5.3x magnification already in effect.

Note: If you use the In-Camera Guide help system, which can be assigned to a control button using the Custom Key (Shooting) option, and press that button when this menu item is highlighted, you will see that the help system says that this option controls the initial magnification for the Focus Magnifier option and for the MF Assist option. However, this option controls the initial magnification only for the Focus Magnifier option. The MF Assist screen always displays initially at the 5.3x magnification, regardless of the setting for this option.

Grid Line

With this option, you can select one of four settings for a grid to be superimposed on the shooting screen. By default, there is no grid. If you choose one of the grid options, the lines will appear in your chosen configuration whenever the camera is showing the live view in shooting mode, whether the detailed display screen is selected or not. Of course, the grid does not appear when the For Viewfinder display, with its black screen full of shooting information, is displayed. The four options are seen in Figure 7-8.

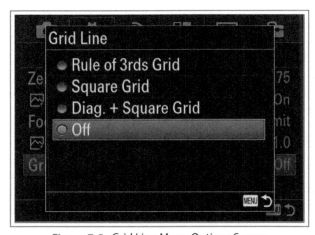

Figure 7-8. Grid Line Menu Options Screen

Following are descriptions of these choices, other than Off, which leaves the screen with no grid.

Rule of Thirds Grid

This arrangement of two vertical and two horizontal lines divides the screen into nine blocks, as seen in Figure 7-9.

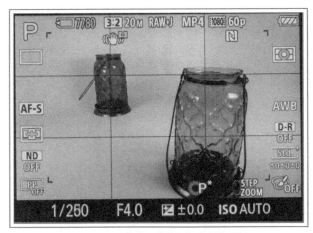

Figure 7-9. Rule of Thirds Grid in Use

This grid reflects a rule of composition that calls for locating an important subject at an intersection of these lines, which will place the subject one-third of the way from the edge of the image. This arrangement can add interest and asymmetry to an image.

Square Grid

With this setting, five vertical lines and three horizontal lines divide the display into 24 blocks, as seen in Figure 7-10.

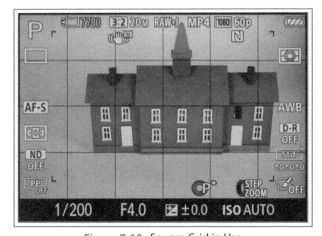

Figure 7-10. Square Grid in Use

In this way, you can still use the Rule of Thirds, but you have more lines available for lining up items, such as the edge of a building, that need to be straight.

Diagonal Plus Square Grid

The last option has a grid of four blocks in each direction and adds two diagonal lines, as shown in Figure 7-11.

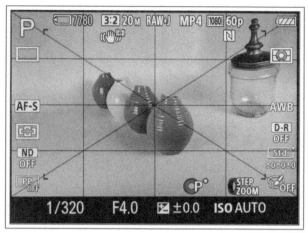

Figure 7-11. Diagonal Plus Square Grid in Use

The idea is that placing a subject or, more likely, a string of subjects along one of the diagonals can add interest to the image by drawing the viewer's eye into the image along the diagonal line.

The second screen of the Custom menu is shown in Figure 7-12.

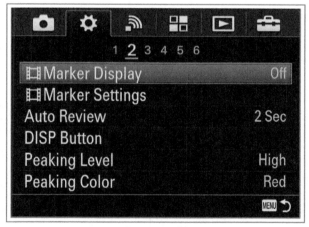

Figure 7-12. Screen 2 of Custom Menu

MARKER DISPLAY

This option, which can be turned either on or off, determines whether or not various informative guidelines, called "markers," are displayed on the camera's screen for movie recording. There are four special markers available, which outline the aspect ratio and other areas on the screen. Any or all of them can be selected for use with the Marker Settings menu option, directly below this one on the Custom menu. If you turn Marker Display on, then, any of the four markers that you have selected will be displayed on the shooting screen while a movie is being recorded in any mode. The

markers also will be displayed while the Mode dial is set to the Movie mode position or the HFR position, even before recording starts.

If this option is turned on, the selected markers will display on the camera's display screen, but they will not be recorded with the movie.

MARKER SETTINGS

This menu option works together with the Marker Display option, discussed above. This option lets you activate any or all of the four available markers—Center, Aspect, Safety Zone, and Guideframe, as shown in Figure 7-13.

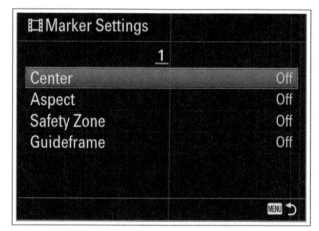

Figure 7-13. Marker Settings Menu Options Screen

If you turn on the Center marker, it places a cross in the center of the display, as illustrated in Figure 7-14. If you are shooting video in a busy or hectic environment, this marker may help you keep the main subject centered in the display so you don't cut it off.

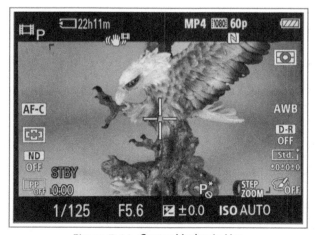

Figure 7-14. Center Marker in Use

The Aspect marker can be off or set to any one of seven settings: 4:3, 13:9, 14:9, 15:9, 1.66:1, 1.85:1, or 2.35:1. Figure 7-15 shows the display with the 2.35:1 setting.

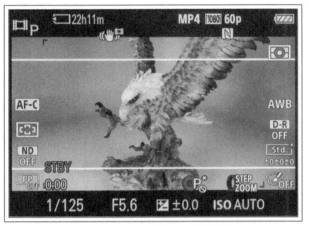

Figure 7-15. Aspect Marker 2.35:1 in Use

This setting places vertical white lines at the sides of the frame or horizontal white lines at the top and bottom of the frame, to outline the shape of the movie frame for the chosen aspect ratio. These lines are useful if you plan to alter the aspect ratio of your footage in post-production, to show what parts of the image will be cut off and help you frame your shots accordingly.

The Safety Zone marker can be off or set to 80% or 90%. The guidelines outline either 80% or 90% of the area of the display. The purpose of these lines is to provide a margin for safety because the average consumer television set does not display the entire broadcast signal provided to it.

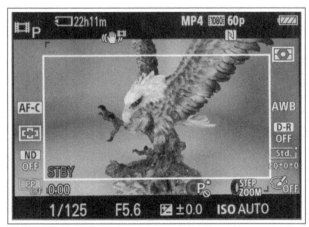

Figure 7-16. Safety Zone Marker Set to 80%

If you set these lines to mark a safety zone, you can make sure that your important subjects are included in the area that definitely will be displayed on most

television sets. Figure 7-16 shows the display with the 80% safety zone activated.

Finally, the Guideframe option, if turned on, displays a grid that is similar to the Rule of Thirds grid for still images with the Grid Line option, discussed earlier in this chapter. That option uses thin, black lines, which may be hard to see when you are shooting video under difficult conditions. The bold, white lines of the Guideframe setting should be more useful for video shooting. You cannot use both options at the same time; Grid Line is not available when Marker Display is turned on. Figure 7-17 shows the Guideframe option in use.

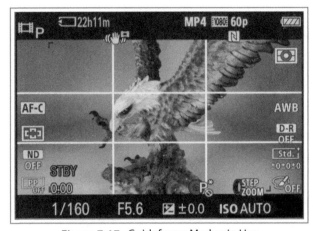

Figure 7-17. Guideframe Marker in Use

AUTO REVIEW

With the Auto Review option, shown in Figure 7-18, you can set the length of time that a still image appears on the display screen immediately after you capture it.

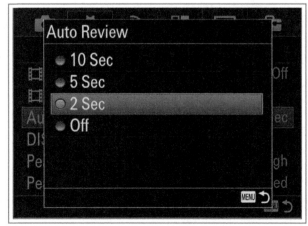

Figure 7-18. Auto Review Menu Options Screen

The default is two seconds, but you can set the time to five or 10 seconds, or you can turn the function off. If you turn it off, the camera will return to shooting mode as soon as it has saved a new image to the memory card. When this option is in use, you can always return to the live view by pressing the shutter button halfway. The Auto Review option does not apply to movies; the camera does not display the beginning frame of a movie that was just recorded until you press the Playback button.

While a new image is displayed, you can use functions of playback mode such as enlarging the image, displaying index screens, or moving to other images. If you start one of these actions before the camera has reverted to shooting mode, the camera will stay in playback mode. You also can delete an image using the Delete button while it is displayed with this option.

DISPLAY BUTTON

This option lets you choose what screens appear in shooting mode as you repeatedly press the Display button. There are sub-options that let you select the screens for the monitor (LCD) and the electronic viewfinder, as seen in Figure 7-19.

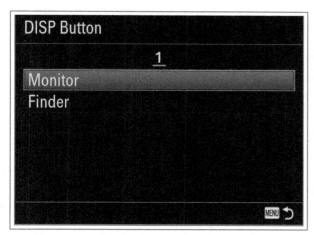

Figure 7-19. Display Button Menu Options Screen

You can make different choices for the LCD and the viewfinder, so pressing the Display button when you are using the monitor may bring up a different set of screens than when you are using the viewfinder.

After you decide to choose display screens for the monitor or the viewfinder, you will see a screen like that shown in Figure 7-20. This screen shows the six display screens you can select for the monitor. The selection screen for the viewfinder is identical to this one, except that the sixth choice, For Viewfinder, is not available as a choice to appear in the viewfinder. That

display screen is designed to appear on the monitor to provide shooting information when you are viewing the live view through the viewfinder.

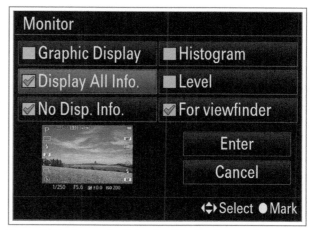

Figure 7-20. Screen for Selecting Display Screens for Monitor

Five of the six display screens available for the monitor are shown in Figure 7-21 through Figure 7-25. The screen displaying just the image with very little information is not shown here.

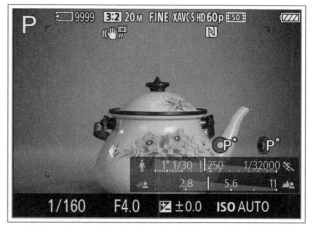

Figure 7-21. Graphic Display Screen in Use

Figure 7-21 shows the screen with the Graphic Display in the lower right corner. That display illustrates the use of faster shutter speeds to stop action and wider apertures to blur backgrounds. I find it distracting and not especially helpful, but if it is useful to you, by all means select it.

I find the Display All Information screen, shown in Figure 7-22, to be cluttered, but it has useful information.

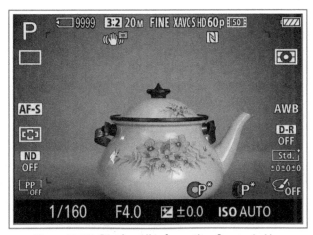

Figure 7-22. Display All Information Screen in Use

You can always move away from this screen by pressing the Display button (if there is at least one other display screen available), and I like to have it available for times when I need to see what settings are in effect. In addition, if you don't have this screen available, you won't be able to see icons that indicate the status of certain features, such as the ND Filter.

The third option, displaying minimal information, isn't shown here. That display is helpful for focusing and composing your shot, and I always include it in the cycle of display screens. If Focus Area is set to an option that displays a focus frame, such as Center, the frame is displayed on this screen. Also, the SteadyShot warning icon will flash if the camera is set to Auto, Program, or Aperture Priority mode, if the camera needs to set a slow shutter speed. The icon alerts you that you may need to use flash or a tripod, or to change a setting such as ISO to avoid motion blur from camera shake.

The next option, in Figure 7-23, is the histogram screen.

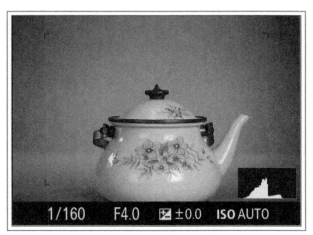

Figure 7-23. Histogram Screen in Use

This shooting mode histogram, unlike the one displayed in playback mode, shows only basic exposure information with no color data. However, it helps you decide whether your image will be well exposed, letting you adjust exposure compensation and other settings as appropriate while watching the live histogram on the screen. If you can make the histogram display look like a triangular mountain centered in the box, you are likely to have a good result.

You should try to keep the body of the histogram away from the right and left edges of the graph, in most cases. If the white area of the histogram runs into the left edge, that means shadow areas are clipping and details in those areas are being lost. If it hits the right edge, you are losing details in highlights. If you have to choose, it is best to keep the graph away from the right edge, because it is harder to recover details from clipped highlights than from clipped shadows.

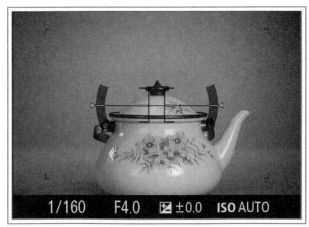

Figure 7-24. Level Screen in Use

The fifth available display screen, shown in Figure 7-24, shows the RX100 V's level, which is a useful tool for leveling the camera both side-to-side and front-to-back.

Watch the small orange lines on the screen; when the outer two ones have turned green, the camera is level side-to-side; when the inner two lines are green, the camera is level front-to-back.

The sixth choice, shown in Figure 7-25, which is available only for the monitor, is called For Viewfinder. This option is the only one that does not include the live view. Instead, it displays a black screen with detailed information about the camera's settings, so you can check your settings after (or before) you look at the live view in the viewfinder. In addition, as I discussed in Chapter 5, this screen is the basis for the Quick Navi system.

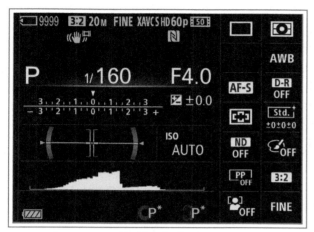

Figure 7-25. For Viewfinder Screen in Use

When you press the Function button, the settings on the screen become active. You can navigate through the settings using the direction buttons and adjust them using the Control wheel or the Control ring. The For Viewfinder screen does not appear while recording a movie or when the camera is in Movie mode.

Once you select the Display Button option and choose whether to select screens for the monitor or viewfinder, you can scroll through the six (monitor) or five (viewfinder) choices using the Control wheel or the direction buttons. When a screen you want to have displayed is highlighted, press the Center button to put an orange check mark in the box to the left of the screen's label, as seen in Figure 7-20.

You can also press that button to unmark a box. The camera will let you un-check all six of the items (or all five for the viewfinder), but if you do that, you will see an error message as you try to exit the menu screen. You have to check at least one box so that some screen will display when the camera is in shooting mode.

After you select from one to six screens for the monitor and one to five for the viewfinder, highlight the Enter block and press the Center button. Then, when the camera is in shooting mode, those screens will be displayed; cycle through them by pressing the Display button. If you have selected only one screen, pressing that button will have no effect in shooting mode when the live view is displayed.

Even if you select only the screen with practically no information, the LCD always displays shutter speed, aperture, exposure compensation, and ISO in the black strip below the image. With the viewfinder, the camera always displays those values at the bottom and displays Aspect Ratio, Image Size, Quality, File Format, and a few other values in a strip at the top of the screen.

PEAKING LEVEL

The Peaking Level option, shown in Figure 7-26, controls the camera's use of the Peaking display to assist with manual focus.

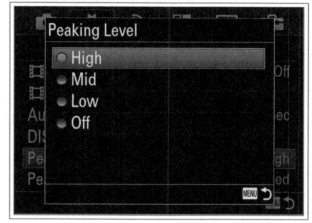

Figure 7-26. Peaking Level Menu Options Screen

By default, this option is turned off. You can turn the feature on with a level of Low, Mid, or High. When it is on and you are using manual focus or DMF, the camera places an outline with the selected intensity around any areas of the image that have edges the camera can distinguish. As focus becomes sharper, the lines become thicker. Figure 7-27 illustrates this feature with a composite image in which Peaking Level is turned off for the left image and set to Mid for the right image.

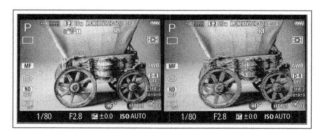

Figure 7-27. Peaking Level Composite Image

The idea is that these lines provide a clearer indication that focus is sharp than just relying on your judgment of sharpness. When I first used a camera with this feature, I found it distracting and not as useful as options such as MF Assist and Focus Magnifier that enlarge the screen for a clearer view when using manual focus. However, after further experience, I have come to appreciate the usefulness of the Peaking feature for some situations.

For example, as discussed in Chapter 9, I took some shots of the moon through a telescope connected to the RX100 V. I used manual focus and fine-tuned the focus using the controls on the telescope. The image on the camera's screen was unsteady because of the high magnification, and the moon did not have any features with edges that I could see clearly in the enlarged view. When I turned on Peaking Level to High with the red color selected, I found it much easier to focus; the camera displayed a broad band of red around the edge of the moon with red dots in craters when focus was sharp.

Some photographers set Creative Style to black and white while focusing so the Peaking color will stand out, and some like to set Peaking Level to Low so the color is not overwhelming, letting them see when the color just starts to appear. Some like to turn on MF Assist to enlarge the screen when using Peaking. You should experiment to find what approach works best for you.

For an excellent demonstration of how Peaking works, see this YouTube video posted by a participant in the Sony Cyber-shot Talk forum at dpreview.com at http://youtu.be/jMAlMQev7Kw.

Note that Peaking also works with DMF, even if you are using the autofocus function of that setting.

PEAKING COLOR

This option lets you choose red, yellow, or white for the color of the lines that the Peaking Level feature places around the edges of in-focus areas of the image. The default color is white. The Peaking Level feature is likely to be most useful when the color you choose for the effect contrasts with the main colors in your subject. As noted above, I found that the red color worked very well for shots of the moon; yellow or white may work well with darker subjects.

Screen 3 of the Custom menu is shown in Figure 7-28.

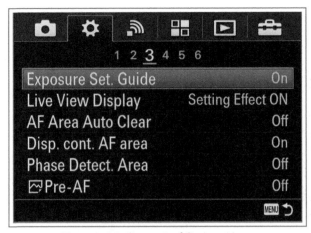

Figure 7-28. Screen 3 of Custom Menu

EXPOSURE SETTINGS GUIDE

The next option on the Custom menu, when turned on, places a circular display on the screen to simulate one or two rotating wheels showing the settings for aperture, shutter speed, or both, when you adjust those settings using the Control wheel. (When you adjust any of the above values using the Control ring, the camera always displays a circular scale in the top half of the screen.)

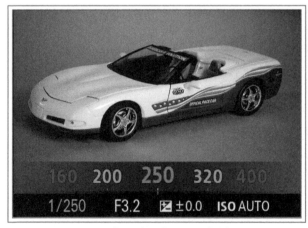

Figure 7-29. Exposure Settings Guide in Use

The display varies according to the shooting mode. In Program mode, two wheels display aperture and shutter speed when you activate Program Shift using the Control wheel. In Shutter Priority mode, a single wheel displays shutter speed as you adjust it. In Aperture Priority mode, a single wheel shows the aperture as you adjust it. In Manual mode, the display varies according to which value is currently being adjusted by the Control wheel. Figure 7-29 shows the display when shutter speed is being adjusted. I find this display distracting, so I leave it turned off, but it might be useful to see this display to let you know what value is being set, in some circumstances.

LIVE VIEW DISPLAY

This menu option can be important for getting results that match your expectations. It lets you choose whether or not the camera displays the effects that certain settings will have on your final image, while you are composing the image.

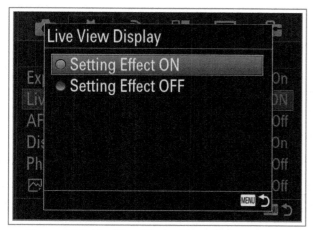

Figure 7-30. Live View Display Menu Options Screen

This option has two sub-options: Setting Effect On and Setting Effect Off, as seen in Figure 7-30. With Setting Effect On, the camera's display in shooting mode will show the effects of exposure compensation, white balance, Creative Style, and Picture Effect settings. In addition, it will show the effects of your aperture and shutter speed settings in Manual exposure mode and other advanced modes, including Movie mode.

In some cases, it may be helpful to see what effect a particular setting will have on the final image, and in other cases that display might be distracting or might make it difficult to take the shot.

For example, when you are setting white balance, it can be helpful to see how various options will alter the appearance of your images. If you have selected Setting Effect On, then, as you scroll through the white balance options, you will instantly see the effect of each setting, such as Daylight, Shade, and Incandescent. That change in the display is informative and not distracting.

However, if you are using the Picture Effect option and experimenting with a setting such as Posterization, which drastically alters the appearance of your images,

you might find it difficult to compose the image with Setting Effect On selected.

There is one use for the Live View Display menu option that I find practically indispensable. On occasion, I use the RX100 V to trigger external flash units using optical slaves, with the camera set to Manual exposure mode. For some of these shots, I may use settings such as f/11.0, 1/200 second, and ISO 80. Such a shot will be exposed properly with the flash units I am using, but, with Setting Effect On selected, the camera's screen is completely dark as I compose the shot. That is because the camera's programming does not account for the fact that flash units will be fired.

With Setting Effect Off, the camera displays the scene using the available ambient light, ignoring the settings I have made. In this way, I can see the scene on the camera's display in order to compose the shot properly.

The Setting Effect On option, though, can be useful when using Aperture Priority, Shutter Priority, or Manual exposure mode when you are shooting in unusually dark or bright conditions, because the camera's display screen will change its brightness to alert you that a normal exposure may not be possible with the current settings. (You should see the aperture, shutter speed, ISO, or other value flashing to alert you to this situation, also.)

With the Picture Effect setting, some of the options will not change the appearance of the display, even with this setting activated, because the effects are added while the image is being processed. Those options are Soft Focus, HDR Painting, Rich-tone Monochrome (the display will appear black and white, but without the rich-tone processing), Miniature, Watercolor, and Illustration.

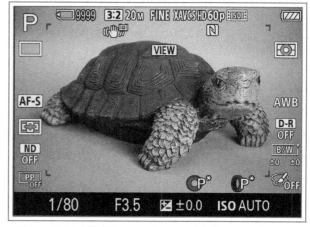

Figure 7-31. VIEW Icon on Screen with Setting Effect Off

When the Setting Effect Off option is selected, the camera will display a VIEW icon on the screen, as shown in Figure 7-31, to remind you that the camera's display is not showing the effects of all your settings.

My recommendation is to leave this option at Setting Effect On unless it is difficult to compose a shot, either because the display is too dark or light, or because a setting such as Picture Effect interferes with your ability to view the subject clearly.

In the Auto, Scene, Sweep Panorama, Movie, and HFR shooting modes, this option is forced to Setting Effect On and cannot be changed.

AF Area Auto Clear

This option controls whether or not the camera continues to display one or more green focus frames after it has achieved sharp focus when the focus mode is set to single AF. By default, this option is turned off, so the autofocus area is not cleared from the display when focus is achieved; the green frame or frames remain on the display until you press the shutter button all the way down to capture an image. If you turn this option on through the menu, then the frame or frames will disappear from the display after about one second, so you can have a clear view of the subject before you press the shutter button all the way down to take the picture.

What setting you use for this option is a matter of personal preference. I usually don't mind seeing the green focus frames on the display, so I leave this option turned off most of the time. There could be situations, though, when you want to confirm focus by viewing the green frames, but then want to see the subject clearly again without the frames, before you actually capture an image.

Display Continuous AF Area

This option can be turned either on or off. When it is turned on, it controls whether the camera displays small, green focus blocks to show what area of the scene is in focus, when the focus mode is set to continuous autofocus and the Focus Area menu option is set to Wide. If this option is turned off, the camera does not display any focus frames or blocks under those conditions.

I find this option useful, because, without it, there is no obvious way to tell what part of the scene or subject is

currently in focus. With continuous autofocus in effect and Focus Area set to Wide, the camera's autofocus mechanism adjusts constantly as you half-press the shutter button, and there is no frame or other indicator that shows where the focus is being set, other than judging with your own eyes what parts of the image look sharper than others. When this menu option is turned on, the camera displays a constantly changing set of focus blocks, as shown in Figure 7-32, as the autofocus mechanism selects a main subject to focus on within the boundaries of the Wide Focus Area setting.

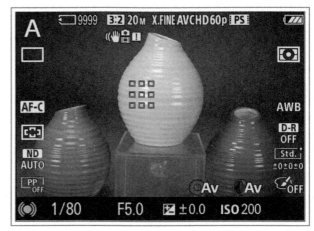

Figure 7-32. Focus Blocks on Display for Continuous AF

Phase Detection Area

One of the prime features of the Sony RX100 V camera is its fast and efficient autofocus system. The RX100 V uses both contrast detection and phase detection for autofocus. With contrast detection, which uses 25 focus points, the camera looks for areas of contrast in the subject and focuses the image by checking the contrast level as the focus distance changes. With phase detection, the camera uses 315 individual focus points, at which the camera checks to see if the image is in focus by comparing two signals to see if they are in phase. Phase detection is considerably faster than contrast detection, so it can be useful to know exactly where the phase detection focus points are located. Phase detection functions only when the aperture is set to f/8.0 or wider (lower f-numbers).

With this menu option, you can turn on or off a display that shows the area where the 315 phase detection focus points are located. When it is turned on, the shooting screen looks like Figure 7-33, with a large frame that shows the boundaries of the area containing the 315 focus points. When this option is turned off, that frame is not displayed. The frame is not displayed while recording movies.

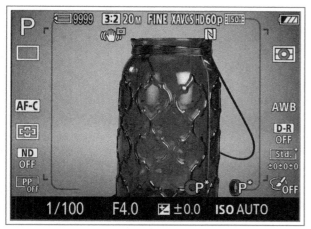

Figure 7-33. Phase Detection Area Turned On

Whether or not to display this frame is a personal preference. For general use, you may not need it, and it could prove slightly distracting. If you are photographing a difficult subject and may need to know whether the phase detection focus points will cover the subject, this option could be worth using.

PRE-AF

The Pre-AF setting affects the way the RX100 V uses autofocus for still images. When this option is turned on and the focus mode is single AF or continuous AF, the camera continuously tries to focus on a subject, even before you press the shutter button halfway. With this setting, the camera's battery is depleted more quickly than normal, but the final focusing may be speeded up because the camera can reach an approximate focus adjustment before you press the shutter button to evaluate focus and take the picture. If this setting is turned off, the camera makes no attempt to focus until you press the shutter button halfway to check focus.

This setting has no effect for recording video. When recording video, the camera always focuses continuously when autofocus is turned on.

I usually leave the Pre-AF setting turned off to avoid running the battery down. But, if I were taking pictures of moving subjects, I might activate this setting to speed up the focusing process.

Screen 4 of the Custom menu is shown in Figure 7-34.

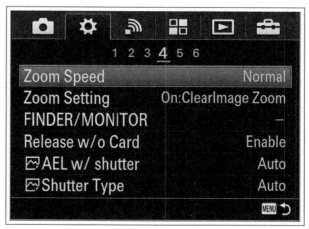

Figure 7-34. Screen 4 of Custom Menu

ZOOM SPEED

This option, which can be set to Normal or Fast, controls how quickly the lens zooms in or out when you move the zoom lever. It also controls the speed of zooming the lens when you are using an optional wired remote control, as discussed in Appendix A. The setting for this item depends on your preference. You may prefer the smoother zooming of the Normal setting, especially if you like to find an intermediate focal length for your shots. But, if you like to change focal lengths quickly to zoom all the way in or out, the Fast setting will save some time.

If you want to increase the speed of zooming using the Control ring, use the Zoom Function on Ring option on screen 6 of the Custom menu, discussed later in this chapter, and set the value to Quick instead of Standard.

ZOOM SETTING

The Zoom Setting option provides two ways to give the RX100 V extra zoom range, using features called Clear Image Zoom and Digital Zoom. To explain these features in context, I will discuss all three zoom methods that the camera offers—optical zoom, Clear Image Zoom, and Digital Zoom. I will also discuss a fourth feature that is related to these, called Smart Zoom.

Optical zoom is the camera's "natural" zoom capability—moving the lens elements so they magnify the image, just as binoculars do. You can call optical zoom a "real" zoom because it increases the information that the lens gathers. The optical zoom of the RX100 V operates within a range from 24mm at the wide-angle setting to the fully zoomed-in telephoto setting of 70mm.

To complicate matters a bit, the actual optical zoom range of the RX100 V's lens is 8.8mm to 25.7mm; you can see those numbers on the end of the lens. You also see the actual zoom range numbers on the detailed screen in playback mode. But the numbers that are normally used to describe the zoom range of a compact camera's lens are the "35mm-equivalent" figures, which translate the actual zoom range into what the range would be if this were a lens on a camera that uses 35mm film. This translation is done because many photographers are familiar with the zoom ranges and focal lengths of lenses for traditional 35mm cameras, on which a 50mm lens is considered "normal." I use the 35mm-equivalent figures throughout this book.

The Digital Zoom feature of the RX100 V magnifies the image electronically without any special processing to improve the quality. This type of zoom does not really increase the information gathered by the lens; rather, it just increases the apparent size of the image by enlarging the pixels within the area captured by the lens. On some cameras, the amount of digital zoom can be very large, such as 100 times normal, but such a large figure can be considered as a marketing ploy to lure customers, rather than a feature of real value to the photographer.

The other option on the RX100 V, Clear Image Zoom, is a special type of digital zoom developed by Sony. With this feature, the RX100 V does not just magnify the area of the image; rather, the camera analyzes the image and adds pixels through interpolation. This system produces a smoother, more realistic enlargement than the Digital Zoom feature. With Clear Image Zoom, the camera achieves greater quality than with Digital Zoom, though not as much as with the "pure" optical zoom.

Finally, there is another way the RX100 V can use a zoom range greater than normal optical zoom with no loss of image quality. The standard range of 24mm to 70mm is available when Image Size is set to Large. However, if Image Size is set to Medium, Small, or VGA, the camera needs only a portion of the pixels on the image sensor to create the image at the reduced size. It can use the "extra" pixels to enlarge the view of the scene. This process, which Sony calls Smart Zoom, is similar to what you can do using software such as Photoshop. If the image size does not need to be

Large, you can crop out some pixels from the center (or other area) of the image and enlarge that area, thereby retaining the same overall image size with a magnified view of the scene.

With Smart Zoom, if you set Image Size to M, S, or VGA, the camera can zoom to a greater range than with Image Size set to L and still keep the full quality of the optical zoom. You will end up with lower-resolution images, but that may not be a problem if you are going to post them on a website or share them via e-mail.

In short, optical zoom provides the best quality for magnifying the scene; Clear Image Zoom gives excellent quality; and Digital Zoom produces magnification with reduced image quality. Smart Zoom gives you greater zoom range with no image deterioration, but at the expense of resolution.

Here is how to use these settings. I will assume for this discussion that you are leaving Image Size set to L, because that is the best setting for excellent results in printing and editing your images.

When you select the Zoom Setting menu option and press the Center button, the camera displays the screen shown in Figure 7-35, giving you the choice of Optical Zoom Only; On: Clear Image Zoom; or On: Digital Zoom. If you turn on Digital Zoom, Clear Image Zoom will automatically be activated also. Optical Zoom is always available, no matter what settings are used.

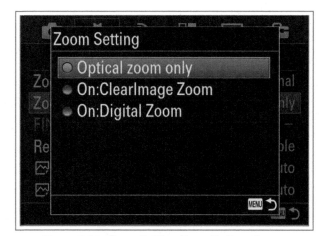

Figure 7-35. Zoom Setting Menu Options Screen

If you turn on only Clear Image Zoom, you will have greater zoom range than normal, as discussed above, with minimal quality loss. If you also turn on Digital Zoom, you will get even greater zoom range, but quality will suffer as the lens is zoomed past the Clear Image Zoom range. When these various settings are in effect, you will see different indications on the camera's display.

In Figure 7-36, Image Size is set to L and both Clear Image Zoom and Digital Zoom are turned off. The zoom indicator at the top of the screen goes only as far as 70mm.

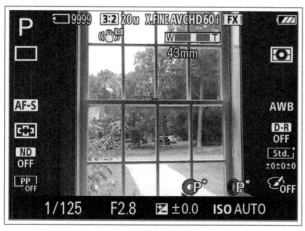

Figure 7-36. Zoom Scale with Optical Zoom Only

In Figure 7-37, Clear Image Zoom is turned on. The zoom indicator shows the lens can zoom to 2.0 times the normal range. There is a small vertical line in the center of the zoom scale showing where the zoom changes from optical-only to expanded (Clear Image Zoom or Digital Zoom, depending on the settings). The magnifying glass icon with the "C" beneath the scale means Clear Image Zoom is turned on.

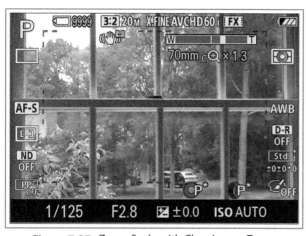

Figure 7-37. Zoom Scale with Clear Image Zoom

Once the lens zooms past the optical zoom range, the sound of the zoom mechanism stops, so you can tell by listening when the camera has entered the range of Clear Image Zoom and Digital Zoom.

In Figure 7-38, both Clear Image Zoom and Digital Zoom are turned on, and the zoom indicator can go up to four times normal magnification. The magnifying glass icon beneath the scale has a "D" beside it, indicating that Digital Zoom is now in effect.

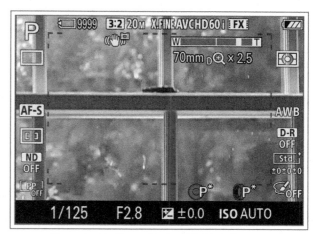

Figure 7-38. Zoom Scale with Digital Zoom

With an Image Size setting smaller than Large, the zoom indicator will use a letter S to show that the camera is using Smart Zoom, as the zoom range extends beyond the standard optical zoom range. For example, in Figure 7-39, with Image Size set to Small, the lens is zoomed in to 1.6 times the optical range, and the zoom indicator displays an S to indicate that Smart Zoom is in effect. With smaller image sizes, the ranges of Clear Image Zoom and Digital Zoom also are expanded.

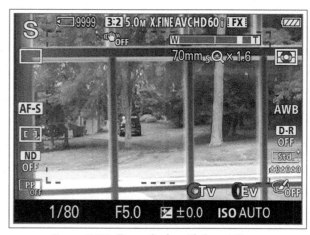

Figure 7-39. Zoom Scale with Smart Zoom

For example, as shown in Figure 7-40, with Image Size set to Small and Digital Zoom turned on, the lens can be zoomed in to 8.0 times the normal optical range.

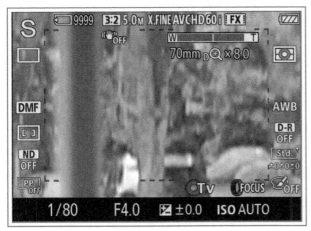

Figure 7-40. Zoom Scale with Digital Zoom and Small Image Size

Table 7-1 shows the zoom ranges available with Image Size set to Large, Medium, and Small, with settings of Optical Zoom, Clear Image Zoom, and Digital Zoom. In all cases, Aspect Ratio is 3:2; with other Aspect Ratio settings, results would be different. (If Aspect Ratio is set to 4:3, the VGA setting for Image Size becomes available, which would add other values to the table.)

Table 7-1.   **Maximum Zoom Range at Various Image Sizes**

	Large	Medium	Small
Optical Zoom (with no deterioration)	70mm	98mm	140mm
Clear Image Zoom (with minimal deterioration)	140mm	196mm	280mm
Digital Zoom (with significant deterioration)	280mm	392mm	560mm

To summarize the situation with zoom, when Image Size is set to Large, you can zoom up to 70mm with no deterioration using optical zoom; you can zoom to about 140mm with minimal deterioration using Clear Image Zoom; and you can zoom to about 280mm using Digital Zoom but with significant deterioration.

My preference is to limit the camera to optical zoom and avoid any deterioration. However, many photographers have found that Clear Image Zoom yields surprisingly good results, and it is worth using when you cannot get close to your subject. I do not like to use Digital Zoom to take a picture. However, it can be useful to zoom in to meter a specific area of a distant subject, or to check the composition of your shot before zooming back out and taking the shot using Clear Image Zoom or optical zoom.

Clear Image Zoom and Digital Zoom are not available when shooting Raw images, when the Smile Shutter or face detection is in use, or in Sweep Panorama mode. They also are unavailable when you are recording a video with Record Setting set to 120p (100p for PAL settings) or when the Mode dial is set to HFR. Smart Zoom is not available when recording movies.

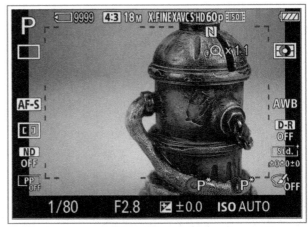

Figure 7-41. Dotted Focus Frame for Non-optical Zoom

Whenever the lens is zoomed into the range of Clear Image Zoom or Digital Zoom, the Focus Area option is disabled and the camera uses a broad focus frame, which is represented by the dotted area seen in Figure 7-41. Any Metering Mode setting other than Multi is set to Multi when non-optical zoom is in use, but only once the lens is actually zoomed past the optical zoom range. It reverts back to the previous setting if the lens is zoomed back within the optical zoom range.

FINDER/MONITOR

This next option on the Custom menu, shown in Figure 7-42, lets you choose whether to view menus and shooting and playback displays on the RX100 V's LCD screen or in the viewfinder. The viewfinder can provide the same information as the LCD screen (depending on menu settings), but its display is viewed inside an eye-level window that is shaded from daylight, giving you a clear view of the shooting, playback, and menu screens.

By default, this option is set to Auto, which means the camera switches the view to the viewfinder automatically when you move your head near the camera, if the viewfinder has been popped up. The camera turns on the viewfinder display and blacks out the LCD. (There is a small eye sensor to the right of the viewfinder that detects the presence of an object nearby.)

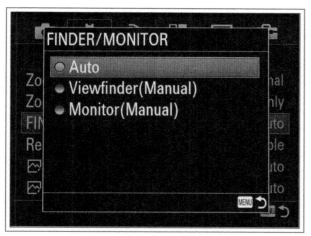

Figure 7-42. Finder/Monitor Menu Options Screen

If you prefer to use the viewfinder at all times, set this option to Viewfinder (Manual). With that setting, the camera will turn off the LCD and will leave the viewfinder active at all times while it is popped up.

To put this another way, with the Auto setting the camera will activate the LCD screen when you are not using the viewfinder; with the Viewfinder setting, the camera will never activate the LCD screen, unless you retract the viewfinder. When you retract the viewfinder, the camera will always use the LCD screen.

My preference is to use the Auto setting because I find it convenient to view the image on the LCD unless conditions are quite bright. If you prefer to use the viewfinder, you may want to use the Viewfinder (Manual) setting so the camera will never turn off the viewfinder until you press it back down into the camera. You may want to use the Monitor (Manual) setting if, for example, you have the camera on a tripod and are moving your head (or hands) close to the camera while composing your shots, but don't want the view to shift to the viewfinder. Of course, you could just retract the viewfinder in that case, but it's good to have this option for occasions when it might be useful.

RELEASE WITHOUT CARD

This option can be set to either Enable or Disable. If it is set to Enable, you can operate the camera's shutter release button even if there is no memory card inserted in the camera. In that case, the camera will display a NO CARD warning message, but it will let you operate

the shutter and an image will be saved temporarily. This setting is useful if the camera is on display in a retail store, so customers can operate the controls and see how a saved image would look, without having to have an expensive memory card left in the camera. As I noted in Chapter 1, there is no easy way to save an image taken when this setting is active, although in an emergency you may be able to send the image through the HDMI port to a video capture device.

If you select Disable, the NO CARD warning still appears. In addition, if you try to press the shutter button, the camera will display a warning message advising that the shutter cannot be operated with no memory card inserted, as shown in Figure 7-43. This setting may be best to protect against operating the camera when there is no card inserted to save images or videos.

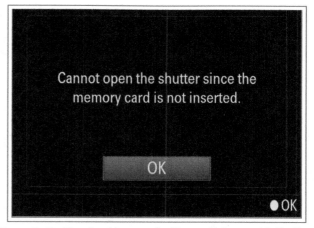

Figure 7-43. Warning Message for Shutter Release with No Card

AEL WITH SHUTTER

This menu item, whose options screen is shown in Figure 7-44, controls how the shutter button handles autoexposure lock for still images. There are three possible settings for this feature: Auto, On, and Off.

With the default option, Auto, pressing the shutter button halfway locks exposure when the focus mode is set to AF-S for single-shot autofocus or DMF for direct manual focus. When the focus mode is set to AF-C for continuous AF or MF for manual focus, pressing the shutter button halfway does not lock exposure. When the focus mode is set to AF-A for automatic AF, pressing the shutter button halfway locks exposure if the subject and camera are motionless. However, if the camera detects motion, it switches into continuous AF mode, and pressing the shutter button does not lock focus or exposure.

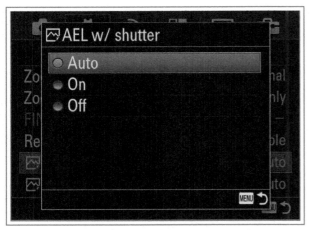

Figure 7-44. AEL w/Shutter Menu Options Screen

If AEL with Shutter is On, pressing the shutter button halfway locks exposure in all situations, regardless of what focus mode is in effect. So, for example, if the focus mode is set to continuous autofocus, pressing the shutter button halfway locks exposure, though the focus mechanism will continue adjusting focus.

If this option is set to Off, pressing the shutter button halfway never locks exposure, in any focus mode. You may want to use this setting when you need to press the shutter button halfway to lock focus and then move the camera to change the composition somewhat. You might want the camera to re-evaluate the exposure, even though you have already locked the focus.

If this option is set to Off or Auto with continuous autofocus in use, a half-press of the shutter button locks the aperture setting but does not lock the overall exposure.

One important use for this option is with the continuous shooting settings of Drive Mode. As I discussed in Chapter 4, if you want the camera to adjust exposure for each shot in a burst, you need to set AEL with Shutter to Off, or Auto if using continuous AF or automatic AF. Otherwise, the camera will lock exposure with the first shot and will not adjust it if the lighting changes during the burst.

Of course, you may not want to use those settings in that scenario, because exposure adjustment can slow the burst of shots, and, depending on the situation, it may not be likely that lighting will change during a

brief burst of shots. But this option is available for times when you want the camera to keep evaluating and adjusting exposure while you take a burst of shots.

SHUTTER TYPE

This last option on screen 4 of the Custom menu lets you determine whether the RX100 V uses its mechanical shutter or its electronic shutter for still images. One of the many advanced features of this camera is that it is equipped with both types of shutter, giving you flexibility for various types of still photography.

With the mechanical shutter, the camera can use shutter speeds from 1/2000 second to 30 seconds, plus the BULB setting, with which you can hold the shutter open as long as you need to. In addition, the camera can synchronize its flash with the mechanical shutter at any setting, including 1/2000 second. With the electronic shutter, the camera can use shutter speeds from 1/32000 second to 30 seconds, but with no BULB setting, and it can synchronize with its flash only at speeds of 1/100 second or slower.

There are several considerations for choosing mechanical or electronic for the shutter type. First, if you need a super-fast shutter speed such as 1/20000 second, you need to use the electronic shutter. You might want a speed in that range if you are taking photos in very bright conditions but still want to use a fairly wide aperture to blur the background. You also might want to use a very fast shutter speed in order to maximize the rate of continuous shooting, or to ensure that you get sharp images of fast action at a sporting event. Also, you can use the electronic shutter when you want to minimize the sounds made by the camera, such as if you are shooting in a museum or other place where sounds should be kept to a minimum. The mechanical shutter makes a sound that cannot be disabled; you can disable the sound of the electronic shutter using the Audio Signals option on screen 1 of the Setup menu. However, the sound of the mechanical shutter is quite faint, and I have not found the shutter sound to be a major factor in choosing a shutter type.

You might use the mechanical shutter if you need the BULB setting for exposures longer than 30 seconds, or if you need to synchronize the flash with a shutter speed faster than 1/100 second. You also might use the mechanical shutter to avoid distortion that can take place in some cases from use of the electronic shutter, such as when shooting under fluorescent lighting.

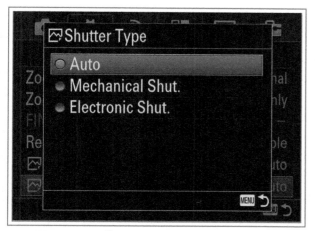

Figure 7-45. Shutter Type Menu Options Screen

This option has three choices, shown in Figure 7-45: Auto, Mechanical Shutter, or Electronic Shutter. With Auto, the camera determines which shutter type to use based on the current conditions, including what shutter speed is called for by the exposure reading. With Mechanical Shutter or Electronic Shutter, the specified shutter type is always used, with a few exceptions. Specifically, even if Shutter Type is set to Electronic Shutter, the mechanical shutter will be used if a custom white balance is being used or if Face Registration is turned on. When Shutter Type is set to Electronic Shutter, Long Exposure Noise Reduction is not available.

Screen 5 of the Custom menu is shown in Figure 7-46.

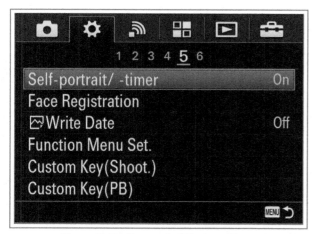

Figure 7-46. Screen 5 of Custom Menu

SELF-PORTRAIT TIMER

This first option on screen 5 of the Custom menu can be turned either on or off. If it is turned on, then,

when you flip the LCD screen up and around so it faces forward, the camera will display a large three-step countdown timer when you press the shutter button, so you can get ready for a self-portrait. The timer screen is shown in Figure 7-47. It includes a three-second self-timer icon in the upper left corner. If this menu option is turned off, you can still take a self-portrait, but without the on-screen timer.

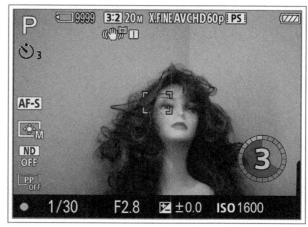

Figure 7-47. Self-portrait Timer Countdown Screen

When you use this option, the camera locks focus when you press the shutter button to start the timer, and, if your position changes during the countdown, the focus may be incorrect.

To avoid this problem, you can turn off this option and take the picture with no delay. Another approach is to use the Smart Remote Embedded app to control the camera, as discussed in Chapter 9, or a wired remote control as discussed in Appendix A. Or, you can just make sure your face does not change its distance from the camera after you press the shutter button to start the self-portrait timer.

FACE REGISTRATION

This next option lets you register human faces so the RX100 V can give those faces priority for face detection. You can register up to eight faces and assign each one a rank from one to eight, with one being the highest. Then, when you set the Shooting menu option for Smile/Face Detection to On (Registered Faces), the camera will try to detect the registered faces first in the order you have assigned them. This feature can be useful if, for example, you take pictures at school functions and you want to make sure the camera focuses on your own children.

To use this menu option, select it and on the next screen, shown in Figure 7-48, select New Registration. Press the Center button, and the camera will place a square frame on the screen.

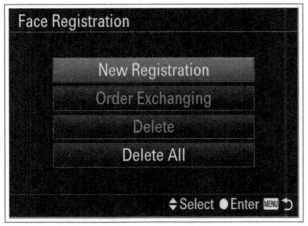

Figure 7-48. Face Registration Menu Options Screen

Compose a shot with the face to be registered inside that frame, as shown in Figure 7-49, and press the shutter button to take a picture of that face.

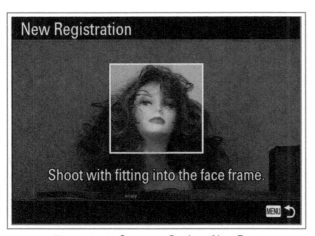

Figure 7-49. Screen to Register New Face

If the process works, the camera will display that face with the message "Register face?" Highlight the Enter bar on that screen and press the Center button to complete the registration process. Later, you can use the Order Exchanging option to change the priorities of the registered faces, and you can delete registered faces individually or all at once using other menu options.

WRITE DATE

This next setting on the Custom menu embeds the date in the lower right corner of your still images, as shown in Figure 7-50. This embedding is permanent, so

the information cannot be deleted other than through cropping or other editing procedures. Use this option only if you want the date recorded permanently on your images, perhaps for a scientific research project.

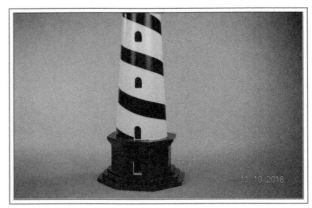

Figure 7-50. Write Date Option in Use

Be careful that you do not leave this setting turned on when you don't want the date imprinted on your images; the camera does not put any indication on the display screen that this setting is in effect. This option is not available when Quality is set to Raw or Raw & JPEG, with panoramas, bracketing, continuous shooting, or in Movie or HFR mode.

FUNCTION MENU SETTINGS

When you press the Function button in shooting mode, the camera displays up to 12 options in blocks at the bottom of the display, as shown in Figure 7-51.

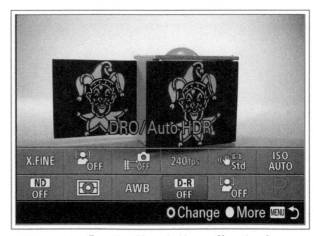

Figure 7-51. Function Menu in Use on Shooting Screen

You move through those options with the direction buttons. Adjust the main settings with the Control wheel or the Control ring. To make secondary settings, press the Center button to go to the regular menu screen for the option being adjusted.

Use the Function Menu Settings menu item to assign options to the Function menu. When you select this option, the camera initially shows the screen in Figure 7-52, listing the assignments for the upper six blocks of the Function menu.

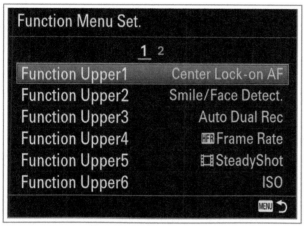

Figure 7-52. Screen to Assign Function Menu Blocks

On screen 2 of the menu item, you can make assignments for the lower six blocks. When you press the Center button on any one of these 12 lines, you will see a screen like that in Figure 7-53, listing the options that can be assigned to that block.

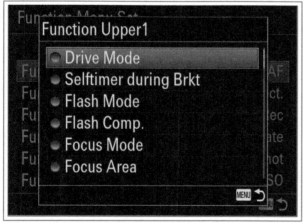

Figure 7-53. Screen Listing Possible Assignments for Function Menu Block

For each menu block, the possible assignments are:

- Drive Mode

- Self-timer During Bracketing

- Flash Mode

- Flash Compensation

- Focus Mode

- Focus Area

- Exposure Compensation

- ISO

- ISO Auto Minimum Shutter Speed

- ND Filter

- Metering Mode

- White Balance

- DRO/Auto HDR

- Creative Style

- Shoot Mode

- Picture Effect

- Picture Profile

- Frame Rate [for HFR Movies]

- Center Lock-on AF

- Smile/Face Detection

- Auto Dual Recording

- Soft Skin Effect

- Auto Object Framing

- Image Size

- Aspect Ratio

- Quality

- SteadyShot (Still Images)

- SteadyShot (Movies)

- Zebra

- Grid Line

- Marker Display

- Peaking Level

- Peaking Color

- Gamma Display Assist

- Not Set

Press the Center button when the option you want to assign to a given block is displayed, and the camera will place an orange dot on that line to indicate that that feature is assigned to that block.

I recommend assigning a function to each of the 12 blocks and experiment to find the best setup. Remember that you can use the Control ring and the Custom, Center, Left, and Right buttons for your most important settings, such as, perhaps, ISO, Creative Style, Drive Mode, ND Filter, and Focus Area, so you can reserve these 12 blocks for other options.

CUSTOM KEY (SHOOTING)

I described this menu option in Chapter 5, in discussing physical controls that can have settings assigned to them. Now I will discuss the settings that can be assigned to these controls.

When you select the Custom Key (Shooting) option, you will see the screen shown in Figure 7-54.

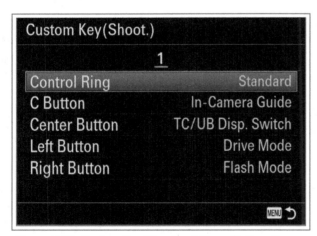

Figure 7-54. Custom Key (Shooting) Menu Options Screen

Navigate to the line for a control and press the Center Button. You will see a screen listing all the options that can be assigned to that control. In most cases, these assignments are self-explanatory. When you assign a function, such as ISO, to a button, pressing the button calls up the menu screen for the option, which lets you adjust it as if you had selected it from the Shooting menu.

However, there are differences for some controls, and there are some items that can be assigned through this option that are not available through any menu. I will discuss these details below.

Control Ring

The first control on the Custom Key (Shooting) menu screen is the Control ring. This control is a special case, because, of course, it is not a button but a ring. The options that can be assigned to the ring are Standard, Exposure Compensation, ISO, White Balance, Creative Style, Picture Effect, Zoom, Shutter Speed, Aperture, or Not Set, the first six of which are shown in Figure 7-55. You have to scroll down to see the remaining options.

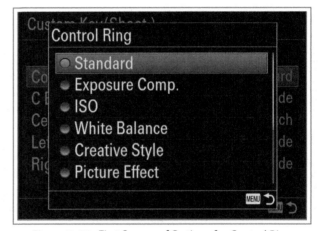

Figure 7-55. First Screen of Options for Control Ring

This feature is powerful because, when you assign a setting such as ISO to this ring, you can use the ring to adjust the setting instantly. For example, if you choose ISO, then, when the camera is in shooting mode, all you have to do is turn the Control ring and the ISO setting will change. You can then immediately press the shutter button to take a picture with the new setting.

However, you cannot get access to all aspects of these settings by turning the ring. For example, if you assign ISO to the ring, you can select a numerical ISO value or Auto ISO, but you cannot set the minimum and maximum settings for Auto ISO, and you cannot select a value for the Multi Frame Noise Reduction setting.

Similarly, if you assign white balance to the Control ring, you can select a white balance setting, including Custom or Color Temperature, but you cannot set a new Custom White Balance or choose a new Color Temperature setting, and you cannot fine-tune the white balance using the color axes. For those options, you need to use the White Balance menu option. Likewise, with Creative Style assigned to the ring, you cannot adjust the contrast, sharpness, and saturation parameters of a selected setting.

However, with Picture Effect, you can select any of the settings or sub-settings, because the Control ring will cycle through all of the options, including, for example, the sub-settings for Toy Camera, which are Normal, Cool, Warm, Green, and Magenta.

When the Control ring has been assigned to a function, the camera puts an icon representing the ring in the bottom right of the screen next to an icon or label indicating the setting currently assigned to the ring. For example, Figure 7-56 shows the screen as it appears when ISO has been assigned to the Control ring.

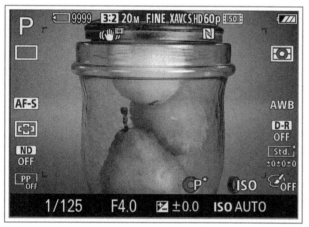

Figure 7-56. Icon Showing Control Ring Adjusts ISO

By default the Control ring's function is set to Standard. In that case, the ring controls various functions in the various shooting modes, as shown in Table 7-2.

Table 7-2. Control Ring: Standard Setting—Shooting Modes vs. Assigned Functions

Shooting Mode	Assigned Function
Intelligent Auto	Zoom
Superior Auto	Zoom
Program	Program Shift
Aperture Priority	Aperture
Shutter Priority	Shutter Speed
Manual Exposure	Aperture
Scene	Scene Selection
Sweep Panorama	Direction

Table 7-2. Control Ring: Standard Setting—Shooting Modes vs. Assigned Functions

Movie/HFR	Depends on Movie or HFR exposure mode setting
Memory Recall	Depends on saved setting

Or you can choose the final option, Not Set, in which case the ring will control only manual focus from the shooting screen. (It also will select items with the Function menu and Quick Navi system.) In my opinion, the Standard option is the most useful, but you might prefer to use the Control ring for one specific purpose, such as controlling exposure compensation, ISO, or zoom for all shooting modes.

C (Custom) Button

If you select C Button from the Custom Key (Shooting) menu screen, the camera will display a screen like that shown in Figure 7-57, which lists the first six of the many options that can be assigned to the Custom button.

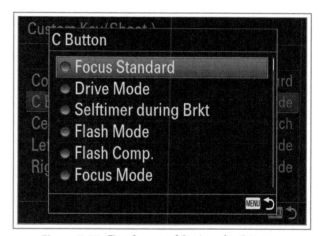

Figure 7-57. First Screen of Options for C Button

The complete list, which is much longer than a single screen, includes all of the following choices, any one of which can be assigned to this button:

- Focus Standard

- Drive Mode

- Self-timer During Bracketing

- Flash Mode

- Flash Compensation

- Focus Mode

- Focus Area
- Exposure Compensation
- ISO
- ISO Auto Minimum Shutter Speed
- ND Filter
- Metering Mode
- White Balance
- DRO/Auto HDR
- Creative Style
- Picture Effect
- Picture Profile
- Frame Rate [for HFR movies]
- Smile/Face Detection
- Auto Dual Recording
- Soft Skin Effect
- Auto Object Framing
- SteadyShot (Still Images)
- SteadyShot (Movies)
- Image Size
- Aspect Ratio
- Quality
- In-Camera Guide
- Memory
- AEL Hold
- AEL Toggle
- Spot AEL Hold
- Spot AEL Toggle
- AF/MF Control Hold
- AF/MF Control Toggle
- Center Lock-on AF

- Eye AF
- Bright Monitoring
- Focus Magnifier
- Deactivate Monitor
- Movie [duplicates function of red Movie button]
- Zebra
- Grid Line
- Marker Display Selection
- Peaking Level
- Peaking Color
- Finder/Monitor Selection
- Send to Smartphone
- Download Application
- Application List
- Monitor Brightness
- Gamma Display Assist
- TC/UB Display Switch
- Not Set

Scroll through the list and press the Center button to make your selection. The dot next to the chosen option will turn orange to mark the choice.

Many of these options are self-explanatory because, when the button has the option assigned, pressing the button will simply call up the menu screen for that option, if the option is available in the current shooting mode. For example, if the Custom button is assigned to Drive Mode, then, when you press the button, the camera displays the Drive Mode menu, just as if you had used the Menu button to get access to that option. (In some cases the screen looks different from the menu screen called up with the Menu button, but the regular menu options are available in every case.) I will not discuss those options here; see Chapter 4 for discussion of the Shooting menu, Chapter 7 for discussion of the Custom and Setup menus, and Chapter 9 for discussion of the Wi-Fi and Application menus. The In-Camera Guide option is not available from a menu, but it is the default setting for this button; I discussed it in Chapter 5. When this function is assigned, you can press the C button when a menu option is highlighted to bring up a help screen with information about that option.

In a few cases, the assigned button switches between menu options without first calling up a menu screen. For example, this is the case with the Marker Display Select, Finder/Monitor Select, and TC/UB Display Switch options.

There are several other selections for the Custom button (and the other control buttons) that do not call up a menu screen. Instead, they perform a function that is not available from a menu option. I will discuss those selections below.

Focus Standard

I discussed this option in Chapter 5, where I discussed the physical controls, because this option is assigned by default to the Center button. If you wish, you can assign it to the C button instead, and free up the Center button for another assignment. When either button is assigned to the Focus Standard option, it has two functions when pressed while the shooting screen is displayed. First, if Focus Area is set to Flexible Spot or Expand Flexible Spot, pressing the Focus Standard button makes the focus frame movable, allowing you to re-position it on the display. Second, if Center Lock-on AF is turned on with single AF in effect and Focus Area set to Wide or Center, pressing the assigned button initiates tracking of the subject in the center of the display.

AEL Hold

If you set the Custom button to the AEL Hold (Autoexposure Lock Hold) option, then, when the camera is in shooting mode, pressing this button will lock exposure at the current setting as metered by the camera, as long as you hold down the button. You also can lock exposure by pressing the shutter button halfway, if AEL with Shutter is in effect, as discussed earlier in this chapter. If that option is not in effect, you can use AEL Hold instead.

You might want to use AEL Hold to calibrate exposure for an object that is part of a larger scene, such as a dark painting on a light wall. You could lock exposure while holding the camera close to the painting, then move back to take a picture of the wall with the locked exposure ensuring the painting will be properly exposed.

Assuming the camera is in Program mode, hold the camera close to the painting until the metered aperture and shutter speed appear on the screen. Press and hold the Custom button and an asterisk (*) will appear in the lower right corner of the screen, as shown in Figure 7-58, indicating that exposure lock is in effect.

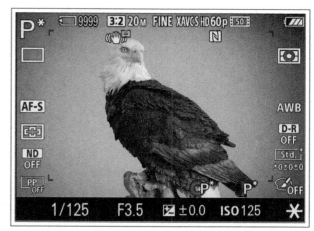

Figure 7-58. Shooting Screen When AEL Hold in Effect

Now you can move back (or anywhere else) and take the photograph using the exposure setting that you locked in. Once you have finished using the locked exposure setting, release the Custom button to make the asterisk disappear. The camera is now ready to measure a new exposure reading.

If the camera is set to Manual exposure mode, pressing a control button assigned to AEL Hold activates Manual Shift, which I discussed in Chapter 3. While you hold down the button for AEL Hold, if you change the aperture or shutter speed, the camera will select a corresponding shutter speed or aperture to maintain the original exposure. This feature operates whether ISO is set to ISO Auto or to a numerical value.

AEL Toggle

If you set the Custom button to the AEL Toggle option, then, in shooting mode, pressing the button will lock exposure just as with AEL Hold. The difference with this setting is that you just press and release the button; the exposure will remain locked until you press the button again to cancel the exposure lock.

Spot AEL Hold

The next option for the Custom button is AEL Hold with a spot icon before the name. The spot icon means that, with this setting, when you press the button and hold it, the camera will lock exposure as metered by the spot-metering area in the center of the display, no matter what metering method is currently in effect. This option can be useful if you want to switch to spot-metering just for one or two shots. You can hold down the Custom button, make sure the center of the display covers the area you want to use for evaluating exposure, and take the shot with the exposure adjusted for that spot.

Spot AEL Toggle

The Spot AEL Toggle option is similar to the AEL Toggle option, except that the camera meters only in the spot area in the very center of the display, as with the Spot AEL Hold option.

AF/MF Control Hold

If you select AF/MF Control Hold for the Custom button's function, pressing the button switches the camera between autofocus and manual focus, but only while you hold down the button. If the camera is set to any autofocus mode, pressing and holding the Custom button will switch the camera into manual focus mode. Releasing it will switch to the autofocus mode that was originally set. If the camera is set to manual focus mode, pressing and holding the button will switch to single-shot AF mode. In this situation, when you press the Custom button, the camera will also evaluate the focus and lock focus, if possible. Releasing the button will switch back to manual focus mode. If the camera is set to DMF mode, pressing the button will toggle between DMF and manual focus.

This function is useful in situations when it is difficult to use autofocus, such as dark areas, extreme closeups, or areas where you have to shoot through obstructions such as glass or wire cages. You can switch quickly into manual focus mode and back again, as conditions warrant.

Also, this capability is helpful if you want to set zone focusing, so you can shoot quickly without having to wait for the autofocus mechanism to operate. For example, if you are doing street photography, you can set the camera to single-shot autofocus mode and focus on a subject at about the distance you expect to be shooting from—say, 25 feet (7.6 meters). Then, once focus is locked on that subject, press and hold the Custom button to switch the camera to manual focus mode, and the focus will be locked at that distance in manual focus mode. You can then take shots of subjects at that distance without having to refocus. If you need

to set another focus distance, release the Custom button to go back to autofocus mode and repeat the process.

Finally, it is convenient to quickly get the camera to use autofocus when it is set to manual focus mode. With this function, as noted above, when you press and release the Custom button, the camera will quickly focus using autofocus, and then go back to manual focus mode for any further adjustments you may want to make. This capability is sometimes called "back button focus," meaning you can press a button on the back of the camera to force it to use its autofocus mechanism.

AF/MF Control Toggle

If you select AF/MF Control Toggle for the setting of the Custom button's function, pressing the button switches the camera between autofocus and manual focus. This option works the same as AF/MF Control Hold, except that you do not hold down the button; you just press it and release it. The switched focus mode then stays in effect until you press the button again. However, with this setting, the camera will not use its autofocus to focus on the scene when you press the assigned button. For that "back button focus" operation, you have to use the AF/MF Control Hold option, discussed above.

Eye AF

If you assign Eye AF to the Custom button, then, if the camera is set to an autofocus mode, when you press this button the camera will look for human eyes and focus on them if possible. If the camera detects an eye, it will display a small green frame to show that it has focused on the eye, as shown in Figure 7-59. Continue to hold down the assigned button to lock focus on the eye while you press the shutter button to take the picture. The camera does not have to have face detection activated for this option to work, and it functions with single AF, automatic AF, continuous AF, and DMF. It does not function when manual focus is in effect.

Eye AF can be especially useful when depth of field is shallow, such as when the lens is zoomed in to a long focal length or you are shooting a closeup, to make sure the focus is sharpest on the subject's eyes rather than on the nose or some other feature. A portrait generally looks best when the eyes are in sharp focus.

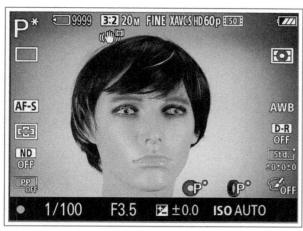

Figure 7-59. Eye AF in Use

This option also is useful to give you an instant way to focus on a face when you were not expecting to take a portrait. You can just press and hold the assigned button to focus on the nearest eye, which should result in a well-focused portrait. Eye AF is not available when recording movies.

Bright Monitoring

This option is intended for a specific situation: when you are using manual focus in dark conditions that make it difficult to evaluate the focus on the LCD screen or in the viewfinder. In that situation, when you press the button assigned to the Bright Monitoring option, the camera changes the display to increase its brightness and sets the Live View Display option to Setting Effect Off, if it was not already set that way. With Setting Effect Off, the display does not darken or brighten to show the effects of exposure settings; instead, it maintains a normal brightness if possible.

If you have the focus mode set to any option other than manual focus, this key assignment will have no effect. It works only with manual focus, and it does not work if either MF Assist or Focus Magnifier is turned on. When you have finished using this feature, press the assigned button again to turn it off.

This setting is designed for use when you really can't see the LCD screen, such as when you are trying to make a long exposure outdoors at night or you need to take a portrait in very dim light.

Deactivate Monitor

This is the next non-menu option for the Custom button. (Remember that I'm skipping over settings that are duplicates of menu options, such as Focus Magnifier.)

If you assign the Custom button to the Deactivate Monitor option, pressing the button while the camera is in shooting mode will turn off the LCD, leaving only a single line of information at the bottom of the screen. You might want to use this option if you are in a darkened area and don't want to distract others or attract attention with the brightness of the monitor. This feature can also help save power if your battery is running down. By pressing the assigned button, you can quickly turn off the monitor temporarily, and recall it just as quickly with the same button.

To deactivate the monitor on a longer-term basis, you can use the Finder/Monitor option on screen 4 of the Custom menu. If you select Viewfinder (Manual) for that option and pop up the RX100 V's viewfinder, the LCD monitor will be turned off at all times, and will not display even the single line of information that appears when the Deactivate Monitor option is used.

MOVIE

The MOVIE setting does not call up a menu option, and it is not equivalent to the similarly named Movie option on Screen 8 of the Shooting menu. Instead, when you assign a button to this setting, the button takes on the same role as the camera's red Movie button. This option gives you another way to start and stop the recording of a video. If you set the Movie Button menu option to Movie Mode Only, this button will start recording a video only if the Mode dial is set to Movie mode.

Download Application

When you select Download Application for the Custom Key (Shooting) option for the Custom button, the camera will display a screen showing the applications that have been downloaded to the camera from Sony's website for camera apps, as discussed in Chapter 9. Scroll through these applications and press the Center button to select the application you want. Then, when you press the assigned button in Shooting mode, the camera will launch the application you selected when you assigned the button to this function.

Not Set

The last option that can be assigned to the Custom button is called Not Set. If you choose this option, then the button will not be assigned any special function.

You may want to select this option if you will be using a limited number of settings and don't want to risk activating a different setting by pressing the button accidentally.

Center Button

Next, you can assign the Center button to any of the same options as for the Custom button, except In-Camera Guide. However, I recommend that you leave this button assigned to its default option, Focus Standard, so it will carry out its focus-related duties.

Left Button

The choices of assignments for the Left button are the same as for the Custom button, except that six of the choices are not available. The unavailable options are Focus Standard, AEL Hold, Spot AEL Hold, AF/MF Control Hold, Eye AF, and In-Camera Guide. So, if you want to set the Left button to lock exposure or to switch between autofocus and manual focus, the button will act only as a toggle, not as one that you have to hold down. Presumably, Sony made this choice because it would be awkward to hold down the Left button while pressing the shutter button. (Eye AF also requires that you hold down the control button while pressing the shutter button.)

Right Button

The Right button has the same options available for assignment as the Left button.

CUSTOM KEY (PLAYBACK)

This final option on screen 5 of the Custom menu lets you change the assignment of the Function button for playback mode. By default, that button is assigned to the Send to Smartphone option, as indicated by the icon next to the button on the camera's back. With this menu option, you can change that assignment to any of the following options instead:

- Finder/Monitor Selection

- Download Application

- Application List

- Delete

- Image Index

- Rotate

- Enlarge Image

- Beauty Effect

- Photo Capture

- TC/UB Display Switch

I have not found a reason to use this option. However, if you know you are not going to be using the Send to Smartphone function, you might want to assign the Function button to a different option, to avoid accidentally activating a Wi-Fi connection between the camera and a smartphone. You might find it useful to use the Function button to call up an index screen or to delete an image.

The sixth and final screen of the Custom menu is shown in Figure 7-60.

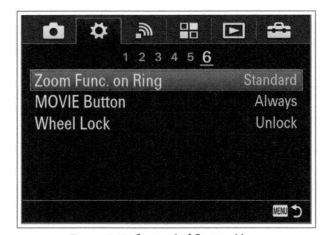

Figure 7-60. Screen 6 of Custom Menu

ZOOM FUNCTION ON RING

This first item on the last screen of the Custom menu determines the way the Control ring operates when you are using it to zoom the lens in and out. As I discussed earlier in this chapter, when its function is set to Standard, the Control ring controls zoom in Auto mode. In any other shooting mode, you have to set the Control ring's function to zoom to enable it to zoom the lens. You set the ring's function using the Custom Key (Shooting) menu option, discussed above.

When the ring is set to control zoom, you can use the Zoom Function on Ring menu option to choose between Standard, Quick, and Step for the way the zoom operates, as shown in Figure 7-61. With Standard, when the Control ring is used to zoom the lens, it does so continuously, just as the zoom lever does. That is, as you turn the ring, the lens zooms through all focal lengths that are available.

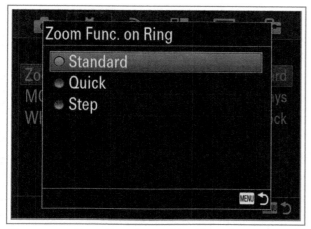

Figure 7-61. Zoom Function on Ring Menu Options Screen

With optical zoom, that means it will zoom from the 24mm wide-angle setting to the 70mm telephoto setting in continuous increments. With Clear Image Zoom and Digital Zoom, the zoom levels increase beyond the 70mm point.

If you choose Quick, the Control ring still zooms continuously, but at a faster rate. You might choose this option if you often need to zoom the lens all the way in or all the way out and are not so concerned with setting intermediate focal lengths or making precise adjustments. (There is a similar setting called Fast for the zoom lever, with the Zoom Speed option on screen 4 of the Custom menu.)

If you set this menu option to Step, then the Control ring zooms the lens only to certain preset values: 24mm, 28mm, 35mm, 50mm, and 70mm. When you nudge the ring toward the wide-angle or telephoto side, the zoom will move to the next preset focal length. You should give the ring a quick nudge and then release it; if you keep turning it, it will move past the next value and go on to the one after that.

There are some limitations with the Step Zoom function on the RX100 V. First, if you set the camera for manual focus or DMF using the Focus Mode menu option, the Control ring will control manual focus and will not zoom the lens.

Next, the Step Zoom feature works only for the Control ring; the zoom lever will always zoom the lens continuously. Also, the Step Zoom feature does not work when shooting movies.

Finally, if you turn on Clear Image Zoom or Digital Zoom using the Zoom Setting option on screen 4 of the Custom menu, or use Smart Zoom, the Step Zoom feature will not include specific increments for the zoom range beyond the optical limit of 70mm. Instead, as shown in Figure 7-62, where Smart Zoom is in use, the camera displays the range of preset increments along with an area at the right side of the scale extending from the 70mm mark to a magnifying glass icon at the far right, showing a general area of extended zoom range.

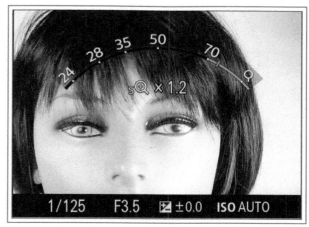

Figure 7-62. Zoom Scale with Smart Zoom and Step Zoom in Use

Step zoom is a valuable feature in some situations. For example, if you want to set a specific focal length for a shot, using Step Zoom is an excellent way to make sure you have the lens zoomed to the exact focal length you want. Of course, this feature is of use only if your desired focal length is 28mm, 35mm, or 50mm; it is easy to set the focal length to 24mm or 70mm using the normal zoom method because those focal lengths are at the two extremes of the camera's optical zoom range.

You might want to choose a focal length of 35mm, for example, to compare shots from the RX100 V against shots from another camera using that same setting.

MOVIE BUTTON

This option, shown in Figure 7-63, lets you lock out the operation of the red Movie button to avoid accidentally starting a video recording. The two choices are Always and Movie Mode Only.

If you want to be able to start recording a video at any time without delay, you should leave the Movie Button option set to Always. With that setting, you can start recording a movie by pressing this button, no matter what shooting mode is set on the Mode dial (except HFR). This is a convenient system, because you can start shooting a video at a moment's notice without having to turn the Mode dial to the Movie position. If you choose Movie Mode only, the Movie button will not operate unless the Mode dial is at the Movie mode position.

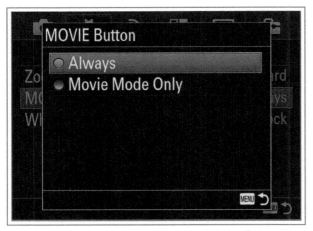

Figure 7-63. Movie Button Menu Options Screen

If you have used the Custom Key (Shooting) option on screen 5 of the Custom menu to assign one of the control buttons to the MOVIE function, so it acts as another Movie button, the setting of the Movie Button menu option will also affect the operation of that button. If the menu option is set to Movie Mode Only, that other button will not start a movie recording unless the Mode dial is at the Movie position.

As I discussed in Chapter 5 in the section on the Movie button, the main reason to choose the Movie Mode Only option is if you are afraid you may press the Movie button by mistake. I have pressed it by mistake several times myself, so, unless I am on a trip when I may want to record movies quickly, I leave this menu option set to Movie Mode Only, to avoid having to stop and delete unwanted recordings.

Wheel Lock

This final option on the Custom menu has two possible settings, Lock and Unlock, as seen in Figure 7-64. If you select Lock, you can lock the functioning of the Control wheel to avoid having exposure settings change by accident.

To engage the actual lock, after this menu item is set to Lock, press and hold the Function button for several seconds until a Locked message appears on the screen.

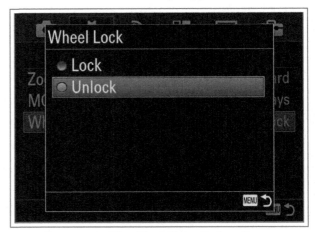

Figure 7-64. Wheel Lock Menu Options Screen

After that, you will see an icon in the lower right corner of the display indicating that the lock is in effect, as shown in Figure 7-65.

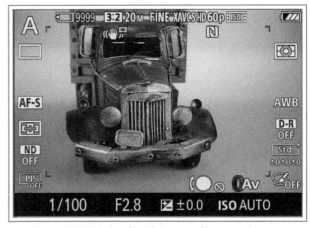

Figure 7-65. Wheel Lock Icon on Shooting Screen

Once the lock is in effect, turning the Control wheel will not change the camera's settings. For example, in Shutter Priority or Manual exposure mode, turning the Control wheel will not adjust shutter speed as it normally would. In Scene mode, turning it will not select a scene setting. However, the wheel will still navigate through menus, and the buttons at the edges of the wheel will operate, even with the lock in effect.

If you have made an important adjustment to your settings, you can lock the wheel so the setting will stay in place. When you are ready to change settings, press and hold the Function button again to remove the lock.

Even when the Lock option is turned on, the Function button can call up or dismiss the Function menu or activate the Quick Navi system. A quick press of the button will carry out that action; a longer press-and-hold will lock or unlock the Control wheel.

Setup Menu

The next menu to be discussed is the Setup menu, marked by the toolbox icon. Its first screen is shown in Figure 7-66.

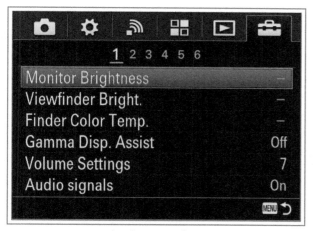

Figure 7-66. Screen 1 of Setup Menu

This six-screen menu has options for matters like USB connections, display brightness, audio options, file numbering, formatting a memory card, video settings, and others. I will discuss each menu item below.

MONITOR BRIGHTNESS

With this option, the camera displays a screen that shows the current setting, as seen in Figure 7-67.

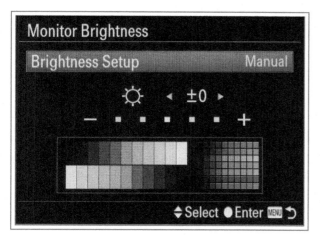

Figure 7-67. Monitor Brightness Main Menu Screen

If you press the Center button on that screen, you will see a screen for choosing one of two available settings for controlling the brightness of the LCD display: Manual or Sunny Weather, as shown in Figure 7-68.

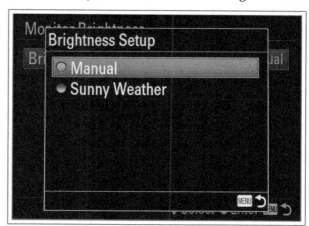

Figure 7-68. Brightness Setup Options for Monitor

If you choose Manual, the camera displays the screen in Figure 7-69. Using the controls on that screen, you can adjust brightness to one or two units above or below normal. After pressing the Down button or turning the Control wheel to highlight the brightness scale, press the Left or Right button to make the adjustment.

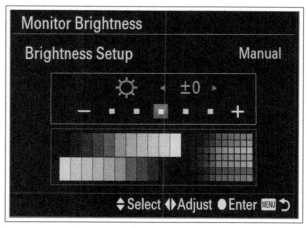

Figure 7-69. Monitor Brightness Manual Adjustment Screen

If your battery is running low and you don't have a spare, you may want to set the monitor to its minimum brightness to conserve power. Conversely, you can increase brightness if you're finding it difficult to compose the image on the screen.

If you are shooting outdoors in bright conditions, you can choose Sunny Weather, which sets the display to a very bright level. Of course, you can switch to using the viewfinder in bright conditions, but there may be times when you want to hold the camera away from your head as you compose the shot, even in bright sunlight. Or, you may want to play back your images for friends while outdoors. The Sunny Weather setting drains the camera's battery fairly rapidly, so you should turn it off when it is no longer needed.

The monitor's brightness will be fixed at the zero level when the camera is recording video with File Format set to XAVC S 4K or with File Format set to XAVC S HD and Record Setting set to either 120p option (100p for PAL systems). Brightness is fixed at the -2 level when Wi-Fi operations are active, to conserve battery power.

VIEWFINDER BRIGHTNESS

This second option on the Setup menu is similar to Monitor Brightness, with some differences. With this option, you have to look into the viewfinder to make adjustments. There is no Sunny Weather setting, because the viewfinder is shaded from the sun and there is no need for a super-bright setting. You can set the brightness to Auto or Manual. With Auto, the camera adjusts the brightness based on a reading of ambient light from a light sensor. If you select Manual, you can make the same adjustments as with the LCD screen.

This option has the same restrictions as the previous one with respect to settings for File Format.

FINDER COLOR TEMPERATURE

This option lets you adjust the color temperature of the view through the viewfinder. As with the Viewfinder Brightness setting, you have to look into the viewfinder to make adjustments. You can use the camera's controls to lower the color temperature by one or two units, which will make the view appear slightly more reddish, or "warmer," or you can raise it by one or two units to make it more bluish, or "cooler." I have not found a reason to take advantage of this adjustment, but it is easy to use and it may be helpful to you.

GAMMA DISPLAY ASSIST

This option is a specialized one that is intended for use only if you are using a Picture Profile setting that includes the S-Log2 setting for gamma. As I discussed in Chapter 4, S-Log2 is a special setting that enables the camera to record video with an extended dynamic range, so it can record scenes clearly even if there is

considerable contrast between shadowed areas and bright ones. One characteristic of the S-Log2 setting is that the image on the camera's display screen will appear quite dark and low in contrast. In order to take advantage of the high dynamic range available with this setting, the footage needs to be processed with video software that can deal with S-Log2 properly.

Therefore, Sony has provided the Gamma Display Assist setting so you can clearly view a scene being recorded or played back while the S-Log2 gamma setting is in effect. When this setting is activated, the images on the camera's display will be boosted in contrast to a level that makes it appear as if a more standard setting was used—specifically, the ITU709(800%) setting.

This menu option has three settings: Off, Auto, and S-Log2, as shown in Figure 7-70.

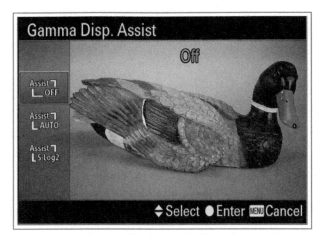

Figure 7-70. Gamma Display Assist Menu Options Screen

If you choose Off, the option is not activated in any case, and video shot with the S-Log2 gamma setting will appear rather dark and low in contrast, as it normally would. If you choose Auto, then the camera will boost the contrast of the display only if the Picture Profile setting in use includes the S-Log2 gamma setting. (The PP7 setting for Picture Profile includes that setting by default, but you can change any Picture Profile setting to include S-Log2, as discussed in Chapter 4.)

If you choose the third setting, called S-Log2, the camera always boosts the contrast of the image on the display, regardless of the Picture Profile setting.

My preference is to leave this option turned off. I do not have difficulty viewing the display when S-Log2 is in use. However, in a situation where you are having a problem viewing the scene on the display screen when using S-Log2, this setting might be useful.

VOLUME SETTINGS

This option, whose settings screen is shown in Figure 7-71, lets you set the volume for playback of movies at a level from zero to 15. The default level is seven. You can also set this level when a movie is playing by pressing the Down button to get access to the detailed controls, which include a volume setting option.

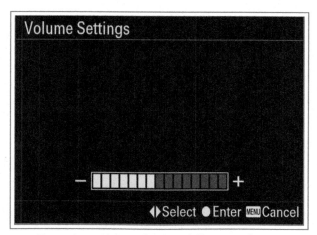

Figure 7-71. Volume Settings Adjustment Screen

When a movie is on the screen in playback mode before playback starts, pressing the Down button calls up the volume adjustment screen immediately. Pressing that button when a still image is displayed in playback mode also calls up the volume screen, if View Mode is set to Date View, which includes videos as well as stills.

AUDIO SIGNALS

This option's main screen is shown in Figure 7-72.

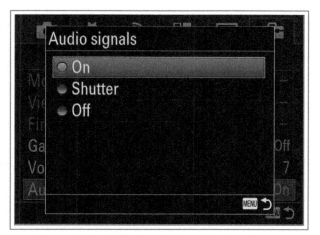

Figure 7-72. Audio Signals Menu Options Screen

It lets you choose whether or not to activate the various sounds the RX100 V makes when an operation takes place, such as pressing the shutter button, confirming focus, or pressing a control button.

By default, the sounds are turned on, but it can be helpful to silence them during a religious ceremony, or when you are doing street photography and want to avoid alerting your subjects. There is a separate entry for Shutter, so you can leave the shutter sound turned on while silencing sounds such as focus beeps if you want.

Screen 2 of the Setup menu is shown in Figure 7-73.

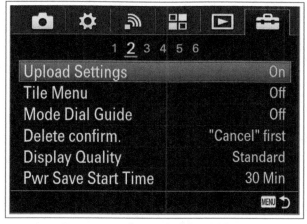

Figure 7-73. Screen 2 of Setup Menu

UPLOAD SETTINGS

This first item on the second screen of the Setup menu, as seen in Figure 7-73, appears only when an Eye-Fi card is in the camera. If no Eye-Fi card is present, this menu option does not display at all, leaving a blank space at the bottom of this menu screen.

As discussed in Chapter 1, an Eye-Fi card is a memory card with a transmitter to send images to a computer over a Wi-Fi network. This menu item has only two settings—On or Off. You might want to use the Off setting if you are on an airplane where you may be required to turn off radio transmitters. Or, if you know you will not be using the Eye-Fi uploading capability for a while, you can turn this menu option off to save some battery power.

Of course, the RX100 V has built-in Wi-Fi capability, which makes it less likely you will use an Eye-Fi card.

TILE MENU

If you turn this option on, the camera displays a screen with six tiles representing the various menu systems, as shown in Figure 7-74, when you press the Menu button.

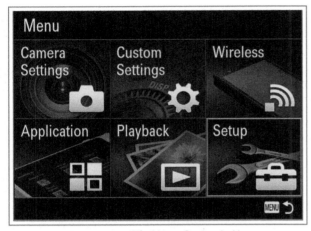

Figure 7-74. Tile Menu Option in Use

This screen gives you a graphic representation of which menu is which, and it lets you get quick access to the menu of your choice. You navigate through the six blocks using the direction buttons or the Control wheel. I prefer to leave this option turned off, because, without it, pressing the Menu button takes me directly to the last menu option I was using. From there, I can navigate quickly to any other menu system. But for those who are new to this camera or who like having a large display to show the menu choices clearly, the Tile Menu option may be worth using.

MODE DIAL GUIDE

This menu item lets you turn on or off the Mode Dial Guide, a display that appears when you turn the Mode dial to select a shooting mode, as shown in Figure 7-75. This guide is helpful when you first start using the camera, but it can be annoying if you don't need the reminders, and you have to press the Center button or Menu button, or press the shutter button halfway, to dismiss the screen. I leave this option turned off to speed up my shooting.

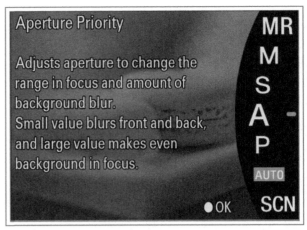

Figure 7-75. Mode Dial Guide Option in Use

DELETE CONFIRMATION

This menu item has two possible settings, as shown in Figure 7-76: "Delete" First or "Cancel" First.

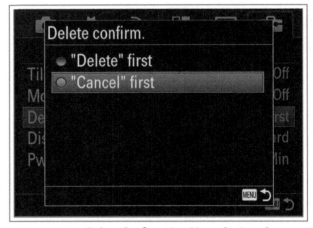

Figure 7-76. Delete Confirmation Menu Options Screen

This option lets you fine-tune how the camera operates for deleting images. Whenever you press the Delete button to delete an image in playback mode, the camera displays a confirmation screen, as shown in Figure 7-77, with two choices: Delete or Cancel.

One of those choices will be highlighted when the screen appears; you can then press the Center button to accept that choice and the operation will be done. You also can use the Control wheel or the Up or Down button to highlight the other option before you press the Center button to carry out your choice.

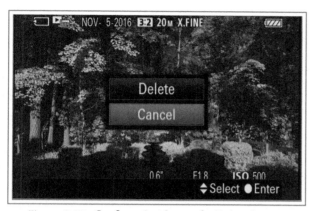

Figure 7-77. Confirmation Screen for Delete Button

Which setting you choose for this menu item depends on how careful you want to be to guard against the accidental deletion of an image. If you like to move quickly in deleting images, choose "Delete" First. Then, as soon as the confirmation screen appears, the "Delete" option will be highlighted and you can press the Center button to carry out the deletion. If you prefer to have some assurance of avoiding an accidental deletion, choose "Cancel" First, so that, if you press the Center button too quickly when the confirmation screen appears, you will only cancel the operation, rather than deleting an image.

Unless you use the Delete button often and need to save time, I recommend you leave this menu item set at the "Cancel" First setting to be safe.

DISPLAY QUALITY

This menu item lets you choose Standard or High for the quality of the display. According to Sony, with the High setting the camera displays the live view on the LCD screen or in the viewfinder at a higher resolution than with the Standard setting, at the expense of additional drain on the battery.

I have tried several experiments with these settings, viewing small print in a catalog using both the viewfinder and the LCD display with both Display Quality settings, and I have not found a noticeable difference. There may be situations in which this option has a more noticeable impact on the display, but my recommendation is to leave it at Standard to conserve battery life.

POWER SAVE START TIME

This option lets you set the interval before the camera turns off automatically to save power, when no controls have been operated. The default is two minutes; with this option you can also choose one, five, or 30 minutes, as shown in Figure 7-78. After the designated time, the camera does not just go into a "sleep" mode, it powers off. You have to turn it back on by pressing the power button, the Playback button, or the Finder switch.

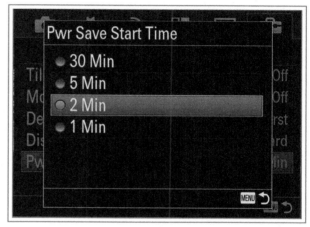

Figure 7-78. Power Save Start Time Menu Options Screen

You cannot turn the power-saving function off. However, the camera will not power off automatically when you are recording movies, when a slide show is playing, when the camera is connected to a computer to upload images, or when the camera is being powered through the Multi port.

The setting you use depends on your preferences. I am usually well aware of the camera's status, and I like to use the maximum 30-minute period for this option so the camera does not power down just when I am about to use it again. I always have extra batteries available and I'm not too concerned if I have to replace the battery. If you are out in the field and running low on battery power, you might want to choose a shorter time for this option, to conserve battery life.

The options on screen 3 of the Setup menu are shown in Figure 7-79.

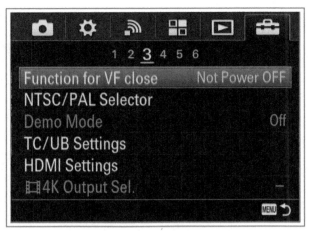

Figure 7-79. Screen 3 of Setup Menu

FUNCTION FOR VF CLOSE

This first option on screen 3 of the Setup menu controls what happens when you push the viewfinder back down into the camera. The choices are Power Off or Not Power Off. If you choose Power Off, the camera will turn off when you stow the viewfinder back in its housing. If you choose Not Power Off, the camera will stay powered on. I prefer the Not Power Off option so I can keep shooting or using playback functions after the viewfinder has been retracted. But, if you use the viewfinder primarily, you may like the convenience of turning the camera on and off by lifting the viewfinder into place and pushing it back into its slot.

NTSC/PAL SELECTOR

This menu option controls which television system the camera uses for recording videos—NTSC or PAL. The NTSC system is used in the United States and other parts of North America, as well as Japan, South Korea, and some other countries. The PAL system is used in many parts of Asia, Africa, and Europe.

For purposes of using the RX100 V camera, the difference between the two systems is that the NTSC system primarily uses multiples of 30 for frame rates (such as 30, 60, or 120 frames per second), while the PAL system uses multiples of 25 (such as 25, 50, or 100 frames per second). You will see these differences in the options for the Record Setting item on screen 2 of the Shooting menu. If you choose NTSC, the options will be mostly in multiples of 30, although there will be some entries for 24 fps, another NTSC standard. If you choose PAL, the options will be in multiples of 25.

In general, you should use the setting that is standard for the area where you will be using the camera. I live in the United States, so I set the camera to NTSC, where the frame rates are in multiples of 30.

It is important to choose this setting before you start recording files on your memory card. Once you have started using a card under one of these systems, you cannot change to the other system without re-formatting the memory card. When you select this menu option, you will see the message shown in Figure 7-80, warning that you will have to re-format the card to continue.

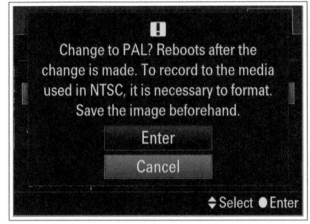

Figure 7-80. Warning Message for Changing from NTSC to PAL

If you select Enter and press the Center button, the camera will format the card for the new system.

DEMO MODE

The Demo Mode menu item automatically plays a movie if the camera has not had any controls operated for about one minute. This feature is designed for use by retail stores, so they can leave the camera turned on with a continuous demonstration on its screen. But you can use it for your own purposes, if you want to create a movie that demonstrates the camera's features for friends, for example, or if you just like the idea of having the camera play a movie when it's not otherwise occupied.

For this feature to be available for selection on the menu screen, the camera has to be powered by the AC adapter or another power source through the Multi port. Otherwise, this line on the menu will be dimmed.

When this option is turned on and the camera is in shooting mode, after one minute of inactivity the camera will enter Demo Mode. At that point, the camera will automatically play a movie, which you have to provide. It cannot be just any movie. The movie the camera will play in Demo Mode must be recorded in the AVCHD format, it must be protected using the Protect option on the Playback menu, and it must be the oldest AVCHD movie on the memory card. So, if you have a reason to use this option, you may want to use a fresh memory card and record a single AVCHD movie on the card, and then use the Protect function to protect it. When the movie plays, it plays audio as well as video, and it will keep repeating in a loop. To exit from Demo Mode, you can press the Center button or just turn the camera off.

TC/UB (Time Code/User Bit) Settings

This menu item provides several sub-options that are helpful if you use the RX100 V for advanced video production. For example, because of its ability to shoot 4K video (discussed in Chapter 8), this camera can be used as part of a multi-camera setup for shooting a professional production. In such a setup, it can be useful to control whether and how the camera outputs time code, a type of metadata that is used when editing video sequences. The user bit is another form of metadata that also can be used as an organizing aid.

This menu option is available only if File Format is set to XAVC S 4K, XAVC S HD, or AVCHD; it is not available if you are recording video in the MP4 format. Even when the TC/UB Settings option is available for selection, all but one of the sub-options are unavailable unless the Mode dial is set to the Movie or HFR position. If it is in any other position, you can get access to the first sub-option only, TC/UB Display Setting.

I will not discuss the nature and use of time code in detail in this book, but I will give a brief overview. Time code for video files includes numbers in a format like the following: 02:12:23:19, which stands for hours, minutes, seconds, and frames. In this example, the time code shown would mark the point in the video clip at two hours, 12 minutes, 23 seconds, and 19 frames into the next second.

Because video (in the NTSC system) is played back at 30 fps or 24 fps, the number in the final position is based on those values, even if the video is recorded in a format such as XAVC S HD with Record Setting set to 120p 100M. With a Record Setting value of 120p, 60p, 60i, or 30p, the number of frames can be set from 00 to 29. When Record Setting is set to 24p, the number of

frames can be set only to 00, 04, 08, 12, 16, or 20. For PAL areas, the numbers of frames can go from 00 to 24, because the video is played back at 25 fps.

When you see a time code like the one in this example, you know what frame of the video is being identified, so you can make an edit at that point or synchronize this video clip with another video clip, as long as both clips are using the same time code format and had the time code recorded in synchronization.

If you are not going to use your camera for that sort of video production, you can largely ignore this menu option, though it is helpful to know what settings you can control. The sub-options are discussed below.

TC/UB Display Setting

This first option controls what figures display in the lower left corner of the camera's screen during video recording. There are three choices—Counter, TC, or U-Bit, for user bit, as shown in Figure 7-81.

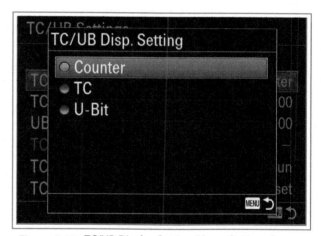

Figure 7-81. TC/UB Display Setting Menu Options Screen

No matter which you choose, the display appears on the screen only during video recording. The characters are not recorded visibly with the video and will not appear during playback, although they can be used as reference points in appropriate video-editing software.

The first choice, Counter, produces a simple display of minutes and seconds of elapsed recording time, as shown in Figure 7-82. This is the default choice, and it is what you probably will want to leave in place for general use. As I noted above, the only reason to use time code (or user bit) is for professional-level video production.

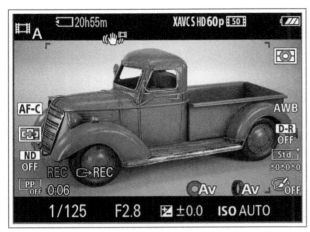

Figure 7-82. Counter in Use on Recording Screen

The second choice places time code on the screen, as shown in Figure 7-83. You may want to use this setting for professional video production, not just to display on the screen but also to output to another device, such as a video recorder, through the camera's HDMI cable, as I will discuss later in this chapter.

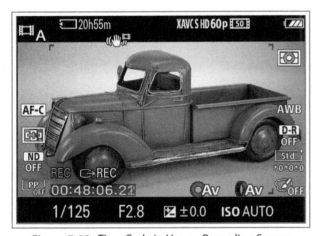

Figure 7-83. Time Code in Use on Recording Screen

The third choice, user bit, lets you set the camera to display a set of four figures in hexadecimal notation, in the format 0B 76 11 F8. This amounts to a string of four numbers, each of which, in hexadecimal notation, can range from 00 (0 in decimal notation) to FF (255 in decimal notation).

In practice, I have never used the user bit for video production. Some videographers use this capability to place notes in the video file, using the few available letters (A through F) and the numbers to make notations like C1 for camera one.

If you don't need to include a customized notation using the user bit option, the RX100 V gives you a

way to have the user bit provide a running display of the current time. To do that, go to the last sub-option under TC/UB Settings, UB Time Record, and set it to On. That option sets the user bit to display the current time in the lower left corner of the display. To make that display appear, you also have to set the TC/UB Display Setting option to U-Bit.

TC Preset

This next option lets you set the initial time code for your video recording. You can set the code anywhere from all zeroes, the default, to 23:59:59:29 for some NTSC formats. As I noted earlier, the final figure can go as high as 29 for most NTSC settings and 20 for the 24p settings. For PAL systems, the highest value is 24.

You might want to use this option if you need to start with a particular time code for a technical reason, in order to synchronize your footage with existing footage or that from another camera. In addition, in some production environments the practice is to set the hours position to a particular value, such as 01, to designate some item, such as the reel number. Unless you have a need to make a setting of that nature, you can leave these values all at zero.

UB Preset

This option lets you set the user bit, as discussed above. Each of the four positions can be set anywhere from 00 to FF, using the hexadecimal system.

TC Format

This option lets you select either DF (drop-frame) or NDF (non-drop-frame) format for the time code, assuming you are using time code and are using the NTSC video system. (Drop-frame time code is not used for PAL video.)

This is a technical setting that you may need to use in order to make sure the time code you use is compatible with that of other cameras and with your editing facilities. Drop-frame time code is used because the NTSC standard of 30 frames per second does not record exactly 30 frames every second. For technical reasons, the actual rate is 29.97 frames per second. To count the frames accurately, video editors use the drop-frame system, which drops a few frames at specified intervals from the counting process, so the actual number of frames is counted accurately.

You can leave this option set to DF if you are using the NTSC system, unless you know of a specific reason to use NDF.

TC Run

This option lets you choose either Rec Run or Free Run for the time code. With Rec Run, the time code increases only while the camera is actually recording. With Free Run, the time code continues to run all the time. Which system to choose is a matter of preference, depending on how you will use the time code for editing. With Rec Run, there should be no gaps in the time code, which can be an advantage. With Free Run, you can set up the time code to match the time of day, which can be useful if you need to find a clip that corresponds to a particular time during the day's video recording.

Free Run time code continues to run even when the camera is powered off. When you turn it on again and set it to Movie mode, the current time should be displaying in the lower left corner of the display, assuming you set the initial value for the time code to the current time.

You may have to take some additional steps to get the time code to appear in your editing software. For example, with AVCHD recordings from the RX100 V, if you are using Adobe Premiere Pro CC, you have to copy the entire AVCHD folder to the disk from which you will be importing the video into Premiere, and then use the Media Browser within Premiere to copy the time code.

TC Make

This option is what you use to set the camera to record the time code option you have selected. The two choices are Preset or Regenerate. If you choose Preset, the camera starts recording time code using the value you entered for TC Preset, discussed earlier. If you choose Regenerate, the camera starts the time code recording based on the last value recorded previously.

UB Time Record

This last option, found on the second screen of the TC/UB Settings menu item, lets you choose whether or not to set the user bit option to display and record the time instead of a user bit formula that you set yourself. If you select On for this option and set the TC/UB Display Setting option to U-Bit, the camera will display the current time in the lower left corner of the screen as the video is recorded, as shown in Figure 7-84.

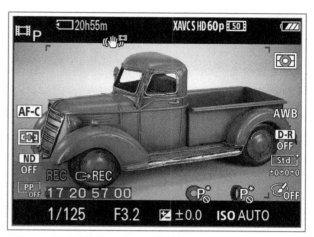

Figure 7-84. UB Time Record in Use on Recording Screen

The display shows the hour (in the 24-hour format), minute, and second; the last set of digits is left at zeroes. In this case, the time was shortly after 5:20 p.m.

HDMI Settings

The HDMI Settings menu option has seven sub-options on its two screens.

HDMI Resolution

The HDMI Resolution option can be set to Auto, 2160p/1080p, 1080p, or 1080i. This setting controls how the camera displays images and videos on an HDTV in playback mode. Ordinarily, the Auto setting will work best; the camera will set itself for the optimum display according to the resolution of the HDTV it is connected to. If you experience difficulties with that connection, you may be able to improve the image on the HDTV's screen by trying one of the other settings. The 2160p/1080p setting is designed for connection to 4K-capable TV sets, which often have a resolution of 3840 x 2160 pixels.

24p/60p Output

This menu option is labeled with a movie-film icon, meaning it is for use when the camera is set to Movie mode. This option, which is available only for cameras using the NTSC system, has a very specific use. It is applicable when you have recorded video using one of three Record Setting formats that include the 24p frame rate: 24p 24M, 24p 17M (using the AVCHD File Format setting), or 24p 50M (using the XAVC S HD File Format setting or the HFR settings). It also applies only if you have set the HDMI Resolution item, under HDMI Settings on screen 3 of the Setup menu, to 1080p or 2160p/1080p.

If the above conditions are met, that means you have some video (or HFR) footage recorded at 24 frames per second. As I will discuss in Chapter 8, that setting is slower than the standard NTSC setting of 30 frames per second, and produces what some people consider to be a more "cinematic" look for the footage.

When you send your 24p video footage out through an HDMI cable to an HDTV set, you may prefer to send it in a way that looks more like standard TV video, using the 60p setting. That is the function of this menu option. If all of the conditions described above are met, you can select 60p for the 24p/60p Output option, and your 24p footage will be sent out through the HDMI cable to the HDTV in a way that simulates 60p video.

This option also may be of use when you are sending video footage out through the HDMI cable to an external video recorder, if 60p footage is a better option for use by the recorder.

HDMI Information Display

This feature controls the behavior of the camera when you connect it to an HDTV set or other external device using an optional micro HDMI cable. However, unlike the HDMI Resolution option discussed above, which controls what happens when the camera is in playback mode, playing your images and videos on an HDTV set, this menu option controls what happens in shooting mode when the HDMI connection is active.

If this menu option is set to On, which is the default setting, then, when the camera is connected to an HDTV or external recorder in shooting mode, the screen of the external device displays exactly what you would see on the camera's display in that mode if the camera were not connected to the device, including icons and figures showing camera settings.

With the On setting, the HDTV acts as a large, external monitor for the RX100 V, and the screen of the RX100 V itself is blank. I use this setting a great deal myself, because this is how I capture screen shots for this book. Once the camera is connected, I can capture all of the information and settings that appear on the shooting screens and menu screens of the camera, with a few exceptions for special settings that are not output through the HDMI port, such as the Zebra stripes.

If this menu option is set to Off, then, when the camera is connected to an HDTV or other external device in

shooting mode, the external device's screen displays only the image that is being viewed by the camera, with no shooting information displayed at all. If you press the Display button, nothing will happen on the external screen; the view will not switch to another display with more information on it. However, at the same time, the camera's screen continues to display all of the shooting information it normally would, including the image and whatever information is chosen by presses of the Display button.

You might use the Off setting when you want to display images from the camera's shooting mode on a large HDTV screen, possibly at a wedding or other gathering, and not have the images cluttered or marred by any shooting information at all. For example, I have seen occasions where a camera is used to focus on an unsuspecting person in the audience, and that person's image suddenly appears on the large screen for everyone to see.

Also, this option is useful for video production when you need to output a "clean" video signal that does not include any shooting information from the camera. That signal can be sent through an HDMI cable to a video recorder for recording to another medium, or for display on a large monitor being viewed by the production team. For example, you can record video directly from the camera to a computer by outputting the clean HDMI signal to a device such as the Intensity Pro by Blackmagic Design. There are similar devices available from companies such as AverMedia, Hauppage, and Elgato. You also can send the clean signal to an external video recorder such as the Atomos Shogun, as I will discuss in Chapter 8.

With the On setting, you can press the Display button to show a screen with very minimal shooting information, but that screen still shows the basic information of aperture, shutter speed, exposure compensation, and ISO value at the very bottom of the screen, and shows the shooting mode in the upper left corner. If you don't want even that minimal level of information to interfere with the video display, choose the Off setting.

This setting does not change the behavior of the camera for playback of images and video; its only effect is on the display of information in shooting mode through an HDMI connection.

TC Output

This option works together with the TC/UB Settings option discussed earlier. If you have set up the camera to record time code, you can use this option to have the time code output through the HDMI cable to an external recorder, so the time code will be available in the recorded footage for use in editing. The choices are On or Off.

Rec Control

This next sub-option for HDMI Settings is another one that applies only when recording to an external device by sending a clean signal through the HDMI cable. In this case, the option controls whether the camera sends a start-recording or stop-recording signal through the cable. If you turn this option on, then you can control the external recorder using the camera's controls, if the external recorder is compatible with this camera.

For example, you can connect the Atomos Shogun 4K recorder and control the recorder's starting and stopping using this option. However, one issue with the RX100 V is that it can record in 4K mode to a memory card only for five minutes or less in one sequence; you then have to pause and wait for the camera to cool down. If you want to record 4K video to the Shogun recorder for longer periods of time, you have to remove the memory card from the camera, as discussed later in this chapter and in Chapter 8. You can use the camera's controls to start and stop an external recorder without this limitation if you are recording video in most other formats, though the RX100 V still has other duration limits on recording.

The Rec Control option can be turned on only if the TC Output option, discussed above, also is turned on.

CTRL for HDMI

This sub-option is of use only when you have connected the camera to an HDTV and you want to control the camera with the TV's remote control, which is possible in some situations. If you want to do that, set this option to On and follow the instructions for the TV and its remote control. This option is intended to be used when you connect the camera to a Sony Bravia model HDTV.

HDMI Audio Output

This option, the only one on the second screen of the HDMI Settings menu, can be turned either on or off. This setting controls whether or not the sound being picked up by the camera's microphone is sent to an external device through the HDMI cable while the camera is recording video. If this option is turned on, the sound goes through to the other device and can be monitored before the recording starts (while the camera is in standby mode), as well as during the recording. The sound is recorded to the external device, if that device is set up to record it. If this option is turned off, then no audio is transmitted through the HDMI cable. You might want to use that option if you are shooting silent footage and you don't want any extraneous sounds recorded by the external recorder, or if you are displaying silent footage and still images on an external HDTV and don't need to have any sounds included.

4K Output Select

This next option on the Setup menu is for use only when the camera is connected to a 4K-capable external video recorder, such as the Atomos Shogun. Unless that connection is active, this option will be dimmed and unavailable for selection. Once the connection to the external recorder is made, the following sub-options are available:

Memory Card + HDMI

With this option, the camera will record video to the memory card in the camera and also output the signal to the external recorder through the HDMI cable. This option gives you an immediate backup copy of your footage.

HDMI Only (30p)

With this option, the camera sends a 4K video signal in 30p format to the external recorder but does not record the video to the camera's memory card. This option and the next one give the camera an important capability—the ability to record 4K video without regard to the five-minute upper limit for recording 4K video to the memory card. These options also let you record 4K video without having a memory card that meets the specifications for that format, and, in fact, it lets you record with no memory card in the camera at all.

If you choose either this option or the next one, for recording 4K/24p video with no card in the camera, the File Format and Record Setting items on the Shooting menu become unavailable, because either of these settings requires use of 4K video, either 30p or 24p.

I tried using this option with the RX100 V connected by an HDMI cable to an Atomos Shogun external 4K recorder, and the camera sent its clean 4K signal through the HDMI cable for a video that lasted about 18 minutes before the camera stopped because of overheating. One advantage of using this setup is that, if you turn on the Rec Control menu option on the camera, you can control the operation of the Shogun recorder by pressing the Movie button on the camera to start and stop the recording. If you are recording 4K video to a memory card inserted in the camera, you can use the Rec Control function, but then you will be limited to the five-minute restriction on recording 4K video.

HDMI Only (24p)

This option is the same as the previous one, apart from the use of the 24p frame rate instead of 30p.

Screen 4 of the Setup menu is shown in Figure 7-85.

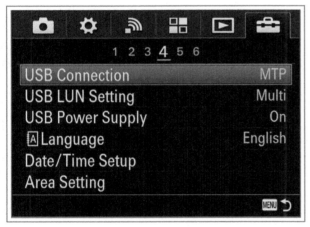

Figure 7-85. Screen 4 of Setup Menu

USB CONNECTION

This option sets the technical standard that the camera uses for connecting to a computer using the USB cable. This menu item has four choices, as shown in Figure 7-86: Auto, Mass Storage, MTP, which stands for Media Transfer Protocol, and PC Remote.

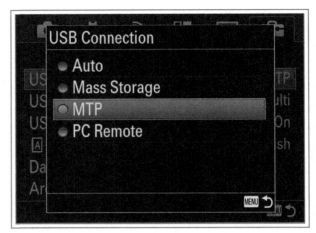

Figure 7-86. USB Connection Menu Options Screen

You ordinarily should select Auto, and the RX100 V should detect which standard is used by the computer you are connecting the camera to. If the camera does not automatically select a standard and start transferring images, you can try one of the other settings to see if it works better than the Auto setting. You may find it necessary to use the MTP option when connecting your camera to the computer to download apps from the playmemoriescameraapps.com site.

The fourth setting, PC Remote, adds an important function to the camera. If you select this option, you can then connect the camera to a computer with the camera's USB cable, and control the camera from the computer using Sony's Remote Camera Control software. That software can be downloaded at no charge from http://www.sony.co.jp/imsoft/Win/ for Windows-based computers and from http://www.sony.co.jp/imsoft/Mac/ for Macintosh computers.

Once this software is installed on your computer, set this menu option to PC Remote, connect the camera to the computer with the Sony USB cable, and turn the camera on. Then start the software application. You will see on the computer a window like that in Figure 7-87, showing the various items you can control from the computer.

You will have to turn the camera's Mode dial to select the shooting mode, but you can control quite a few items from the software, depending on what mode is selected. These include Drive Mode, including all varieties of continuous shooting and bracketing; white balance; Picture Effect; DRO/Auto HDR; Quality; Image Size; and Aspect Ratio.

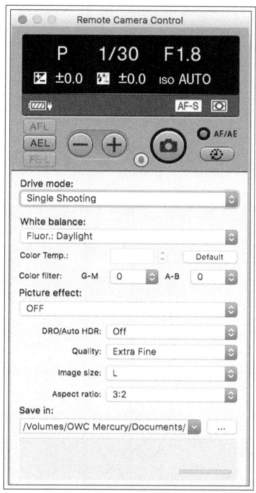

Figure 7-87. Computer Window for PC Remote Connection

You can set autoexposure lock by clicking on the AEL button icon. To control exposure compensation, click on the exposure compensation icon in the black window at the top of the screen, and then click on the large plus or minus sign in the gray area below the black window. The same technique works for flash exposure compensation. You also can control ISO by clicking on the ISO reading in the black window and then on the plus or minus sign in the gray control area.

When the mode dial is set to Aperture Priority, Shutter Priority, or Manual exposure, you can control the aperture and/or shutter speed, depending on the shooting mode, by clicking on the setting in the large black block and then clicking on the plus or minus sign in the gray area. You also can click on the AF or AE in the block labeled AF/AE in the gray area to simulate a half-press of the shutter button.

You can click on the red button at the bottom of the gray control area to start or stop a video recording.

(However, this operation won't work if the Movie Button option on screen 6 of the Custom menu is set to Movie Mode only, unless the Mode dial is at Movie mode.) Click on the camera icon to the right of that button to take a still image. Click and hold down on the camera icon to fire a burst of shots when continuous shooting is selected for Drive Mode.

Finally, if you click on the small button with a timer dial, below the AF/AE button, a new window will open up with options for interval shooting. In that window, you can set the interval between shots to a value from 10 seconds to 180 minutes and the number of shots from two to 1000. Or, you can click on the option for capturing an unlimited number of shots. Using this feature, you can create a time-lapse movie. For example, if you set the camera up on a tripod and aim it at a construction project, taking one picture per minute for 600 minutes, you will end up with 600 images that cover a period of 10 hours. If you assemble those images into a movie and play it back at 30 frames per second, the actions for those 10 hours will play back in 20 seconds.

If you use this capability for a fairly long sequence, you will probably need to power the camera with the AC adapter or another external power source, as discussed in Appendix A.

Also, you should note that there are other ways to carry out interval shooting or time-lapse photography with the RX100 V. You can do this without connecting the camera to a computer using the Time-Lapse app that is available for download, as discussed in Chapter 9. Or, you can use a wired intervalometer, as discussed in Appendix A.

USB LUN Setting

This is an option that should not often be needed. LUN stands for logical unit number. This item has two possible settings—Multi or Single. Ordinarily, it should be set to Multi, the default. In particular, it should be set to Multi when the RX100 V is connected to a Windows-based computer and you are using Sony's PlayMemories Home software to manage your images. If you encounter a problem with a USB connection to a computer, you can try the Single setting to see if it solves the problem.

USB POWER SUPPLY

The USB Power Supply option, which can be turned either on or off, controls whether or not the camera's battery will be charged or the camera will be powered through the USB cable when the camera is connected by its USB cable to a computer.

If you use the AC adapter provided with the camera or an external USB battery, as discussed in Appendix A, to provide power to the camera, you do not need to have this menu option turned on. When the USB cable is connected to an external power supply, power will be provided to the camera even with this option turned off.

Turning this option on gives you another avenue for keeping the RX100 V's battery charged. The only problem is that if your computer is running on its battery, then that battery will be discharged more rapidly than usual. If you are plugging the camera into a computer that is plugged into a wall power outlet, there should be no problem in using this option.

As I will discuss in Appendix A, I recommend that you get an external battery charger and at least one extra battery for the RX100 V, because even if you can charge the battery in the camera using the USB cable, you don't have the ability to insert a fully charged battery into the camera when the first battery is exhausted.

I recommend leaving this option at its default setting of On, unless you will be connecting the camera to a battery-powered computer or other device and you don't want to run down the battery on that device.

LANGUAGE

This option gives you the choice of language for the display of commands and information on the camera's LCD screen and in the viewfinder. Once you have selected this menu item, scroll through the language choices using the Control wheel or the direction buttons and press the Center button when your chosen language is highlighted.

DATE/TIME SETUP

I discussed this item in Chapter 1. When the camera is new or has not been used for a long time, it will prompt you to set the date and time and will display this menu option. If you want to call up these settings on your own, you can do so at any time.

When you press the Center button on this menu line, you will see a screen like that in Figure 7-88, with the choice of adjusting Daylight Savings Time (On or Off), Date/Time, or Date Format.

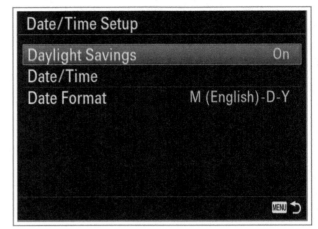

Figure 7-88. Date/Time Setup Menu Options Screen

To adjust Date/Time, select that option and press the Center button. The camera will display a screen like that shown in Figure 7-89.

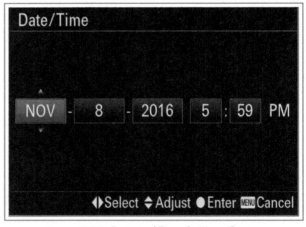

Figure 7-89. Date and Time Settings Screen

Scroll through the options for setting month, day, year, and time by turning the Control wheel or pressing the Left and Right buttons. As you reach each item, adjust its value by using the Up and Down buttons. When all of the settings are correct, press the Center button to confirm them and exit from this screen.

From the first menu screen, you can also turn Daylight Savings Time on or off depending on the time of year, and you can choose a date format according to your preference.

AREA SETTING

The last option on screen 4 of the Setup menu, Area Setting, lets you select a location so you can adjust the date and time for a different time zone when you are traveling. When you highlight this item and press the Center button, the camera displays the map shown in Figure 7-90.

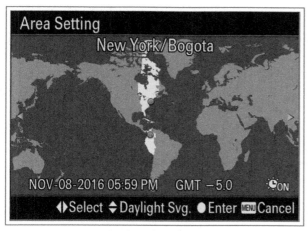

Figure 7-90. Area Setting Map Display

Turn the Control wheel or press the Left and Right buttons to move the light-colored highlight over the map until it covers the area of the location you want to set. If you want to adjust the setting for Daylight Savings Time, press the Up or Down button to make the adjustment. Then press the Center button and the date and time will be adjusted for that location until you change the location again using this menu item.

Screen 5 of the Setup menu is shown in Figure 7-91.

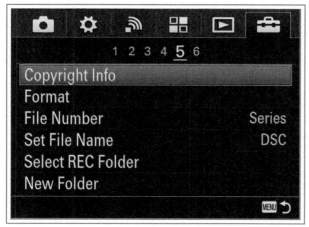

Figure 7-91. Screen 5 of Setup Menu

COPYRIGHT INFO

This first item on screen 5 of the Setup menu lets you add information about the photographer and copyright holder to the metadata for images taken with the camera.

The first sub-option, Write Copyright Info, determines whether the copyright information entered for this item will be written to still images that you take. If you turn this option on, then the copyright information (names of photographer and copyright holder) will be added to the metadata for any still images captured after the option is turned on. The information will not appear on the images themselves, but can be read by any program that reads EXIF data for images, such as Adobe Bridge.

The second option, Set Photographer, lets you enter the name of the photographer. When you select this option, you will see a screen with a window for entering the name. Press the Center button when the window is highlighted and you will see the data-entry screen. Use that screen to enter any name you want. Use the control wheel or the direction buttons to move the orange highlight bar to the first block on the left under the name window. When that block is highlighted, press the Center button to toggle between letters, numbers and symbols. Then move the highlight bar to the block for the letter you want. Move to the up arrow to shift to uppercase letters. Press the Center button repeatedly to choose the letter you want from each group of letters.

For example, to type the letter "e," move the highlight bar to the "def" block and press the Center button quickly two times to select e. After a second or two, the blinking white cursor will move to the right, and you can repeat this process. You can move the cursor forward or back using the left and right arrows at the upper right in the blocks of characters.

When you have finished entering the name, highlight OK and press the Center button to accept the name.

The third option, Set Copyright, lets you set the name of the company or person who holds the copyright for the images to be taken with the camera.

Finally, the Display Copyright Info option lets you see the names now entered in the camera for these items.

FORMAT

This next option on screen 5 of the Setup menu is used to prepare a new memory card to store images and videos with the correct data format. This command also is useful when you want to wipe all the data off a card that has become full or you have copied a card's images to your computer or other storage device. Choose this process only when you want or need to completely wipe all of the data from a memory card. When you select the Format option, as shown in Figure 7-92, the camera will warn you that all data currently on the card will be deleted if you proceed.

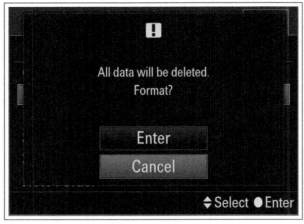

Figure 7-92. Format Confirmation Screen

If you reply by highlighting Enter and pressing the Center button to confirm, the camera will format the card that is in the camera, and the result will be a card that is empty and properly formatted to store new images and videos.

With this procedure, the camera will erase all files, including those that have been protected from accidental erasure with the Protect function on the Playback menu. It's a good idea to periodically save your images and videos to your computer or other storage device and then re-format your card to make sure it is properly set up for recording new images and videos. It's also a good idea to use the Format command on any new memory card when you first insert it into the camera. Even though it likely will work without that procedure, it's best to make sure the card is set up with Sony's method of formatting for the RX100 V.

FILE NUMBER

This option controls how the camera assigns file numbers to images and MP4 movies. The choices are Series or Reset, as seen in Figure 7-93.

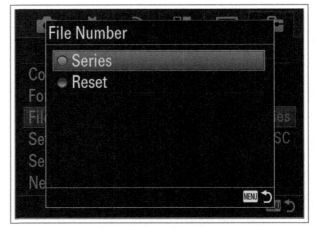

Figure 7-93. File Number Menu Options Screen

If you choose Series, then the camera continues numbering where it left off, even when the camera creates a new folder for images or you put a new memory card in the camera. For example, if you have shot 112 images on your first memory card, the last image likely will be numbered 100-0112: 100 for the folder number (the first folder number available) and 0112 for the image number. If you then switch to a new memory card with no images on it, the first image on that card will be numbered 100-0113 because the numbering scheme continues in the same sequence. If you choose Reset instead, the first image on the new card will be numbered 100-0001 because the camera resets the numbering to the first number.

SET FILE NAME

This menu option, which is highlighted in Figure 7-94, lets you specify the first three characters for file names of your images. By default, those characters are DSC, so a typical image might be named DSC00150.jpg. You can choose any other characters by using the data-entry screen for this option, shown in Figure 7-95. Those three characters will then appear at the beginning of the file name for any images captured after you change this setting, if the images use the sRGB color space. If the images use the Adobe RGB color space, the camera will add an underscore character before the file name, as shown in Figure 7-95.

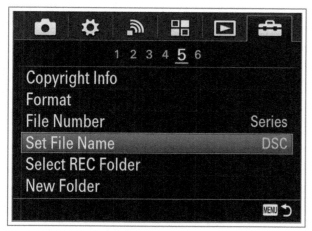

Figure 7-94. Set File Name Menu Option

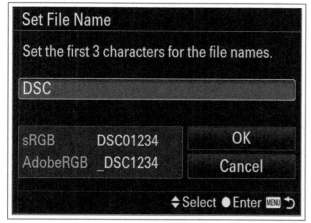

Figure 7-95. Data Entry Screen for Set File Name Menu Option

SELECT REC FOLDER

When you select this menu item, the camera displays an orange bar with the name of the current folder, as shown in Figure 7-96.

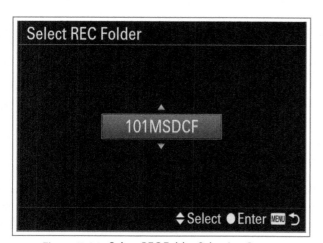

Figure 7-96. Select REC Folder Selection Screen

You can use the Up and Down buttons or turn the Control wheel to choose another folder on the memory card if one exists, so you can store future images in that folder. For example, if you take some photos for business and some for pleasure, you could create a new folder for business shots (see the next menu item, below). The camera would then use that folder. Afterward, you could use the Select REC Folder option to select the folder where your personal images are stored and take more images that will be stored there. This option is not available if you use Date Form for the File Name option, discussed later in this section. This option also selects the folder number for storing MP4 videos, though that folder is different from the one for still images.

NEW FOLDER

This next item lets you create a new folder on your memory card for storing images. After you highlight this item on the menu screen and press the Center button, you will see a message announcing that a new folder has been created, as shown in Figure 7-97. The camera will store new images in that folder until you select another folder with the Select REC Folder option, discussed above, or create another folder using this option.

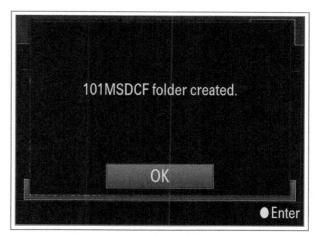

Figure 7-97. New Folder Confirmation Screen

The camera will create a new folder for storing MP4 videos at the same time. The camera also will create a new folder once a folder contains 4,000 images. Folders for still images are created within the DCIM folder, and folders for MP4 videos are created within the MP_ ROOT folder. (AVCHD videos and XAVC S videos are stored in different folders that are not affected by this command.)

I find this option useful for organizing images. When I go on a trip to take photos at a particular location, I often create a new folder to store the photos from that trip so I can easily find them and upload them to my computer when I return.

The sixth and final screen of the Setup menu is shown in Figure 7-98.

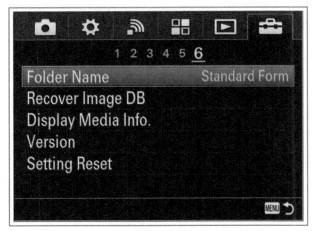

Figure 7-98. Screen 6 of Setup Menu

FOLDER NAME

This option gives you a choice of two methods for naming folders that store still images on your memory card, as seen in Figure 7-99: Standard Form or Date Form.

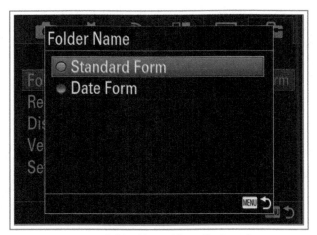

Figure 7-99. Folder Name Menu Options Screen

Standard Form uses the folder number, such as 100, 101, or higher, followed by the letters MSDCF. An example is 100MSDCF. If you choose Date Form, folder names will have the same 100 or higher number followed by the date, in a form such as 10061124 for a

folder created on November 24, 2016, using only one digit to designate the year.

I find the date format confusing and hard to read, and I am used to the MSDCF format. If you use the date format, you will end up having a folder for every date on which you record still images. You may prefer having your image folders organized in that way so you can quickly locate images from a particular date. I prefer having fewer folders and organizing the images using software on my computer according to my own preferences.

RECOVER IMAGE DATABASE

This menu item activates the Recover Image Database function. If you select this option and press the Center button to confirm it on the next screen, as shown in Figure 7-100, the camera runs a check to test the integrity of the file system on the memory card.

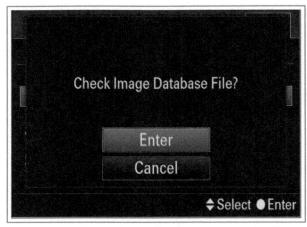

Figure 7-100. Recover Image Database Confirmation Screen

I have never used this menu option, but if the camera is having difficulty reading the images on a card, using this option might recover the data.

DISPLAY MEDIA INFORMATION

The next item on this menu screen gives you another way to see how much storage space is remaining on the memory card that is currently in the camera.

When you select Display Media Information and press the Center button, the camera displays a screen like that in Figure 7-101, with information about the number of still images or the minutes of video that can be recorded using current settings. It is nice to have this option available, although the number of images that can be recorded is also displayed on the detailed shooting screen, and the number of minutes of video that can be recorded is displayed on the video recording screen once a recording has been started.

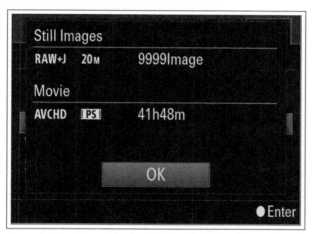

Figure 7-101. Display Media Information Screen

The available storage time for video files is displayed before a recording starts, if the Mode dial is set to the Movie or HFR position.

VERSION

This menu option displays the current version of the firmware installed in your camera. The Sony Cyber-shot DSC-RX100 V, like other digital cameras, is programmed at the factory with firmware, which is a set of computer instructions electronically implanted in the camera. These instructions control all aspects of the camera's operation, including the menu system, functioning of the controls, and in-camera processing of your images. The reason you may want to check to see what version is installed is that, in many cases, the manufacturer will release an updated version of the firmware that may fix problems or bugs in the system, provide minor enhancements, or, in some cases, even provide major improvements, such as adding new shooting modes or menu options.

To determine the firmware version installed in your camera, highlight this menu option and press the Center button, and the camera will display the version number, as shown in Figure 7-102.

To see if firmware upgrades have been released, visit Sony's support website at http://esupport.sony.com. Find the link for Drivers and Software, then the link for Cyber-shot Cameras, and then a link to any updated

version for the RX100 V (often referred to by Sony as the RX100M5). The site will provide instructions for downloading and installing the new firmware.

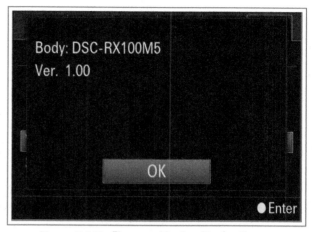

Figure 7-102. Firmware Version Display Screen

SETTING RESET

This final option on the Setup menu is useful when you want to reset some or all of the camera's settings to their original (default) values. This action can be helpful if you have been playing around with different settings and you find that something is not working as expected.

With this item, the camera presents you with two sub-options: Camera Settings Reset and Initialize, as shown in Figure 7-103.

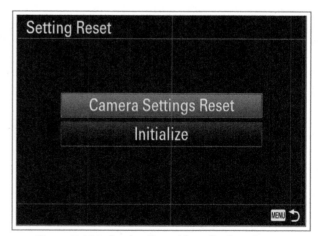

Figure 7-103. Setting Reset Menu Options Screen

If you choose Camera Settings Reset, only the settings that directly affect the shooting of images and videos are reset. If you select Initialize, all settings, including items such as Audio Signals and Monitor Brightness, are reset to their factory values.

CHAPTER 8: MOTION PICTURES

The RX100 V is a stellar performer for capturing still images, and it must be considered primarily a camera for stills. But Sony has included a solid set of movie-recording features in this camera. Although a camera this small is not one you might think of for professional-level video shooting, it comes with features that would allow you to produce footage for many high-end applications. Before I discuss specific settings you can make for your movies, I'll begin with a brief overview of the process.

Movie-Making Overview

In one sense, the basics of making movies with the RX100 V can be stated in four words: "Push the red button." (That is, the red Movie button at the upper right corner of the camera's back.) In most situations, you can press and release that button while aiming at your subject, and you will get results that are likely to be quite usable. You do not need to worry about special settings, particularly if you set the camera to one of the more automatic modes, such as Auto or Scene. (You can record a normal-speed movie with the Mode dial at any position except HFR, as discussed later in this chapter.)

To stop recording, press the red button again. If you prefer not to run the risk of recording unwanted movies by pressing the Movie button accidentally, you can change the button's operation so it activates movie recording only when the camera is in Movie mode, as discussed in Chapter 7.

If you're mainly a still photographer with little interest in movie making, you don't need to read further. Be aware that the red button exists, and if an interesting event starts to happen, you can turn the Mode dial to Auto, press the Movie button, and capture footage to post on YouTube or elsewhere with a minimum of effort. But for those RX100 V users who want to use this camera's amazing motion picture capabilities, there is much more information to discuss.

First, there is a requirement that may decide what memory card you get for your camera. To record movies in the high-quality XAVC S formats, you have to use a memory card with a capacity of at least 4 GB and a speed of at least Class 10 or UHS Speed Class 1. If you do not use a card with those specifications, the camera will display an error message and will not record video using that format.

To record XAVC S video using a Record Setting value of 100M, meaning 100 megabits per second, you have to use a card with a speed in UHS Speed Class 3. Because all 4K videos recorded with this camera use the XAVC S format, this means you have to use a card in UHS Speed Class 1 or SD Speed Class 10 for any 4K video, and a card in UHS Speed Class 3 for 4K video using the 100M setting. (As I will discuss later in this chapter, 4K is a designation for video files of higher resolution than high-definition video.)

I have used the SanDisk Extreme PRO 32 GB SDHC card, the SanDisk Extreme 256 GB SDXC card and the SanDisk Extreme Pro 512 GB card, shown in Figure 8-1, all of which are rated in UHS Speed Class 3, for recording the highest-level formats with no problems, but there are other choices available.

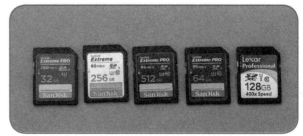

Figure 8-1. High-speed SD Cards for Video Recording

If you are not going to use the highest-level formats, you can use a less-powerful card, such as the SanDisk Extreme PRO 64 GB card or the Lexar 128 GB card, both rated in UHS Speed Class 1, also shown in Figure 8-1. And, as I'll discuss later in this chapter, you can actually record 4K video with no card at all, if you connect the RX100 V to an external video recorder.

Also, it's important to note that the RX100 V, like most cameras in its class, has built-in limitations that prevent it from recording any sequence longer than about 29 minutes (20 minutes for the MP4 format using the 1920 x 1080 60p 28M Record Setting option). And, because of issues with overheating from recording at the highest quality levels, the camera can record for only five minutes at a time when using the XAVC S HD format with the 120p 100M Record Setting option or when recording 4K video. You can, of course, record multiple sequences adding up to any length depending on the amount of storage space available on your memory cards. After five minutes of recording at the highest-quality formats, though, you have to pause for a while to let the camera cool down. (As I'll discuss later, you can avoid this time limitation if you record 4K video to an external recorder.)

If you plan to record a large amount of HD video, you should get a high-capacity and high-speed card. A 64 GB card can hold about one hour and 15 minutes of the highest quality of 4K video, five hours of the highest quality of AVCHD video, or about 22 hours of the lowest quality of MP4 HD video. (I will discuss these video formats later in this chapter.)

Details of Settings for Shooting Movies

As I noted above, the one step that is a necessity for recording a movie with the RX100 V is to press the Movie button. However, there are numerous settings that affect the way the camera records a movie when that button is pressed.

I will discuss four categories of settings: (1) the movie-related selections you make on the Shooting menu; (2) the position of the Mode dial on top of the camera; (3) the other selections you make on the Shooting menu and other menus; and (4) the settings you make with the camera's physical controls.

Movie-Related Shooting Menu Options

First, the movie-related options on the Shooting menu control the format and other important settings for movies you record with the RX100 V. I discussed this

menu in Chapter 4, but I did not provide details about all of the movie-oriented options in that chapter.

As noted above, you can press the Movie button to start a normal-speed video recording at any time and in any shooting mode (except for HFR), as long as the Movie Button option on screen 6 of the Custom menu is set to Always. Because of this ability to shoot movies in almost any shooting mode, you can always change the settings for movie recording using the Shooting menu, no matter what shooting mode the camera is set to. I will discuss each item on the Shooting menu that has an effect on your shooting of videos.

At this point, I will discuss the Shooting menu options that apply only to movies; later in this chapter, I will discuss options on this menu and other menus that affect movies as well as still images, such as White Balance, ISO, Creative Style, Picture Effect, and others.

File Format

The first item on screen 2 of the Shooting menu, File Format, gives you a choice of the four available movie recording formats on the RX100 V—XAVC S 4K, XAVC S HD, AVCHD, and MP4, as shown in Figure 8-2.

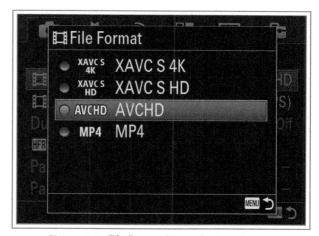

Figure 8-2. File Format Menu Options Screen

This setting determines the format the camera will use for movies when you press the Movie button. The characteristics of the formats are discussed below.

XAVC S 4K

The XAVC S format is a consumer version of the XAVC format, developed for use with 4K video recording, sometimes known as Ultra HD. The term "4K" refers to a horizontal resolution of roughly 4,000 pixels, instead of the 1920 pixels in standard HD video. On the

RX100 V, video recorded with the 4K format has a pixel count of 3840 x 2160. Because of its high resolution, this option provides excellent quality for your videos. To enjoy the full benefit of the format, you need to view the videos on a TV set that is equipped for 4K viewing. However, even without that type of TV, you can edit 4K videos with appropriate software, such as Adobe Premiere Pro, Sony Vegas Pro, and others. In the editing process, you can downsample the 4K video clips to a standard HD format, such as 1920 x 1080 pixels, and they will have greater quality than videos originally recorded in an HD format.

As noted earlier, there are restrictions on the use of this format. First, you have to use a memory card with a capacity of 4 GB or greater, rated at least in Speed Class 10 or UHS Speed Class 1. If you use the highest-quality Record Setting option, the card must be rated in UHS Speed Class 3. Second, because of heat buildup caused by using this format, the camera will not record 4K video to an internal memory card for more than five minutes in any one sequence, and it may stop recording even before that time. After that, you will have to wait for the camera to cool down before starting to record more video.

However, as I will discuss later in this chapter, you can avoid both of these restrictions for 4K video if you connect the RX100 V to an external video recorder, such as the Atomos Shogun, using an HDMI cable, and record to the Shogun recorder without recording to the camera's memory card. With that system, you can record a sequence somewhat beyond the normal limit of five minutes. I'm not suggesting that that system is simple or inexpensive, but it is available if you need to use the RX100 V for extended 4K video recording.

XAVC S HD

This second option for File Format also uses the high-quality XAVC S format, but records using an HD resolution of 1920 x 1080 pixels rather than the higher 4K resolution. This option will give you excellent quality without requiring the use of a 4K-capable TV set. However, it carries with it the same requirements for a high-speed memory card as the 4K format. If you record in this format using the highest-quality option for Record Setting, this format also has the five-minute restriction for recording time.

AVCHD

If you don't want to purchase the high-speed memory card required for the XAVC S formats, but you still want high quality for your movies, you can choose AVCHD. This format, developed jointly by Sony and Panasonic, has become increasingly common in advanced digital cameras. It provides excellent quality, and movies recorded in this format on the RX100 V can be used to create Blu-ray discs.

MP4

If you want to record movies with excellent video quality but in a format that is easier to edit with a computer than the first three options and easy to share on the Internet or by e-mail, you can choose MP4. The MP4 format is compatible with Apple Computer's QuickTime software, and the files can be edited with various software programs, including QuickTime, iMovie, Windows Movie Maker, and many others.

Record Setting

The Record Setting item on the Movie menu is another quality-related option for recording video. (The accent is on the second syllable of "Record.") The choices for this item are different depending on whether you choose XAVC S 4K, XAVC S HD, AVCHD, or MP4 for File Format. I will discuss these options assuming you have your camera set for NTSC, the video standard used in the United States, using the NTSC/PAL Selector option on screen 3 of the Setup menu, as discussed in Chapter 7. If you have set the camera for PAL, the choices for Record Setting will include numbers such as 50p and 25p instead of 60p, 30p, and 24p.

XAVC S 4K

If you choose XAVC S 4K for File Format, the four options for Record Setting are 30p 100M, 30p 60M, 24p 100M, and 24p 60M, as shown in Figure 8-3. For these choices, the letter "p" is for progressive, which means the camera records 30 or 24 full video frames per second. (The other option, used with some AVCHD formats, as discussed below, is designated by the letter "i," standing for interlaced. With those options, such as 60i, the camera records 60 fields, or half-frames, per second, which yields lower quality and fewer possibilities for editing.) The standard speed for recording video in the United States is about 30 frames per second, and using the 30p setting will yield excellent quality.

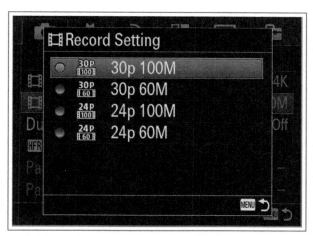

Figure 8-3. Record Setting Options for XAVC S 4K Format

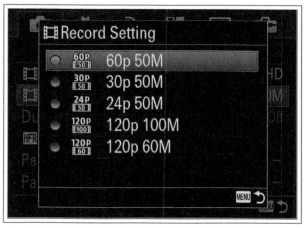

Figure 8-4. Record Setting Choices for XAVC S HD Format

If you select either of the 24p options, your video will be recorded and played back at 24 fps. The 24p rate is considered by some people to be more "cinematic" than the 30p format. This may be because 24 fps is a standard speed for movie cameras that shoot with film. My preference is to use the 30p format, but if you find that 24p suits your purposes better, you have that option with the RX100 V.

The 60M or 100M designation means that these formats record video with a bit rate up to a maximum of 60 or 100 megabits per second, which are very high rates that yield excellent quality. As noted earlier, when you record using the 100M setting, you have to use a memory card rated in UHS Speed Class 3.

My recommendation for this setting is to use 30p 60M unless you have a definite need for the super-high quality of the 30p 100M setting.

XAVC S HD

If you choose XAVC S HD, the five choices for Record Setting are 60p 50M, 30p 50M, 24p 50M, 120p 100M, and 120p 60M, as shown in Figure 8-4. If you use one of the 60p or 120p options, the camera will record at two or four times normal speed, and so will record two or four times as much video information as with the 30p choice. If you use one of those higher speeds, you can produce a slow-motion version of your footage at high quality. This possibility exists because the 60p or 120p footage is recorded with twice or four times the number of full frames as 30p footage, so the quality of the video does not suffer if it is played back at one-half or one-quarter of the normal speed.

If you think you may want to slow down your footage significantly for playback, you should choose the 60p setting, or, for even slower motion, the 120p setting.

Video recorded with the 60p or 120p setting will play back at normal speed in the camera. To play it back in slow motion, you can use a program such as iMovie for the Mac or Movie Maker for Windows. Just set the playback speed to a factor such as 0.5x or 0.25x to play the footage at the slower speed.

All of these options are recorded in full HD, meaning the pixel count for each video frame is 1920 x 1080. The 120p selections (100p for the PAL system) are not available with the Auto and Scene shooting modes. Also, while actually recording a video with either of the 120p options, the camera cannot use face detection, DRO/Auto HDR, a Monitor Brightness setting greater than zero, a Viewfinder Brightness greater than zero, or non-optical zoom. Any of those settings can be made with the 120p setting in place, but once a recording starts using the 120p setting, the conflicting option (face detection, DRO, etc.) will stop working.

Here again, as with the 4K settings, you have to use a UHS Speed Class 3 card if you use the 100M setting, and at least a Speed Class 10 or UHS Speed Class 1 card for the other settings in this format. Any card you use for this format must have a capacity of 4 GB or greater.

AVCHD

With AVCHD for File Format, the five choices for Record Setting are 60i 24M(FX), 60i 17M(FH), 60p 28M(PS), 24p 24M(FX), and 24p 17M(FH), as seen in Figure 8-5.

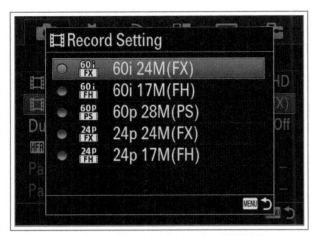

Figure 8-5. Record Setting Choices for AVCHD Format

60i and 60p Video Formats

There are three formats that use 60 fields or frames per second. As noted above, the letter "i" or "p" stands for interlaced or progressive. With interlaced video, the camera records 60 fields per second; a field is equal to one-half of a frame, and the two halves are interlaced to form 30 full frames. The video frame rate of about 30 frames per second (fps) is the standard video playback rate in the United States.

If the letter is "p," for progressive, the camera records 60 full frames per second, which yields higher quality than interlaced video. The 60 frames are later translated into 30 frames for playback at the standard rate of 30 fps. However, as with the XAVC S HD format, if your video-editing software has this capability, you can play back your 60p footage in slow motion at one-half the normal speed and still maintain full HD quality.

The 28M, 24M, or 17M designation states the "bit rate," or volume, of video information that is recorded—either 28, 24, or 17 megabits per second. The higher-numbered settings provide greater quality at the cost of using more storage capacity on the memory card and requiring greater computer resources to edit.

The final designations, FH, FX, and PS, are proprietary labels used by Sony for these various qualities of video. They have no particular meanings; they are just labels for various levels of video quality—PS is the highest, then FX, and then FH.

Choose 60p 28M if you want the highest quality (including slow-motion capability), 60i 24M for excellent quality, or 60i 17M for excellent quality that takes up fewer resources.

24p Video Formats

As with the XAVC S options discussed above, the 24p formats are available if you want a more "cinematic" look for your footage. (If you set your camera to use the PAL system, it will offer 25p formats instead of 24p.)

MP4

If, instead of XAVC S or AVCHD, you choose MP4 for File Format, you are presented with three choices for Record Setting: 1920 x 1080 60p 28M, 1920 x 1080 30p 16M, and 1280 x 720 30p 6M, as shown in Figure 8-6.

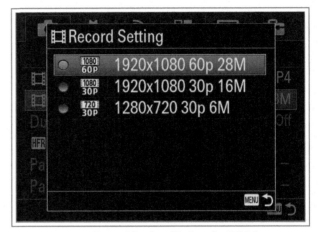

Figure 8-6. Record Setting Choices for MP4 Format

The first two settings provide full HD resolution with the same pixel count as XAVC S HD or AVCHD. The third setting, 1280 x 720, has a lower resolution, but is still HD. As you can see from the bit rate values for these settings, 28M, 16M, and 6M, the bit rates are lower than those of the highest-quality AVCHD or XAVC S settings. Therefore, the quality is not as great, but the MP4 formats take up less storage space than AVCHD or XAVC S and, as noted above, are easier to manipulate with a computer and to send by e-mail.

If you choose the MP4 file format, I recommend you select the 1920 x 1080 60p 28M option to get maximum quality from this setting, unless you are recording a video of household possessions for an inventory or shooting another subject that does not require such high quality. However, you should recall that because of a four GB limitation on file size, the RX100 V can record only 20 minutes of MP4 video at a time in this high-quality HD format. So, if you need to record for a time longer than that in one sequence, you should choose the 1920 x 1080 30p 16M setting, which will still yield excellent quality and record for 29 minutes at a time.

Dual Video Recording

This next menu option, which can be turned either on or off, sets the camera to record an MP4 movie at the same time that it records an XAVC S or AVCHD movie. This feature is like a video version of the Raw & JPEG setting for Quality, for still images. It gives you a video file in a high-quality format for later editing on a computer, along with a lower-quality MP4 version that is easier to manipulate quickly and post to social media sites.

This option is available only when File Format is set to XAVC S 4K, XAVC S HD, or AVCHD. For XAVC S movies, it is available only when Record Setting is set to 30p or 24p; for AVCHD movies, it is available only when Record Setting is set to one of the 60i or 24p formats. It is not available when SteadyShot (Movies) is set to Intelligent Active.

I have not yet found a need to use this setting, but it could be useful if you want to record a video in one of the high-quality formats and also have a second copy available that is easier to edit or share.

HFR Settings

This menu option lets you set up the camera for super-slow-motion video, which you can record when you turn the Mode dial to the HFR position, for high frame rate shooting. I will discuss these options later in this chapter, in a section on HFR shooting.

AF Drive Speed

This option, on screen 4 of the Shooting menu, controls the speed at which the camera's autofocus system changes focus when recording video. The choices are Fast, Normal, or Slow. The Fast option is suitable for sports or other activities when the most important goal is to keep the subject in focus, and quick focus shifts are not a problem. The slower options are for use when you are shooting static or slow-moving subjects, when it may be preferable for focus to adjust more gradually, to avoid jarring the audience with abrupt focus changes. The setting you choose depends on your preference; you may want to experiment with all three and see which one suits your taste best for a given situation. This

option is not available when Record Setting is set to a 120p setting (100p for PAL systems).

AF Tracking Sensitivity

This option, located after AF Drive Speed on the menu, controls how quickly the autofocus system tracks a moving subject when recording video. The choices are Fast and Normal. With Fast, the focus will shift quickly, to track a fast-moving subject. With Normal, the focus shifts at a moderate pace. With the Normal setting, there is less risk that the camera will shift focus when an unwanted subject comes between the camera and the actual subject. For example, if a person walks in front of the camera while you are recording a scene in the distance, with the Normal setting the camera is likely to maintain focus on your actual subject, rather than quickly shifting focus to the person who is temporarily in the way. I recommend using the Normal setting unless you need to track a fast-moving subject, such as a runner in a track meet or a moving vehicle. This option is unavailable with the 120p/100p settings.

Picture Profile

This option, found on screen 6 of the Shooting menu, is applicable for both still images and video recording, though it is really oriented for shooting video. I discussed the details of these settings in Chapter 4. If you want to have the greatest amount of dynamic range available in your video sequences and are willing to go through the effort of color grading your clips with post-processing software, you can choose PP7 for the Picture Profile setting, to take advantage of the S-Log2 setting for gamma curve. Otherwise, choose one of the lower-numbered profiles, or no profile at all. If you want to get involved with parameters such as gamma, black level, detail, and knee, you can create your own profile with the settings you prefer.

If you want to experiment with different Picture Profile settings, you can assign this menu option to one of the control buttons using the Custom Key (Shooting) option on the Custom menu or to the Function menu. You can then call up different Picture Profile settings while recording a video, to see how they affect the recording.

Auto Dual Recording

This third option on screen 7 of the Shooting menu lets you set up the camera to capture still images automatically when a video sequence is being recorded. I will discuss this menu item later in this chapter, in a section on shooting stills during movie recording.

HIGH FRAME RATE

This third option on screen 8 of the Shooting menu is different from the HFR Settings option on screen 2 of that menu. This High Frame Rate option is available for selection only when the Mode dial is at the HFR position. I will discuss this option in the section on HFR shooting, later in this chapter.

MOVIE (EXPOSURE MODE)

This item on screen 8 of the Shooting menu can be selected only when the camera's Mode dial is set to Movie mode, as shown in Figure 8-7. In other shooting modes, this menu option cannot be selected.

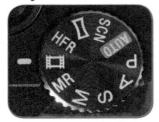

Figure 8-7. Mode Dial at Movie

When the camera is in Movie mode, the Movie option on the menu lets you select an exposure mode for shooting movies. If you have the Mode Dial Guide option turned on through screen 2 of the Setup menu, you won't need to use the Movie option when you first select the Movie mode. When you turn the Mode dial to the Movie position and then press the Center button, the screen with choices for the Movie item will appear automatically. If the Mode Dial Guide option is not active or if the Mode dial is already set to Movie mode, you get to this screen by selecting Movie from the Shooting menu.

With the Mode dial set to Movie mode, navigate to screen 8 of the Shooting menu, select the fourth item, Movie, and a screen will appear with four options: Program Auto, Aperture Priority, Shutter Priority, and Manual Exposure, as shown in Figure 8-8. Move through these choices by turning the Control wheel or by pressing the Up and Down buttons.

You also can call up this screen of options by assigning Shoot Mode to the Function menu using the Function Menu Settings option on screen 5 of the Custom

menu. If you do that, then, with the Mode dial set to Movie, you can press the Function button to activate the Function menu, scroll to the Shoot Mode item, and select your choice of Movie exposure mode. (The Shoot Mode item will be labeled Movie in the Function menu when the Mode dial is at the Movie position.)

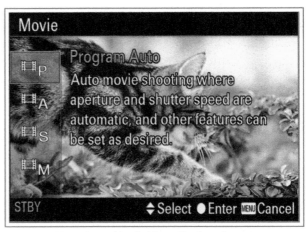

Figure 8-8. Movie Menu Options Screen

Following are details about the behavior of the RX100 V when shooting movies with each of these settings.

Program Auto

With the Program Auto setting, which is highlighted in Figure 8-8, the RX100 V sets aperture and shutter speed according to its metering, and it uses settings from the Shooting menu that carry over to video recording, including ISO, White Balance, Metering Mode, Face Detection, and DRO.

In this mode, the camera can set the aperture anywhere from f/1.8 to f/11.0, depending on the focal length, and it can use a shutter speed as fast as 1/12800 second. The camera will normally not use a shutter speed slower than 1/25 second, 1/30 second, 1/50 second, 1/60 second, or 1/125 second, depending on the settings for File Format and Record Setting. It can use a slightly slower speed in most cases if you turn on the Auto Slow Shutter option, discussed later in this chapter.

Aperture Priority

With the Aperture Priority setting, shown in Figure 8-9, you can set the aperture, just as in the similar mode for still images, and the camera will set the shutter speed based on its metering. You can set the aperture anywhere from f/1.8 to the most narrow f/11.0, depending on the focal length setting of the lens. As with the Program Auto exposure mode for movies, discussed above, the camera will not use shutter speeds slower than those listed for that mode, unless you turn on the Auto Slow Shutter option.

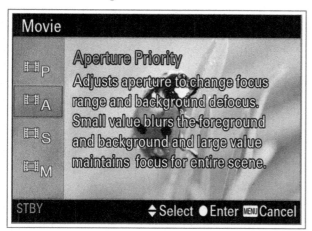

Figure 8-9. Aperture Priority Setting for Movie Option

With this setting, you can adjust the aperture during a video recording. This may not be something you need to do often, but it can be useful in some situations.

For example, you may be recording at a garden show, and at some point you may want to open the aperture wide to blur the background as you focus on a small plant. Afterward, you may want to close the aperture down to a narrow value to achieve a broad depth of field to keep a large area in focus.

Also, you can use aperture control to do a fadeout. For example, in indoor lighting you may start with aperture at f/1.8 and ISO at 200, with Auto Slow Shutter off. Press the Movie button to start recording. When you're ready, turn the Control ring or Control wheel to f/11.0. (I'm assuming the Control ring is set to the Standard option). The scene should fade to black. In brighter light, you may need to turn on ND Filter on screen 5 of the Shooting menu, and you may need to reduce ISO to its minimum setting for movies, which is 125.

Shutter Priority

With the Shutter Priority mode for movies, shown in Figure 8-10, you set the shutter speed and the camera will set the aperture.

Unlike the situation with the Aperture Priority exposure mode for movies, in which the camera normally will not set the shutter speed slower than 1/25 second (or a higher value for some formats), you are able to set the shutter speed as slow as 1/4 second in this mode in most cases, even if Auto Slow Shutter is

turned off. (If Record Setting is set to 120p for XAVC S HD video, the slowest shutter speed available is 1/125 second.) You can select a shutter speed from 1/4 second all the way to the maximum shutter speed for movies, which is 1/12800 second.

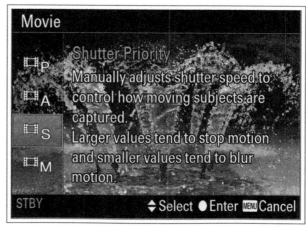

Figure 8-10. Shutter Priority Setting for Movie Option

Of course, to expose your video normally at a shutter speed of 1/12800 second, you must have bright lighting, a high ISO setting, or both. Using a fast shutter speed for video can yield a crisper appearance, especially when there is considerable movement, as when shooting sports or other fast-moving events. In addition, having these very fast shutter speeds gives the camera flexibility for achieving a normal exposure when recording video in bright conditions.

With slower shutter speeds, particularly below the normal video speed of 1/30 second (equivalent to 30 fps), footage can become blurry with the appearance of smearing, especially with panning motions. If you are shooting a scene in which you want to have a drifting, dreamy appearance that looks like motion underwater, this option may be appropriate. You will not be able to achieve good lip sync at the slower shutter speeds, so this technique would not work well for realistic recordings of people talking or singing.

One interesting point is that you can preview this effect on the camera's display even before you press the Movie button to start recording. If you have the shutter speed set to 1/4 second in Movie mode, you will see any action on the screen looking blurry and jerky as if it had already been recorded with this slow shutter speed. (The Live View Display option on screen 3 of the Custom menu is forced to the Setting Effect On option in Movie mode, and you cannot change it.)

With the Shutter Priority exposure mode for movies, you also can achieve a fadeout effect, as with Aperture Priority mode, discussed above. Just turn the Control ring or Control wheel smoothly to increase the shutter speed to its fastest speed of 1/12800 second, and the scene may go black, depending on the lighting conditions. You may need to turn on the ND Filter to achieve full darkness.

Manual Exposure

The last setting for the Movie item, shown in Figure 8-11, gives you more complete control over the exposure of your videos.

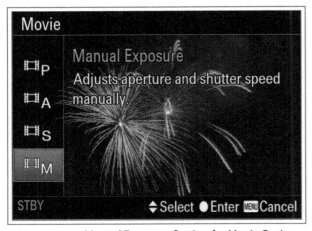

Figure 8-11. Manual Exposure Setting for Movie Option

As with Manual exposure mode for stills, you can adjust both the aperture and the shutter speed to achieve your desired effect. With video shooting, you can adjust the aperture from f/1.8 to f/11.0, depending on the focal length set for the lens, and you can adjust the shutter speed from 1/12800 second to 1/4 second. (If Record Setting is set to 120p for XAVC S HD video, the slowest shutter speed available is 1/125 second.) Using these settings, you can create effects such as fades to and from black as well as similar fades to and from white.

For example, if you begin a recording in normal indoor lighting using settings of 1/60 second at f/3.2 with ISO set to 800, you can start recording the scene, and, when you want to fade out, start turning the Control wheel slowly to the right, increasing the shutter speed smoothly until it reaches 1/12800 second. (You may have to press the Down button to let the Control wheel control shutter speed.) Depending on how bright the lighting is, the result may be complete blackness. Of course, you can reverse this process to fade in from black.

If you want to fade to white, here is one possible scenario. Suppose you are recording video with shutter speed set to 1/400 second and aperture set to f/2.8 at ISO 3200. When you want to start a fade to white, make sure the Control wheel is setting shutter speed, and turn the Control wheel smoothly to the left until the shutter speed decreases all the way to 1/4 second. In fairly normal lighting conditions, as in my office as I write this, the result will be a fade to a bright white screen.

There are, of course, other uses for Manual Exposure mode when recording videos, such as shooting "day for night" footage, in which you underexpose the scene by using a fast shutter speed, narrow aperture, or both, to turn day into night for creative purposes. Also, you might want to use Manual Exposure mode when you are recording a scene in which the lighting may change, but you do not want the exposure settings to change. In other words, you may want some areas to remain dark and some to be unusually bright, rather than have the camera automatically adjust the exposure. In some cases, having a constant exposure setting can be preferable to having the scene's brightness change as the metering system adjusts the exposure.

Note that you can set ISO to Auto ISO with the Manual Exposure setting if you want. With the Auto ISO setting, you can maintain a constant aperture and shutter speed, but the camera will adjust exposure using the ISO setting to the extent that it can. You might want to use that setup if you need to maintain a narrow aperture to have a broad depth of field.

STEADYSHOT (MOVIES)

The second SteadyShot item on screen 8 of the Shooting menu, shown in Figure 8-12, is different from the SteadyShot (Still Images) item above it. (The Movies and Still Images designations are indicated by icons on the menu—a movie-film icon for Movies and a mountain/landscape icon for Still Images.)

As shown in Figure 8-13, the SteadyShot (Movies) setting offers four options: Off, Standard, Active, and Intelligent Active, unlike the Still Images version, which is limited to being turned on or off. With the Movies version, if you select Standard, the camera uses the same stabilization system used for shooting stills. If you select Active or Intelligent Active, the camera uses an additional electronic stabilizing system that can compensate for unwanted camera movement to a greater extent.

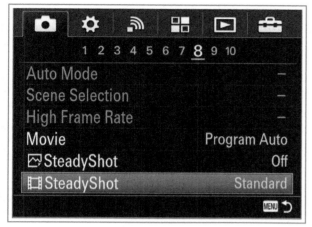

Figure 8-12. SteadyShot (Movies) Highlighted on Menu

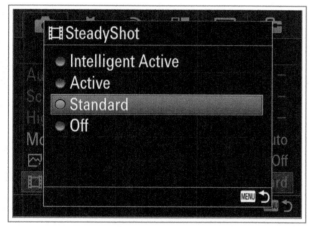

Figure 8-13. SteadyShot (Movies) Menu Options Screen

The Active and Intelligent Active settings are not available when File Format is set to XAVC S 4K.

With the Active setting, the camera crops out parts of the image at the edges to compensate for the required processing of the image. With Intelligent Active, the camera uses an even stronger stabilizing effect and crops the frame even more heavily.

Figures 8-14 through 8-17 illustrate the cropping that results with the various settings of SteadyShot (Movies), using the same scene in each case. In Figure 8-14, SteadyShot (Movies) was turned off; in Figure 8-15 it was set to Standard; in Figure 8-16 to Active; and in Figure 8-17 to Intelligent Active.

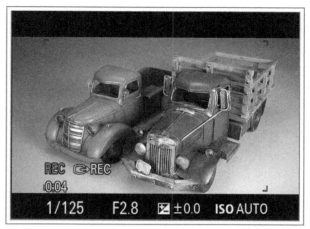

Figure 8-14. SteadyShot (Movies) Turned Off

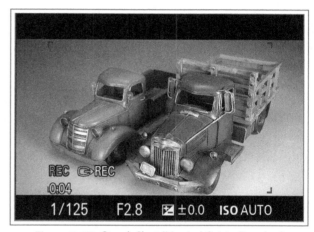

Figure 8-15. SteadyShot (Movies) Set to Standard

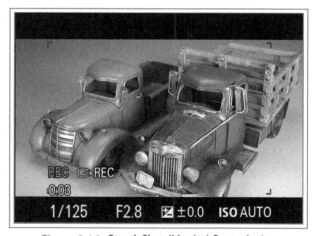

Figure 8-16. SteadyShot (Movies) Set to Active

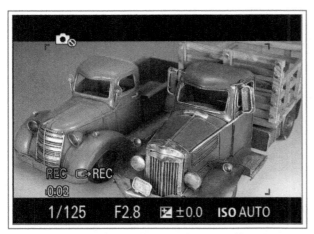

Figure 8-17. SteadyShot (Movies) Set to Intelligent Active

As you can see, the Standard setting does not crop the frame, but the Active setting crops pixels from all four sides of the frame, and Intelligent Active crops even more pixels from all four sides. I recommend using Standard in most cases to avoid the cropping that comes from using the Active or Intelligent Active setting. If you need to shoot movies when there is a great likelihood of camera movement, though, those two settings can be useful. They can be especially helpful if you need to hand-hold the camera as you walk.

Auto Slow Shutter

This item on screen 9 of the Shooting menu can be turned either on or off. When this option is turned on and the RX100 V is recording a movie using automatic exposure, the camera will automatically use a slower shutter speed than normal if the lighting is too dim to achieve a proper exposure otherwise.

The details of this option depend on the setting for Record Setting on screen 2 of the Shooting menu. (The File Format setting does not matter; the rules stated here apply for all File Format settings.)

If Record Setting is at a 60p or 60i setting, the camera normally will not use a shutter speed slower than 1/60 second. (This makes sense, because, in order to record 60 fields or frames per second with good quality, a shutter speed of 1/60 second is needed.) If Auto Slow Shutter is on, the camera can use a shutter speed as slow as 1/30 second.

If Record Setting is at one of the 30p settings, the camera ordinarily will use a shutter speed no slower

than 1/30 second, but it will go down to 1/15 second with Auto Slow Shutter turned on.

If Record Setting is at one of the 24p settings, the camera ordinarily will use a shutter speed no slower than 1/50 second, but it will go down to 1/25 second with Auto Slow Shutter turned on.

However, if Record setting is at one of the 120p settings (available only when File Format is set to XAVC S HD), the slowest shutter speed available is 1/125 second, and the Auto Slow Shutter option is not available.

Rather confusingly, the camera will let you turn on Auto Slow Shutter when the Mode dial is set to Movie and the Movie exposure mode is set to Shutter Priority or Manual Exposure. However, the setting you make for shutter speed will stay in place and the Auto Slow Shutter option will have no effect, even when the menu item is turned on. The same situation is true when the Mode dial is set to the Shutter Priority or Manual exposure mode for stills. You can shoot video in those modes while adjusting the shutter speed and you can turn on Auto Slow Shutter, but that setting will have no effect; the shutter speed you set will take priority.

In addition, for the Auto Slow Shutter option to work, ISO must be set to Auto ISO.

The use of an unusually slow shutter speed can produce a slurred or blurry appearance because the shutter speed may not be fast enough to keep up with the motion in the scene. But, if you are recording in a dark area, this option can help you achieve properly exposed footage, so it is worth considering in that situation.

Audio Recording

This next option on screen 9 of the Shooting menu determines whether or not the RX100 V records sound with its movies. If you are certain you won't need the sound recorded by the camera, you can turn this option off. I never turn it off, because you can always turn down the volume of the recorded sound when playing the video, or if you are editing the video on a computer, you can delete the sound and replace it as needed, but you can never recapture the original audio after the fact.

Micref Level

The next movie-related option is Micref Level, the fourth item on screen 9 of the Shooting menu.

This option, whose screen is shown in Figure 8-18, can be set to Normal or Low.

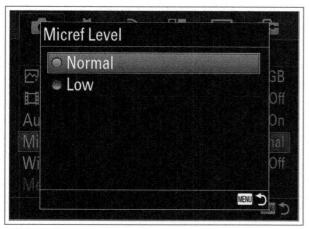

Figure 8-18. Micref Level Menu Options Screen

This setting controls how the camera records audio for movies using its built-in stereo microphone. With Normal, the default setting, the camera uses an automatic gain control to boost the level of quiet sounds to an audible volume. However, it also boosts the level of ambient sounds from sources such as heating or air conditioning equipment. You might want to use this setting if you are recording a speech or a small, relatively quiet event, so the camera will not miss any important sounds.

The Low setting would be more appropriate when you are recording an event such as a concert, and you want to let the sound level vary according to the sound levels of the music without any artificial boosting or limiting.

WIND NOISE REDUCTION

This option, if turned on, activates an electronic filter designed to reduce the volume of sounds in the low frequencies of wind noise. I recommend not activating this feature unless the wind is quite strong, because it limits the sounds that are recorded. With video (or audio) editing software, you can remove sounds in the frequencies that may cause problems for the sound track, but using the camera's built-in wind noise filter may permanently remove or alter some wanted sounds.

Effects of Mode Dial Position on Recording Movies

The second factor that affects video recording with the RX100 V is the position of the Mode dial. As I discussed

above, you can shoot normal-speed movies with the dial in any position except HFR (if the Movie Button menu option is set that way), and you can get access to many movie-related menu items no matter what position the dial is in. However, as I noted above, the shooting mode does make some difference for your movie options.

First, the position you select on the Mode dial determines whether you can adjust the aperture and/or shutter speed for your movies. If the dial is set to the Auto, Scene, Program, or Sweep Panorama mode, the camera will set both aperture and shutter speed automatically. However, if the dial is set to the Aperture Priority, Shutter Priority, or Manual exposure position, you will be able to adjust the aperture, shutter speed, or both aperture and shutter speed, just as you can when shooting still images. The range of available shutter speeds is different for movies than for still images, but you can make these adjustments at any time.

You also can make those adjustments when the Mode dial is set to the Movie position and you select one of the more advanced exposure modes using the Movie item on screen 8 of the Shooting menu. For example, if you select Manual Exposure for the Movie menu item with the Mode dial at the Movie position, you can adjust both aperture and shutter speed for your movies, in the same way as if the Mode dial were set to the M position. (If you set the Mode dial to the HFR setting, you can shoot high frame rate movies, which will play back as slow-motion movies. I will discuss those options in an HFR section later in this chapter.)

Because of the ability to adjust aperture and shutter speed in the advanced still-shooting modes, you might wonder why you would ever use the Movie position on the dial—why not just set the dial to A, S, or M if you want to adjust aperture and/or shutter speed while recording a movie, or to P if you want the camera to set the aperture and shutter speed automatically?

The answer is that several options or settings are available only when the Mode dial is at the Movie position. For one thing, you will see how the video recording will be framed before you press the Movie button to start recording. If the Mode dial is at one of the still-oriented positions such as Auto, Scene, or one of the PASM modes, the display will show the live view according to the current setting for Aspect Ratio on screen 1 of the Shooting menu. If that setting is 3:2,

4:3, or 1:1, it will not correspond to the framing of the video, which will be recorded in a widescreen format, until you press the Movie button to start recording. (If Aspect Ratio is set to 16:9, the framing will show approximately how the video framing will look before you press the Movie button.)

When the Mode dial is at the Movie position, the camera adjusts the live view to show how the video will look before you press the Movie button, so you will know before you start the recording how to set up the shot to include all of the needed background and foreground elements.

In addition, when the Mode dial is at the Movie position, you can take advantage of the Movie Button menu option, on screen 6 of the Custom menu, to limit normal-speed video recording to that one shooting mode. In this way, you can make it impossible to start a recording accidentally by pressing the Movie button when the Mode dial is set to a still-oriented mode such as Auto, Scene, or one of the PASM modes. If that setting is turned on, you will need to turn the Mode dial to the Movie position in order to record a video.

Moreover, several menu options are not available when the Mode dial is at any position other than Movie. In particular, on screen 3 of the Setup menu, the 4K Output Select option is not available, nor are most of the sub-settings of the TC/UB Settings option. All of these settings can be useful when recording to an external video recorder. In addition, the Marker Display option on screen 2 of the Custom menu can be selected in any shooting mode, but any marker you have selected for display will not appear in still-oriented modes until you actually start recording. When the Mode dial is at the Movie position (or the HFR position), you will see the marker on the display before the recording starts, so you can set up your composition ahead of time.

Also, the camera's shooting mode has an effect on what options are available on the Shooting menu and with the control buttons, as discussed in following sections of this chapter. For example, if the Mode dial is set to Auto, Sweep Panorama, or Scene, the Shooting menu options are limited. If the Mode dial is set to Program, Aperture Priority, Shutter Priority, or Manual exposure, the options are greater. This point is important for video shooting because, as discussed below, several

important Shooting menu options carry over to movie recording.

If the camera is set to Program mode (P on the Mode dial), you can make several settings that will control the recording of videos while the Mode dial is in that position. The camera will set the aperture and shutter speed automatically, as it does with still-image shooting. You can use exposure compensation to vary the exposure, but only within the range of plus or minus 2.0 EV, instead of the 3.0-EV positive or negative range for still shooting.

If the camera is set to Aperture Priority mode (A on the Mode dial), you will have the same Shooting menu options as in Program mode, and you can also set the aperture; the camera will set the shutter speed automatically, but the range of available shutter speeds will be somewhat different than for still images. That range is determined by the Record Setting option selected and the setting of the Auto Slow Shutter menu option, as discussed earlier in this chapter.

If the camera is set to Shutter Priority mode (S on the mode dial), you will have the same Shooting menu options as in Program mode, and you can also set the shutter speed. In this case, you can set the shutter speed anywhere from 1/4 second (the camera's slowest setting for movies) to 1/12800 second (the camera's fastest setting for movies), regardless of the Record Setting or Auto Slow Shutter settings, with one exception. The one exception is that the slowest setting available is 1/125 second when Record Setting is set to either of the 120p settings (100p for the PAL system), which are available when File Format is set to XAVC S HD.

If the camera is set to Manual exposure mode (M on the mode dial), you will have the same Shooting menu options as before and you can set both shutter speed and aperture, with the same restrictions for shutter speed settings noted above for Shutter Priority mode.

If the camera is set to Sweep Panorama mode, it will act largely as if it were set to Movie mode with the Program Auto exposure mode selected. If it is set to Scene mode, it will shoot movies as if it were set to Intelligent Auto mode, in which limited menu options are available. It will not recognize any specific scene settings, such as Portrait, Sports Action, or Sunset.

There is a lot of information involved in outlining the differences in the RX100 V's behavior for video recording in different shooting modes, so I am including here a table that lays out the more important differences, for reference.

Table 8-1. Behavior of RX100 V for Video Recording in Various Shooting Modes

Shooting Mode:	Auto	Scene	Panorama	HFR	Movie	M	S	A	P
Adjust Aperture During Video Recording	No	No	No	Yes, before recording, depending on High Frame Rate menu option setting	Yes, depending on Movie menu option setting	Yes	No	Yes	No
Adjust Shutter Speed During Video Recording	No	No	No	Yes, before recording, depending on High Frame Rate menu option	Yes, depending on Movie menu option setting	Yes	Yes	No	No
See Video Framing Before Recording Starts	No	No	No	Yes	Yes	No	No	No	No
Use 4K Output Select	No	No	No	No	Yes	No	No	No	No
Use All TC/UB Settings Options	No	No	No	All except TC Run	Yes	No	No	No	No
See Marker Display Items Before Recording Starts	No	No	No	Yes	Yes	No	No	No	No
Use 120p/100p Record Settings Options	No	No	Yes	No	Yes	Yes	Yes	Yes	Yes
Can record video if Movie Button Menu Option is set to Movie Mode Only	No	No	No	HFR video only	Yes	No	No	No	No

Effects of Other Shooting Menu Settings on Recording Movies

Next, I will discuss other Shooting menu options that have an effect on movie recording, beyond the options that are applicable only to movie recording, such as File Format, Record Setting, Auto Slow Shutter, and the others discussed earlier in this chapter.

One of the main reasons the shooting mode is important for movies is that, just as with still photography, some menu options are not available in some shooting modes. For example, in an advanced still-shooting mode such as Aperture Priority or Program, video recording will be affected by such settings as Focus Mode, Focus Area, Exposure Compensation, ISO, ND Filter, Metering Mode, White Balance, DRO, Creative Style, Picture Effect, Picture Profile, Focus Magnifier, Center Lock-on AF, and Face Detection, among others.

In some cases, you can adjust these settings while the video is being recorded. You cannot get access to the Shooting menu by pressing the Menu button; you have to use a control button or the Control ring to call up the item to adjust. Of course, you have to have that setting assigned to the button or ring ahead of time.

For example, you can adjust ISO while recording a video, but only if ISO is assigned to the Control ring or one of the control buttons using the Custom Key (Shooting) menu option on screen 5 of the Custom menu, or to the Function menu. Table 8-2 shows which of these settings can be adjusted while a video recording is in progress.

Table 8-2. Shooting Menu Items that Affect Movies, and Items that Can Be Adjusted During Video Recording

Shooting Menu Item	Can Adjust During Video Recording
Image Size (Dual Rec)	No
Quality (Dual Rec)	No
File Format	No
Record Setting	No
Dual Video Recording	No
HFR Settings	No
Focus Mode	Yes
Focus Area	Yes
AF Drive Speed	No

AF Tracking Sensitivity	No
Exposure Compensation	Yes
ISO	Yes
ISO Auto Min SS	No
ND Filter	Yes
Metering Mode	No
White Balance	No
DRO/Auto HDR	No
Creative Style	No
Picture Effect	No
Picture Profile	Yes
Focus Magnifier	Yes
Center Lock-on AF	Yes
Smile/Face Detection	No
Auto Dual Recording	Yes
HFR Frame Rate	Yes
Movie (Shoot Mode)	No
SteadyShot (Movies)	No
Auto Slow Shutter	No
Audio Recording	No
Micref Level	No
Wind Noise Reduction	No

There are built-in limitations with some of these settings. Focus Mode can be set to continuous autofocus or manual focus only. Exposure compensation can be adjusted to plus or minus 2.0EV only, rather than the 3.0EV range for still images. The ISO range includes Auto ISO and specific values from 125 to 12800, omitting the lowest settings. You cannot set ISO to Multi Frame Noise Reduction, which would cause the camera to take multiple shots. With Picture Effect, you can use some of the sub-settings, but you cannot use Soft Focus, HDR Painting, Rich-tone Monochrome, Miniature, Watercolor, or Illustration. (As noted on the table, you cannot get access to the Picture Effect settings during video recording.)

There are some other options on the Shooting menu that have no effect for recording movies. Some of these settings are clearly incompatible with shooting movies, such as Drive Mode, Flash Mode, and Auto Object Framing. Some are less obvious, including AF Illuminator and Scene Selection.

There are two other points to make about using Shooting menu settings for movies. First, you have a great deal of flexibility in choosing settings for your movies, even when the camera is not set to the Movie position on the Mode dial. You can set up the camera with the ISO, Metering Mode, White Balance, Creative Style, Picture Effect (to some extent), or other settings of your choice, and then press the Movie button to record using those settings. In this way, you could, for example, record a black-and-white movie in a dark environment using a high ISO setting. Or, you could record a movie that is monochrome except for a broad selection of red objects, using the Partial Color-Red effect from the Picture Effect option, with the red color expanded using the color axis adjustments of the White Balance setting. (Note that you can't use Creative Style and Picture Effect settings at the same time.)

Second, you have to be careful to check the settings that are in effect for still photos before you press the Movie button. For example, if you have been shooting stills using the Posterization setting from the Picture Effect menu option and then suddenly see an event that you want to record on video, if you press the Movie button, the movie will be recorded using the Posterization effect, making the resulting footage practically impossible to use as a clear record of the events. Of course, you may notice this problem as you record the video, but it takes time to stop the recording, change the menu setting to turn off the Picture Effect option, and then press the Movie button again, and you may have missed a crucial part of the action by the time you start recording again.

One way to lessen the risk of recording video with unwanted Shooting menu options is to switch the Mode dial to the Auto position before pressing the Movie button. That action will cause the camera to use more automatic settings and will disable the Creative Style and Picture Effect options altogether. (Of course, you have to have the Movie Button item on screen 6 of the Custom menu set to Always for this approach to work.)

Effects of Physical Controls When Recording Movies

The next settings that carry over to some extent from still-shooting to video recording are those set by the physical controls. In this case, as with Shooting menu items, there are differences depending on the position of the Mode dial. I will not try to describe every possible combination of shooting mode and physical control, but I will discuss some settings to be aware of.

First, you can use the exposure compensation button while recording movies when the Mode dial is set to the P, A, S, M, Movie, or Sweep Panorama setting. That setting is not available during video recording in the Auto or Scene modes. The range of exposure compensation for movies is plus or minus 2.0 EV, rather than the plus or minus 3.0 EV for still images. If you set exposure compensation to a value greater than 2.0 (plus or minus), the camera will set it back to 2.0 after you press the red Movie button to start shooting a movie.

Second, the Function button operates normally. For example, if the Mode dial is set to P for Program mode, then, after you press the Movie button to start recording a movie, you can press the Function button and the Function menu will appear on the screen. This menu will let you control only those items that can be controlled under current conditions, as seen in Figure 8-19.

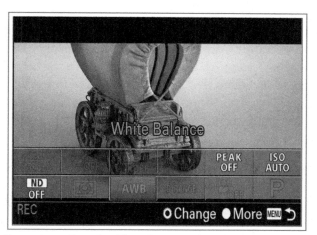

Figure 8-19. Function Menu During Video Recording: P Mode

If you start recording a movie while the Mode dial is set to a mode such as Auto in which most options on the Function Button menu are not available, the RX100 V will display the menu, but few items can be selected, as shown in Figure 8-20.

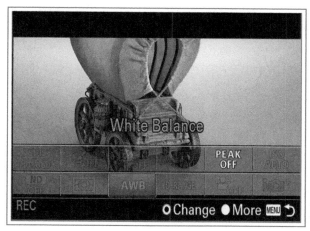

Figure 8-20. Function Menu During Video Recording: Auto Mode

Third, if you assign the Custom, Center, Left, or Right button or the Control ring to carry out a particular operation using the Custom Key (Shooting) option on screen 5 of the Custom menu, you can use that button or wheel to perform the operation while recording a movie if the action is compatible with movie recording in the current shooting mode.

For the Control ring, the functions that can be assigned and controlled during video recording are exposure compensation, ISO, zoom, shutter speed, and aperture. Although White Balance, Creative Style, or Picture Effect can be assigned to the ring and controlled before the recording starts, those listed above are the only items that can be controlled by the ring during the recording.

In addition, there are numerous options that can be assigned to a control button that will function during video recording, if the current context permits that control. For example, if the Left button is set to control ISO and you are shooting a movie with the Mode dial set to P, pressing the Left button will bring up the ISO menu and you can select a value while the movie is recording. If the Mode dial is set to Auto, though, pressing the button will have no effect during recording, because ISO cannot be adjusted in that shooting mode.

If the Center button is assigned its Focus Standard setting through the Custom Key (Shooting) menu option and Center Lock-on AF is turned on through screen 7 of the Shooting menu, you can press the Center button during video recording to activate tracking focus. Of course, to use tracking focus, you have to have an autofocus mode selected using the Focus Mode menu option. You also can press the button to activate the focus frame for moving and resizing, if

Focus Area is set to Flexible Spot or Expand Flexible Spot. (And you can control Focus Area with a control button during video recording as well.) You can turn the Control wheel to resize the frame once it is activated.

If you set the Right button (or some other button) to the AEL Toggle function, you can press that control while recording a movie to lock the exposure setting. This ability can be useful when recording a movie, when you don't want the exposure to change as you move the camera over different areas of a scene.

Following is a list of functions that can be assigned to one of the control buttons and that can be controlled during video recording by pressing the button:

- Focus Standard

- Self-timer During Bracketing

- Focus Mode

- Focus Area

- Exposure Compensation

- ISO

- ND Filter

- Picture Profile

- HFR Frame Rate

- Auto Dual Recording

- SteadyShot (Still Images)

- AEL Hold

- AEL Toggle

- Spot AEL Hold

- Spot AEL Toggle

- AF/MF Control Hold

- AF/MF Control Toggle

- Center Lock-on AF

- Focus Magnifier

- Movie (acting as red Movie button)

- Zebra

- Grid Line

- Marker Display Selection

- Peaking Level

- Peaking Color

- Finder/Monitor Selection

- Gamma Display Assist

- TC/UB Display Switch (switches among counter, time code, and user bit displays)

Some of the items on this list are not useful during video recording, such as Self-timer During Bracketing and SteadyShot (Still Images). However, Sony for some reason has made these items available for use with an assigned button during movie recording, so I have included them on the list.

Some more notes about physical controls: First, Program Shift does not function during video recording. If you turn the Control ring while the camera is set to Program mode (when the Control ring is assigned the Standard setting), the exposure settings will not change while the camera is recording a movie.

Second, the Photo Creativity feature, described in Chapter 2, works during movie recording in a limited way. When the camera is set to Intelligent Auto or Superior Auto mode, you have to press the Down button before the recording starts, to put the Photo Creativity controls on the screen. Then, after you press the Movie button to start recording, you can control Background Defocus, but no other Photo Creativity settings.

High Frame Rate Recording

As discussed earlier in this chapter, the Record Setting options for the RX100 V include several options for recording at higher-than-normal frame rates, including 60 frames per second (fps) and 120 fps (50 fps and 100 fps for PAL systems). In addition, the camera has a special HFR (high frame rate) mode for recording at even higher rates, which produces slow-motion sequences when played back at a normal rate. If you are using the NTSC system, you can record at a rate as high as 960 frames per second (fps); with the PAL system, you can record at up to 1000 fps. With either system, you can create a video sequence to be played back in the camera at up to 40 times slower than normal. Because there are several settings and steps to be taken to use this feature, I will provide a step-by-step guide.

1. Set the Mode dial to HFR, as shown in Figure 8-21.

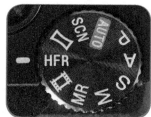

Figure 8-21. Mode Dial at HFR

2. On screen 8 of the Shooting menu, highlight the third option, High Frame Rate, and select one of the available exposure modes, as shown in Figure 8-22—Program Auto, Aperture Priority, Shutter Priority, or Manual Exposure. These modes are similar to those for normal-speed movie shooting, discussed earlier in this chapter. Note that the shutter speeds that can be used will depend on the Frame Rate setting you make in Step 6. For example, if you select 480 fps for the Frame Rate, the shutter speed will have to be 1/500 second or faster.

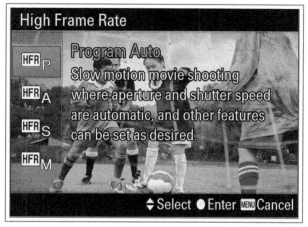

Figure 8-22. High Frame Rate Menu Options Screen

3. Make any control or menu adjustments that are needed. For example, if you selected Aperture Priority for the exposure mode, set the aperture. Set ISO, Focus Mode, and any other available settings, if needed. Select the zoom range for the lens and adjust the focus for your subject. None of these items can be adjusted after the screen has been switched to standby mode for HFR shooting.

4. On screen 2 of the Shooting menu, highlight HFR Settings and press the Center button. You will see a screen like that in Figure 8-23.

5. On this screen, set Record Setting as you want it. This setting is not related to the Record Setting option on screen 2 of the Shooting menu. This setting sets the frame rate for playback of your slow-motion videos. If your camera is set for the NTSC system, the choices for Record Setting are 60p, 30p, or 24p. The bit rate is set at 50M for each of the three settings. The video will be recorded using the XAVC S HD format.

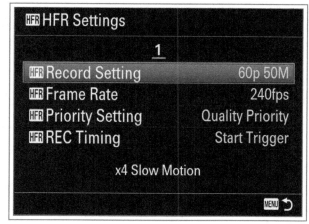

Figure 8-23. HFR Settings Menu Options Screen

6. Go back to the menu options and select Frame Rate. Select 240 fps, 480 fps, or 960 fps. You can determine how slow the slow-motion footage will be by dividing this number by the Record Setting figure. For example, if Frame Rate is 480 and Record Setting is 30, the resulting footage will be slowed down 16 times when played back in the camera.

7. Go back to the menu options and select Priority Setting. Choose either Quality Priority or Shoot Time Priority. This setting lets you decide whether it is more important to be able to shoot for a longer time or with higher image quality. If you choose Quality Priority, you can record for about three or four seconds, depending on the frame rate; if you choose Shoot Time Priority, you can record for about six or seven seconds, depending on the frame rate but at considerably lower resolution.

8. Go back to the menu options and select Rec Timing. Choose either Start Trigger or End Trigger. If you choose Start Trigger, the camera will start the

recording when you press the red Movie button, and will record for the next three-to-four or six-to-seven seconds. If you choose End Trigger, it will end the recording when you press the Movie button, and will capture whatever action it was aimed at for the previous three-to-four or six-to-seven seconds. If the action you are trying to record is predictable, you can use the Start Trigger option. If you need to wait and see which few seconds are most worth capturing before you decide, choose End Trigger and push the Movie button quickly after seeing the action you want to record. Press the Menu button to return to the live view.

9. You will see a screen like that in Figure 8-24, with a message indicating to press the Center button to enter Shooting Standby mode. At this point, you can still press the Menu button to adjust various menu options if necessary. (If you don't see this screen, press the Display button until it appears.)

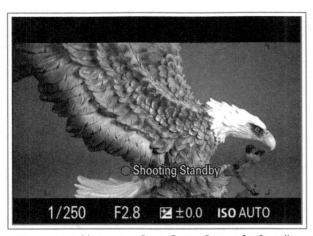

Figure 8-24. Message to Press Center Button for Standby

10. When you are ready to start recording, press the Center button. The camera will briefly display a Preparing . . . message, followed by a message saying Starts Recording with MOVIE Button, and then the screen shown in Figure 8-25, with a green STBY label, for Standby, in the lower left corner.

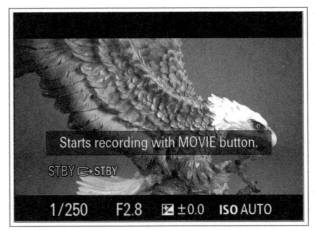

Figure 8-25. HFR Screen in Standby Mode

11. The camera is now in standby mode, waiting for you to press the Movie button to mark the start or end of the brief sequence. (To adjust settings at this point, press the Center button to exit standby mode and make the settings; press the Center button again to return to standby mode.)

12. If you selected Start Trigger for the recording option, wait until you believe the few seconds of action you want to capture is about to start, and press the Movie button just before it starts, if possible. If you selected End Trigger, wait until the few seconds of action has just happened, and immediately press the Movie button. In either case, the camera will display a red Recording . . . label near the top of the screen and a red REC label in the lower left corner. It will then show a recording screen for a fairly long time—much longer than the duration of the action that was captured. You can press the Center button to cancel the recording while that screen is displayed.

13. When the live view returns, you can press the Playback button to view your recording. On your memory card, the video will have a file path such as Untitled:PRIVATE:M4ROOT:CLIP:C0114.mp4.

The HFR feature can produce beautiful videos under the right conditions. Because of the very fast recording rate, it is important to have as much light as possible to achieve excellent quality. I recommend using Quality Priority for the Priority Setting option, unless you have a definite need to record for six or seven seconds instead of three or four seconds. Note that the video quality decreases as the slowdown factor increases, so take that factor into consideration when choosing settings. Finally, note that high frame rate videos are recorded with no sound.

Recording to an External Video Recorder

For recording everyday videos such as clips of vacations or family events, the RX100 V will serve you well. However, Sony also has equipped this camera with options that make it suitable for some aspects of professional video production. Several of these options are designed for use when the camera sends video to an external video recorder. I will not try to discuss all possible scenarios for using the RX100 V with a recorder, but I will describe the steps I took to record video with the camera connected to an Atomos Shogun 4K recorder, discussed in Appendix A. I will describe a process for doing this, with the caveat that there undoubtedly are other approaches that will work; this happens to be one that worked for me.

First, make sure the Shogun is powered by a battery or power supply and has a formatted storage disk installed. I used a SanDisk Extreme Pro 480 GB solid state drive (SSD). Connect headphones to monitor sound. On the Input menu, enable HDMI and Timecode Trigger. I selected Apple ProRes HQ as the recording format.

Connect the HDMI input port of the Shogun to the HDMI output port of the RX100 V using a micro HDMI cable. Then turn on both the camera and the recorder, set the camera's Mode dial to Movie mode, and make the settings on the camera shown in Table 8-3.

Table 8-3. Recommended Settings on RX100 V Camera for Recording 4K Video to an Atomos Shogun Recorder

SHOOTING MENU	
File Format	XAVC S 4K
Record Setting	30p 100M
Dual Video REC	Off
Focus Mode	AF-C
Focus Area	Wide
AF Drive Speed	Normal
AF Tracking Sensitivity	Normal
ISO	ISO Auto
Metering Mode	Multi
White Balance	Auto White Balance
Picture Effect	Off

Table 8-3. Recommended Settings on RX100 V Camera for Recording 4K Video to an Atomos Shogun Recorder

Picture Profile	PP1
Movie	Program Auto
SteadyShot (Movies)	Standard, or Off if camera on tripod
Auto Slow Shutter	Off
Audio Recording	On
Micref Level	Normal
Wind Noise Reduction	Off
CUSTOM MENU	
Zebra	Off unless needed
Grid Line	Off unless needed
Marker Display	Off unless needed
Marker Settings	Off unless needed
Zoom Speed	Normal
Zoom Setting	Optical Zoom Only
SETUP MENU	
NTSC/PAL Selector	NTSC (in U.S., etc.)
TC/UB Settings	
TC/UB Display Setting	TC
TC Preset	00:00:00:00
TC Format	DF
TC Run	Rec Run
TC Make	Preset
UB Time Rec	Off
HDMI Settings	
HDMI Resolution	Auto
24p/60p Output	60p
HDMI Info Display	(not available)
TC Output	On
REC Control	On
HDMI Audio Out	On
4K Output Select	Memory Card +HDMI (cannot be turned on until camera and recorder are connected with proper settings)

Some of the above settings are optional or unnecessary and some, such as White Balance, Metering Mode, and Focus Mode, can be changed according to your preferences. The important ones are File Format, Record Setting, the TC/UB settings, the HDMI settings, and the 4K Output Select setting, which makes the HDMI Info Display setting unavailable.

Once these connections are made, press the Movie button on the RX100 V. The screen on the Shogun recorder should indicate that the recording has begun. Use the controls on the camera to zoom or adjust settings as needed. When you are ready to stop the recording, press the Movie button again, and the recorder should stop. When I tested this setup, the recording stopped after four minutes and 59 seconds, because of the five-minute limitation of the camera for recording time. The file recorded by the Shogun was about 32 GB in size.

I also tried a modified version of these settings with no memory card in the camera, setting 4K Output Select to HDMI Only (30p). In that case, I was able to record 4K video continuously for about 18 minutes before the camera displayed an overheating warning and shut down. The resulting video file was more than 115 GB in size, but it imported readily into Adobe Premiere Pro CC for viewing and editing.

Using an External Audio Recorder

One decision Sony made for the RX100 V that seems puzzling is the omission of a jack for plugging in an external microphone to record audio for movies. An earlier model, the RX100 II, accepts external microphones through the Multi Interface Shoe, but the RX100 V has no such option.

The stereo microphone built into the RX100 V records good-quality sound, but, with the superior video quality available with this camera, you may want to record audio using higher-quality microphones.

Fortunately, it is not difficult to do this with the RX100 V, using current technology and software. One way to do this is to use an external video recorder such as the Atomos Shogun, discussed in the previous section. You can connect high-quality microphones to the Shogun using an optional breakout cable with two XLR input jacks.

If you are not using an external video recorder, another approach is to use a separate digital audio recorder and then synchronize the sound from the recorder with the video from the camera. If you use good equipment and software, it can be easy to use this type of system. I'll outline the steps I used; you may find equivalent techniques that work as well.

1. Get a good digital recorder like the Zoom H1, the Zoom H6, the Shure VP83F, the Tascam DR-40, or the Tascam DR-100mkII, which is discussed in Appendix A.

2. Make sure the camera is set to record audio by turning on the Audio Recording option on screen 9 of the Shooting menu.

3. Set the audio recorder to record high-quality audio in a .wav file and place it, or one or more microphones connected to it, in a location to receive the sound clearly.

4. Start the audio recorder, then start the camera recording video and audio.

5. When the recording is done, load the video file and its attached sound track into a video-editing program such as Adobe Premiere Pro CC, Final Cut Pro, or others. You also can use Plural Eyes, a program from redgiant.com that synchronizes audio and video.

6. The software will compare the waveforms from the camera's sound track and the external audio track to move them into sync. With Premiere Pro CC, which I use, the procedure is to select the video track and the two audio tracks, right-click on them, and select Synchronize–Audio–Mix Down. The software will move the external audio track into sync with the video track.

7. Once the external audio track has been synchronized with the video track, you can delete the audio track recorded by the camera.

Of course, this system introduces more complexity and expense into your video-recording process. But, if you want the highest quality audio for your movies, it is worth exploring this method.

Shooting Still Images During Video Recording

The RX100 V has the ability to shoot still images while you are recording a video sequence, though this feature has certain limitations. You cannot capture stills when File Format on screen 2 of the Shooting menu is set to the XAVC S 4K format. If File Format is set to XAVC S HD, Record Setting cannot be set to either of the 120p options. You can use any Record Setting values for AVCHD or MP4 videos. The camera can be set to any shooting mode, except HFR. If the camera is set to Movie mode, you can capture still images during video recording, but you cannot capture still images when the camera is not recording video. If you press the shutter button when the camera is not recording, you will see an error message.

Also, certain menu settings are incompatible with this feature. For example, if Picture Profile is turned on through screen 6 of the Shooting menu, you cannot capture still images during movie recording.

To control the size and quality of the still images you capture, use the Image Size (Dual Recording) and Quality (Dual Recording) items on screen 1 of the Shooting menu. The choices for size are L:17M, M:7.5M, or S:4.2M. The choices for quality are Extra Fine, Fine, or Standard. The images will be captured in the widescreen format of the video. There is no option for capturing Raw images during video shooting.

Assuming you have the Mode dial set to a compatible shooting mode and File Format and Record Setting set to compatible values, with no other conflicting settings in place, once the movie is recording, just press the shutter release button at any time to capture a still image. The camera will display a green CAPTURE message at the top of the screen. There is no limit on the number of still images you can capture in this way, other than the space available on the memory card. If you press the shutter button halfway down during recording, the camera will display the number of still images that can be captured, in the upper left corner. You cannot use the camera's built-in flash when shooting still images during video recording.

There is another option to be aware of for shooting still images during video recording—the Auto Dual Recording feature, found on screen 7 of the Shooting menu. I discussed the details of this setting in Chapter 4. When you turn this option on, the camera is programmed to capture still images during video recording when it detects what it determines to be an "impressive" composition including people. As I noted in Chapter 4, I do not often use this feature, but it might be useful if you were to have a camera set on a tripod, unattended, at a gathering and wanted to have some interesting stills captured while the video was being recorded. This option has the same limitations as

shooting stills by pressing the shutter button. You can still press the shutter button to capture images when this option is activated.

Finally, there is one other way to record still images in connection with video recording—by capturing still frames from a video sequence. For example, if you record video using the XAVC S 4K format, the video clips will have the high resolution of 4K video, giving you the option to save a still frame that is of high enough quality to stand on its own. You can save the frame with the Photo Capture option on screen 3 of the Playback menu or with video editing software. If you use an exposure mode that lets you set the shutter speed, you can choose a fast shutter speed to stop action, and use this technique as a sort of super burst shooting.

Summary of Options for Recording Movies

As I have discussed, there is some complication in trying to explain all of the relationships among the controls and settings of the RX100 V for recording movies. To cut through that complication, I will provide a summary of your options for recording movies with the RX100 V.

To record a video clip with standard settings, set the Mode dial to the Auto or Scene position and press the Movie button. The camera will adjust exposure automatically, and you can use either continuous autofocus (set in this mode using the AF-S or AF-C setting for Focus Mode) or manual focus (MF setting). In those shooting modes, you cannot adjust many shooting options, such as ISO, White Balance, DRO, Creative Style, or Picture Effect. You can use options such as Center Lock-on AF, Face Detection, and SteadyShot (Movies). You can choose File Format and Record Settings options to control the video quality.

For more control over video shooting, set the Mode dial to the P, A, S, or M position. Then you can control several additional Shooting menu options, including ISO, White Balance, Metering Mode, Creative Style, and Picture Effect, among others. You can choose continuous autofocus or manual focus in the same way as for the more automatic shooting modes. You can adjust aperture, shutter speed, or both, or let the camera set them, depending on which shooting mode you select.

For maximum control over movie recording, set the Mode dial to the movie film icon for Movie mode. Then select an option for the movie exposure mode from the Movie item on screen 8 of the Shooting menu. To control aperture, choose Aperture Priority; to control shutter speed, choose Shutter Priority; to control both aperture and shutter speed, choose Manual Exposure. Other options can be selected from the Shooting menu.

Control buttons operate during movie recording if the context permits, as discussed earlier. There are many possibilities for assigning settings to them. If you want a good set of functions tailored for video recording, use the list in Table 8-4 to start, and adjust it for your own needs:

Table 8-4.   **Suggested Control Assignments for Movie Recording**

Control	Function
Control ring	ISO
Custom button	ND Filter
Center button	Focus Standard
Left button	Zebra
Right button	Focus Magnifier

If you want the RX100 V to be ready to record good, standard video footage at a moment's notice without having to remember a lot of settings, I recommend that you set up one of the seven registers of the Memory Recall shooting mode with a solid set of movie-recording settings. Table 8-5 lists one set of settings to consider. (Settings not listed here can be set however you like.) The Record Setting option and the Picture Profile setting in this table make some other settings unavailable, as noted in the table. If you want to use those settings, turn Picture Profile off and use a different option for Record Setting. You also need to turn off Picture Profile if you want to capture still images while recording video.

Table 8-5.   **Suggested Shooting Menu Settings for Recording Movies**

File Format	AVCHD
Record Setting	60p 28M (PS)
Dual Video Recording	Off (not available)
Focus Mode	AF-C
ISO	ISO Auto
ND Filter	Off
Metering Mode	Multi

Table 8-5.   **Suggested Shooting Menu Settings for Recording Movies**

White Balance	Auto White Balance
DRO/Auto HDR	Off (not available)
Creative Style	Standard (not available)
Picture Effect	Off
Picture Profile	PP1
Center Lock-on AF	On
Smile/Face Detection	On
Movie	Program Auto
SteadyShot (Movies)	Standard
Auto Slow Shutter	Off
Audio Recording	On
Micref Level	Normal
Wind Noise Reduction	Off

Other Settings and Controls for Movies

There are several other points to be made about recording and playing back videos that don't concern the Shooting menu or the major physical controls. Here are brief notes about these issues.

The Step Zoom function is not available for video recording, even if the Zoom Function on Ring option is set to Step on screen 6 of the Custom menu. The zoom operates continuously for movies. (Actually, if Zoom Function on Ring is set to Step, the camera will display the Step Zoom scale, but the zoom will operate continuously during video recording despite the presence of the scale on the screen.)

The Display button operates normally to change the information that is viewed during video recording. The screens that are displayed are controlled by the Display Button option on screen 2 of the Custom menu. However, the For Viewfinder screen does not appear for video shooting, even if it was selected through that menu option.

In playback mode, the Display button operates normally for movies. The screen with space for a histogram will display, but the spaces for histogram and other information will be blank.

The MF Assist option on screen 1 of the Custom menu does not operate for video recording, so the camera will not magnify the display when you turn the Control ring to adjust manual focus. However, you can assign the Focus Magnifier function to one of the control buttons and use that capability to enlarge the screen when using manual focus. After you press the assigned control button to put the orange frame on the display, press the Center button to enlarge the area within the frame to 4.0 times normal. (This is less than the 5.3x and 10.7x enlargement factors for still shooting.) Then turn the Control ring to adjust the focus. Half-press the shutter button to dismiss the Focus Magnifier frame.

The Setting Effect Off choice for the Live View Display option on screen 3 of the Custom menu does not function for video recording; the Setting Effect On choice is locked in. So, for example, if you are shooting movies in Movie mode using Manual Exposure for the Movie setting and you have the aperture and shutter speed set for strong underexposure, you cannot adjust this option to make the display more visible.

Movie Playback

As with still images, you can transfer movies to a computer for editing and playback or play them back in the camera, either on the camera's display or on a TV connected to the camera.

If you want to play your movies in the camera, there is one basic aspect of the RX100 V to be mindful of. As I discussed in Chapter 6, the View Mode option on screen 1 of the Playback menu controls what images or videos you will see in playback mode. If you don't see the video you are looking for, check to make sure this menu option is set to display all files from a certain date (Date View), Folder View (MP4), AVCHD View, XAVC S HD View, or XAVC S 4K View.

Once you have selected the proper mode to view your video, navigate to that file by pressing the direction buttons or turning the Control wheel. Once the first frame of the selected video is displayed on the screen, you will see a playback triangle inside a circle, as shown in Figure 8-26. In the lower right corner of the screen will be a Play prompt with a white circle icon indicating that you can press the Center button to play the video. (If you don't see that prompt, press the Display button one or more times until it appears.)

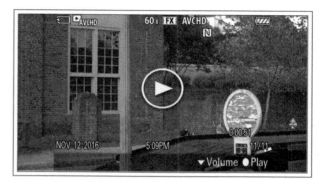

Figure 8-26. Movie Ready to Play in Camera

After you press the Center button to start playback, you will see more icons at the bottom of the screen, as in Figure 8-27. From the left, these icons indicate: Rewind/ Fast Forward; Pause; Open Control Panel; and Exit.

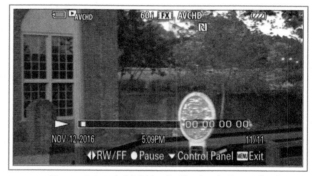

Figure 8-27. Initial Movie Playback Controls

From this screen, you can press the Left or Right button repeatedly to play the movie rapidly forward or backward; multiple presses increase the speed up to four times.

While the video is playing, if you press the Down button, you will see a new line of controls at the bottom of the screen, as seen in Figure 8-28.

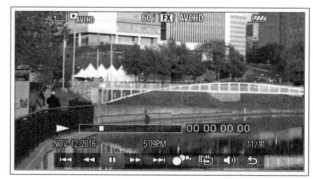

Figure 8-28. Detailed Playback Controls While Movie Playing

When the movie is playing, these icons indicate, from left to right: Previous Movie; Fast Reverse; Pause; Fast

Forward; Next Movie; Motion Shot; Photo Capture; Volume; and Close Control Panel.

When the movie is paused, the icons change, as in Figure 8-29. Those icons indicate, from left to right: Previous Frame; Reverse Slow; Normal Playback; Forward Slow; Next Frame; Motion Shot; Photo Capture; Volume; and Close Control Panel.

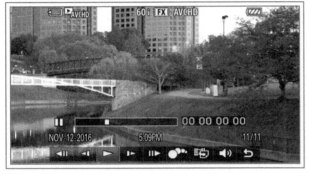

Figure 8-29. Detailed Playback Controls While Movie Paused

In either case, move through the icons with the Left and Right buttons, and press the Center button to select the function for that icon.

When a movie is playing, you can fast-forward or fast-reverse through a video at increasing speeds by turning the Control wheel right or left or by pressing the Right or Left button.

MOTION SHOT FEATURE

The icon on the movie playback control panel that is a series of shrinking circles represents the Motion Shot feature. With this option, you can slow down the playback of a movie and display a motion sequence as a series of multiple exposures on the camera's screen, or on a TV screen if you have the camera connected to one.

This feature works only with AVCHD and MP4 movies, not with movies recorded in the XAVC S formats. To use the feature, let the movie play up to the point where you want to start the effect. For example, suppose you recorded some children playing basketball. You could play the movie up to the point where a child shoots the ball toward the basket. At that point, or just before it, use the Right button to scroll to the Motion Shot icon, highlight it, and press the Center button to select it.

The camera will then play back the video as a series of multiple exposures tracing the path of the object

in motion. For example, Figure 8-30 shows how the camera processed a video sequence of a basketball shot.

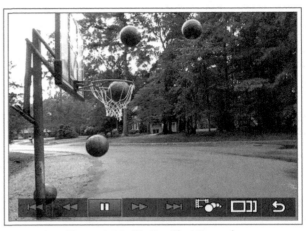

Figure 8-30. Motion Shot Example

If the images of the moving object overlap too closely on your first attempt, you can make an adjustment using the Motion Interval Adjustment option. On the video control panel, once you have selected the Motion Shot icon, the line of icons will change, as shown at the bottom of Figure 8-31. The Motion Shot icon will change to an icon for exiting the Motion Shot mode, which looks like a smaller version of the Motion Shot icon.

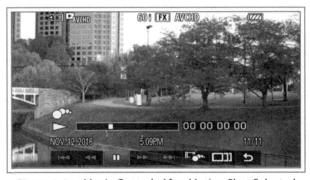

Figure 8-31. Movie Controls After Motion Shot Selected

The icon to the right of that one, which looks like a set of rectangular frames, lets you adjust the interval between the images. Select that icon and adjust the scale to a lower number to place the images closer together and to a higher number to place them farther apart. You also can adjust the interval using the Motion Interval Adjustment option on screen 2 of the Playback menu.

You cannot save the results of your work with the Motion Shot feature unless you connect the camera to a video capture device using an HDMI cable, as I did for Figure 8-30. I view this feature as an interesting novelty that lets you examine the path of an object in motion in some detail. It might be helpful for checking your golf swing or for adding interest to a video demonstration.

If you like the general idea of the Motion Shot feature, you can purchase an application (app) called Motion Shot+ from the Sony website, http://www.playmemoriescameraapps.com. That app lets you save the composite image that shows the motion trail. I will discuss the use of in-camera apps in Chapter 9.

Editing Movies

The RX100 V camera cannot edit movies in the camera. (At least, not with the options that come with the camera. It may be that an application will be developed for in-camera movie editing in the future.) If you want to do any editing, you will have to do it with a computer. For Windows, you can use software such as Windows Movie Maker. If you are using a Mac, you can use iMovie or any other movie editing software that can deal with MP4 and AVCHD files, and with XAVC S 4K or XAVC S HD files, if you record movies using those formats. I use Adobe Premiere Pro CC on my Mac, and it handles all of these file types well.

You also can use the PlayMemories Home software that is available for free from Sony for use with the RX100 V. To install PlayMemories Home on your computer, you need to download the software from the internet. For Windows-based computers, go to http://www.sony.net/pm. For Macintosh computers, go to http://www.sony.co.jp/imsoft/Mac/. This software is updated with new features periodically, so be sure to keep checking the website for updates.

One issue you may encounter when first starting to edit movie files from the RX100 V is finding the files. When you insert a memory card into a card reader, the still images are easy to find; on my computer, the SD card shows up as No Name or Untitled; then, beneath that level, there is a folder called DCIM; inside it are folders with names such as 100MSDCF, which contain the still images. (If you use the Folder Name option on screen 6 of the Setup menu to select Date Form, the folder names will be based on dates the images were taken; an example is 10061106 for images taken on November 6, 2016.)

The movie files are a bit trickier to find. The XAVC S files that you need to find and import into your software for editing have an .mp4 extension, but they are not the same as the more ordinary .mp4 files. Here is the path to a sample XAVC S file: Untitled\Private\M4ROOT\CLIP\C0007.MP4.

Here is the path to an AVCHD movie file: Untitled\Private\AVCHD\BDMV\Stream\0006.MTS. These files can be difficult to find on a Macintosh, because the Finder may not immediately show the contents of the AVCHD folder. You may have to right-click on the AVCHD item in the Finder and select Show Package Contents in order to view the BDMV folder. You may have to repeat that process to see the contents of the BDMV folder.

Here is the path to an ordinary MP4 movie file: Untitled\MP_ROOT\100ANV01\MAH00180.MP4.

You can avoid the complications of finding the movie files on a memory card by connecting the camera to your computer using the USB cable. Most video-editing software should detect the camera and import the movie files automatically, ready for you to edit them.

Also, with the RX100 V, you can transfer your files to your computer using the Wi-Fi capabilities that are built into the camera, as discussed in Chapter 9.

Chapter 9: Wi-Fi, Applications, and Other Topics

Connections Using Wi-Fi and NFC

The RX100 V has the ability to connect to computers, smartphones, and tablets using a Wi-Fi network. As noted in Chapter 1, you can transfer images and videos wirelessly using an Eye-Fi card or other memory card that includes Wi-Fi connectivity, but having Wi-Fi circuitry built into the camera gives you features that are not available with a card. Also, with some devices, the RX100 V can use NFC technology to establish a Wi-Fi connection without going through the steps that are ordinarily required. In this section, I will describe these features and give examples of how you can use them.

First, here is one note to remember when using any of the camera's Wi-Fi features: The Wi-Fi menu has an option called Airplane Mode near the bottom of its first screen. If that option is turned on, no Wi-Fi features will work. Make sure that menu setting is turned off when setting out to use the Wi-Fi options.

Sending Images to a Computer

Although you can edit and print images and edit videos to some extent using a smartphone or tablet, the easiest way to work with them is to transfer them to a computer. The traditional ways to do this are to connect the camera to the computer with the camera's USB cable or to use a memory card reader. However, there are two methods you can use to transfer your images and videos to a computer over a wireless network, eliminating the need to use a USB connection or a card reader.

First, as discussed in Chapter 1, you can use an Eye-Fi card or a similar memory card with the capability to transfer your files wirelessly to the computer. This system works well, but it requires the purchase and use of this special type of memory card.

The other approach for wireless transfer is to use the Wi-Fi capability built into the RX100 V. Once you have the camera and computer set up to communicate over a wireless network, you can use the Send to Computer menu option to transfer images and videos from the camera's memory card over that network, regardless of what type of memory card is installed. Here are the steps to set up the camera and computer:

1. Install the appropriate Sony software on the computer. For Windows-based computers, the software is PlayMemories Home, available for download at http://www.sony.net/pm/.

–or–

For Macintosh computers, install Wireless Auto Import, available for download at http://www.sony.co.jp/imsoft/Mac/.

2. Run the software you downloaded in Step 1. Follow the program's prompts to connect the camera to the computer using the camera's USB cable, and select the option to designate this computer to receive images from the camera. (That step needs to be done only once, unless you later switch to a different computer.) Then disconnect the USB cable.

3. Make sure the camera is within range of a wireless access point, also known as a Wi-Fi router. Normally, this will be a private, secured network at your home or office.

4. If the router has a button labeled WPS (Wi-Fi–protected setup), use that button to connect the camera to the network. Select the WPS Push option on the second screen of the Wi-Fi menu, and the camera will display the screen in Figure 9-1.

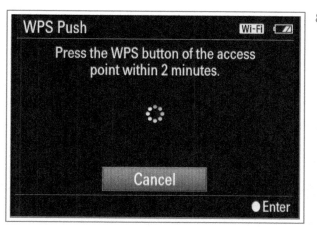

Figure 9-1. Camera's Screen After WPS Push Selected

5. Within two minutes, press the WPS button on the router. Figure 9-2 shows an example of that sort of button.

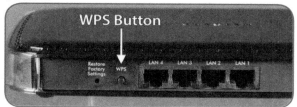

Figure 9-2. WPS Button on Router

6. If the setup is successful, the camera will display a message saying the access point has been registered. Proceed to Step 10.

–or–

If the router does not have a WPS button, or if pushing the button does not work, go to Step 7.

7. Locate the name of the network and its password. (This information may be on a label on the router or modem.)

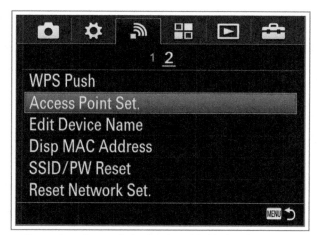

Figure 9-3. Access Point Settings Highlighted on Menu

8. Select the Access Point Settings option on the second screen of the Wi-Fi menu, as shown in Figure 9-3.

9. If the name of your network appears on the camera's screen, as shown in Figure 9-4, enter the network's password, as shown in Figure 9-5. The camera will display a virtual keyboard to let you enter the necessary characters.

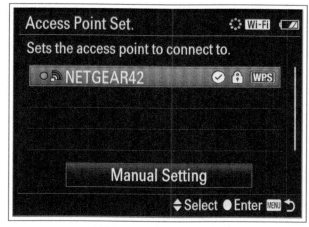

Figure 9-4. Wi-Fi Network ID on Camera's Screen

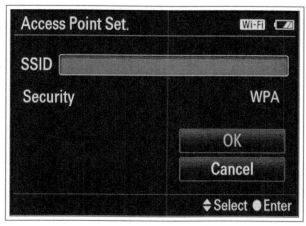

Figure 9-5. Screen for Entering Network Password

–or–

If the access point does not appear on the camera's screen, enter its SSID (network ID), using the Manual Setting option on the menu screen, as shown in Figure 9-6, and then enter the network's password, as shown in Figure 9-5.

10. On the Wi-Fi menu select Send to Computer, as shown in Figure 9-7.

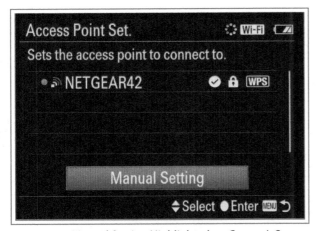

Figure 9-6. Manual Setting Highlighted on Camera's Screen

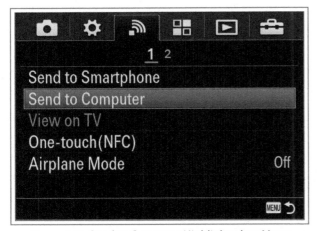

Figure 9-7. Send to Computer Highlighted on Menu

11. The camera will display a screen like that in Figure 9-8, reporting the name of the computer it is connecting to.

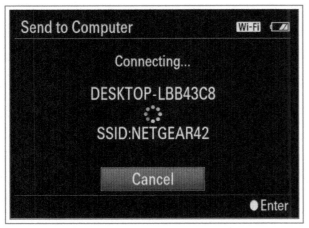

Figure 9-8. Local Network ID Displayed on Camera's Screen

12. Depending on what computer you are using, the computer may display an Importing dialog box. The images and videos will be uploaded to the

appropriate folder on your computer. You can designate that folder using the software installed in Step 1. On my Macintosh, the default folder is the Pictures folder; the computer places the images and videos in a sub-folder bearing the date of the transfer. The process also worked well with a Windows-based computer using Windows 10.

13. The camera will only transfer images and videos that have not previously been transferred wirelessly to the computer, but there is no way to select which items will be transferred. The transfer may take a very long time, especially if the transfer includes AVCHD and XAVC S videos. In fact, Sony does not recommend transferring XAVC S videos using the Send to Computer option. I ran a test using two brief videos, one recorded with the XAVC S HD format and one with the XAVC S 4K format. The camera did manage to send both files to my computer, but it took several minutes to transmit each video, each of which was less than 60 seconds in length.

I have not found this option to be as useful as transferring images and videos using a card reader or a USB cable, because of the time it takes for the transfer. However, if you have only a few items to transfer, it can be convenient to have this option available.

SENDING IMAGES TO A SMARTPHONE

If you don't need to print your images or do heavy editing, you may want to transfer them to a smartphone or tablet so you can send them to social networks, display them on the larger screen of your tablet, or otherwise share and enjoy them.

You can transfer your images and MP4 videos (not XAVC S or AVCHD videos) wirelessly from the RX100 V to a smartphone or tablet that uses either the iOS (iPhone and iPad) or Android operating system. These two systems have different capabilities. With iOS devices, you have to use the camera's menu system to connect. With many Android devices, you can use NFC technology, which establishes a Wi-Fi connection automatically when the camera is touched against the smartphone or tablet.

Here are the steps for connecting using the menu system, using an iPhone as an illustration:

1. Install Sony's PlayMemories Mobile app on the phone; it can be downloaded from the App Store for

the iPhone or from Google Play for Android devices. Figure 9-9 shows the app's icon on an iPhone.

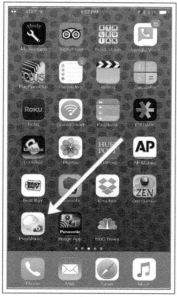

Figure 9-9. Icon for PlayMemories Mobile App on iPhone

2. Put the camera into playback mode and select an image or MP4 video to be transferred to the phone.

3. On the Wi-Fi menu, select Send to Smartphone, and from that option choose Select on This Device, as shown in Figure 9-10. On the next screen, you can choose to transfer This Image, All Still Images (or All Movie (MP4)) on Date, or Multiple Images.

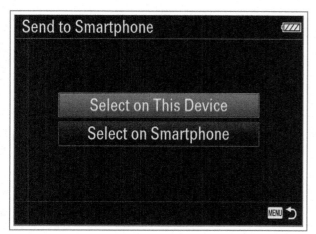

Figure 9-10. Select on This Device Highlighted on Camera

4. On the next screen, as shown in Figure 9-11, the camera will display the SSID (name) of the Wi-Fi network it is generating along with a QR code that can be scanned by the phone's camera.

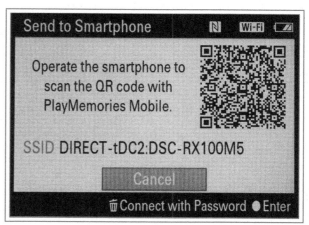

Figure 9-11. Screen Generated by Camera for Connecting to Phone

5. On the phone, open the PlayMemories Mobile app and select the option for scanning the QR code, as shown in Figure 9-12. After scanning the code, you may have to follow some prompts on the phone to install a profile, and then go to the Settings area on the phone.

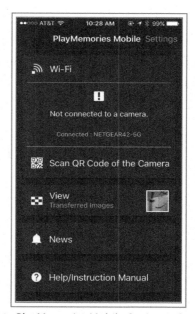

Figure 9-12. PlayMemories Mobile Option to Scan QR Code

6. On the phone, go to the Settings app, select Wi-Fi, and select the network displayed on the camera's screen, as shown in Figure 9-13. The first time you connect to that network, you may have to enter the password displayed on the camera's screen. After that initial connection, you can connect to that network without entering the password.

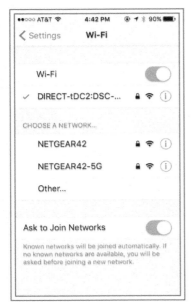

Figure 9-13. Camera's Network ID Displayed on iPhone

7. The camera will then display a message saying "Connecting." At this point, start the PlayMemories Mobile app on the iPhone.

8. The phone will display a message saying it is copying the images or videos from the camera, and will confirm the copying with a screen like that in Figure 9-14. The images or videos will appear in the Camera Roll area on an iPhone.

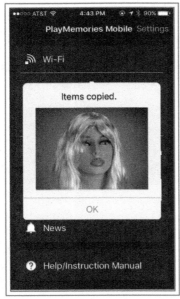

Figure 9-14. Confirm Copying Screen on iPhone

Connecting with NFC

If you are using an Android phone or tablet that has NFC capability built in, the steps for connecting that

device to the RX100 V are easier. I tested the procedure using a Samsung Galaxy S6 smartphone, but the same process should work with many Android devices that have NFC included. Here are the steps:

1. On the Android device, go to the Google Play Store and find and install the PlayMemories Mobile app, as shown in Figure 9-15.

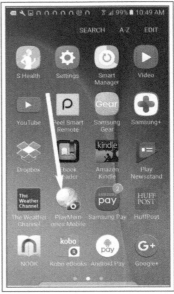

Figure 9-15. Icon for PlayMemories Mobile App on Samsung Phone

2. On the Android device, go to the Settings app, and under the NFC and Payment item, make sure NFC is turned on and Android Beam is turned on, as shown in Figure 9-16.

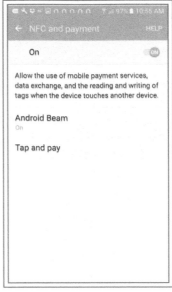

Figure 9-16. Samsung Phone Screen Showing NFC Active

3. Put the RX100 V into playback mode and display an image you want to send to the Android device.

4. Find the NFC icon on the left side of the camera, which looks like a fancy "N," as shown in Figure 9-17.

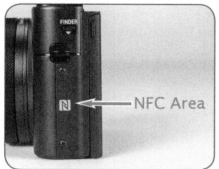

Figure 9-17. NFC Active Area on Camera

5. While both devices are active, touch the N on the camera to the NFC area on the Android device. (On the Galaxy S6, this area is on the back, as shown in Figure 9-18.) Be sure the two areas touch; you cannot have the two NFC spots separated by more than about a millimeter, if that.

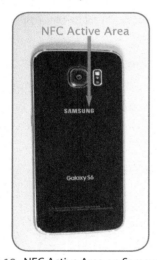

Figure 9-18. NFC Active Area on Samsung Phone

6. Hold the devices together, and within a couple of seconds you may hear a sound, depending on settings, and the camera will transfer the image to the Android device; you should see a display saying the transfer is complete, as in Figure 9-19.

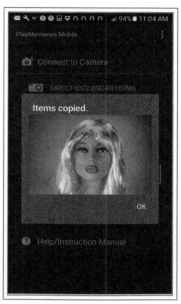

Figure 9-19. Confirm Copying Screen on Samsung Phone

7. The image will appear in the Photos app on the Android device.

8. If you want to transfer multiple images, select that option from the camera's menu before touching the camera to the Android device to start the transfer.

9. By default, when you transfer images to a smartphone or tablet, the maximum image size will be 2.0 MP. If the image originally was larger than that, it will be reduced to that size. You can change this setting to send the images at their original size or at the smaller VGA size, if you want. To do that on your device, find the settings for the PlayMemories Mobile app. On an iPhone, go to Settings, then scroll to find PlayMemories Mobile. On an Android device, open PlayMemories Mobile, then tap the Settings icon. If the images were taken with Raw quality, they will be converted to JPEG format before being transferred to the smartphone or tablet, even if the device is set for transfer at the original size.

USING A SMARTPHONE OR TABLET AS A REMOTE CONTROL

You can use a smartphone or tablet as a remote control to operate the RX100 V from a distance of up to about 33 feet (10 meters), as long as the devices are in sight of each other. Here are the steps to do this with an iPhone:

1. Go to the camera's Application menu, marked by an icon with white and black blocks. Highlight the first item, Application List. Press the Center button

to display the list of applications, or apps, currently loaded into the camera.

2. Use the direction buttons or the Control wheel to highlight the app called Smart Remote Embedded, as shown in Figure 9-20.

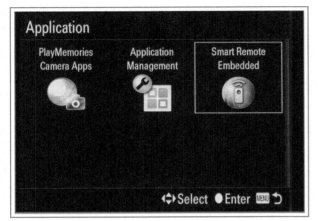

Figure 9-20. Icon for Smart Remote Embedded App in Camera

(If you have downloaded an updated version of this app, it may be called Smart Remote Control instead of Smart Remote Embedded.)

3. Start the app by pressing the Center button, and the camera will display a screen with the identification information for its own Wi-Fi network and a QR code that you can scan with the PlayMemories Mobile app, as shown in Figure 9-21.

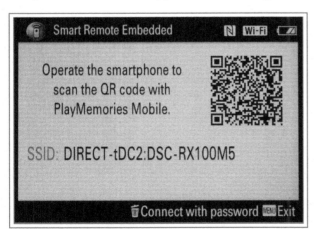

Figure 9-21. Screen Generated by Camera for Remote Connection

4. On the phone, go to the Wi-Fi tab of the Settings app and select the network ID displayed by the camera, as shown earlier in Figure 9-13. Or, if you have not connected previously, you can open the PlayMemories Mobile app on the phone and use the

app's option to scan the QR code on the camera's screen.

5. If that does not work, press the Delete button on the camera to move to another screen, shown in Figure 9-22, which lets you use the network ID from the camera's screen along with the password to connect the phone to the camera's network.

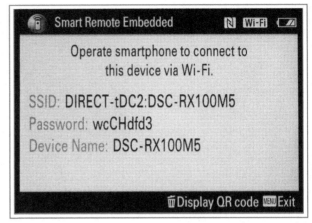

Figure 9-22. Camera's Screen to Connect with Password

6. Set up the camera on a tripod or just place it where you want it, aiming at your intended subject.

7. Open the PlayMemories Mobile app on the iPhone if it is not already open.

8. The camera will display a screen like that shown in Figure 9-23, with an icon in the upper left corner showing that the camera can now be controlled from the phone.

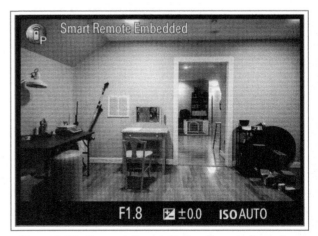

Figure 9-23. Camera's Screen During Remote Operation

9. The phone will display a screen like that in Figure 9-24, with the view from the camera's lens and several control icons.

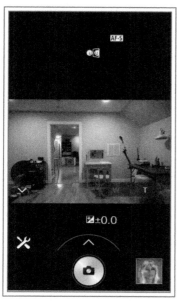

Figure 9-24. iPhone's Screen During Remote Operation

10. Using these controls, you can zoom the lens and control exposure compensation. You can press the wrench-and-screwdriver icon to get access to settings for the self-timer, image review, and save options, as shown in Figure 9-25. You also can adjust several menu options using the camera's controls. For example, you can use the Mode dial to change the shooting mode and you can use the Creative Style menu option.

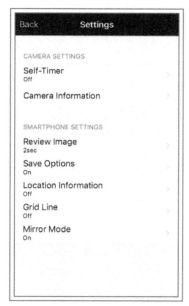

Figure 9-25. Settings Screen for Remote App on iPhone

11. If you want to record a movie from the phone, you have to turn the Mode dial to the Movie mode position and select an exposure mode, at which point the camera

icon on the iPhone app will change to a red button for starting a video recording. If you download the updated Smart Remote Control version of the app, you can focus by touching the screen with your finger. You also can use the settings panel to turn on the Touch Shutter function, which lets you trigger the shutter as the focus is set, when you touch the phone's screen with your finger. The updated app also has additional controls for exposure.

12. By default, images saved to the phone will be resized down to 2.0 MP unless they already were that small or smaller. Movies will be saved only to the camera; they cannot be displayed on the phone.

13. When you have set up the shot as you want it, press the camera icon on the iPhone app to take the picture or the red icon to start the video recording.

14. If you are using an Android device with NFC capability, you should be able to connect to the camera by touching the device to the camera, as discussed above in connection with transferring images. To do this, though, you first have to register the Smart Remote Embedded (or Smart Remote Control) app using the One-touch (NFC) menu option on screen 1 of the camera's Wi-Fi menu.

15. Once the connection has been made, you can separate the devices to the standard remote-control distance of up to about 33 feet (10 meters). If you have difficulty making an NFC connection, start the PlayMemories Mobile App on the Android device before touching the camera to that device. The camera can then be controlled using the PlayMemories Mobile app on the Android device, as noted in the numbered steps above.

The features of the remote control app are likely to change as Sony updates this and other apps; you can download updated versions at www. playmemoriescameraapps.com.

You can use the remote-control setup if you want to place your camera on a tripod in an area where birds or other wildlife may appear, so you can control the camera from a distance without disturbing the animals. (The wireless remote will work through glass if you are indoors behind a window.)

Also, you can try pole aerial photography, which involves attaching the camera to a painter's pole or other pole about 10 to 16 feet (3 to five meters) long, as shown in Figure 9-26, to get shots from a higher vantage point than would otherwise be possible. See polepixie.com for information about equipment for making this sort of attachment.

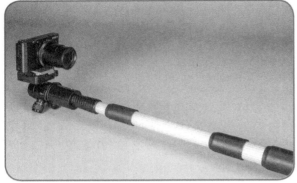

Figure 9-26. Sony RX100 V Camera Attached to Pole

I took the image shown in Figure 9-27 using this pole, which allowed me to get a shot of a fountain from an angle that would not have been possible otherwise.

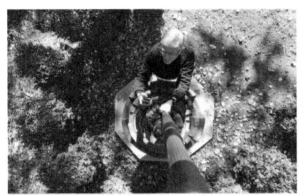

Figure 9-27. Photograph Taken from Pole Using Remote App

With this system, I could see exactly where the camera was being aimed. It was difficult holding the pole steady while using the iPhone, but if you have another person to help, this setup can be useful for higher-angle photos of properties being sold, viewing above crowds, and other applications. Being able to control the camera remotely also might be useful in other situations in which you want to have the camera set up unattended, such as when you want to capture images in a classroom or other group setting without calling attention to the camera.

Wi-Fi Menu

I have discussed some of the options on the Wi-Fi menu, whose first screen is shown in Figure 9-28, but there are several other options to discuss.

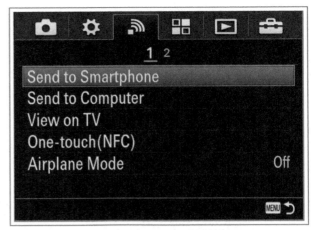

Figure 9-28. Screen 1 of Wi-Fi Menu

Following is information about each of the items on this menu.

SEND TO SMARTPHONE

This first Wi-Fi menu option lets you transfer images or MP4 videos to a smartphone or tablet. I discussed the steps for using this option earlier in this chapter.

SEND TO COMPUTER

This next option lets you send images and movies directly from the RX100 V to a computer via a Wi-Fi network. I discussed this process earlier in this chapter.

VIEW ON TV

This option sets up the RX100 V to transmit still images (not movies) wirelessly to a Wi-Fi–enabled TV, such as a Sony Bravia TV. The procedure will vary with the TV set you are using. Once the connection is established, you can browse through the images using the controls on the camera or the remote control of the TV if the TV is compatible with this setup.

This is a useful option once it is working properly, but I found it hard to set up. After trying various approaches with little success, I got it to work using WD TV Live, a media player made by Western Digital. I connected that device to an HDTV using an HDMI cable, and configured the device to connect to my home network. Then I connected a laptop computer running Windows 10 to the same network. I configured the Windows Media Player software on the computer to allow streaming of media over the network. I also downloaded a program called Serviio from http://serviio.org and configured this system to work as a DLNA streaming media server on my network. (DLNA stands for Digital Living Network Alliance; see www.dlna.org.)

Once everything was working together, I selected the View on TV menu option and the camera displayed the screen shown in Figure 9-29 as it connected to the WD TV Live device. Then the camera began sending still images to the TV through the wireless network.

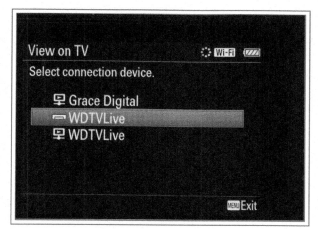

Figure 9-29. Camera's Screen when Detecting TV Device

The camera displayed the screen shown in Figure 9-30, with a few control icons at the bottom.

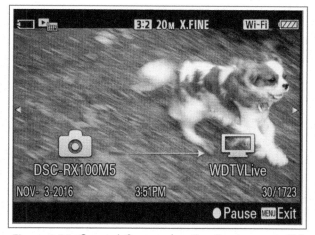

Figure 9-30. Camera's Screen when Sending Images to TV

Once this screen appeared, I pressed the Center button to pause the transmission, and pressed the Down button to display the screen shown in Figure 9-31, with additional options, including 4K display mode, found under the Playback Image Size option.

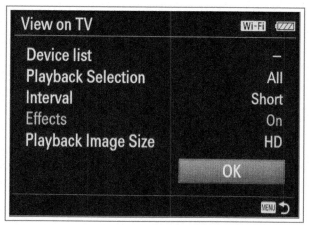

Figure 9-31. Screen with More Options for View on TV

If you are familiar with setting up a DLNA server, this option may be great for you. Otherwise, I recommend that you view your images on a TV using an HDMI cable, a USB flash drive, or some other direct connection.

ONE-TOUCH (NFC)

The RX100 V has built-in near field communication (NFC) functionality, which means it can establish a wireless connection just by touching a smartphone or tablet that also has NFC built in. As of this writing, many Android phones and tablets have this feature, but Apple devices, such as iPhones and iPads, do not.

To use the NFC feature to start a camera app, you first have to use this menu option to register that app. Then, with the smartphone or tablet turned on and the camera in shooting mode, touch the N mark on the left side of the camera to the NFC area on the smartphone or tablet. The two devices should immediately start to establish a connection, and the application you registered using this menu option should launch. For example, you might want to register the Smart Remote Embedded application or another application that you have downloaded from Sony's site.

You don't have to use this menu option before using the camera to connect to a phone or tablet to transfer images.

AIRPLANE MODE

This option is a quick way to disable all of the camera's functions related to Wi-Fi, including Eye-Fi card activity and the camera's own internal Wi-Fi network. As indicated by its name, this option is useful when you are on an airplane and you are required to disable electronic devices. In addition, this setting can save battery power, so it may be worthwhile to activate it when you are on an outing with the camera and you won't need to use any Wi-Fi capabilities for a period of time.

If you are trying to use any of the camera's built-in Wi-Fi functions such as Send to Smartphone or Send to Computer and notice that the menu options are dimmed, it may be because this option is turned on. Just turn it back off and the Wi-Fi options should be available again.

The second and final screen of the Wi-Fi menu is shown in Figure 9-32.

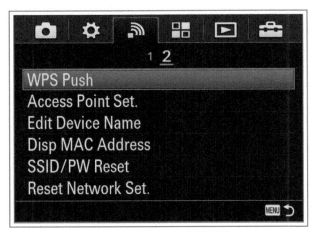

Figure 9-32. Screen 2 of Wi-Fi Menu

WPS PUSH

The WPS Push option gives you an easy way to set up your camera to connect to a computer over a Wi-Fi network. Ordinarily, to connect to a wireless network using the camera's menu system, you have to use the Access Point Settings option and then enter the network password into the camera to establish the connection. The WPS Push option gives you a shortcut if the wireless access point or wireless router you are connecting to has a WPS button. That option, if it is present, is likely to be a small button on the back or top of the router, and it is likely to have the WPS label next to it or on it. For example, one router I connect to has the button shown earlier in Figure 9-2.

If the router has a WPS button, you will not have to make any manual settings or enter a password. All you have to do is select the WPS Push menu option on the RX100 V, and then within two minutes after that, press the WPS button on the router. If the operation is successful, the

camera's display screen will show that the connection has been established, as shown in Figure 9-33.

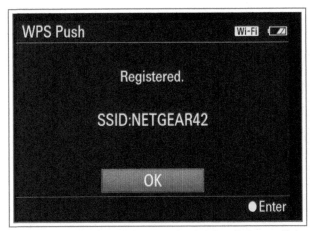

Figure 9-33. Camera's Screen After WPS Push Successful

Once that connection has been made, you will be able to connect your camera to a computer on that network to transfer images using the Send to Computer option.

If the connection does not succeed using WPS Push, you will need to use the Access Point Settings option, the next item on screen 2 of the Wi-Fi menu.

ACCESS POINT SETTINGS

This option is for connecting the camera to a router if WPS Push, discussed above, is not available or does not work. I discussed the use of this option earlier in this chapter, in connection with sending images and videos to a computer wirelessly.

EDIT DEVICE NAME

This next option, shown in Figure 9-34, lets you change the name of your camera as it is displayed on the network. The default name is DSC-RX100M5, and I have found no reason to change it, especially because doing so would require me to use the camera's laborious data-entry system. This option could be useful, though, if you are in an environment where other RX100 V cameras are present and you need to distinguish one camera from another by using different names.

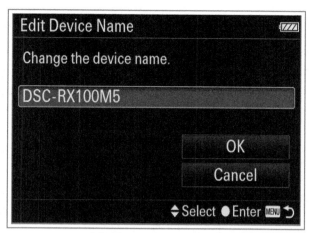

Figure 9-34. Edit Device Name Menu Options Screen

DISPLAY MAC ADDRESS

If you select this menu option, the camera will display a screen like that seen in Figure 9-35, which provides the MAC address of your camera. MAC stands for media access control.

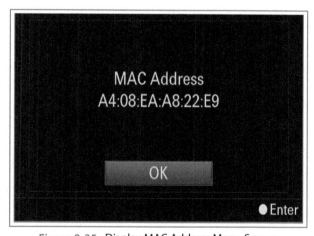

Figure 9-35. Display MAC Address Menu Screen

The MAC address is a string of characters that identifies a physical device that can connect to a network. In some cases, a router can be configured to reject or accept devices with specified MAC addresses. If you are having difficulty connecting your camera to your Wi-Fi router using the options discussed above, you can try configuring your router to recognize the MAC address of your camera, as reported by this menu item. I have not had to use this option, but it is good to have it available in case it is needed.

SSID/PW RESET

When you connect your RX100 V to a smartphone or tablet, either to transfer images or to control the camera remotely with the other device, the camera generates its own Wi-Fi network internally. With this option, whose main screen is shown in Figure 9-36, you can force the camera to change the SSID (name) and password of its own wireless network.

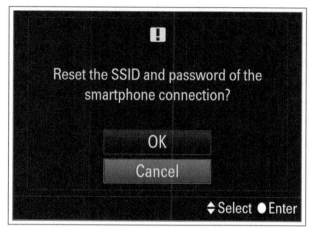

Figure 9-36. SSID/PW Reset Menu Screen

You might want to do this if, for example, you have attended a conference where you allowed other people to connect their smartphones to your camera, and now you want to reset the camera's network ID so they will no longer have access to the camera's network.

RESET NETWORK SETTINGS

This final item on the Wi-Fi menu lets you reset all of the camera's Wi-Fi network settings, not just the SSID and password. This option is useful if you are having problems and need to get a fresh start with the wireless functions, if you are switching to a new wireless network where you use the camera, or if you are selling the camera and want to erase these settings.

APPLICATIONS AND APPLICATION MENU

The one menu system I have not yet discussed in any detail is the Application menu, represented by an icon with white and black blocks, to the right of the Wi-Fi menu's icon. This menu system opens the door to expansions of the RX100 V's features through applications, or apps, that you can download from a Sony website. I will give a brief introduction to this capability, though there undoubtedly will be changes to the website and the available options as time goes by.

The apps available from Sony are similar to apps for smartphones and tablets. Each camera app provides a separate function or set of functions, and is represented by a name and an icon. The apps are found on the RX100 V by going to the Application menu and selecting the first item, Application List, shown in Figure 9-37.

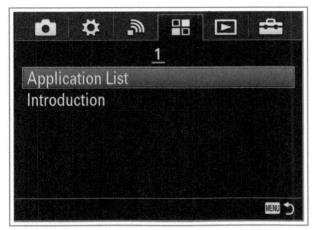

Figure 9-37. Application List Highlighted on Menu

When you highlight that item and press the Center button, you will see a screen like that in Figure 9-38, with icons for all apps currently loaded in the camera. If you highlight any of those icons and press the Center button, you will activate that app.

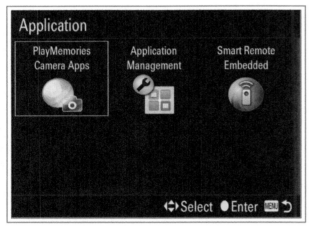

Figure 9-38. Icons for Apps Currently Loaded in Camera

Although it is likely that the set of initial apps will change over time, when my camera was new it came with just one actual camera app installed—Smart Remote Embedded, which lets you use a smartphone or tablet to control the camera. (The camera included two other apps that involve downloading and management of camera apps.) Sony has updated that app to add new features in a version called Smart Remote Control, and I won't be surprised if it is updated further in the future.

Besides the app that came pre-installed, Sony has, as of this writing, made available several other apps,

some free and some for prices up to $9.99. These apps include Sky HDR ($9.99); My Best Portrait (free); Photo Retouch (free); Picture Effect+ (free); Star Trail ($9.99); Motion Shot+ ($4.99); Smooth Reflection ($4.99); Time-Lapse ($9.99); Multiple Exposure ($4.99); Light Painting ($4.99); Stop Motion+ ($4.99); and Bracket Pro ($4.99), among others. You can read about these apps at Sony's site, mentioned in the next paragraph. Some of them, like Picture Effect+, add enhancements to features that already exist in the camera, and others, like Time-Lapse, add new features.

In order to install and use any of these apps, you first have to go to Sony's site at www.playmemoriescameraapps.com and create an account. Then you can obtain information about the apps and download them by connecting your camera to the computer using the camera's USB cable. You may have to set USB Connection to MTP on screen 4 of the Setup menu to get these steps accomplished.

Once the account is set up and you have your camera registered with a Wi-Fi access point, you can also download an app directly to your camera. The camera has about 100 MB of capacity to install apps, and each of the ones I have downloaded so far has used about six MB, so you may be able to have about 15 apps installed altogether. To manage installed apps and view how much storage space has been used, you use the administrative app called Application Management, whose icon is shown in Figure 9-38.

To purchase an app directly from the camera, use the PlayMemories Camera Apps icon, also shown in Figure 9-38. With that method, you need to connect the camera to a wireless network and then sign in to the playmemoriescameraapps.com site with your username and password. That can be a laborious process using the on-screen keyboard, but the system does work effectively for downloading apps if you are not able to use a computer for that purpose.

Once you have installed an app and highlighted its icon on the camera's screen, press the Center button and follow the on-screen instructions to use the app. If you press the camera's Menu button while the app is running, the camera may display a special menu with options that apply while that app is in use. For example, when the Smart Remote Embedded app is running, if you press the Menu button you will see one of the five menu screens for that app, as shown in Figure 9-39.

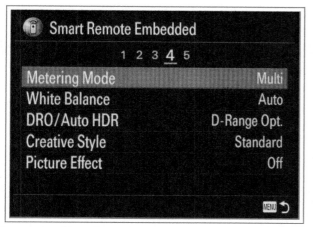

Figure 9-39. Menu Screen in Camera During Remote Operation

The other four menu screens for this app display standard camera options that can be controlled when the app is in use, such as Image Size, Quality, ISO, and the like. In other cases, an app may just use icons to let you choose various functions. If you expect to use in-camera apps often, you can assign the Application List menu item to the Custom, Center, Left, or Right button so it can be called up quickly.

The second line of the Application menu, Introduction, provides some general information about applications.

Other Topics

ASTROPHOTOGRAPHY AND DIGISCOPING

Astrophotography involves photographing sky objects with a camera connected to (or aiming through) a telescope. Digiscoping is the practice of using a digital camera with a spotting scope to get shots of distant objects such as birds and other wildlife.

There are many types of scope and several ways to align a scope with the RX100 V's lens. I will not describe all of the methods; I will discuss the approach I used and hope it gives you enough guidance to explore the area further.

I used a Meade ETX-90/AT telescope with the RX100 V connected to its eyepiece. To make that connection, you need a filter adapter, such as one sold by Lensmate, which uses 52mm filters, or one from Sony, model number VFA-49R1, which uses 49mm filters, and

adapter rings to connect the filter adapter to the telescope's eyepiece. You can get the proper rings for the Lensmate adapter by purchasing the 52mm DigiKit, part number DKSR52T, from telescopeadapters.com. That is the setup shown in Figure 9-40.

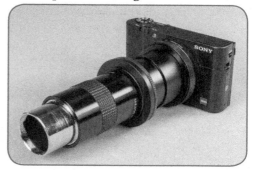

Figure 9-40. Telescope Eyepiece Connected to RX100 V

I took the image of the moon in Figure 9-41 with the RX100 V connected to the telescope using the 52mm adapter rings with the Lensmate adapter.

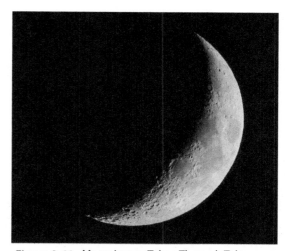

Figure 9-41. Moon Image Taken Through Telescope

I set the camera to Manual exposure mode with settings of 1/400 second, f/4.5, and ISO 1600. I needed a fast shutter speed to avoid motion blur from the unsteadiness of the telescope. I used manual focus, adjusting the telescope's focus control until the image was sharp on the camera's LCD. At first I used the MF Assist option, so I could fine-tune the focus with an enlarged view of the moon's craters. After some experimenting, I found I got better results using the Peaking Level function at High, and Peaking Color set to red. When focus was sharp, I saw a bright, red outline on the outer edge of the moon, which made focusing much easier than relying on the normal manual focus mechanism, even with MF Assist activated.

I set the self-timer to five seconds to minimize camera shake. I set Quality to Raw & JPEG so I would have a Raw image to give extra latitude in case the exposure seemed incorrect. As you can see in Figure 9-41, the RX100 V did a good job of capturing the crescent moon. Because of the relatively large sensor and high resolution of the RX100 V, this image can be enlarged to a fair degree without deteriorating.

You can use a similar setup for digiscoping. I attached the RX100 V to a Celestron Regal 80F-ED spotting scope, shown in Figure 9-42, using the same eyepiece I used with the telescope.

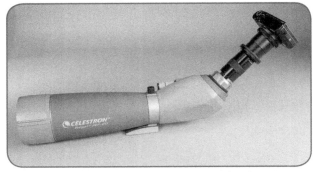

Figure 9-42. Spotting Scope Connected to RX100 V

Figure 9-43 is a shot of a bird at a feeder, taken with the RX100 V through this scope. I turned on continuous shooting to catch various views of the bird. I used manual focus with Peaking at its mid level set to red, and that worked well.

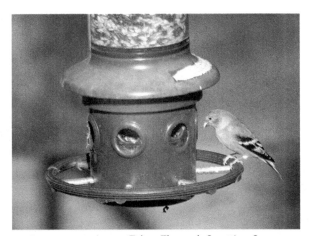

Figure 9-43. Image Taken Through Spotting Scope

STREET PHOTOGRAPHY

The RX100 V is well suited for street photography—that is, shooting candid pictures in public settings, often without the subject being aware of your activity. It is small, lightweight, and unobtrusive in appearance,

so it can easily be held casually or hidden in the photographer's hand. Its 24mm wide-angle lens takes in a broad field of view, so you can shoot from the hip without framing the image carefully on the screen. You can tilt up the LCD screen and look down at it to frame your shot, which further hides your actions. The f/1.8 lens lets in plenty of light, and it performs well at high ISO settings, so you can use a fast shutter speed to avoid motion blur. You can silence the camera by turning off its beeps and shutter sounds.

The settings you use depend in part on your style of shooting. One technique that some photographers use is to shoot in Raw, and then use post-processing software such as Photoshop or Lightroom to convert their images to black and white, along with any other effects they are looking for, such as extra grain to achieve a gritty look. (Of course, you don't have to produce your street photography in black and white, but that is a common practice.)

If you decide to shoot using Raw quality, you can't take advantage of the image-altering settings of the Picture Effect menu option. You can, however, use the Creative Style option on the Shooting menu. (You may have to use Sony's Image Data Converter software for the Creative Style setting to be effective.) You might want to try using the Black and White setting; you can tweak it by increasing contrast and sharpening if you want. Also, try turning on continuous shooting, so you'll get several images to choose from for each shutter press.

You also can experiment with exposure settings. I recommend you shoot in Shutter Priority mode at a fairly fast shutter speed, 1/100 second or faster, to stop action on the street and to avoid blur from camera movement. You can set ISO to Auto, or use a high ISO setting, in the range of 800 or so, if you don't mind some noise.

Or, you can set the image type to JPEG at Large size and Extra Fine quality to take advantage of the camera's image-processing capabilities. To get the gritty "street" look, try using the High Contrast Monochrome setting of the Picture Effect item on the Shooting menu, with ISO set somewhat high, in the range of 800 or above, to include some grain in the image while boosting sensitivity enough to stop action with a fast shutter speed. You also can use the High Sensitivity setting of Scene mode to convey a gritty feeling.

One interesting approach is to take advantage of the camera's ability to shoot 4K video. You can shoot video in an exposure mode such as Shutter Priority that lets you use a fast shutter speed to avoid motion blur, and record a street scene for several seconds, or even a minute or two. You can then use video-editing software to extract a single frame. You also can use the Photo Capture option on screen 3 of the Playback menu to extract a frame from a movie. Because of the high resolution of 4K video, the quality is likely to be quite acceptable.

For Figure 9-44, I was shooting various scenes with different settings when these two people appeared in front of me. I switched the camera to Program mode with continuous shooting turned on and grabbed 18 quick shots, of which I chose this one as the best.

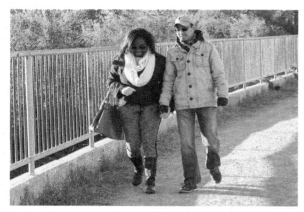

Figure 9-44. Street Photography Example

INFRARED PHOTOGRAPHY

The RX100 V camera is capable of taking infrared photographs if you use an infrared filter to block visible light from the lens. I use a Hoya R72, but there are other options. Figure 9-45 shows that filter attached to the RX100 V using the Lensmate filter adapter discussed earlier in this chapter and in Appendix A. Infrared photography can produce unusual-looking images, with the sky turned dark and green leaves and grass turned white. For Figure 9-46, I used Manual exposure mode with a shutter speed of five seconds and an aperture of f/5.6, with ISO set to 250. I set a custom white balance with the filter on the lens, aiming at green leaves and bushes as the base area for white.

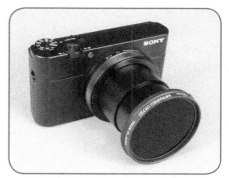

Figure 9-45. Infrared Filter Attached to Sony RX100 V

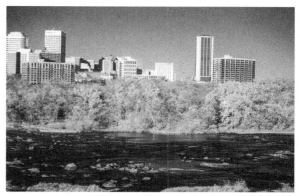

Figure 9-46. Infrared Image Taken by Sony RX100 V

CONNECTING TO A TELEVISION SET

The RX100 V can play back its still images and videos on an external television set, as long as the TV has an HDMI input jack. The camera does not come with any audio-video cable as standard equipment, so you have to purchase your own cable, with a micro HDMI connector at the camera end and a standard HDMI connector at the TV end. These cables are available through online retailers.

To connect the cable to the camera, you need to open the little flap marked HDMI on the right side of the camera and plug the micro HDMI connector into the port underneath that flap, as shown in Figure 9-47.

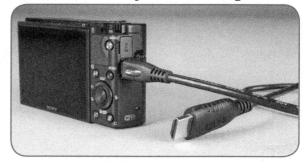

Figure 9-47. HDMI Cable Connected to Sony RX100 V

Then connect the large connector at the other end of the cable to an HDMI input port on an HDTV set.

Once you have connected the camera to the set, the camera not only can play back images and videos; it also can record. When the RX100 V is hooked up to a TV while in recording mode, you can see on the TV screen the live image being seen by the camera. In that way, you can use the TV as a large monitor to help you compose your photographs and videos.

You also can use this port and cable to output a "clean" video signal to another device, such as a video recorder.

To do that, you have to turn off the HDMI Information Display option under the HDMI Settings item on screen 3 of the Setup menu, as discussed in Chapters 7 and 8.

As noted earlier in this chapter, the RX100 V also has an option on the Wi-Fi menu called View on TV, which lets you view your images on a Wi-Fi–enabled TV. As I discussed in that chapter, I have found that option to be difficult to use effectively. Unless you are familiar with setting up the special type of network that is needed for that sort of setup, I recommend that you stick to using an HDMI cable for the connection.

Appendix A: Accessories

When people buy a new camera, especially a fairly expensive model like the Sony RX100 V, they often ask what accessories they should buy to go with it. I will discuss several options, with an emphasis on items I have used personally.

Cases

The RX100 V is such a small camera that you may find you don't need a case. There is no separate lens cap to deal with as there is with some models in this class, and when the camera turns off and its lens retracts, the RX100 V is ready to stow easily in your pocket, purse, or other handy location. But I do use a case with my RX100 V, and I know that other users do also, so I will provide some suggestions.

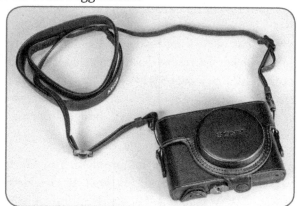

Figure A-1. Sony Case LCJ-RXF Closed

The Sony case made for the RX100 series of cameras, model number LCJ-RXF, is shown in Figures A-1 and A-2. This case is similar to an earlier version that was made for the original RX100 camera. The older version may not fit the newer camera, so be sure to check the model number of the case. This case is roomy enough to hold the RX100 V with its tilting LCD.

This is an attractive case made of synthetic material that looks like leather. It holds the camera securely and comes with a matching shoulder strap. It will hold the camera with a filter adapter attached, but not with an add-on grip installed. It does not have room for holding an extra battery or other items.

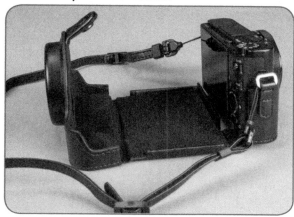

Figure A-2. Sony Case LCJ-RXF Open

A less expensive option is the Camson case, shown in Figures A-3 and A-4.

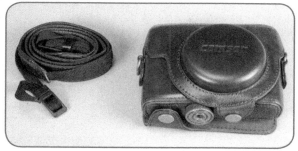

Figure A-3. Camson Case Closed

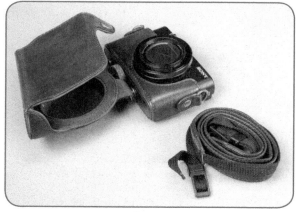

Figure A-4. Camson Case Open

This brown leather case comes with a matching strap and can hold the camera with filter adapter, but not much else. It has a nice appearance and feel and does not display the Sony label, so it may provide a degree of security because it does not reveal the brand of your camera. I purchased this case from Wall Street Photo in New York.

If you want a case with room for other items besides the camera, there are many choices. One I have used successfully is the Lowepro Rezo 110 AW, shown in Figure A-5. This case can hold the camera with grip and filter adapter, and has room for other items such as filters and extra batteries. It has a belt loop, or you can carry it by the padded handle on top. You also could fit a small bottle of water and some snacks for a short trip.

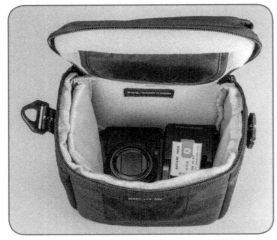

Figure A-5. Lowepro Rezo 110 AW Case

When I am going on a day trip to take photos, I often use a larger pack, such as the Lowepro Inverse 100 AW waist pack, shown in Figure A-6.

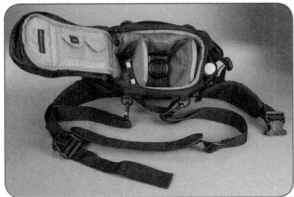

Figure A-6. Lowepro Inverse 100 AW Waist Pack

You can fasten this case around your waist or use its shoulder strap. It holds the camera along with water bottles, batteries, filters, and other items. One feature I

appreciate is that it has straps for attaching a tripod to the bottom of the case.

Another good option is a standard waist pack, not designed just for photography, such as the Eagle Creek pack shown in Figure A-7. It can readily accommodate the camera and some small accessories, and it has two mesh pockets for holding small water bottles.

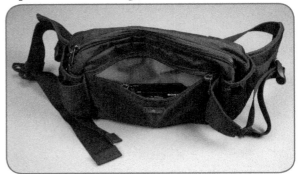

Figure A-7. Eagle Creek Waist Pack

Batteries and Chargers

This is a category of items that I recommend you purchase along with the camera or soon after getting the camera. I use the RX100 V heavily, and I find it runs through batteries fairly quickly. You can't use disposable batteries, so if you're out taking pictures and the battery dies, you're out of luck unless you have a spare battery (or another power source, as discussed below). The model number of the Sony battery is NP-BX1. You can get a spare Sony battery for about $30 as I write this. It won't do you a great deal of good by itself, though, because the battery is designed to be charged in the camera.

There is an easy solution to this problem. You can find generic replacement batteries, as well as chargers to charge the batteries outside the camera, inexpensively from online sellers. I purchased a package including a generic replacement battery and a charger for about $20 on eBay. You also can get the official Sony external charger, model number BC-TRX. Besides charging a battery externally, the Sony charger can be used with its included USB cable to charge a battery inside the camera. Both the Sony charger and a generic charger are shown in Figure A-8, along with a generic battery and a Sony battery.

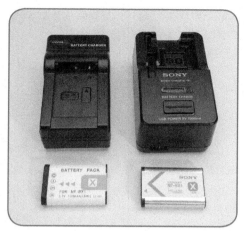

Figure A-8. Battery Chargers and Batteries

Another option for powering the RX100 V is to use the AC adapter that comes with the camera, which is model number AC-UUD12 in the United States. You can plug the micro USB end of the camera's USB cable into the Multi port on the camera and plug the other end into the AC adapter, and then plug the adapter into an electrical outlet, and it will provide constant power to the camera. If the camera is turned off, the battery inside the camera will be charged. If the camera is turned on, you can operate the camera normally. (The battery will not be charged while the camera is powered externally, though.) There must be a battery installed in the camera for this system to work. If there is no battery installed, the camera will not turn on.

Of course, it is usually not convenient to have the camera plugged into an electrical outlet, unless you are taking shots in a studio or otherwise using the camera indoors. If you want to power the camera from an external source when you are in the field, you can get a good-quality USB power source and connect it to the camera, either for charging the camera's battery or for powering the camera. Figure A-9 shows the G-Cord 10000 mAh Boutique Mobile Power Supply.

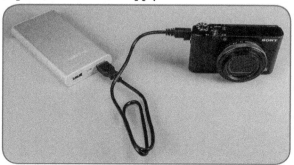

Figure A-9. G-Cord Mobile Power Supply

This device has two standard-sized USB ports. You can plug the camera's USB cable into one of those ports and connect the other end to the camera to provide a long-lasting source of power, or to charge the camera's battery. You can charge the power supply through its own micro USB port, using any compatible AC adapter. In fact, you can use the RX100 V's own AC adapter to recharge the G-Cord device. The G-Cord device is not very large and weighs about 220 grams (8 ounces).

Another device I have found very useful for providing power for the RX100 V is the Anker 40-watt desktop USB charger, shown in Figure A-10, which has five slots for charging devices such as smartphones and tablets. I have used it to charge my iPhone and iPad, and it does a good job of charging the Sony battery inside the RX100 V camera at the same time. You also can use it to charge the G-Cord device, discussed above. There undoubtedly are other USB chargers that can handle this process; just make sure the charger meets the necessary specifications.

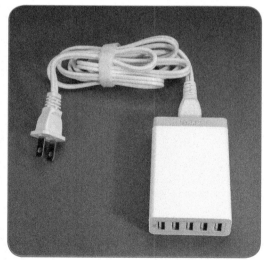

Figure A-10. Anker 40-Watt Desktop USB Charger

Add-On Filters and Lenses

There is no way to attach a filter or other item, such as a closeup lens, directly to the RX100 V's lens, as you can with DSLRs and other cameras whose lenses are threaded to accept filters and auxiliary lenses. With the RX100 V, to add such accessory items you need to get an adapter. One such adapter is sold by a company called Lensmate, at lensmateonline.com, which lets you attach any 52mm-diameter filter to the camera's lens.

The adapter has two parts. The first part, shown already attached to the lens in Figure A-11, is a plastic ring called the "base ring" that you glue onto the front of the lens barrel.

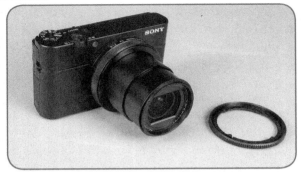

Figure A-11. Lensmate Filter Adapter

This piece stays in place and does not interfere with the lens or the automatic lens cover. To use a filter, you attach a larger piece, the actual "filter adapter," lying beside the camera in Figure A-11, which bayonets onto the base ring as shown in Figure A-12.

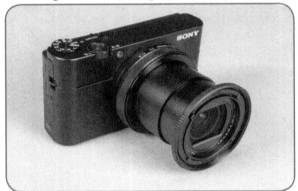

Figure A-12. Lensmate Filter Adapter with Holder in Place

Then you can screw any 52mm diameter filter or other auxiliary lens into the holder. The base ring is removable if you later want to take it off the lens; Lensmate includes a "remover," which is a plastic piece attached to a thread; you work the thread under the base ring and pull it through to remove the ring from the lens.

As you might expect, this system is not as sturdy as the natural screw-on capability of other cameras because everything depends on a plastic ring that is glued in place. So don't expect to attach large items like teleconverters or anything heavier than a standard 52mm filter. Having the ability to attach filters, however, enhances the usefulness of the camera greatly. You can use neutral density filters, polarizers, or any of a wide assortment of closeup lenses, among others. Also, as discussed in Chapter 9, I used this system to

attach the RX100 V to the eyepiece of a telescope and spotting scope to take pictures through the scopes. You have to be careful not to put too much stress on the adapter in that situation, but the adapter worked well for that purpose.

There is a similar system sold for the RX100 series by Sony, model number VFA-49R1, which accepts 49mm filters, but it is not advertised as being compatible with the RX100 V camera. I expect that it would work, possibly with some adjustments, but I have not tested it with this camera.

Grips

Some users find it difficult to get a firm grasp of the RX100 V because it is small and has a smooth front surface with no place to take hold of it. Lensmate, which provides the filter adapter discussed above, also offers a solution to this issue—a custom-made grip designed by Richard Franiec, shown in Figure A-13.

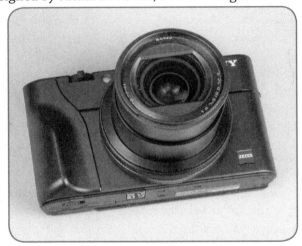

Figure A-13. Franiec Grip on RX100 V Camera

The Franiec grip is well crafted from aluminum and contoured to fit on the camera's body with a low profile. It is attached with a strong adhesive supplied by Lensmate. This grip offers you a solid ridge for keeping a tight hold on the camera. I do not find it necessary, but this is a matter of personal taste.

Sony also offers a grip of its own, model number AG-R2. Figure A-14 shows the Sony grip on the RX100 V.

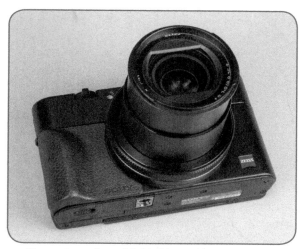

Figure A-14. Sony AG-R2 Grip on RX100 V Camera

This grip has a different shape, appearance, and texture from the Franiec grip, and it is less expensive. There also are other grips available, but I have not tried any of them. Again, I do not use an add-on grip myself, but it is good to have these options available.

Remote Controls

In several situations, it is useful to control a camera remotely. For example, when you are using slow shutter speeds, holding the shutter open with the BULB setting, doing closeup photography, or taking pictures through a telescope, any camera motion during the exposure is likely to blur the image. If you control the camera remotely, you lessen the risk of blurred images from moving the camera as you press the shutter button. Remote control also is helpful when you need to be located away from the camera, as for taking self-portraits or images of wildlife.

As I discussed in Chapter 9, the RX100 V has a built-in Wi-Fi capability for connecting a computer, smartphone, or tablet to the camera wirelessly. Besides using that feature to transfer images from the camera to the other device, you can use a smartphone or tablet as a wireless remote control. However, it can be tricky to establish and maintain the connection between the camera and the phone or tablet.

Fortunately, Sony offers several remote controls that are compatible with the RX100 V camera.

Sony's model number RM-VPR1 is shown in Figure A-15.

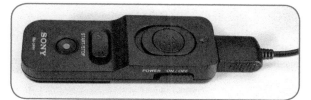

Figure A-15. Sony Remote Control RM-VPR1

You connect this device to the Multi port on the right side of the camera. With this remote, you can turn the camera on and off, use the autofocus system, zoom the lens in and out, take a still image, lock the shutter down for a long exposure, and start and stop video recording.

This remote comes with two cables—one for cameras with a Remote terminal and one for cameras like the RX100 V, which has the Multi terminal. Take the cable that has identical connectors at each end, and plug the end with the smaller plastic housing into the camera. Plug the other end of the cable, which has a larger housing, into the remote. You also can attach the included clip to the underside of the remote, if you want to clip the remote to a tripod or other support.

You can half-press the shutter button to cause the autofocus system to operate (if the camera is in an autofocus mode), and press the button fully to take a still picture. You can press the shutter button down and then slide it back toward the other controls to lock it in place. This locking is useful when you are taking continuous shots using the Drive Mode settings, or when you want to hold the shutter open using the BULB setting in Manual exposure mode. Press the shutter button back up in its original direction to release it.

The red button labeled Start/Stop is similar to the Movie button on the RX100 V camera. Press it once to start recording a movie and press it again to stop the recording.

The power button on the side of the remote control can be used to turn the camera on and off, and to wake it up from power-saving mode. Press the switch back toward yourself as you hold the control to power the camera either on or off.

A more sophisticated remote, Sony model number RMT-VP1K, is shown in Figure A-16.

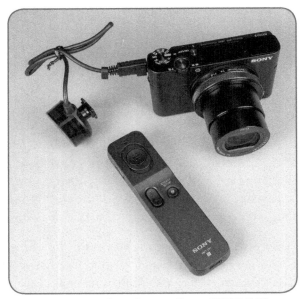

Figure A-16. Sony Remote Control RMT-VP1K

This remote comes with an infrared receiver that plugs into the camera's Multi port. The receiver, a small cylinder, has a foot for attaching to a camera's shoe, but, of course, the RX100 V has no shoe, so you have to let the receiver dangle or attach it somewhere else. The remote kit comes with a clip that you can use to attach the receiver to a tripod leg or other support.

The remote control itself is similar to the wired remote discussed earlier, RM-VPR1, though there are some differences. You can press the shutter button, and you can lock it down for BULB shooting. You can zoom the lens and start and stop a video recording. The remote has a slide switch labeled TC Reset on the left side, which you can operate to reset the camera's time code to zero. With the camera's Mode dial at the Movie position, press the TC Reset switch on the remote, and the time code displayed in the lower left corner of the display will be reset to the zero point. The way to accomplish this reset in the camera is to go to the TC Preset option under TC/UB Settings on screen 3 of the Setup menu. With TC Preset highlighted, press the Center button to bring up the screen showing the values of the current time code. While that screen is displayed, press the Custom/Delete button, and the time code will be reset. It is considerably easier to just press the TC Reset button on the remote if you need to reset the time code.

Figure A-17 shows another option, Sony model number RM-SPR1. This device is a very simple wired remote that also connects to the Multi port. It has only one large button, which acts as a remote shutter button.

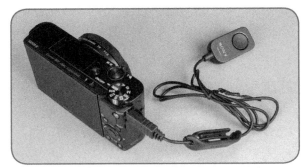

Figure A-17. Sony Remote Control RM-SPR1

You can press it halfway to evaluate focus and exposure, press it all the way to take a still image, or hold it down to fire a burst of shots if Drive Mode is set for continuous shooting. You cannot use this remote to record a movie or carry out any other functions.

One more device, which has more functionality than an ordinary remote control, is the Vello ShutterBoss II, shown in Figure A-18.

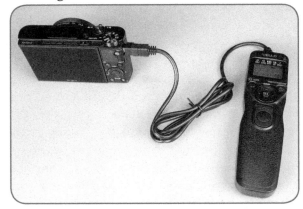

Figure A-18. Vello ShutterBoss II Remote Control

This versatile device can act as a remote control, similar to the Sony devices discussed above. In addition, it can serve as a powerful intervalometer, for setting up the camera for a time-lapse sequence. Using the controls and the small LCD screen on the device, you can set up a sequence of up to 399 shots, or an indefinite series, until you command it to stop. You can set the interval between shots to any value from one second up to 99 hours, 59 minutes, and 59 seconds.

External Flash

When Sony designed the RX100 V, they included the desirable feature of a built-in viewfinder that pops up, but, probably because of that feature, they omitted a hot shoe where you can attach an external flash unit. So, if you want to use an external unit to supplement the light from the camera's small pop-up flash, you have to use an optical slave.

An optical slave is a flash unit that includes a sensor that triggers the flash when it senses the light from the camera's built-in flash. (You also can use a separate optical slave that can be attached to any compatible flash unit.)

One problem with this system is that the RX100 V fires one or more pre-flashes before it fires the main flash burst to expose the image. The camera uses the pre-flashes to measure the amount of light being reflected from the subject so the image can be exposed properly. If the optical slave is not set to ignore the pre-flashes, it will fire as soon as it "sees" a pre-flash, and the external flash will not be synchronized with the actual exposure.

The solution to this problem is to use an optical slave that can be set to ignore the pre-flashes. One of the best ones I have found for use with the RX100 V is the LumoPro LP180, shown in Figure A-19.

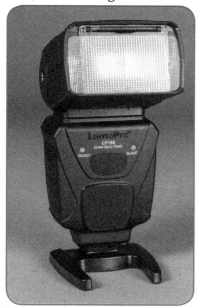

Figure A-19. LumoPro LP180 Optical Slave Flash

This powerful unit has a head that swivels and rotates, a built-in diffuser, variable power, and settings that allow it to ignore a variable number of pre-flashes. I have had good success using this flash with the RX100 V by setting the flash to its S2-1 mode.

With this flash, as with any optical slave, you have to use Manual exposure mode on the camera and determine the proper exposure by trial and error or by using a light meter. You can set up the external flash

on a light stand or tripod at any location where it can sense the light from the camera's built-in flash.

Another good unit for use as an optical slave is the Yongnuo YN560-IV, shown in Figure A-20, which also has a built-in optical slave capability.

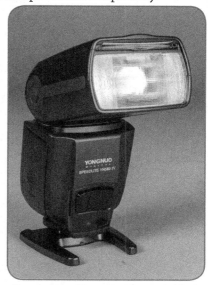

Figure A-20. Yongnuo YN560-IV Flash

I had success using this unit with the RX100 V with the flash set to either its S1 or its S2 optical slave mode. You can attach this, or any, external flash to the RX100 V using a standard flash bracket with a tripod socket.

There is one other issue to be aware of when using an external flash unit. When you set the camera to Manual exposure mode, the camera's display screen (or electronic viewfinder display) is likely to be black or very dark because the exposure settings would result in a dark image if you were not using flash, and the camera will not "know" about the effects of the external flash. Therefore, it may be difficult to compose the shot. The solution is to go to screen 3 of the Custom menu on the camera, and set the Live View Display option to Setting Effect Off. With that setting, the camera's display will not darken to show the effects of the manual exposure settings, and you will probably be able to view the display clearly enough to compose the image.

External Video Recorder

In Chapter 8, I discussed how to take advantage of the RX100 V's excellent video features to output its 4K video signal via the HDMI port to an external video recorder. Using this system, you can bypass the five-minute limit on recording 4K video to a memory card, and you can even make a 4K recording with no memory card in the camera at all.

The recorder I used to test this process is the original Atomos Shogun 4K recorder, a very capable device though an expensive one, available at this writing for $1,495.00. As you can see from Figure A-21, the recorder is considerably larger than the camera, and it can be tricky to mount the two devices together. I ended up attaching the camera on top of the recorder using a Pearstone 4.2-inch (10.7 cm) articulating arm, which has tripod screws on two mounting heads, shown here. (With larger cameras, the Shogun often is mounted on top of the camera; the Shogun has standard tripod sockets on its top and bottom edges.)

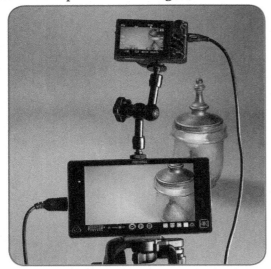

Figure A-21. Atomos Shogun Video Recorder with RX100 V

Apart from the mounting issues, the combination of RX100 V and Shogun performed very well in producing 4K video files. The menu system is easy to work with and the recorder produces high-quality files. At the highest quality, the files can be extremely large (more than 190 GB in one case), so be prepared with a strong computer capability for editing. There are other 4K video recorders that might work as well, such as the Odyssey7 series of recorders from Convergent Design or devices from Blackmagic Design, though I have not tested any of those.

External Audio Recorder

As I discussed in Chapter 8, the RX100 V has excellent video features but no provision for connecting an external microphone for high-quality audio. Although the built-in microphone records good-quality audio, you can get better results if you use an external audio recorder and synchronize the audio track from that recorder with the sound recorded by the camera.

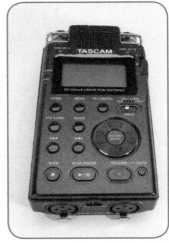

Figure A-22. Tascam DR-100MkII Audio Recorder

One excellent piece of equipment for this purpose is the Tascam DR-100MkII recorder, shown in Figure A-22. This recorder includes two sets of high-quality microphones, one set that is omnidirectional for recording lectures or classes, and another that is directional for recording concerts or other performances. The recorder also has two XLR inputs where you can connect high-quality microphones of your choice.

There are many other options that will work for this purpose, depending on your budget and needs, including the Shure VP83F, the Tascam DR-40, the Zoom H1, and the Zoom H6. Also, if you use the Atomos Shogun video recorder discussed above, you can connect high-quality microphones to that device using an audio connection cable from Atomos.

Tripods

I will mention two tripods that I have found to be excellent for traveling with the Sony RX100 V camera. They are both Manfrotto BeFree tripods, shown in Figures A-23 and A-24. The version in Figure A-23 is the aluminum version, model no. MKBFRA4-BH. It includes a versatile head, reduces to about 20 inches (50 cm) long just by collapsing the legs, and to about 16 inches (40 cm) if you take the trouble to fold the legs backward. It weighs about three pounds five ounces (1.5 kg). The tripod in Figure A-24 is the carbon-fiber version, model no. MKBFRC4-BH, which is lighter and more expensive than the aluminum one.

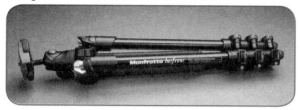

Figure A-23. Manfrotto BeFree Aluminum Tripod

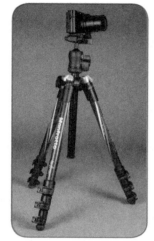

Figure A-24. Manfrotto BeFree Carbon -fiber Tripod

External LCD Monitor

There is another accessory to consider for viewing live and recorded images with the RX100 V. The Sony Clip-On LCD Monitor, model number CLM-FHD5, is an add-on unit with a 5-inch (12-cm) screen. The unit, shown in a closeup view in Figure A-25, includes a short HDMI cable that ends in a micro-HDMI plug at the camera end, for connecting to the HDMI port of the camera.

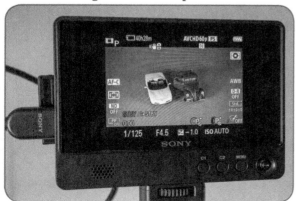

Figure A-25. Sony LCD Monitor, CLM-FHD5

This monitor adds visibility for viewing the shooting screen and for playing back images and videos. The screen can rotate 180 degrees, so you can view the scene from the front of the camera for self-portraits. It also can tilt up or down for viewing from high or low angles. The monitor has numerous controls for settings such as Peaking, brightness, and contrast, and it has a special display mode for boosting the contrast when you are using the S-Log2 gamma curve. This unit costs about $700 at the time of this writing, plus the cost of a battery, but if you need the extra screen size or versatility, it is worth looking into.

With a larger camera, the monitor can be attached to an accessory shoe on the camera's top. With the RX100 V, which has no shoe, you can use a flash bracket or some other accessory to hold the monitor. In Figure A-26, I attached the monitor and the camera to two separate ball heads on a horizontal bar on my tripod, to show how the two devices work together. This image shows the included sunshade attached to the monitor.

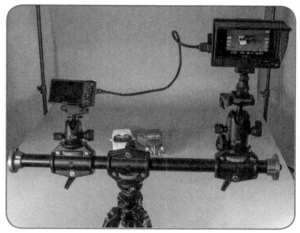

Figure A-26. Sony LCD Monitor with RX100 V Camera

Appendix B: Quick Tips

In this section, I will list some tips and facts that might be useful as reminders. I have tried to include points that you might not remember from day to day, especially if you don't use the RX100 V constantly.

Move the focus frame quickly. To adjust the focus frame for use with autofocus, choose Flexible Spot or Expand Flexible Spot for the Focus Area menu option and Focus Standard for the Center Button option of the Custom Key (Shooting) item on screen 5 of the Custom menu. Then, when the camera is in shooting mode, press the Center button to put the movable focus frame on the screen. Use the direction buttons to move it around the display. You can assign the Custom button to the Focus Standard option if you prefer.

Use Auto ISO with Manual exposure mode. With these settings, you can set the shutter speed and aperture and let the camera choose the ISO value to produce a good exposure. This is like having a new shooting mode that lets you stop action and control depth of field at the same time.

Use continuous shooting. Consider turning burst shooting on as a matter of routine, unless you are running out of storage space or battery power, or have a particular reason not to use it. Even with portraits, you may get the perfect expression on your subject's face with the fourth or fifth shot. Press the Left button (or use the menu system) to call up Drive Mode, scroll to Continuous Shooting, and turn it on. With the High speed setting, the camera can shoot at up to 24 frames per second while adjusting focus. Continuous shooting is not available when the camera is set to Sweep Panorama mode or to any Scene mode setting other than Sports Action.

Use 4K video for super continuous shooting. When you use the 4K video format for recording video, you can extract still frames from the video sequence using editing software such as Adobe Premiere Pro or Final Cut Pro, or with the Photo Capture option on screen 3 of the Playback menu. If you shoot with a fast enough shutter speed to stop action, you can use this system to produce still images with good resolution and image quality. In effect, you can do continuous shooting at 30 frames per second for up to five minutes at a time.

Use tethered shooting. With the RX100 V, you can connect the camera to a Mac or Windows computer and control the camera from the computer using the free Remote Camera Control software from Sony. That software can be downloaded from http://www.sony.co.jp/imsoft/Win/ for Windows-based computers and from http://www.sony.co.jp/imsoft/Mac/ for Macintosh computers. Then, on screen 4 of the Setup menu, select PC Remote for USB Connection. Details are in Chapter 7.

Use shortcuts. Speed up access to many settings by placing them on the Function menu for recall with a press of the Function button. In some cases, as with flash settings and Drive Mode, you can press a button (the Right and Left buttons, respectively) to get access to the features you need. Speed through the Shooting menu using the Control wheel to move rapidly through the items on a screen. Use the Right and Left buttons to move through the menus a screen at a time by highlighting the icons at the top of the screen.

Take advantage of the help system. The RX100 V does a good job of advising you about conflicts between settings. If a menu option is unavailable for selection, you can still highlight it and press the Center button. The camera will display a message telling you what setting is causing the highlighted item to be unavailable. Press the C button when a menu item is highlighted to get information about the item, if In-Camera Guide is assigned to that button through the Custom Key (Shooting) menu option.

Use the Memory Recall shooting mode. The MR position on the Mode dial lets you save seven favorite groups of settings. You also can use it for more specific purposes. I like to have one slot set up to remove all "special" settings, such as Creative Style, Picture Effect, and self-timer, so I can quickly set up the camera to take a shot with no surprises. You can use one slot to set the camera at a particular zoom range, such as, say, 50mm. To do this, press the zoom lever to move the lens, so you see the desired range below the zoom scale in the upper right corner of the display. When the range is set as you want it, save the settings to one of the MR slots. (You also can use the Step Zoom feature to set a particular zoom amount; to do that, set the Zoom Function on Ring option on the Custom menu to Step.)

Use an external power source to power the camera. The RX100 V can be powered by any compatible USB battery, such as the G-Cord unit discussed in Appendix A. A device like that is useful when you need to do extensive photography in the field.

Use the extra settings for White Balance and Creative Style. When you set White Balance, even to Auto White Balance, you can press the Right button and use the amber-blue and green-magenta axes to further adjust the color of your shots. Remember to undo any color shift when you no longer need it. Also, you can press the Right button after selecting a Creative Style option and then adjust the contrast, saturation, and sharpness settings. (Saturation is not adjustable for the Black and White and Sepia settings.)

Play your movies in iTunes, and on iPods, iPhones, and iPads. If you record movies using the MP4 extension (including XAVC S HD and XAVC S 4K movies), you can use iTunes to copy the MP4 files to an iTunes-compatible device, such as an iPad. After transferring the files to your computer, open iTunes on that computer and drag an .mp4 file from the computer's Explorer or Finder window to the Home Movies panel in iTunes. You can then play the movie from iTunes. To play it on an iPod, iPhone, or iPad, select the video in iTunes, and, on the iTunes menu, select File—Convert—Create iPod or iPhone version, or Create iPad or AppleTV version, as appropriate. Then sync iTunes with your device, and the converted movie will play on that device. (If you have trouble locating the .mp4 files on your computer, see the last part of Chapter 8.)

Diffuse your flash. If the built-in flash produces light that's too harsh for macro or other shots, try using translucent plastic pieces from milk jugs or broken ping-pong balls as diffusers. Hold the plastic between the flash and the subject. When using Fill-flash outdoors, use the Flash Compensation setting on the Shooting menu to reduce the intensity of the flash by -2/3 EV. You can bounce the light from the built-in flash off of the ceiling or a wall by holding it back gently with a finger.

Use the self-timer to avoid camera shake. The self-timer is not just for group portraits; you can use the two-second or five-second self-timer whenever you use a slow shutter speed and need to avoid camera shake. It also is useful for macro photography. Don't forget that you can set the self-timer to take multiple shots, which can increase your chances of getting more great images.

Use DMF for focusing. The direct manual focus option combines the camera's autofocus ability with your own manual focus adjustments, to achieve precision for critical focus tasks. You can use the MF Assist option, which enlarges the display when you turn the Control ring to adjust focus, but, with DMF, you have to half-press the shutter button as you turn the Control ring for MF Assist to work.

Try time-lapse photography. With time-lapse photography, a camera takes a series of still images at regular intervals, several seconds, minutes, or even hours apart, to record a slow-moving event such as the rising or setting of the moon or sun or the opening of a flower. The images are played back at a much faster rate to show the whole event unfolding quickly. The RX100 V does not have this feature built in, but you can purchase the Time-Lapse app from Sony through playmemoriescameraapps.com for $9.99 as of this writing. This app includes several preset options for capturing sunsets, night scenes, miniatures, and other traditional time-lapse subjects. You also can use the Remote Camera Control software when the camera is connected to a computer, or the Vello ShutterBoss II intervalometer, discussed in Appendix A.

Avoid the five-minute limit for high-quality video recording. If you record video to an external video recorder, as discussed in Chapter 8, with no memory card in the camera, you can record for longer periods of time, avoiding the five-minute limit for the highest-quality formats.

Use the self-timer for bracketed exposures. To do this, use the Bracket Settings option on screen 3 of the

Shooting menu and select the first sub-option, Self-timer During Bracket.

Use the camera's automatic HDR option. To do this, go to screen 5 of the Shooting menu, select DRO/Auto HDR, then HDR. You cannot use certain other settings with HDR, including Raw for Quality, Picture Effect, or Picture Profile.

Use the settings that are available only when assigned to a control button. Use the Custom Key (Shooting) option on screen 5 of the Custom menu to assign one of these settings to the Custom, Left, Right, or Center button. These include Eye AF, AF/MF Control Toggle, AEL Toggle, Bright Monitoring, Deactivate Monitor, and others, as discussed in Chapter 7. Several options also work during video recording when assigned to control buttons, including Focus Mode, Focus Area, ND Filter, ISO, Focus Magnifier, and Picture Profile, among others, as discussed in Chapter 8.

Use the Playback button to turn on the camera. This is useful if you only need to look at menu items or view your images or videos. The lens will not be activated.

Use the Picture Profile feature to full advantage. If you are really serious about getting the maximum benefit from the Picture Profile feature, including the S-Log2 option for gamma, you need to use color-grading software. A good software package can take advantage of the profiles and bring out the colors, contrast, and other aspects of your video files in the way you intend. An extremely powerful program is DaVinci Resolve 12.5, which is available in a free version as well as a professional one. See https://www.blackmagicdesign.com/products/davinciresolve.

Experiment with Picture Profile for still images. Picture Profile is intended primarily for use with video recording, to achieve consistent results among various video cameras and to manage dynamic range efficiently. However, the RX100 V's Picture Profile menu option includes a wealth of adjustments, some of which might be useful for your still photography. For example, you might take one of the settings, such as PP1, and adjust it for a particular purpose. You could set Color Mode to Black & White, and then adjust the Color Depth options to emphasize the brightness of the various colors (red, green, blue, cyan, magenta, and yellow), in a way similar to the use of glass filters on a camera using black-and white film.

Appendix C: Resources for Further Information

Books

There are many excellent books about photography. Rather than trying to compile a long bibliography, I will list a few especially useful books that I consulted while writing this guide.

C. George, *Mastering Digital Flash Photography* (Lark Books, 2008)

C. Harnischmacher, *Closeup Shooting* (Rocky Nook, 2007)

H. Horenstein, *Digital Photography: A Basic Manual* (Little, Brown, 2011)

H. Kamps, *The Rules of Photography and When to Break Them* (Focal Press, 2012)

J. Paduano, *The Art of Infrared Photography* (4th ed., Amherst Media, 1998)

S. Seip, *Digital Astrophotography* (Rocky Nook, 2008)

Websites and Videos

Since websites come and go and change their addresses, it's impossible to compile a list of sites that discuss the RX100 V that will be accurate far into the future. One way to find the latest sites is to use a good search engine, such as Google or Bing, and type in "Sony DSC-RX100 V."

I will include below a list of some of the sites or links I have found useful, with the caveat that some of them may not be accessible by the time you read this.

Digital Photography Review

Listed below is the current web address for the "Sony Cyber-shot Talk" forum at Dpreview.com. Dpreview.com is one of the most useful sites for reviews, discussion forums, technical information, and other resources concerning digital cameras.

http://www.dpreview.com/forums/1009

For a useful compilation of tips and tricks for effective use of the RX100 and RX100 II, many of which apply for the RX100 V, see the following thread in this forum:

http://www.dpreview.com/forums/post/51991398

Reviews of the RX100 V

The links below lead to reviews or previews of the RX100 V by dpreview.com, imaging-resource.com, and others.

https://www.dpreview.com/reviews/sony-cybershot-dsc-rx100-v-review

http://www.imaging-resource.com/PRODS/sony-rx100-v/sony-rx100-vA.HTM

https://www.cnet.com/products/sony-cyber-shot-rx100-v/preview/

http://www.stevehuffphoto.com/2016/10/07/sony-rx100-mark-v-in-depth-first-look-best-pocket-camera-ever-created/

http://www.photographyblog.com/reviews/sony_cybershot_dsc_rx100_v_review/

Finally, my own site, White Knight Press, provides updates, offers support for download of PDFs and eBooks, and provides a way to contact me with questions or comments.

http://whiteknightpress.com

THE OFFICIAL SONY SITE

Sony provides resources on its websites, including the downloadable user's manual for the RX100 V and other information.

The link below provides general support for the RX100 V camera:

https://esupport.sony.com/US/p/model-home.pl?mdl=DSCRX100M5&LOC=3#/howtoTab

Here is a link to the downloadable Sony user's guide for the RX100 V:

https://docs.sony.com/release//Help_4593794111.pdf

The next link is to a guide for using the Picture Profile feature with the RX100 V:

http://helpguide.sony.net/di/pp/v1/en/index.html

The link below is to the official specifications for the RX100 V camera:

https://docs.sony.com/release//specs/DSCRX100M5_MKSP.pdf

The link below is to the operating instructions for the PlayMemories Mobile app for Android and iOS:

http://support.d-imaging.sony.co.jp/www/disoft/int/playmemories-mobile/en/operation/index.html

The link below leads to the site for downloading camera apps for the RX100 V:

https://www.playmemoriescameraapps.com/portal/

OTHER RESOURCES

The first two links below are to a two-part tutorial on the use of the S-Log2 gamma setting on the Sony A7S camera, which includes a lot of helpful information that is applicable to the use of that setting with the RX100 V:

http://www.xdcam-user.com/2014/08/exposing-and-using-slog2-on-the-sony-a7s-part-one-gamma-and-exposure/

http://www.xdcam-user.com/2014/10/using-s-log2-from-the-a7s-in-post-production/

This next link is to a fairly detailed video seminar by video expert Philip Bloom discussing video settings for the Sony A7S camera, much of which is very useful for the RX100 V.

https://youtu.be/zeX-eZXaRtw

The link below is to more information from Philip Bloom, including insights about the video features of the RX100 IV, a model very similar to the RX100 V.

http://philipbloom.net/blog/rxroadtests/

The link below is to a video that gives general tips about movie settings on the Sony Alpha A7S camera, which has many settings similar to those of the RX100 V.

https://blog.sony.com/2014/10/a7s-movie-setting-tips-for-the-filmmakers-out-there/

The next link gives some helpful discussion of using picture profiles on the Sony FS-700 video camera. Much of the discussion, which explains terms such as gamma, black level, and knee, is applicable to the RX100 V.

http://videogearsandiego.blogspot.com/2013/12/using-picture-profiles-on-sony-fs-700.html

The link below is a YouTube video that gives one person's approach to grading S-Log2 video from the Sony A7S camera using DaVinci Resolve software.

https://youtu.be/WPRiGXF5JKQ

This next link provides some technical information about the S-Log two gamma curve:

http://blog.abelcine.com/2013/01/18/sonys-s-log2-and-dynamic-range-percentages/

If you're interested in using the Atomos Shogun external video recorder, the video in the link below gives a helpful introduction to using that recorder with the Sony A7S and the Panasonic GH4. A lot of this discussion is helpful for users of the RX100 V.

http://nofilmschool.com/2014/12/helpful-crash-course-using-atomos-shogun-4k-recorder-gh4-a7s

This next link has a video with tips on settings for shooting video with the Sony A7S:

http://www.4kshooters.net/2014/10/13/some-useful-sony-a7s-movie-settings-tips-and-tricks/

The link below provides more information about the settings that can be adjusted for Picture Profiles:

http://www.xdcam-user.com/picture-profile-guide/

Finally, the last link below is to a site that has excellent tutorials on many photographic topics.

http://www.cambridgeincolour.com

Index